Metaphysical
Graffiti

Other Books by Randall E. Auxier

Responses to Royce: 1885–1916, three volumes (edited, 2000)

Hartshorne and Brightman on God, Process and Persons: The Correspondence, 1922–1945 (co-edited with Mark Y.A. Davies, 2001)

The Philosophy of Seyyed Hossein Nasr (co-edited with Lewis E. Hahn and Lucian W. Stone Jr., 2001)

The Philosophy of Marjorie Grene (co-edited with Lewis E. Hahn, 2002)

The Philosophy of Jaakko Hintikka (co-edited with Lewis E. Hahn, 2006)

The Philosophy of Michael Dummett (co-edited with Lewis E. Hahn, 2007)

Bruce Springsteen and Philosophy: Darkness on the Edge of Truth (co-edited with Douglas R. Anderson, 2008)

The Wizard of Oz and Philosophy: Wicked Wisdom of the West (co-edited with Phillip S. Seng, 2008)

The Philosophy of Richard Rorty (co-edited with Lewis E. Hahn, 2010)

Time, Will, and Purpose: Living Ideas from the Philosophy of Josiah Royce (2013)

The Philosophy of Arthur C. Danto (co-edited with Lewis E. Hahn, 2013)

Pussycat Blackie's Travels: There's No Place Like Home, by Josiah Royce (co-edited with Robin Wallace, 2014)

The Philosophy of Hilary Putnam (co-edited with Douglas R. Anderson and Lewis E. Hahn, 2015)

The Quantum of Explanation: Whitehead's Radical Empiricism (with Gary Herstein, 2017)

The Philosophy of Umberto Eco (co-edited with Sara G. Beardsworth, 2017)

Metaphysical Graffiti

*Deep Cuts in the
Philosophy of Rock*

RANDALL E. AUXIER

OPEN COURT
Chicago

*This book is dedicated to my wife Gaye.
I'm glad we brought that ship into the shore
and threw away the oar forever.*

To find out more about Open Court books, visit our website at
www.opencourtbooks.com.

Open Court Publishing Company is a division of Carus Publishing Company,
dba Cricket Media.

Printed and bound in the United States of America.

Photographs by Bruce Chandler

Metaphysical Graffiti: Deep Cuts in the Philosophy of Rock

ISBN: 978-0-8126-9964-7

Library of Congress Control Number: 2017933160

This book is also available as an e-book.

Contents

Bonus Tracks: Growing Older but Not Up   275

The Silence in Between

LUKE DICK

Rock and roll is cool, philosophy is wide and deep. No treatise, no essay, no phenomenology of "coolness" is or was ever necessary to drive home the fact. We all know it already. The difference between philosophy and rock is something like the difference between a Rubik's Cube expert and Jimmy Page. But if you're going to make me do some kind of proving, fine. Just do a Google image search of "Prince" while listening to "Kiss" and then go read Descartes's *Meditations*. If you come away from this thinking philosophy is cooler than rock and roll, I'll buy you a beer—scout's honor.

The existentialists came closest to being cool. De Beauvoir and Sartre were both brilliant, and their free love relationship comes close to *Rolling Stone* fodder. Maybe they're the Fleetwood Mac of philosophy. But I'd rather see a Fleetwood Mac show than read *The Ethics of Ambiguity*. And I can't think of anything more punk than the opening pages of Camus's *Myth of Sisyphus*. But if I had to pick, I'd take The Clash over Camus. No philosophy is going to move you like music.

So what are we even doing here? Why read what you're about to read? Why not cuddle up to *Exile on Main Street* right now instead of cracking this cover? Well, if you want to listen to music right this second, I would suggest you stop and plunge into some vinyl—there's nothing like getting lost in music. I've spent a good deal of my life doing just that. But you'll eventually get bored. Everyone has a tipping point—maybe two or three records in—when music turns into noise and silence sounds good. But you've got to do *something* with your silence.

When I started college I was in a band. We would play all over the state on the weekends, and I'd take classes throughout the week. I remember signing up for a philosophy class. I was raised way outside of a city, so just seeing the word "philosophy" on my schedule seemed exotic. Part of me felt like the answers to all life's mysteries were at my fingertips. The truth is, even after a few classes, I didn't really understand what philosophy was—I just knew I kinda liked it, and it seemed to be asking interesting questions, so the author of this book talked me into adding it to my list of majors. Yeah, that, and only one of my philosophy professors came to hear that band. I still know him. He wrote a book on rock and philosophy. Asked me to read it. Then I wrote this foreword.

After a few years studying, I was still playing music, but the purpose of Western philosophy seemed at least a little clearer to me: Ask questions about heady stuff that can't be answered verifiably, then give your answers some thought, bounce it off what some other dead guys say, and then write four hundred to eight hundred pages about it. Despite the inherent futility, the endeavor of philosophy is surprisingly gratifying and unsurprisingly painful. If questions about the nature of right and wrong are what trip your trigger, it turns out there are books on books written over centuries talking about how to systematically determine if something is right or wrong. If it's art you're interested in, thinkers in the field of aesthetics can show you multitudes of ways in which to judge and conceptualize beauty. And so on.

Western philosophy is something of an analytic meditation on stuff that has puzzled humans for millennia. Once we humans got the food thing figured out and had a little free time on our hands, we had a bit of silence we had to fill up with something. Some eccentrics filled it up with wondering about stuff. Some eccentrics filled it up with making music. Both of the impulses are somewhere in our brains and guts and muscles and bones. Some folks are better at wondering and some folks are better at making music. Some folks are not good at either, so they become accountants and forklift drivers, and that's fine too. I used to drive a forklift, and I liked it.

Auxier found a way to convince people to let him wonder about stuff for a living, because he was really, really good at it, and he wasn't good enough at making music. (Well, I guess that depends on how well a person wants to eat.) I found a way to convince people to let me write songs for a living, because I wasn't good enough at wondering. (That also depends on how well a fellow wants to eat.) Suffice to say, we're eating well, or well enough for now.

So here we are, at a paperback crossroad of music and philosophy, still wondering why we're here. The truth of it is, you have to have some way to fill in the silence after your ears are saturated, when you've already listened to a few records on a Sunday and you need something else to do. Chances are, if you're attracted to a word like "philosophy," you're probably attracted to at least some of the things philosophy deals with. Since you love music, why not spend a little time weaving your wonder through a few of your favorite songs to think about why those songs are so important to you to begin with? You might find out something about yourself.

Look, these are great essays. I've read them. At the end of the day, they won't put food on your table or anything, but to some of us music-lovers, there's some solace in the act of reflection. I've had a love-hate relationship with philosophy over the years—it's dense stuff, and I can't help but feel my own intellectual limits when I read it. But, I'm past that now and happy with my lot as a finite little speck who wonders about stuff from time to time. If you love music and have wondered even a little about why you love it so much, turn up your brain to eleven and listen to this record. It's not nearly as cool as music, but it's a more wonderful way to fill your silence.

Sources

Four of these chapters (Chapters 7, 13, 14, and 18) appear for the first time in this volume, as do "Late Summer: Like a Window in Your Heart" and "Afterword: Long Live Rock."

The other chapters (here revised and updated) first appeared in the following publications:

Chapters 1, 2, and 3, "The Glimmer Twins," "When the Whip Comes Down," and "Frenzy," in *The Rolling Stones and Philosophy: It's Just a Thought Away*, edited by Luke Dick and George A. Reisch, Open Court, 2012;

Chapters 4 and 5, "When Jumpin' Jack Flash Met Ziggy Stardust" and "Warm Impermanence" in *David Bowie and Philosophy: Rebel Rebel*, edited by Theodore G. Ammon, Open Court, 2016;

Chapter 6, "Magic Pages and Mythic Plants," in *Led Zeppelin and Philosophy: All Will Be Revealed*, edited by Scott Calef, Open Court, 2009;

Chapter 8, "It's All Dark: The Eclipse of the Damaged Brain," in *Pink Floyd and Philosophy: Careful with That Axiom, Eugene!*, edited by George A. Reisch, Open Court, 2007;

Chapter 9, "A Touch of Grey: Gratefully Dead?" in *The Grateful Dead and Philosophy: Getting High Minded about Love and Haight*, edited by Steven Gimbel, Open Court, 2007;

Chapters 10, 11, and 12, "An Everlasting Kiss: The Seduction of Wendy," "Blinded by the Subterranean Homesick Muse: The Poet as Virtuoso and Virtuous," and "Prophets and Profits: Poets, Preachers, and Pragmatists," in *Bruce Springsteen and Philosophy: Darkness on the Edge of Truth*, edited by Randall E. Auxier and Doug Anderson, Open Court, 2008;

Chapter 15, "Christ in a Sidecar: An Ontology of Suicide Machines," in *Harley-Davidson and Philosophy: Full-Throttle Aristotle*, edited by Bernard E. Rollin, Carolyn M. Gray, Kerri Mommer, and Cynthia Pineo, Open Court, 2006;

Chapter 16, "Yesterday's Tom Sawyers," in *Rush and Philosophy: Heart and Mind United*, edited by Jim Berti and Durrell Bowman, Open Court, 2011;

Chapter 17, "Dead Reckoning and Tacking the Winds of Fortune and Fate," in *Jimmy Buffett and Philosophy: The Porpoise Driven Life*, edited by Erin McKenna and Scott L. Pratt, Open Court, 2009.

The title, *Metaphysical Graffiti*, was used as an album title by the satirical rock band The Dead Milkmen, in 1990, in a reference to the Led Zeppelin album, *Physical Graffiti* (1975).

Late Summer: Like a Window in Your Heart

Late summer, 2011. This is traveling music for sure. We are northbound on "Future I-26 West." You read that right. North Carolina has a quasi-interstate by that name. My traveling companion is the wife of my first marriage, since 1986, a very good year (apart from the politics), and the year we all went to Graceland.

We received a complimentary copy of the silver anniversary edition of Paul Simon's now classic recording. As soon as it landed on the kitchen table, I felt a little tingle I would interpret as "woo-hoo," followed closely by the sinking realization that if this was *Graceland*'s twenty-fifth year, what the hell happened to the last quarter century? Then I looked at the pictures of Paul Simon from 1986. I didn't need to examine any pictures of myself from that year to confirm that both he and I are wearing the evidence. We were surely squinting at the sun and eating dinner for that longish lapse. (Why am *I* so soft in the middle, Mr. Beerbelly?)

So I planned and then anticipated my opportunity to revisit *Graceland* on an upcoming road trip. I suppose I could have waited for a trip down the Delta that looms in my future, but somehow late summer, as the days converge on school-year bustle, is a time for reflections over longer epochs of our durational awareness. Everyone thinks New Year's Eve is the moment for this kind of consciousness, but in truth, that occasion is forced. The length of the epoch is too fixed—a year, a decade, a century, a millennium—all arbitrary numbers and invented occasions, imposed like incidents and accidents on a fluid field of passage.

But a quarter century, or rather, a third of a lifetime, from a milestone moment we shared, as communities, as nations, as a globe . . . well, there's nothing arbitrary about that. Twenty-five years ago (counting back from 2011), Nelson Mandela was still imprisoned, and Truth and Reconciliation was an impossible dream. Now it is the finest accomplishment in human history. Paul Simon's role in the unfolding events of the late-Eighties and early-Nineties, while apartheid was coming to an end, is ambiguous. The heavy lifting was done by tens of thousands of ordinary folks with iron wills and soft hearts, almost none of them from our hemisphere. But the Americans needed a symbol, some vessel from which our collective incomprehension of South African suffering could be poured out over the suburbs, sprinkled on the heads of Protestants and Catholics and Jews, incorporating them into the body of the struggle, however superficially.

What Simon learned during his artistic journey was that we knew more about this distant world than we thought. Something sleeping in the sounds, seeping out of the roots of the Delta rhythms and creeping into our brains. It still remains. It isn't just an analogy between American apartheid and the movement that struck it down. Rather, there is something darker, four hundred years removed, that still calls and answers across the ocean and the centuries, something that wells up in the body when the beat commences.

Our music *is* African music. Some vestige of the simple freedom song flows over the jerky gyrations of colonizers and middle-passage merchants, smoothing it into a heartbeat. That is what *Graceland* feels like, and that is what we felt as a culture when we put it on the turntable. As the writer of this story, the tale of our raised consciousness, maybe Paul Simon claimed credit beyond what was appropriate, but he was undoubtedly the conduit through which this remembrance of four centuries passed from the present into the future. Or so it seems to me a third of a life later, northbound on Future I-26 West.

※　※　※　※　※

Another day, late summer, 2014. A gas station in Pennsylvania, just north of Gettysburg. $3.45 a gallon. There is music beneath the canopy as we feed our machines. I know it well, and so do you. . . . *The Mississippi Delta is shining like a National Guitar.* . . . I hum along. So do you. We are now in this together, wafted in song through the . . . *cradle of the Civil War* . . . What? I never really heard that before. The Civil War was a baby once? In the Delta? I wonder if the grown version of that infant is any less horrible than this stunning image.

And then we aren't together anymore, you and me. *I have been primed. I am listening with new ears.* I hear another lyric, as if for the first time, and it robs me of my present, your company included. I am transported and if you were watching, you'd see it and know it for what it is. I think you've had the ride yourself. Ironies tumble over regrets and disappear into a haze of history, mystic chords of memory, a statesman once said. Yes, she comes back to tell him she's gone. Yes, he knows that, he knows his own bed, and then, like a hammer, it falls:

She said losing love is like a window in your heart . . .
Everyone sees the wind blow

I grew up less than a mile from this songwriter's destination, which is Graceland, which is the name of the song, which is the name of the album, which is the name of the junior high school where I got my first broken heart. I had to walk by the gates to get to school. I can't help the autobiography in this book, but I think my experience is enough like yours to keep us interested in each other. I now realize that some of my experiences were extraordinary, but I didn't know that when they happened. Maybe the occasional indulgences in personal memory won't put you off. I want you to reach back and also forward in your life, your experience with this music. You have your late summers and your own heart's window.

Like a window in your heart. See how devastated the poet really is. He knows you remember when it happened to you. But he has his pride. He has *her* say it. *Losing love* (and I'm not becoming maudlin, just thinking with my keyboard) *is like a window in your heart.* Dammit, but *that's it. That's* how it is. That is *exactly* how it is. Our narrator repeats it in his own voice the second time around in this song. I guess even brokenhearted people in the world can agree, sometimes. Shine until tomorrow, then.

Notice how this gifted poet moves right to the horrifying idea that people can see in, or rather, he has the woman who broke his heart move to that idea, and it is absolutely true. They can. But that isn't what occurs to *me* first—not at all. And maybe not to Paul Simon either. That's his other half speaking, and irony is the trope. Who out there is like this narrator, as I imagine him? (And like me?) Is this Lincoln Duncan, fifteen summers later? Has Princess Leia (RIP) done him in?

I see the woman who said this in my mind's eye. She is pretty, sad eyes, determined chin, and this isn't her first heart-break. She has been on both sides of that symbol. She knows how to do what's necessary, and she is in charge of seeing what that is. Necessity is her possession. Possibility is for children and dreamers and poets and those hopeless poor boys who think they have reason to believe we all will be received. Fools sporting for another broken heart.

For suchlike, that window is not a matter of other people seeing in. Only sad-eyed, determined-chin, pretty ones think about that sort of thing. For me (and for Elvis and Paul, and Lincoln Duncan, as I imagine them), that window is something that lets me see out. *Having* love is like owning one's own heart, and all that is in it. That's why losing love is like watching that same stuff from the window, looking at a world you can't really control, let alone possess. The chances that someone would bother to look in are very small, even if you're Elvis. It doesn't matter that people *could* see you. They won't notice anyway. There's no risk here. And if they do look, so what? You're heartbroken. So is everybody else. They'll have compassion because they are the same. There is no risk, no shame, no problem at all with having people see in, if they ever look.

The whole beauty of the image works in the other direction. To have a hole entices us to see the outside, the beyond. *That's* where the risk is. Can we bear to look? Can I bear to look? Do I just pass the window daily until I no longer notice what's out there? Do I assure myself that nothing really changes out there? Or do I sit in front of the window and watch the seasons change, watch for the smallest detail of the landscape, ask the big scary questions about why it all looks like it does and where it came from?

I don't have enough life left to sit by all of these windows and contemplate the scenery. I have stuff to do before I check out. But losing love is like a window in your heart. It's a mystery how anyone ever gets in, but everybody who leaves does so by way of a window, made to order. Or double doors, in some cases, depending on whatever they take the time to frame.

*   *   *   *   *

I met Elvis when I was nine years old. My mother was driving me and my sister home from swimming at the YMCA in late summer, and my grandmother (born 1896; this was 1970, so you do the math) was with us. Elvis was on his way down the curving driveway as we passed Graceland. That wasn't unusual. I know you're sitting there saying "No way . . ." but the man had to live somewhere. Before he got fat, he used to be out and about town all the time.

People in Memphis left Elvis alone unless he wanted to talk. Everyone understood he was just like anyone else, except much cooler and better looking, which wasn't his fault. Half the people in Whitehaven (that is the area of town he lived in, and yes, that is its actual name) during those years (1959–1977) met Elvis at one time or another, and everybody *saw* him. When he left the building, well, this is where he went.

On this day he was bopping down the driveway and my mother said, "He's going to open the gate." Elvis did that sometimes. He would open the gate and let a crowd gather and talk and joke and sign autographs and kiss the girls. He did it a few times a year, when he was in the mood. Mom could tell from his attitude he was in that mood. My grandmother demanded that my mom pull over. She was from the mountains of eastern Kentucky and only visiting us, but she wanted to meet Elvis. Grandma was more a Hank Williams kind of gal (I mean the real Hank Williams, not the generational copies), and she didn't care for rock and roll, but this was Elvis and she wanted to know what all the fuss was about.

So Mom parked the car by the side of the road (now called Elvis Presley Boulevard, but then it was merely South Bellevue). My sister and I were still wet from the pool, in our swimsuits. We didn't look our best, but who cares? We walked back to the gate as it opened and had Elvis to ourselves for about five minutes. He kissed my mom (a good-looking woman and the same age as Elvis, but he liked the young ones), and my sister (who was eleven—he didn't like them quite that young), and then my grandmother. He shook my hand.

I don't remember the conversation, but if one thing settled into my mind it was "music gets you girls." I haven't had reason to revise that hypothesis, but the full syllogism evaded me at the time: Girls break your heart. Therefore, music breaks your heart. I think Elvis knew it pretty well. But I took up the bass guitar anyway.

*   *   *   *   *

I played my first paying gig four years later, in late summer, at the Moose Lodge. I was substituting on the bass guitar for a guy who had been busted for possession. The band's name? "Busted." They should have chosen another name, I think. The drummer was even younger than I was, but the rest of the band was of age, actual pros. It was cool. There would be girls.

I have played rock and roll in bars ever since that time, branching out into singer-songwriter stuff when I learned the guitar, and played around Memphis on both drums and bass in the early 1980s. My love of rock music is visceral, permanent, and sustaining. I went to college to mark time and dropped out to play all the time—a common enough story. That was a tough couple of years, trying to make a living that way. College might be easier. I went back. It was.

Then philosophy came into my purview. You could get paid for *that*? No shit? What a great country, what an amazing time to live in, when people can get paid for such. And it gives you time to play music in bars, too. All you have to do is stay in school through your entire twenties and into your thirties, and pass many tests and write many boring papers and learn a few languages and then somehow find a job. Piece of cake compared to making a living at music.

I remember thinking, as I was making my way through the undergraduate portion of that path, "I wonder if any of these philosophy people ever think about Jim Morrison?" He seemed pretty profound to me. I have since learned that he did take philosophy classes at Florida State, and he did read Heidegger. So I innocently asked a fellow philosophy major if he thought Jim Morrison was a philosopher. He was scandalized by the suggestion, offended, derided me for even asking. "Okay," I said and backed off, a little confused, chastened. But I thought to myself, in my secret heart "There is something in Jim Morrison's lyrics . . . in the way he sings. That dude is thinking." And *I* wanted to think about it and maybe write about it. I still haven't done Jim Morrison, but I might.

I think there is a lot of philosophically interesting stuff going on in the music that was made from the onset of the rock era and up through the 1980s. I sort of checked out in the 1990s, but then, so did the good music. I'm not saying there was no good music between then and now. There was a lot, but somehow it isn't the same. John Lennon said in about 1968 that all the rock and roll songs had been written and it was just going to be repetition from there on. He was right, but he missed the timing by about twenty years.

I spent the last thirty years on college campuses. Decade after decade I have watched the students discover and then take up *as their own* the music I grew up with. It was better. It just was, and is. So let's wend our way through some of it. You'll see that I have a predilection for Bruce Springsteen and the Rolling Stones are a close second. But whatever your favorites are, I think you might not mind if I dwell on mine, this time around. By all means, substitute your own memories for mine and remake these stories around the moments when that lyric you'd heard a hundred times before suddenly *hit you*. I know it will be strongest when it brings back a lost love and a broken heart. But it is *that* moment, when the lyric hits, when we hear with new ears, notice the groove or the harmony for the first time. That moment is why I think about the music, and because I *have to* think about it, I have to write about it.

The music gets in, you know? Somehow it just worms its way right into the heart of things and becomes the silent urge to look out of one of those windows. There's not much to see out there, after a few heartbreaks, but if you'll notice the contours of the window, you'll feel yourself slip-sliding back. My Mom passed away in late summer. In fact, it was last week, as I type this. It was August 16th, 2016. She was pretty, sad eyes, determined chin. Elvis kissed her once. You know, losing love is like a window in your heart. She left us thirty-nine years, to the day, after Elvis died. Damnable late summer.

I'm not depressed. I'm just not one to pass by a window without looking out. And when I look, there are questions, more of them than answers. Some people are like that. That's how it looks out the window today. Tomorrow? Well, that's another day, right?

Carbondale, Illinois
Late Summer 2016

A SIDE

It's Only Rock and Roll

1
The Glimmer Twins

Sometimes it seems ordained by the gods that certain pairs of people just have to go through the proverbial threescore and ten *together*, the whole damn thing. You know what I'm talking about because you've known people, especially certain couples, who play in the sandbox, date, marry, divorce, remarry, divorce again, and still end up together. Full disengagement isn't among the options, even when they no longer *want* to be entangled. Is it a cosmic joke of some kind? If that occasional feature of human life, alone, isn't weird enough, the phenomenon becomes still more interesting when the entangled pair is famous and artistic. Mick and Keith are not only December's Children. They're destiny's children.

The fact that they were a Stone's throw from each other in the unassuming burb of Dartford, and schoolmates (if not quite friends) even before they hooked up in their teens, adds a bit of romance to our way of imagining their destiny. That also isn't a bad place to start wondering. It invites speculation, for instance, on what might have been if they had been on different buses on a particular day (the point at which the collaboration *really began*). The world with no Rolling Stones? How could that be, and how far-reaching the consequences? I don't know about you, but I can't easily work out how my own life would be different with no Stones. They have been so pervasive as a presence for so long, supplying the soundtrack of my entire life and probably yours too, well, I just don't know. Many of my ideas, especially about rock music, but about a full range of aesthetic topics, used The Stones as a model. Anyway, I don't think I can quite believe in destiny, but cosmic entanglement I have seen first hand. So it's hard to grasp how long the Jagger-Richards tentacles might be, but hardly any part of the world is wholly out of the reach of their collaboration.

When it comes to Mick and Keith, on the one hand, it seems sort of inevitable that two kids with such similar drives and musical tastes, and occupying almost the same space, would eventually hook up, but *meeting* isn't quite enough. The circumstances of meeting needed to be such as to open rather than close the doors. Earlier encounters between Jagger and Richards had failed to produce that "moment of recognition." In the days before The Stones formed, any number of events might have taken them in different directions. And so, in that light, it all seems quite evitable. (My computer actually recognizes that word, so I am deprived of my snarky moment of creative rebellion by the Microsoft Corporation; maybe some things are evitable, but not Microsoft, I add chalantly.)

Pretty Pairs

What makes this more than a matter of idle curiosity is that just this entangled duo turned out to be the Glimmer Twins, the most culturally important *genuine* collaboration in music in the second half of the twentieth century. Lennon and McCartney didn't really collaborate on their songwriting—more of a corporation there than a co-operation, a good business deal. We could certainly take The Beatles as a whole to be a crucial collaboration, but they were not entangled for life, and at the core of that whole effort, John and Paul were mostly writing their songs individually. It's different from the Mick-and-Keith nexus. The kind of creative collaboration that intrigues me goes all the way down and all the way up, which includes dipping into the ether and pulling out the songs together, not just individually, then taking whatever is found forward into recording, performance, and through decades of response and repetition. A song can't "exist" more completely than do some of the Jagger-Richards classics.

When a full-bodied collaboration comes up in the domain of music, at least during the brief 175 years since the "song" became the dominant musical unit, we usually find that one half of the pair writes the music, the other writes the lyrics. The Gershwins, Rodgers-Hart (later Hammerstein), Lerner-Loewe, and, from a later day, John-Taupin or even Garcia-Hunter would be the other pairs one might mention. But fewer were full collaborations, with both members contributing both lyrics and music, and also taking the music from bottom to top. Page-Plant and Waters-Gilmour come to mind along with the Glimmer Twins as partners who also made a living sharing the stage, *presenting* what they had created. And these collaborations were more than songwriting, entering into every phase of the creation of commercial music.

Of those three pairs, the Glimmer Twins were the most enduring and successful, but I'm aware that to say they were the most important, as artists, can be disputed. It's really tough to imagine any commercial music more important, artistically speaking, than Pink Floyd's, and no single project of The Stones had the impact of either *Dark Side of the Moon* or *The Wall*. The artistic impact of Zeppelin's body of work is also very serious, if not as focused or sustained as the Waters-Gilmour creations. What I will say is that while I think the fruits of the Waters-Gilmour partnership are more intense and deeper, I do not believe their overall impact on the world, as artists, was greater, nor do I find their creative process very intriguing, for reasons you may or may not find compelling. But instead of dissecting Waters and Gilmour, let me put it in more positive terms.

I'll just blurt it out: the reason The Stones pair is more interesting, from a philosophical and human point of view, is because it's so very clear that Mick and Keith actually always *loved* each other, being far more than friends and something closer to brothers, nay, actual twin sons of different mothers, as Mick once said. Except they are also a bit like a married couple at the same time, or so it appears when one sees them bickering. Yet, even that characterization sort of understates the matter, if some of the biographers are to be believed. Christopher Andersen basically claims that Mick was *in love* with Keith and depicts a Jones-Jagger-Richards love triangle when the three shared a flat on Edith Grove, in the early days. This triangle was the beginning of a lifetime of jealousies, any time someone else moved in to take Keith away from Mick, or Mick away from Keith, there was going to be trouble.

Frankly, I don't know what to believe about any of that, and I don't much care, but a lot of what people like Andersen say seems to be confirmed in Keith's autobiography. What I'm talking about between them might or might not involve lust, and I wouldn't be surprised if lust is part of the story. It certainly *does* involve jealousy of various kinds. The creative process for artists is inseparable from *eros*, as I understand that ancient idea. Still, there's more to *eros* than sexual desire—it can be directed in many ways—but if *eros* comes to be expressed by artists in sexual activity, no one ought to be surprised. And if that sort of desire is the close companion of jealousy, and perhaps also envy, well, we all know how stories like that go. Things get ugly sometimes. It's not as if The Stones were renowned for their wisdom, maturity, restraint, and circumspection.

My point is that the obvious depth of Mick's and Keith's relationship makes their creative process all the more fascinating (and perhaps easier to understand). Waters and Gilmour had a hard time ever tolerating each other, while Page and Plant apparently didn't even have the decency to argue very much. The Page-Plant pair is considered later, in Chapter 6, but I could add in this context that it looks to me as if almost anyone could probably get on well with Robert Plant, who seems so easygoing as to be almost otherworldly. It also appears that Roger Waters can't even manage to tolerate himself, perhaps that's why others have difficulty (and his art may well require just these problems). I don't know any of these people, so I could be very wrong. I'm just saying how it looks. But I am sure of this much: Mick and Keith both have huge personalities, big enough to fill a stadium, and when you lock something that powerful in a single room, and it doesn't blow up the whole house, *that's interesting*.

Picking a Fight

So we're talking about artistic temperaments here. That has to be a part of the story about the collaboration of the twins. But we want more than psychology from this little exploration. Let's get at something about *creativity*, when it comes from *interaction*, instead of just one person. The kind of creativity that only happens between two people, and *particular* people at that, the interdependence, is fascinating. We have a habit, in this culture, of thinking that "genius" (whatever it is) lives in *individual* artists, but I am convinced that isn't the whole truth. There are people who can only achieve genius together, and who absolutely *cannot* get at that level of creativity alone. I think Mick and Keith are like that. Don't get me wrong. They are both very good alone, and I think they might both have become famous alone, but when they work together, that's when we get into the realm of genius.

There are really two ways philosophers mull over the question of art (including music). There are those who worry mainly about the "work," such as the song or the symphony or the painting or the sculpture. They will argue about the definition of what does or doesn't count as a "work of art," and they will discuss how we can or should interpret the work. This is the stuff most of us are on about. So, if I were like that (and I'm not), I'd try to get you wondering about certain songs or albums, or even certain concerts or videos. It's pretty natural to be curious about those things. We like to take the *product* of our creativity and use it to find the meaning and value of art in our common experience. The work itself is our guide to thinking about what artists *are*, and so forth. In this case the philosophy of art is about *things*, and what things can tell us.

Other philosophers (like me) worry more about the creative process itself, and we want to understand what happens and what *can* happen in the course of *creating* works of art. Such philosophers are often more interested in the artist than in the art, wanting to know what (if anything) makes (good, great) artists different from other folks, and inquiring into why and how they do what they do. From this viewpoint, the key to understanding the *work* is to understand how it came into existence. For folks like us, to think about works of art *without* thinking through the creative process is like building a castle in the air. So this is about processes, not about things.

In fact (and now I'm picking a fight), I would go so far as to say that there isn't a single "thing," strictly speaking, that *is* "the" work of art. Artworks *are* processes, even after they're nominally "finished." Mick's and Keith's song "Street Fighting Man" means one thing in 1968 and something different now, and you can't completely separate one from the other. To speak of that song as an artwork *in the fullest sense* is to begin when it didn't exist—was just a glimmer in the twins' eye—and bring the story up to the present day. You can cut off a slice of time at some point, if you like, and just talk about the song in that context, but don't try to claim that this half-story just *is* the song. You can't really bottle up a work of art in a single slice of time. Artworks don't really work like that.

To give another example, hearing Keith do "Gimme Shelter" with the X-Pensive Winos really transforms the song. They totally jam on that song, and I am really moved by the way Keith sings it. Prior to that new interpretation of the song, it was something less than it is now. Go to YouTube and watch it. See if you don't agree. Artworks are living processes, and the processes are connected with their origins, their creators. Sometimes an artwork awaits the right context—Michelangelo's *David* surrounded by his own unfinished works in the *Academia* in Florence instead of standing in the entrance way for which it was commissioned, or Aretha Franklin singing "You Make Me Feel (Like a Natural Woman)," instead of Carole King (who certainly did a decent job, but anyone can see she wrote it for Aretha, whether she knew it at the time or not—and I'll bet both would agree). So context is a moving target and it matters very much to thinking about works of art.

Only Rock'n Roll

One of the best known among philosophers of the creative process was Susanne Langer (1895–1985). She believed that any philosopher who wanted to talk about art at least needed to try a hand at *making it*, first. That's the only way to prevent "empty or naive generalizations," she said. Really it takes more than that, though, since nobody can be good at all the arts, even enough to get a fair sense of them. What we have to do, if we want to say true or wise things about art, is choose the arts we are good enough at to enjoy a few real moments of successfully creating *within* the art form or medium. But even then, the real artists themselves must be our teachers. So when we later look at art *philosophically*, aiming to understand how it is created, we need to begin with what the artists *say* along with what they show us. The uncomfortable truth is that Mick and Keith are doing something you and I can't do (not at anything like their level), and that's why we have to listen to their version of what's happening.

Artists have peculiar ways of talking about what they do, however. Here is Keith, for example, on the question of rhythm:

> There's something primordial in the way we react to pulses without even knowing it. We exist on a rhythm of seventy-two beats per minute. The train, apart from getting them from the Delta to Detroit, became very important to blues players because of the rhythm of the machine, the rhythm of the tracks, and then you cross onto another track, the beat moves. It echoes something in the human body. So then when you have machinery involved, like trains, and drones, all of that is still built in as music inside us. The human body will feel rhythms even when there's not one. Listen to "Mystery Train" by Elvis Presley. One of the great rock-and-roll tracks of all time, not a drum on it. It's just a suggestion, because the body will provide the rhythm. Rhythm really only has to be suggested. Doesn't have to be pronounced. That's where they got it wrong with "this rock" and "that rock." It's got nothing to do with rock. It's to do with roll. (*Life*, p. 44)

This is all over the place. I think I know what he's getting at here, but this is a string of insights and reports and examples and assertions all tangled together. I'm sure it's all true, in its context, properly qualified, and so on, but it isn't in the artist's temper or among his purposes to explain it all. Langer says:

> The philosopher must know the arts, so to speak, "from the inside." But no one can know all the arts in this way. This entails an arduous amount of non-academic study. [In other words, you have to learn to play guitar or something.] His teachers, furthermore, are artists, and they speak their own language, which largely resists translation into the more careful, literal vocabulary of philosophy. This is likely to arouse his impatience. But it is, in fact, impossible to talk about art without adopting to some extent the language of the artists. The reason why they talk as they do [see Keith above] is not entirely (though it is partly) because they are discursively untrained and popular in their speech; nor [are] they [simply] misled by "bad speech habits" [just the beginning of Keith's bad habits I'm sure] . . . Their vocabulary is metaphorical because it has to be plastic and powerful to let them speak their serious and often difficult thoughts. They cannot see art as "merely" this-or-that easily comprehensible phenomenon; they are too interested in it to make concessions to language. (*Feeling and Form*, p. ix)

Artists really do try to understand what they're doing, and that's because they are in constant pursuit of the end product, trying to nail down whatever it is that can pull the best stuff into concrete existence, from all the possibilities. Maybe it's only rock and roll, but that doesn't matter unless we all like it.

Genius

Even at that, things are still pretty mysterious in the creative process. Maybe it's better to look at a creative *collaboration* because at least you get *two* takes on what happens. That strategy also adds complexities, sure enough, but it may be easier to get at the core of the creative process by triangulating: place yourself at one angle in the triangle and watch the other two move around you. Whatever Mick and Keith may say or do, they are held together by *you* (your question "how'd you do that?") and by the fact that they did really write those songs and play those shows. The songs exist and the shows actually happened. The collaboration occurred. You've heard the results. We can get to the bottom of this, at least in a general way.

The tempting word for what they make together is genius, but I think in their case we're more likely to want to call the outcome—the song, the show, the video—a *work* of genius than pin the label on either of our twins. The word "genius" has a weird sort of history. It used to be thought of as a sort of spirit that comes from beyond and settles on certain people for a time. Then it came to be thought of like a reliable muse of some sort. People would say "he has the genius of writing" or "she has the genius of painting." But nobody said that one person or another was "a genius," in our modern sense, until the late eighteenth century. There was a dude with the unfortunate name of Immanuel Kant (which is pronounced very close to what you think—it's what Keith calls people he really holds in contempt). He made good on his name, some people think, by being one. But he's the guy who wrote about genius in a way that stuck:

> *Genius* is the talent (natural endowment) that gives the rule to art. Since talent is an innate productive ability of the artist, and as such belongs itself to nature, we could also put it this way: *Genius* is the

innate mental disposition through which nature gives the rule to art. . . . For every art presupposes rules . . . [and] since a product can never be called art unless it is preceded by a rule, it must be nature in the subject (and through the attunement of his powers) that gives the rule to art. (*Critique of Judgment*, pp. 174–75)

Admittedly the guy is a little bit stuffy. Okay, he's a twit, but this really is the guy who is responsible for the way we talk about individual people being "geniuses" these days. We added scientists and mathematicians in with the artists somewhere along the way, but at first it was just artists. Something in their subjective natures allows them to produce works that give the rule to the rest of the art. To be genius, Kant goes on to say, talent procures originality, originality leads the work to be an exemplar, and "exemplarity" of the work just is *nature* in the artist. Blah, blah, blah. It's a fancy way of saying they're not supernatural, but they're not exactly like us, either.

Kant goes on to say that geniuses don't understand and can't explain their own powers, and you might as well not bother asking them because all you'll get is bullshit. (That's my summary; Kant himself, being very old-fashioned, rarely used the word "bullshit.") This all seems fine, as far as it goes, but why do some people have this genius and others don't? And also, I think he left out something really crucial, which is that sometimes genius works only when two people are at it together. So we're back to Mick and Keith, together.

Let It Bleed

To get the philosophical stuff worked out, we'll have to rehearse our facts, as far as we can know them. It's sort of like trying to guess what happens inside of a marriage. You never really know, even if you're the marriage counselor. Even if you get to hear both sides and ask any question, you still don't really know. But we do the best we can with what we have, and I'll try not to draw too many conclusions about what really happened between Mick and Keith, when they were being geniuses. (It's a little clearer what to think when they're just being assholes, since we can all pretty well pull *that* off.)

Even though Keith usually wrote the music and Mick the lyrics, there weren't any rules in their collaboration, and these guys never liked rules very much anyway (and we all know what they'd think of Kant). Some songs are all Mick's, some are all Keith's, and every variation in between, and some of those, although largely created alone, are works of genius (or at least rules through which the *nature* of rock and roll gives the rule to the *art* of rock and roll). Keith says, for example, that when Mick would bring in a song that was largely complete, like "Brown Sugar," he (Keith) would start out playing it on a six-string guitar in standard tuning, not his five-string guitar in open G tuning. The reason is that Mick plays standard and Keith didn't want to just assume the song should be crammed into his favorite nook. But often the songs would take on a wonderful new life when Keith did pick up the five-string and say to Mick, "What about this . . . ?"

I have a friend and old band mate, a well-known guitar player in Memphis, who is a Keith Richards expert and has learned to do everything Keith does. I remember him telling me about the first time "Brown Sugar" came on the radio in Memphis in 1968. "From the first chord, you just knew," he said. Knew what? "It was a number one song." I have to agree. That was certainly one that "Mick wrote," but it received some ineffable part of its life, of its nature, of its genius from the five-string tuning and from that tight sound, so different from "Honky Tonk Women" or "Start Me Up," where you can hear just a bit of the separation among the five strings, as the chord is stroked. On "Brown Sugar," not only is the guitar sound a little more like a green cherry than a ripe apple, it's also exactly the tart thing it just *has to be* to convey the song, to *make* it a work of genius. Did Mick write "Brown Sugar"? Not alone, in the important sense, because without that perfect sound, and the perfect riffs (both the three-note and the six-note riffs that punctuate that rhythm guitar), it just isn't genius.

The boundary between what Mick did and what Keith did would be impossible to draw. There were also boundary problems in their partnership, mainly because there apparently weren't any healthy ones ever established, and maybe that was a needed feature for them to succeed. The twins reversed roles of bad guy and good guy even though they always were, to their later and mutual consternation, better together than apart and thus rendered creatively (and emotionally) interdependent early in life. The things they could do only together became, at times, an open wound, so for the sake of better art they just let it bleed. At other times their interdependence was a scab they couldn't resist picking.

Keith says it's "in the DNA code" that "sooner or later the two principals will turn on each other because one of them will be driven crazy by the knowledge that to be at their best they need to perform with the other person and therefore they need that other person to be successful, or even to be heard. It makes you hate that person. Well, it didn't in my case, because I wanted us to depend on each other and carry on" (*Life*, p. 501). It doesn't appear the twins have been genuinely happy with each other since about late 1968 (the Anita Pallenberg film debacle), which is to say that there are people in this world with grandchildren, who weren't themselves even *born* the last time Mick and Keith were really "good mates," as they might put it.

Anyone can see why they "stay together," practically speaking. Each wants what he can get only with the co-operation of the other, sort of like why people stay in difficult marriages to be with their children. In this case it looks more complicated, though, because the creative side of their partnership, especially the songwriting process, requires more than a set of practical decisions concerning the kids, more than détente. It requires at least some genuine vulnerability to the judgments of the other, along with an openness to finding complementary wavelengths. There is a kind of pre-verbal communication that occurs in artistic (and any creative) collaboration, and it seems to require a kind of trust, at least if the songs have any depth (so these are *not* like most of those Nashville-style arranged songwriting dates).

In past years, Keith would stand at the microphone with his musical ideas and sing fragments of lines and make vowel sounds in a semi-linguistic encounter with possible language, while Mick would turn this "voweling" into lyrics. It was speaking in tongues. By the time they did *Bridges to Babylon*, their producer, Don Was, had to bounce between them so they could write the songs. Don Was would try to take notes from Keith's glossolalia, go over to Mick and toss all that nonsense out, while Mick wrote lyrics. In that fashion, if Keith has it right, they made the entire album without even speaking to one another. I'm sorry folks, but that's just strange . . . not that they aren't speaking, but that they're still writing songs without speaking.

So, in a way, it's not that Mick and Keith are staying together for practical reasons, working out the business decisions through lawyers and producers, even though that side of it certainly exists. Rather, even after they decimated and belittled one another on the world stage, to the point of no return, it's like they still agreed to have more children, so to speak, by surrogacy if necessary, and they did so for a long, long time (perhaps now with a new blues album they're post-menopausal, but I don't know; I wouldn't bet on it). Whatever the "genius" is here, it lives outside of the subjective existence of these boys, each taken alone. It's about how sparks fly when two powerful subjectivities clash, and mesh.

This is a classic case of what philosophers like to call "dialectic." It is a simultaneously destructive and creative encounter of standpoints, and if the "dialectical philosophers" are right, pretty much everything in cultural history gets made by means of such strife. You never get anything worth having without a fight. The master of this kind of philosophy was Georg Hegel (1770–1831), and he didn't think very highly of Kant's idea of "genius." There is a spirit of the times (a "Zeitgeist") that moves the world from one stage of history to the next, with or without the co-operation of the individuals involved. The Stones are a pretty fair example of a group of people on the edge of the Zeitgeist of the 1960s, and somehow they were able to surf that wave all the way into the second decade of the twenty-first century—and that's a long ride.

Fifteen Minutes of Fame?

It may be good to remember that Mick and Keith have been famous for over half a century, and it's unlikely that either can remember what it's like to have anonymity. They never were easily embarrassed and they learned early on that their dirty laundry would be on public display (not that it was altogether bad for business), and even though Mick is generally thought of as being image-conscious and sensitive to criticism, I think it's pretty obvious that both of these guys were temperamentally well-suited to the limelight. If they minded at first that their quarrels ended up in the tabloids, that's all over now. These guys have leathery hides and they're tougher than we are. Ordinary folks like us can't really imagine what their lives are like—but then, they also can't imagine our lives, and surely they envy us at least a little that we can pop over to the corner for an ice cream cone whenever we take a notion.

In hindsight, we see that Mick and Keith are (and always were) serious artists, or if that goes too far, serious *about* their art. They weren't just seeking money or fame. They definitely had a sense of the history they were living. They saw their music as being grounded in a thorough understanding of the side of American culture that gave rise to the blues as an art form. Unlike the blues purists, the twins were quite willing to repackage and sell what they had gleaned; the times required it. But their sincere devotion to blues as an art form is beyond questioning. Get the new album. It's not just that these guys loved the blues, as fans. They also approached it with real intellectual curiosity, made themselves true students, and in time, also initiates. They recognized the enduring aesthetic and cultural value of the blues back when Americans themselves did not. The twins didn't just pore over the music because it was cool; they knew it was good art, in the sense of aesthetically and spiritually significant. They were surprised to find out that Americans didn't pay it much attention.

Hegel thought that the movement of history is given its sensuous appearance by art. To put that in clearer language, when you hear Keith's guitar sound, and you see Mick prancing down the runway, that "show" is the very clothes that history wears when it is rolling from one stage to the next. The geniuses are the ones who are a little bit ahead of the wave. They don't really know or understand what they're doing. They're actually hitting a target no one else even sees, and they are showing us what the future looks like, even before it has to be filled in with politics and religion and all sorts of other slower moving innards. Art is out ahead, giving our senses what *will be* before it really *is*. But it doesn't do that out of the pure blue, it uses all the materials that history has already made, and it taps into all the tensions that currently exist, and then it pulls off a reversal so that what was *last* is now *first* and what was on top is now dependent on what came later, up from the swamp.

The Stones used their fame and influence, both with the public and in the art world, to draw attention to the blues, the bottom rung of the cultural ladder. At the time the Rolling Stones were on the rise, pop art was also pulling down the barriers between fine art and commercial/popular imagery, the beat poets wrote seriously about how the other half lived, and all that messiness cleared the way for low culture to become an object of curiosity around the world. Eventually, "high culture" found itself begging at the banquet.

For whatever reason, American low culture seems to have fascinated everyone who had the opportunity to consider the matter. People had been writing about the plight of the poor and painting and sculpting ordinary life since the Romantic era, so it wasn't the subject matter that was new. What had changed is that the sensibilities of the lower classes, their types of expression and even their aesthetic sense was coming to the center of things, slowly crowding out the old dominance of the earlier age (when the bourgeois tried to ape the aristocrats in taste). Suddenly it had become cool to affirm that the people's art was good, nay *better* than the stuffy old crap we were told we should appreciate.

Art for Art's Sake

Even in the midst of a move across the tracks, there is still a place for what philosophers call "aestheticism." People whose moral and even religious values are drawn from the aesthetic realm are "aesthetes." The pure bluesman is a kind of low culture aesthete, *living* the blues so he can *play* the blues, and not expecting anything more from life or from death. Hank Williams is an example of how that view plays out in country music, or see Townes Van Zandt, or Steve Earle. And The Stones are aesthetes in the rock and roll sense, but they came at a time of transition. The worlds of high and low culture were in a dialectical tango in the 1960s. Being a rock and roll version of the aesthete is not enough to conquer the world (and The Stones, *and* their aesthetic, most definitely *did* prevail). The bluesmen and the hillbilly aesthetes hadn't conquered the world, they had been spit on by it. But The Stones were different.

It isn't an accident that Mick and Keith both began to associate very early with visual artists like Andy Warhol, and with mavens of the art world like Robert Fraser. Painting still represented the domain of high art, like ballet and opera did, but painting was changing. While The Stones were treating blues as something to be elevated, painters were becoming curious about how to take painting down a notch. That Keith was drawn to visual art from the first, and that Ronnie Wood, also a recognized painter, would be a natural fit, seems to confirm the idea that the collective *lives* of The Stones have been and remain a generalized artistic project. Andy Warhol would have been among the first to impress upon them that the lines between fine art and pop culture were being erased, and that to be an artist *now* was to embrace many art forms at once and to cultivate celebrity itself.

The new, post-modern art form was to achieve fame *as an artist*, and so painters needed to be acting and actors should be writing musical scores and composers should take up architecture, while the architects are writing novels, and so on. The all encompassing category of "the artist" as a type of celebrated performer was being popularized. This is, in a sense, the very extreme of the idea of genius. It's genius pushed to its limit, so that no longer does the nature of the genius give the rule to art; now, the genius is a powerful subject who tells both nature and culture what art *is* and *isn't*. It's the apotheosis of celebrity as justified by the idea of genius. It was an irresistible role for anyone with the balls to claim it.

Mick has big balls. He took the bait right away. Keith was a pure musician, but he was willing to play the role, and in this I think Mick was probably his guide. Mick saw that being outrageous and re-inventing one's image in successive spurts was *de rigueur* for the world Warhol prophesied. Mick saw how to do that. He needed Keith to remain grounded in the music, to keep him on some kind of tether and bring him back down to what he really does well, which is front The Stones, and Keith needed Mick to be out there doing that Warhol-esque thing so as to keep The Stones on top, so that everyone would listen to the new music. Keith's job was to develop and deepen himself as a serious musician, and to speak in tongues while Mick interpreted for the world. Each of them was very good at his own principal side of the collaboration, and each was nothing short of brilliant in support of the other.

So, although our twins came from the world of music, specifically the blues, there was no reason to assume that being The Stones, or more specifically, being the Glimmer Twins, was just about being good musicians. They never saw it as being only about fame, fortune, celebrity, or even just about music. There was something about what was happening and had happened to the world itself that called forth a new kind of artist. The Stones knew and intended to be artists themselves, first as bluesmen, and then as creators of songs, albums, images, shows, films, books, and all manner of other things, in an age when being an "artist" meant being perceived and received by the public as a creative person and an aesthete. The older lines were fading.

Sweet Home Chicago

Still, making excellent art always involves getting schooled by the masters. If you want to know why the great movement of Romanticism declined after the first generation, it's because being an excellent Romantic poet requires a classical education that is then (supposedly) rejected for the sake of the power of the personal will, blah, blah, blah. As soon as that first generation of Romantics was gone (Byron, Keats, Shelley), all that was running around Europe was a bunch of narcissistic idiots who thought that being cool was all it took to be a genius.

The Stones, especially the twins and Brian Jones, *did* have masters. They were Muddy Waters and Howlin' Wolf and Willie Dixon and Little Walter and a host of others who are only now recognized for their true cultural and artistic importance. So if you want to know why Nickelback sucks, all you need to do is remember that they don't know the blues. If they did, they wouldn't have to suck. Maybe they went to school on The Stones or Zeppelin, but that's not the right school. That's like trying to learn to paint before you know how to draw. Long before ethnomusicology was a recognized discipline, with its own intellectual standing, The Stones studied everything they could find and used their hands and feet and vocal chords to profess what they knew. Anyone who wants to know how they created what they did has to go to the same school, the University of South Chicago. The Stones wasted no time, when it became possible for them, in arranging to go and sit at the feet of their heroes at Chess.

Keith remarks that if The Stones did nothing else for America, at least they introduced us to our own music. It wasn't easy to see at first, through all the bright lights and the purple haze, that The Stones were teaching us something. For example, Joe Walsh talks about how he learned the blues from The Stones, since no one knew about the blues in the various places he grew up. Many Stones fans would tell a similar story. If Joe can play now, it's because he didn't stop with The Stones, but went back and studied the blues.

The Stones themselves always said, repeatedly, and their actions proved, what they regarded as their artistic bedrock, but the truth is, *to us* their music sounded different from Chicago or Delta blues. It's like going to a distant city and over-hearing some strangers have a deep conversation about the place you're from. They see things you never noticed, and if they never mentioned the name of the place, you might not even recognize that they were talking about your hometown.

Even though I come from Memphis and grew up around some of the music The Stones professed to follow (I didn't know much about the Chicago stuff), I really couldn't *hear* what the connection was supposed to be between what The Stones were playing and what I regularly heard in Memphis. I *loved* The Stones too, from the first, but it didn't sound or feel like anything I ever heard coming out of the Delta. I knew it wasn't the Beatles, but it sounded English to me, what The Stones were doing. Like many fans, I only slowly learned to recognize how the two kinds of music were connected, and as I did begin to understand it, my appreciation for (and understanding of) the blues was transformed.

It took still longer for a lot of other Stones fans (and some still haven't made the trip home) to go back and successfully "retrieve" the Chicago and Delta blues traditions, but that train ride is worth the trouble. Led Zeppelin was so much more overt in its appropriation of that music, so it was easier to see how they did what they did. But that came later. After doing some intense ear-study, and then listening to The Stones again, especially beginning with *Beggar's Banquet*, it all starts falling into place. The Stones' music has the sort of relationship to Chicago blues that Impressionist painting has to Post-impressionism. If you look at Monet's flowers next to Van Gogh's you might agree.

Doomed to Repeat It?

My point here is that the genius of the Glimmer Twins can't be separated from its historical setting. I'm not saying history made them what they are, I'm just saying that their genius depended on getting history right and being just ahead of the spirit of the times. When the future historians of art take a look at the second half of the twentieth century, in two or three hundred years, The Stones are going to be remembered as serious artists, partly because of their cultural impact, but also because they created something of their own which has lasting aesthetic value, and that was a kind of music that hadn't existed before. They may end up being mentioned second, after the Beatles, like Mozart and Beethoven, but you could do worse than *that*. Beethoven also inspired riots by breaking the rules, and he most definitely *was* a rock star, as was Mozart, in that day. There is something to the old saw "the Beatles or The Stones?" as a way of getting to know someone, but I can't personally answer the question with finality.

Not that it needs defending, but I don't think anyone ought to sneer if philosophers who specialize in aesthetics take The Stones seriously *as artists*. Critics clearly do, and sociologists, and historians, and musicologists. The engine of that original contribution to culture is the Jagger-Richards collaboration, and *as* a collaboration I think it is probably more important than any other in the same time-frame, and I don't just mean in music. I'm in a good mood, so I'm willing to be argued with about this, but I can't think of a collaborative team in any medium that is clearly and obviously *more* important, although the challengers would almost all come from the world of film (I'd put the Coen brothers on the top of that pile, but the Coen Brothers don't come close to The Stones in cultural impact). I've been wracking my brain trying to come up with any two artists whose joint achievement raises as many philosophical questions as this one does. Maybe there's an obvious pair I haven't thought of, so help me out here if I missed something.

In the Shadows

Some of the other puzzles about the Glimmer Twins include their sometimes contradictory accounts of the collaboration itself. They agree on many points, of course, but their views of what they were doing, how it happened, who did what, well, it isn't easy to decide what to believe. How can people who were both there, and who collaborated so successfully, many thousands of times, disagree so thoroughly on what was happening, and where, and when? This practical question becomes theoretically interesting, too, when we ask, to what extent is *anyone* really a good or reliable or authoritative interpreter of his or her own experience—especially *creative* experience? I think this is the key to the whole thing: how well anyone really understands his own experiences, especially the creative ones.

Hegel thinks the artists don't understand at all what they do when they give sensuous expression to the "objective spirit" moving in history. And they don't *need to*, according to him. So he thinks history made The Stones what they were and are, and it had nothing to do with what they set out to do, or took themselves to be doing. On the other hand, Langer thinks artists do understand what they're doing and how to do it, but they are discursively "untrained," and their "difficult thoughts" resist clear formulation. These two philosophers can't both be right. Or can they?

Like some of you, I am old enough to remember when everybody thought Mick *was* the Rolling Stones. Keith was quiet and a little bit menacing, but he was just "in the band" as far as most people knew. It took the world quite some time to begin to discern what was really happening within the group. Keith just wasn't the sort to draw our particular attention to himself, and back in those days people didn't think of The Stones with the sort of seriousness and questioning we now take for granted. Their importance has come partly from their stamina at the top of the heap of pop art, and partly from our growing hindsight. We have enough distance now to see how very important this music was. We thought it was just the soundtrack of our lives, but now we're in a position to see that the music, and these artists, were also changing our consciousness, our ideas about value, about social acceptability, about art.

So The Stones were great, but until Keith stepped out of the shadows (the last ten years or so) they weren't a puzzle that needed a solution or an enigma that demanded a theory. All we *saw* was an unusually good English rock band with an image of being rough around the edges, with a prancing, leaping fool in the front; and what we *heard* was pop songs that were edgy and irreverent. The mediator of all we saw and heard was Mick's twitchy, big-lipped, strained, in-your-faceness. Keith was, at most, a brooding, dangerous, semi-animal, whose black eyes flashed in a challenge to any and all. He didn't seem much different from the rest of the band, and he certainly didn't fit our preconceived notion of a creative force in pop culture. His name went second behind Mick's. That's what we knew.

Saviors of Rock and Roll

Things have really changed, nowadays. We didn't get tired of Mick, but slowly we also became more fascinated by Keith. We knew Mick was an intellectual, that he aspired to elite circles, that he navigated the full range of possible social domains from dope dealers to Knight of the Realm. (Can you believe that shit? The guy with his hand down his pants, licking Ronnie Wood on live network TV, that dude is "Sir Michael Jagger"?) He got away with it all, the court jester who is smarter than the court. Meanwhile, Keith was and is mysterious and dangerous, and he had a talent for suffering, for taking into his body all of our sins and somehow rising from the dead every night at show time, not redeemed, but certainly ready to party. Both Mick and Keith actually lived the sort of life we could barely imagine—and they survived when we were all certain they'd never grow old. Keith's talent for suffering, and for rejecting the very society Mick courted, was every bit as important as Mick's public climbing. It kept things grounded and kept them real. The saviors of rock and roll have to be real and they also have to be able to get behind the gilded doors in order to rip the joint.

I'm not saying we quite have the needed historical distance to begin drawing conclusions, but we wouldn't have been wondering about the Glimmer Twins twenty years ago like we do now, because so much of Keith's personality has begun bubbling to the surface. And there is something about the way that Johnny Depp, an artist everyone takes seriously, captured what we hadn't quite managed to put our fingers on. He modeled the character of Jack Sparrow—the look, the physical movements and gestures, even the accent—on Keith Richards. How could we have missed this? Keith is a sort of pirate, and that's what we had always responded to in his Stones persona. Having been shown Keith in a two-dimensional form, by Johnny Depp, we began to become more aware that this guy really had to be something else, even to have survived. It dawned on us how smart he must be, too, in spite of his earthy vocabulary. I've never met a truly good artist who was anything less than killer smart, and Mick and Keith both have that.

Keith is now pretty much out of Mick's shadow these days. His autobiography has surprised the world. We didn't really expect something so insightful, even intellectual. It is so well written that I have to wonder how much is Keith and how much is James Fox. On the other hand, I now realize I should have been wondering about the Jagger-Richards pair long ago, and I can see that I never tended to think of Keith as a creative force until Johnny Depp drew my attention in that direction. I was told by those wiser than I to pay attention to Keith, long ago, and I tried, but I now see how far behind the curve I was. It's a good thing I don't agree with Hegel about history. If he was right, I'd be totally screwed. I can't even figure out what has already happened, let alone what's going on now or coming next.

Anyhow, it's now pretty clear that the shadow Mick was casting, which was large, was also part of the total package. It wasn't important that the public know how the art was being made, and in a way, it was actually more important that we *not* know. Some of The Stones' mystique would disappear if we knew too much about the nuts and bolts. That Stones mystique is like the secret of the varnish on a Stradivarius violin. It may or may not really make the thing good, but it makes us wonder, and that's more important. I had the strange fortune to learn from my college roommate, who later became one of the sound crew for The Stones for the Steel Wheels tour, how very *un*-mysterious it all is. "All business," he reported to me some twenty years ago. "It's a show and these guys are businessmen." That sort of burst the bubble, but what did I expect? It's art, and this art is about creating illusions—that's what Langer says—and in this case, where the artist is an all-pervading public persona, it's about creating *that* illusion, a public perception, while disguising the mundane realities is as much a part of the arts as is the finish on a violin.

The Songs

But there has to be something real in the illusion, and in the case of The Stones, it's the songs that are real, which is to say, the songs are the primary illusions that give life to the rest of it. Your life is not a song, and neither is anyone else's. Rather, the songs symbolize in an artistic work, how it *feels* to be living our lives in our times. In the next chapter I will talk about how the rhythm section contributes to the aesthetic value of The Stones' music, and I avoided talking about songwriting there because it is a very different art. Writing a song doesn't even have to involve learning how to *play* the song. Any songwriter will tell you that after a song is written, it still has to be *learned*. It's like the difference between successfully creating perfect pigments and learning to paint with them. Certain kinds of changes will occur in the learning process that are finishing the work of writing the song, but the collaborative process between the Twins, as it originates in songwriting, is a different process.

Beginning with *Aftermath*, we began to see the credit Jagger-Richards after nearly all the songs, and The Stones stepped into the company of the Beatles at that point as creative forces, more than just glitzy personas. That was a huge step into history. It made it obvious then, as now, that these guys intended to say something of their own. If they hadn't made the move into being songwriters, The Stones would have faded after two or three years, along with many other groups whose names now only show up in trivia questions.

Andrew Oldham, their "producer" is credited with putting Mick and Keith together and insisting they write songs. I would guess that he had an eye for talent, and he had scoped out the situation and saw where the creative energy in the band was. Long before we could tell which of The Stones was Keith, and point him out, Oldham had worked out that the pairing of Mick and Keith was his own personal retirement plan. And maybe he saw even more than that. Who knows? What people saw on stage was a presentation, in highly organized space and for very limited time, of something quite real that was happening in a complex and interesting way back behind the scenes.

But the outcome wasn't just forty or fifty songs that were works of cultural genius—and with the self-destruction of the fine arts, these songs became works of cultural genius, historically contextualized, since that is all the genius that was left. There were, in addition to the songs, a dozen albums that were works of genius. And there were shows and tours of cultural genius. In the latter category, it is really hard to imagine cultural events that would or could ever top the great tours between Steel Wheels and A Bigger Bang. The Rolling Stones perfected the "tour" as an art form, which wouldn't even have occurred to me as a *possibility*, frankly.

Beyond that, we have the personas of Mick and Keith as art forms. Unlike so many of today's pop icons, who have to reinvent their personas every three years or so (Marilyn to Cher to Madonna, or Michael Jackson, et al.), Mick and Keith each worked on perfecting the one persona they had initiated in 1962 , and have found that plumbing the depths of what they *really are* is better than trying to make up something superficial and new. That "something real" is the way they write the songs, which is the basic building block of the whole shebang. Keith describes this process at the time the band was working on *Exile on Main Street*, where the twins were writing the material as they were recording it, which they have done many times. People would be coming to the studio, expecting to record, but the songs didn't exist yet. Mick or Keith might be tempted to panic when they realized they had nothing to offer the other studio performers, who might be expecting ready-made material straight from the gods, when in reality it could come only from Mick and Keith. But the twins knew they could come up with something new every day or two—even if it was just the bare bones of a riff, it would be something to go on. And as the band tried to shape this elemental idea, the song would just fall into place:

> Once you're on a roll with the first few chords, the first idea of the rhythm, you can figure out other things, like does it need a bridge in the middle, later. It was living on a knife edge as far as that's concerned. There was no preparation. . . . The idea is to make the bare bones of a riff, *snap the drums in and see what happens*. It was the immediacy of it that in retrospect made it even more interesting. There was no time for too much reflection, for plowing the field twice. It was "It goes like this" and see what comes out. And this is when you realize that with a good band, you only really need a little spark of an

idea, and before the evening's over, it will be a beautiful thing. (*Life*, pp. 305–06, my italics)

The secret, then, to the creative power of the Glimmer Twins is that the dialectic between Mick and Keith just builds in its tension until Charlie kicks in. I don't mean to pull a cheap one on you, but the twins aren't enough by themselves to pull off what The Stones did. It would be cheating to end the chapter this way, except that you can keep reading and I'll try to explain in another chapter how this rhythm section of The Stones channels the creative energy to ground and makes it rock. The works of art in question originate with Keith and Mick, but their genius lies beyond the dialectic and in the group. What Mick is to Keith, or what Keith is to Mick, is the left and right ventricles of the heart of rock and roll, exchanging blood between sixty and 160 times a minute, but the body that dances to that beat is the band.

2
When the Whip Comes Down

One thing drives another in a band. It all has to melt together. Basically it's all liquid.

—KEITH RICHARDS, *Life*

Rock music isn't supposed to be healthy or wholesome, but it's got its own satisfaction(s). It's all about energy and what to do with it. To organize energies you have to constrain them for a moment, to store up some excess, to hold that excess (against its natural tendency to flow out and diffuse itself into moments of pure enduring), and then release it again in little bursts of suffering life. To rock and roll is to release that pent-up power in tiny explosions, between sixty and a hundred sixty times per minute, in groups of four.

You can tell it's rock and roll when every explosion destroys as much as it creates. It has to do that to rock. You might swing or two-step without hurting anything, but you'll never rock until you are willing to whip the moment into submission even as you make time. Keith Richards calls it the "discipline" of a rhythm section. You have to chain something up, and whip it until it feels bad enough to be good. That is the rhythm of rock and roll. It stings the hindside of the gods, because even they don't get to live forever without at least dying a little death at the end of every bar.

Mad Men

Whenever the music gets too acceptable, too commercial, too packaged, whenever it starts to look too sanitary, you can bet that some kind of upheaval is in the offing. Rock re-invents itself by pulling down whatever it has built. It's easy to see the pattern now, that for every Hall and Oates chart-topper, there is a sneering Johnny Rotten take-down, or if you can't quite handle any more Culture Club, there is Kurt Cobain to take a bullet for you and for many.

And so it goes. That balance between pop swill and rock music has always been uncomfortable, but it's clearer now what rock does to cleanse itself of the disgusting sweet excrescence that just is the music business. It makes your fingers sticky, no matter who you are. But back in the day, you know, 1965 or so, it was difficult to know what to do about Herman's Hermits, and the ridiculous Freddie and the Dreamers, and the list goes on.

But rock and roll is able to survive its occasional confinement in that thin air, high above Madison Avenue and Fleet Street. It's like electricity trapped in the clouds; somehow rock music finds its way to ground. The Mad Men devise their insulators, little three-minute morsels of mind-numbing neutrons, weighing down the real protons, with only a few sugary electrons in orbit, and they sell it to the kids. But the kids are already jumping with their own charges and pretty soon, well, let's just say they'll get their ya-yas out. When they do what all of nature commands and commends, Herman's Hermits won't turn the tricks anymore. They need some real rhythm, and that means something has to be under the whip. Enter their Satanic Majesties. I promise to reveal, in the end, what gets sacrificed on that altar.

"It"

For now let's concentrate on the energy, that electricity that always finds its way to ground. It's difficult to offer a schematic of the circuit path. Whatever it is that makes a man or a woman into a conduit of all that energy isn't captured in any theory, or even any folk wisdom I know of. But it's obvious when it's working. Celebrity, star power, may intensify that energy, make it shine, but the basic stuff, whatever "It" may be, is something apart from that. It isn't the glitz that draws the lightning down. I'm sure of that because I know that this "It" can live in obscurity and often does. By chance some night, maybe you drop into some joint by the wayside, and some guys you never heard of are there just rocking the place, wailing and rattling the walls, and everybody is gripped by "It." These cats aren't headed anywhere, but they have the present moment tied to the post, already black and blue and begging for more of the same. I know you've been there.

This is a chapter about "It." I don't mean the "it" in "it's raining" or "it's too hot," and this is not just one of the words the Knights of Ni cannot hear. I'm talking about the what-ness and the that-ness of the It in "he has It" or, in the case of The Stones, "they have It." What It is, in no uncertain terms, is a path to ground for whatever floats in the atmosphere as potential energy, and then suddenly finds a circuit completed, when the right components are hooked up and tied down in the right order. This is musical metaphysics, and we can't rest until we find the very bottom of the being of the beat.

There was this dude named Alfred North Whitehead (1861–1947), and he spent a lot of time and energy thinking about, well, time and energy. He was part of an earlier British invasion, when Harvard stole him from his London gig in 1925, and he came over the pond and started writing awesome books about how the whole cosmos is really sort of rocking and rolling. It was called "process philosophy." It hovers on the edge of being well understood, because it's very difficult and pretty radical, but every time you thinks it's done for, it keeps coming back for another US tour. Consider this the advance billing. Google the dude. Or just keep reading.

Musical Metaphysics

One idea Whitehead hit upon pretty early was that experience is made of little bursts of energy. Energy vibrates, and when it comes into more or less regular repeating patterns, we have "rhythm." Things that appear to be solid are really patterns of vibrations. Back then (1925 or so), most people thought things were made of "atoms," little indivisible bits of matter, arranged in "molecules," but Whitehead thought they were wrong. There really aren't any "things," like atoms and molecules, there are dances that just look like stones and guitars and people. Everything that exists in time is a repeating rhythm of some sort, so molecules just are shakings and rattlings in patterns, like little rock bands of Being. So molecules aren't "things" made of "stuff," they're more like performances; little Stones concerts in tiny stadiums having a huge party. Whitehead even talked about The Stones themselves (before they were born), and said there was more "Rolling" than "Stones" in the rock and roll of existing. Check out what the dude says when he was using the example of a stone:

> The [mistaken] molecular theory has robbed the [rolling] stone of its continuity, of its unity, and of its passiveness. The [rolling] stone is now [in that very uncool theory] conceived as a society of separate molecules in violent agitation. But the metaphysical concepts, which had their origin in a mistake about the [rolling] stone[s], were now applied to the individual molecules. Each atom was still [wrongly supposed to be some] stuff which retained its self-identity and its essential attributes in any portion of time—however short and however long, provided that it did not perish. (*Process and Reality*, p. 78—I've helped the dude say what he meant to say with the stuff in the brackets.)

But you'll never rock and roll that way, Whitehead says. Each member of the band just being his own individual self, bringing to the stage whatever he already has, all by his lonesome. When you see a band that doesn't have "It," you're probably looking at a collection of individuals failing to connect and not channeling anything from sky to ground. They're surrounded with a layer of individuality that insulates them from the sky and from each other. And you just can't rock in rubber shoes; you all have to dig your toes into Mother Earth and raise a hand to Father Sky. Nothing rocks and nothing rolls when it's not like that. But Whitehead goes on:

> The [uncool] notion of undifferentiated endurance of substances with essential attributes and with accidental adventures was still applied. This is the root doctrine of materialism [boo, hisssss] . . . but this materialistic concept has proved to be as mistaken for the atom as it was for the stone[s]. The atom is only explicable as a society with the activities involving rhythms with their definite periods . . . The mysterious quanta of energy [Keith, Charlie, and Bill] have made their appearance, derived, as it would seem, from the recesses of protons [called "grooves"], or electrons [called "riffs"] . . . Further, the quanta of energy are associated by a simple law with the periodic rhythms

which we detect in the molecules [called "concerts"]. Thus the quanta are, themselves, in their own nature, somehow vibratory; but they emanate from the protons and electrons. Thus there is every reason to believe that rhythmic periods cannot be dissociated from the protonic and electronic entities [or the grooves and riffs]. (*Process and Reality*, pp. 78–79)

What Whitehead is saying (with some help from me) is that it's not what we are that makes us do what we do, it's what we are doing that makes us what we are, for a short while, and then the show is over, fading ever so gradually into the past. I will now use this theory to describe why The Stones totally rock. There are three quanta (Keith, Charlie, and Bill), and their "rhythmic periods" are going to get the names Whitehead gave them:

1. Keith = the "dative dater" of the divine data.

2. Charlie = the co-ordinator and organizer of the data Keith dates, called the "synthesis."

3. Bill = the distributor and contributor of the all goods Keith and Charlie achieve, called by Whitehead (and I swear to God I'm not making this up) the "satisfaction."

Their "rhythmic periods" are called by Whitehead "the phases of concrescence," and the "groove" and "riff" are the varying patterns of "intensity," the protonic and electronic vibes from which these wondrous quanta cannot be separated. I speak henceforth of the rock and roll rhythm section, and by anyone's account, The Stones have the best one that ever existed.

The Sum of the Parts

One of the great mysteries associated with The Stones is that of the group-ness of It—how well It works when they are all in one place and time, and how not much happens when they separate and make music with others, or even when they try to go it alone. Of course Keith's Winos and Bill's Rhythm Kings can rock, but we all know It isn't the same. Why is that? I think it's a genuine question, and an important one—and not just for rock history or music criticism. The question is about "It," and touches on the value of one kind of existing over another, and what that costs those who would pursue "It" over some more neutral equilibrium.

Somehow The Stones together are greater than the parts, and not by just a little bit. But it never was the easy choice to keep rocking and rolling, so the value they achieve by hanging in there for one more record, one more tour, comes with risks and costs. The lure of some sort of experience has drawn them back into the dance with death again and again.

The Stones "experiment" is now well over fifty years old and we've had an opportunity to test what "It" was that completes the circuit. The comparatively early exit of Brian Jones showed that It wasn't the triumvirate of Jagger-Richards-Jones, as some people initially thought. "It" had little to do with Jones. The nearly seamless entry and exit of Mick Taylor, followed by the permanent installment of Ronnie Wood, showed that at least the "other guitar" was a modular component. In his auto-biography, Keith says he had worked out well before Jones finally vacated that what he needed was just one other gui-tarist for "weaving," and that he could adapt to a whole range of styles and levels of ability in that other player.

So, for thirty-odd years (and they certainly were odd years), the other four Stones were a constant, although their recording process often did not reflect the live line-up, even from the beginning. Some of the more memorable recordings may lack one or another member of the magic circuit. Keith is generally on all the good records, but Charlie and Bill aren't always, although the results seem indistinguishable from the core group. That's probably because the other drummers or bass players are generally playing "the sort of thing" Charlie or Bill would play, and not introducing a foreign element into the Stones' sound, but reveling in being a contributor to that dis-tinctive sound.

Yet, the permanent departure of Bill Wyman in 1993 seems to have weakened the circuit, if my perceptions are at all trust-worthy. I'm not finding their stuff since then quite as satisfy-ing, to say it as Whitehead might. The power still flows through, but I don't think the Stones could have done what they did without the full rhythm section, and I would claim that the special something-or-other they possess as a trio, is the It that Is, when all three quanta become components connected in series—and the series is Keith-Charlie-Bill, in that order; data-synthesis-satisfaction. More on that in a minute.

And here I'm going to go out on a limb. I think that even without Mick Jagger, this would have been a famous rock band, if not at all the same band. The reason has to do with what happens when Keith, Charlie, and Bill strike a groove. Mick is more like the light bulb or the box fan (or any other dirty, pretty thing you might plug in) that actually draws the current and "works" when it is flowing. Mick isn't pulling the power down from the air, he's just using it on its way to the ground. He's a symbol of what's happening in the rhythm section, and he is, as a Stone, the presentation of the rhythm section's causal effect on the world. Mick's musicality, his delivery, his showmanship, even his athleticism, is pretty much fluff when he tries to plug himself into any other circuit. He can't adorn just any musicians hooked up in series, at least not with the same depth and meaning. And unlike David Bowie, whom Mick has apparently always envied a bit (if Keith is to be believed), Mick is not a musical force unto himself. He has to have the Stones to strut his stuff and make us all believe it.

Some people can do the whole thing alone, like Elvis or Robert Johnson, or some can do it with almost anyone, like Chuck Berry. There's no denying Mick Jagger is a natural front man, a visible presentation of what jumps across the abyss from being nothing to becoming "It," from one moment to the next. Alone, Mick just isn't very "important," to use Whitehead's word for it. But put him in front of Keith-Charlie-Bill, and at least one other guitar player who "gets It," he becomes one of the most important interpreters of the existence and meaning of "It" who has ever lived. I don't know whether he chafes at being dependent on that circuit or not, but I can certainly see that he isn't the cause of the cool, even if he is just the right dirty, pretty thing to spring into view as soon as Keith hits the first chord. Don't get me wrong. They aren't The Stones without Mick, by any stretch, and I wouldn't change a hair on their graying heads, but Keith-Charlie-Bill surely would have been a famous band without him.

And, as Whitehead says, the whole is always greater than the sum of the parts, even when all the parts are functional alone, as in the Beatles, and even though clearly each component has its own energy supply. But then sometimes you have the thing that only works when it's hooked up in series, just so, like the Stones. So, structurally and functionally, The Stones are a bit like lithium, with three inseparable protons in the nucleus, an electron (Mick) down and dirty, and another electron (that second guitar) spinning opposite Keith in a more distant orbit, and a whole cloud of saxes and pianos and black girls singing in the ionized spaces. Like lithium, they're loosely bound in the middle, unstable, and highly flammable. So next time you want to know what mother's little helper really is, well, she's doing lithium, but it's about taking out the right record and dropping the needle into the groove. An interesting way to stabilize your mood, huh?

The thing about the rhythm section for The Stones is that all three of those protons are very quirky. None of these guys plays quite "right." Let me explain, but I have to begin with a crucial point, and if you don't get this, if you can't find a way to hear this, most of what I say later won't resonate: Charlie interprets Keith, and then Bill interprets Charlie and closes back on Keith, and it happens in that order, pretty much all the time. That's what is between the buttons. Now let's divide up what can't really be divided and move among the vibrations that make It happen.

A Date with Keith

Keith just is Prometheus with a five-stringed lightning rod. He's the one who pulls the grooves and riffs in from the atmosphere and shares them with the band. Until Keith arrives, it's all just the bare past and lame possibility, just data for a world that may never exist, nothing happening. And if Keith is off, the Stones will be off, but that doesn't happen too much. Almost no matter what Keith is on, he's almost never off. He can call down the lightning even in a stupor. (And Keith having an off night is like other people having the best night of their lives.)

But Keith doesn't play "right" and he doesn't play "nice." He's usually just a little bit (in other words, perfectly) out of tune, and he doesn't bother much with details, and he doesn't fret about the frets. It's a little sloppy, if you only notice what it sounds like and forget to notice what it does. He doesn't play flashy at all, and once the song kicks in, it's difficult to descry exactly what Keith is playing and what the other guitarist is adding. Keith isn't even describable as either a lead or a rhythm player, he's a little bundle of pure activity confronting a wide universe of possibilities and memories and taking just what he wants for a little date, by force if necessary.

To the guitar purist, and to the critics who are expecting something to gratify their critical reflections, Keith is something of an enigma. I have heard so many people, the types whose rock understanding is just the conventional cool, and whose actual rock experience is limited to garage bands at most, say that they don't understand why Keith's name is mentioned in the same company as the greatest guitar players of the age—Clapton, Hendrix, Page, Beck. How does Keith Richards command the respect, even the awe, of such virtuosos, and their successors like Eddie Van Halen? Is it just because he's one of the Stones and so he's automatically in the club? That isn't it. The people who will tell you Keith isn't really a great guitar player (I have even heard some say he sucks) have no clue what a guitar really does in the context of creating the rhythmic feel of a band. They think of great guitar playing as the fast and flashy more than the furious and gutsy, and they probably have no notion of the promethean groovemaker and riffmaster. And they imagine that it's more challenging to be creative with lead lines than with great grooves and amazing, ear catching simple riffs.

They're wrong. And if they don't at least admit that they can hear the greatness, if not account for it, then they are also fools. Even just finding (let alone discovering) the grooves that make your body jump, involuntarily, and creating the riffs people can't get out of their heads is far, far more difficult, musically speaking, than playing fast or freaky lead lines. The riff and groove are the batter and bake of the rock and roll cake, and it's more important, and tougher to master, than making a batch of tasty icing from the butter and sugar of those hot licks (that you probably copped from somebody else) to put on top of the finished product.

Anyone who has played in a serious band, a band that has enjoyed at least some real power to draw in the people, knows that you might have a trillion hot licks, but no one wants to listen to that for more than about two minutes. What every lead player and lead singer has to have is a promethean lightning rod in the band, a point of origin in the rhythm section. For The Stones, that is and always was Keith. He's the one who kidnaps the silence itself, with his leathery sneak attack and then herds it around at his whim. You think you can handle a date with that? If not, stay well out of his range. The whip is long and the lightning rod is very stiff, and he'll keep you up for six days straight.

Maestro Tempo and Mr. Groove

But even Keith has to bend a knee at the right altar to receive the energy. He exists way beyond you, but he isn't a god. It's one thing to discover the grooves, and another thing to be able to call them up again, on demand. The power to recall a groove isn't that rare—every good bar band has one or two members who can do as much. Sometimes it's the drummer or the bass player, but commonly it's the rhythm guitar player (and quite often he is also a singer). Watch next time you go to a bar. The "grooves guy" will be the one who starts most of the songs, whether with a count, or an intro lick, or even just a nod of the head. This is "finding" a groove again, not technically discovering it. From rehearsal, and huge repetition, the groove is already down inside his body. He doesn't have to call it down from the air; he pulls it back up from the ground and re-connects it to its source.

Before the song starts, you will see one guy get still, for just a second; maybe he'll look up, or look down, or close his eyes; then he will start moving his foot, or bob his head, or he might wave his pick above the strings in a rhythmic pattern. When the groove has made its way from the edges of his body to the center, has planted itself in the center as a pulse, and has worked its way back out to his extremities, he will move, as one unified being, into that groove. He will become the groove. All this only takes a second. That is how it happens, and this part isn't too much different in a rock band than for the conductor of a symphony orchestra or the leader of a jazz band, or even a church choir director.

There is a difference, though. Whereas the conductor or choir director is finding the tempo from a full range of interpretive possibilities, and that initial tempo will then flow into and out of regular bends and eddies, the rock guitarist is just looking for the groove, which is an uneducated, hard-drinking, poor relation of tempo, who lives in a trailer across the tracks and wants to boink your underage daughter. Grooves are built on raw repetition in a way that tempos are not. The altogether "proper" determination of a tempo ought to consider how the music will sound. So Maestro Tempo treats Miss Sound like a lady, asks her for a proper date, spends some serious bucks on her, chats her up and listens to her titter and gossip, offers her the best wine, hopes for a peck on the cheek at the end of the night. Nobody gets hurt. Herman's Hermits are looking for a tempo, and they'll walk you to the door when they're done with the song and tell Mrs. Brown's daughter what a lovely time they had.

But Mr. Groove operates independently of how things sound. Sounds are a dime a dozen, and they'll need to go to their knees if they want a ride on the wild horses. Mr. Groove has had plenty of sounds in his paws, and he isn't easily impressed and never tamed, even when he decides to be gentle. In rock music, Mademoiselle Sound must conform to what Mr. Groove wants, and what he needs, to make it all feel good, and said Sound need not be, ought not be, clean or pristine. It's better if she's been around the block a time or two and has an attitude about it. Groove knows what he likes, and it isn't a sorority girl saying "ewwww"—unless she's got another side she isn't showing. And Groove will have his way with Sound before it's all said and done. In short, for rock and roll, Sound is Groove's "Bitch," and when her name is called, she salivates like Pavlov's best friend.

Who Could Hang a Name on You?

So that is how you find a groove again, but discovering a groove is a different deal. That is the promethean moment in rock and roll. Truly novel grooves are out there, but you can't really make a groove out of nothing. It has to be possible for you, and you have to take it in from what you are and what you can be, but in discovering a groove, you can make it your own. Whitehead calls it the "self-creative act," in which nothing that came before and nothing that comes later wholly explains the act. So you can't really name it.

For rock and roll, there aren't so very many possibilities. They're constrained by the choice to rock rather than flow. Yet, the tiniest variation in terms of how the four beats are rushed or relaxed in mutual relations will make the difference between a groove that is erotic or invigorating, and one that is limpid or relaxing. Keith describes this in the 2011 issue of *Rolling Stone* magazine (as I write this), in a tribute to Bob Dylan:

> Before he went electric and submitted himself to that relentless discipline of a rhythm section, there was a beautiful flow in Bob's songs that you can only get with just a voice and guitar. He can float across the bar here and there. You let certain notes hang longer, and it doesn't matter because it all goes with the song. . . . I love the man—and I love that he rock and rolls too. (26th May 2011, p. 66)

Some people may think it's sloppy, but the rhythm section of a rock band is in truth a highly structured and disciplined unit. It cannot slide around and still be any good. To rock and roll is to let yourself be whipped, a relentless repeating kick and slap.

The typical rock groove has a kick (bass drum) on the first and third beats of each bar, and a snare slap on the second and fourth beats. The bass guitar is at the mercy of beats one and three. His dominatrix likes to kick him around. The rhythm guitar is owned by beats two and four, and she slaps him when he gets out of line. The variations are built from there, stretching, pulling, switching, dragging those four beats apart and pushing them back together. I wouldn't exactly say that there is a finite number of arrangements of those four beats that "work," but I will say that all the most obvious variations are already familiar to you—that is, they've already been found and used many times in many songs you know.

Alright Now

Yet, Keith has contributed perhaps a dozen new grooves to the common repertoire. The groove to "Start Me Up" comes immediately to mind, as well as the "kick in" on "Jumpin' Jack Flash"—which makes every beat seem like the start of a new measure, like it's going one-one-one-one, at the front edge of each iteration. You want to talk about relentless driving, especially since the intro groove, before the kick-in, is all way, way back, flowing around, at the tail-end of the beat, like a primeval soup, with paramecia flitting around, barely coalescing at all. Then boom, out jumps Mick fully evolved, with no tail at all, and ready to screw anything foolish enough to move. It's a gas (the more you read about the structure and habits of lithium, the clearer all this chemistry becomes).

The song "Honky Tonk Women" is an important contribution to grooves—it's so much slower than most people realize, although this is a song they play at different speeds live. Frankly I think it diminishes the song—the recorded speed was the right speed, and the gin-soaked barroom queens of Memphis do not hurry, you or themselves. To play that song "right" (so that it does its proper work) is almost excruciating, the way you just keep having to hold back. You have to think about golf or something between thrusts to keep your load in. How can something that slow so totally rock? And how can it not? And then even beyond that, there is "Wild Horses," which is the slowest rock groove I know of (I can't believe Keith got this to be so very cool).

Not all distinctive Stones grooves are Keith's, probably, but these are among Keith's most distinctive grooves. For example, there is also "Beast of Burden," which is devilishly hard to get right, and that is partly because it's actually much faster than it seems like it would be, it's just that the snare slap is trailing in an almost unnatural way, but I have a feeling this groove was Charlie's doing more than Keith's. And there's the stupendous groove of "Shattered," but I think that one may need to be credited to Ronnie Wood, who played the bass on that track. More on all that in a minute.

There are lesser known original Stones grooves, like "She Said Yeah," which was way ahead of its time. It only re-emerged in the era of the Ramones, and the list could go on. I say these are "original grooves" but what I mean is that I haven't heard anything earlier that was precisely the same, and when rock musicians communicate grooves to each other, they often call these grooves by their Stones names. ("It's goes like 'Start Me Up'" they'll say, and so on.) I haven't made an exhaustive survey, but I'm fairly confident about these grooves I've named. Of course, plenty of Stones songs have ordinary rock grooves, or blues grooves, or even country (like "Far Away Eyes") or disco (like "Miss You"). It's not like our boys discovered them all.

There may be no definite limit to how many rock grooves

there are, but I doubt any other single person has contributed more previously undiscovered grooves to rock music than Keith Richards. Maybe Chuck Berry did, and he is a great study in grooves because if you don't hit exactly the right groove in playing one of his songs, they all sound too similar to one another. Apart from being a daring and brilliant lyricist and tremendous innovator on the guitar, the third prong of Chuck Berry's great genius lies in the tiny variations in the rock grooves he discovered. But with the Stones concert, it is Keith who first draws the grooves down from the atmosphere to the ground, and then back from the ground and out into the ionosphere, and we all just have to hop around like worms on a hot rock—especially Mick, who shows us just how It should be done. I defy you to stay still when "Brown Sugar" kicks in.

Riffing

In spite of the dominance and heedlessness of Mr. Groove, Mademoiselle Sound does get her say, because only she knows what she likes. Maybe it's the Stockholm Syndrome. Having been captured and tied down by Bad Boy Groove, she says, not so coyly, "not like that, do it like this . . . if you wanna hear me squeal . . ." and suddenly she has all his attention. After all, he does want to hear her squeal. (And so do I, at this point. Is it getting warm in here, or is that just me?) Anyway, when it comes to the Mistress Sound (as she now calls herself), she'll only get happy for a fellow if you turn all her knobs the right way and caress her taut body just so. Keith knows the right moves, most nights. He had the gift, but it takes patience and practice too. At least, judging by what I hear, I'd say the good Lady Sound actually likes to go slumming with him.

So the riff has two legs, and one of them is the tone. You have to get a hold on that leg first, adjust it this way and that until you hear something you can work on. There are so many different things an electric guitar can sound like, from these smooth Chet Atkins country hollow-body tones, to Duane Eddy's reverb-laden, rebel rousing pluck tone, to Jimi's famous feedback-on-the-edge-of-forever, to Tom Petty's cool clean "Breakdown," to the Malcolm Young "fuck-tone" in "You Shook Me All Night Long." All electric guitar players explore tones, and it's common for them to be very picky about it. Keyboard players once shared in this arcane science, but then they got spoiled by the electronic overhaul of the keyboarding world, synthesizers and samplers. The keyboard player who is a master of amplifier and instrument tones is rare these days, and probably over fifty years old. But true rock guitarists will never give in to this kind of ones-and-zeroes mentality.

If you're looking to be in a good band, your guitarists need to be the kind of people who can patiently screw around with tone adjustments and reverb knobs until everyone else has given up and gone home. It helps if you can stay up for days and days in a row. Both the devil and the good god are trapped in there, down in the protons and electrons, in the signals exchanged by the instrument and the amplifier, and how each responds to the slightest variations in the other. If you want something to feel like "Nineteenth Nervous Breakdown" (and I can hardly imagine a riff that sounds more like what it is supposed to be than that one), you had better know how to get that exact sound from your equipment, and that can only be done by very patient experimentation. But if you go looking for that sound, just remember, Keith is the one who made it first, and he was the one who first heard that this—just this and only this—was the tone for the guitar on that particular riff in this one song. He regularly creates unique tones, and then in some cases he doesn't re-use them, because they are too identifiable. So there's a vast range of tones he creates with the choices of amplifiers and knobs and guitars, even though there really is no recognizable set of tones we would usually identify with Keith's work. He knew very well after he had used that fuzz pedal for "Satisfaction" that he couldn't go there again. And for him, getting the tones was and remains an endless quest.

To be a rock guitarist in our day you have to go to school on the tones Keith made and learn how he used them. It's Rock 101. The story in his autobiography about how he found the tone for the guitars on "Jumpin' Jack Flash" is a keen piece of rock history. It had been a mystery. Anyone could play the actual licks (they are easy), but people couldn't find a way to re-create those tones. So finally Keith revealed that there are no electric guitars on that recording. He played acoustic guitars into the condenser mic that was built-in on an early model Phillips cassette tape recorder, and to achieve a distortion in the tone, he played the guitars too close to the mic and too loud.

He listened back to the cassette and said, in effect, "that's it, that's the sound." He didn't provide the further details in his book, but I assume he then hooked up the same mic to his four-track machine, and the result you have heard. Or maybe he just played the cassette sound into his four-track recorder. Clean sound isn't always the best sound. He re-enacted this for the documentary based on his autobiography.

You Make a Dead Man . . .

So let's say the groove and the tone are jiving, but you're not riffing yet. Mademoiselle Sound is giving you that look, but she isn't there yet. The riff has another leg dangling and kicking, so you've got to get a hold on it. You still have to figure out what to play, and here is what we will call the "sig lick" (the signature lick is the full name). Get this right and she'll squeal, if she's going to squeal at all—I mean, who doesn't like a great lick? A sig lick is an identifiable musical phrase that belongs exclusively to a single song, and which usually starts the song, and it makes the most of what the groove and the tone have brought together. It may be just a violin arpeggio (like "Ruby Tuesday"), or it may be a little melodic phrase (like "Nineteenth Nervous Breakdown"), or it may be a chord change (like "Start Me Up" or "Honky Tonk Women"). A song can have more than one sig lick and it can also come later in the song, like the six ascending notes that precede the words "brown sugar." Whatever it is, it's supposed to tell you in a split second what song you're hearing. It's the culmination of pulling the lightning down. It uses the tone and the groove and it makes you lose yourself in both anticipation and memory. You die a little death in that moment, for sure. But it's worth it.

No matter how many Stones songs you've heard, you know which one you're hearing within a couple of seconds because of the riff, and there is always a different combination of groove and tone and sig lick that brings it home. It takes genuine talent and amazing patience to make all this—indeed, it takes a fair amount of ability just to recreate it, even after someone like Keith has done all the pioneering work. Keith, with his rhythm section, has probably created more truly great riffs than any other rock and roller, maybe up to six dozen utterly recognizable, one of a kind, winning sig licks. And somehow he not only dated all these delicate beauties, he also knew they were winners when he first set ears on them. You have to be prescient to know when you've got one. Some of these conquests were simply bizarre, twisted trysts, like the "Jumpin' Jack Flash" riff, while others were a risky rendezvous, like the "Nineteenth Nervous Breakdown" riff, which is actually painful to listen to, and is intended to be. "Ouch Keith. Turn it up, would you? Oh yes, here it comes." She loves the way you play that guitar.

The Singer, Not the Song

All of what I'm trying to get at is completely apart from and basically unrelated to Keith's songwriting, both with and without Mick. The songwriting isn't a wholly separate activity for the Stones, because sometimes the riff and groove produced the occasion and inspiration for the song. Commonly Keith would have a hook line to go with the riff and groove and say to Mick what the hook was, and show him the riff and groove, and then Mick would just start singing it or jotting down the words. That is, for sure, its own kind of promethean feat. But the songwriting part, even as it touches on the issue of rhythm, is a different matter than the "It" I am chasing right now.

I'm still trying to explain why Keith's peers regard him as among the greatest guitarists of his generation. And when you consider that the same song can be played (successfully, consider Clapton's slow version of "Layla") with many different grooves, and that the riff can be varied and re-interpreted as needed, it becomes clear that this isn't so much about songs as about the "how" the song comes to feel like rock and roll. Christopher Guest, Michael McKeon, and Harry Shearer (The Folksmen) have made it clear enough that even a song as tied to its groove as "Start Me Up" can be played in a bluegrass groove (if "groove" is even the right word for it) . . . and the less said about that, the better.

So this isn't about being a great songwriter, it's about exploring the possibilities that the invention of the electric guitar made available, in amazing and unexpected ways. These sounds had never been heard by human ears, as Keith points out. Keith was in the first generation of musicians who really saw how rich the possibilities were, and who set off into that *terra incognita* and returned with some of the best treasure. It requires a peculiar curiosity, a certain tenacity, a singular power of focus and concentration, and above all a complete passion for just this kind of journey, to explain what Keith Richards did. The people who have tried to explore this territory, and who really understand what it takes to succeed, rightly stand in awe of Keith Richards as a guitar player. To say Keith Richards isn't a great guitar player is sort of like saying Christopher Columbus wasn't a great sea captain. Whatever the faults, we're all permanently changed by the exploration, for better and for worse.

A Steady Synthesis of the Data

I confess: For years I believed Charlie Watts wasn't a great drummer—hell, I didn't even think he was very good. I admitted, along with everyone, that he certainly was rock steady, and there is a lot to be said for that. But steady drummers are out there. Every city has a dozen or so, and the good bands stand in line to try to capture such drummers, especially if they don't have debilitating drug habits or personality problems. But even then, if they can be counted on to show up for the gig, the rest can be dealt with as needed. Rock drummers don't have to be extra-ordinary, but if they don't speed up and can play a decent quick shuffle beat, well, that's all you have to have.

But watching Charlie, back in the day, when I was young and stupid and arrogant (now I'm not young), I observed all kinds of uneconomical movement in Charlie's hands and feet. There were hitches and jerks, like parries and feints at the drums, and then there was that totally annoying habit where he lays off the hi-hat with the right hand on the second and fourth beats and just slaps the snare drum by itself. That basically looked to me like no one ever told him how to play the drums. But he was pulling it together all along, wasn't he? The second phase of Stones concrescence, just as Whitehead said.

I was deeply and profoundly wrong, and my thinking and interpretation were clouded by conventional expectations and at least some pure boorishness. I had to admit even back then that it was just a mystery to me why The Stones so totally rocked. Keith was out of tune, Bill stood like he was made of concrete and I thought I knew two dozen guys who could play at least as well as Charlie. I was an idiot. No, that's not strong enough. A fucking idiot. My little theories and judgments wouldn't have helped one bit in dispelling the mystery of why The Stones have "It."

I stupidly thought "It" was about "knowing" something, as in consciously knowing it and being able to act on what you know. So I believed I understood what I was hearing and it didn't dawn on me that I had missed a whole universe of music fermenting beneath the radar of my conventional little conscious expectations. Whitehead says consciousness isn't very common in the universe, and it's not very important either, in terms of what's really going down. So it's worth remembering, just as a principle for life, that if something is very good and your pet theories say it shouldn't be, you need to dump your pet theories.

The River of Tight

The Stones were doing everything wrong, not by the rules (or the conventions), and there was all sorts of apparent looseness in how the rhythm section went about its business and I foolishly believed that everyone wants to be tight, not loose. What I didn't understand back then is that there is a kind of looseness that's on the other side of tight. It doesn't come from being a virtuoso player, it comes from being a truly great listener and responder. And here is where we could have the Grateful Dead argument, if anyone is so inclined. The Dead were (and wanted to be) even looser than The Stones, and so loose that they defied people to believe they were even capable of playing tight. But they were more than capable of that. The recorded evidence exists. They chose an outward trajectory for their rhythmic mode of being, on the farthest wilds across the River of Tight, to see what was there. By comparison, The Stones found some nice spots for partying just on the other side of the River of Tight, and they went straight to those places when they played. And they certainly could play utterly tight when they wanted to. I speak in the past tense because I feel that this changed when Bill left the band, as I will get to in a minute.

What I needed to learn is that tight doesn't rock. It's impressive, for sure, but it's for your ears and your head, not for your ass and your feet. Tight is for Rush and Styx and Kansas and Yes. It's cerebral to play tight. It's discursive and advisory, a little detached; playing tight won't solve your problems and it won't guide your life. It's good to rehearse your part in life, by all means; but when it comes time to act, to decide, to do something you can't take back, you need to be in the moment. You can plan your life until you think you have every detail under control, but the minute you step out on the stage of life, it's not going to go like you planned. If you try to make it all conform to your plan, your life will surely suck, and if you'll be honest with yourself, you'll have to admit you really wanted it to rock. So get out of your fucking head, would you? Learn how to play tight, that's good. But then forget about it and go live a little.

Charlie Chuckles

Charlie plays the drums that way. He knows that Keith has been awake for four manic days and needs a little something to pull him back from the next moment into the present one. So Charlie usually lays on the back of the beat, holding back (especially the snare slap, which is the rhythm guitar player's mistress, as I said); he holds that slap to the last possible micromoment when the skin can still be pounded. And here's his secret, the one he discovered entirely by himself, and that everyone identifies as "playing like Charlie Watts": What everyone else would regard as the last micromoment in the range of the beat isn't really the very last micromoment. The one you and I would call "last" is actually only the last *serious* moment. There is another micromoment behind that one, and it is comical, it is a rhythmic snort or a jocular grunt, and it takes all of Keith's gravity and intensity and insane focus and releases it into the room as levity and fun. Charlie hits it and Keith (serious, dangerous, violent, drug-addicted, passionate, hopeless Keith) smiles. That's when the whip comes down. And when the whip comes down, it hurts sort of *good*, doesn't it? I admit that I like it when Keith likes treating me that way. And I'm straight, too.

Charlie Watts is an excellent drummer, and I now know he can play any style he wants to play. He isn't all that limited. (I mean, everyone has limitations.) Charlie's job is to take the grooves and riffs that Keith feeds him and make them congeal into something Bill can distribute around the room, in ways that everyone can use (I'm afraid that only Keith can use his own grooves without Charlie's help). So, even though Charlie's reach is from the first micromoment before one to the last micromoment after four, he always lags behind Keith, and that is very much by design. This keeps Keith on the front edge of the whole sound and still holds him in, makes him available to the rest of us in little bursts. And after all, we need a second to follow Keith's mania. The lag also creates a musical space in which other things can happen. And they do.

I can't think of a better example of how Charlie interprets Keith than "Beast of Burden," which is a song that rarely gets covered successfully, even by bar bands that make their living covering Stones songs. The groove is extremely difficult to capture, and without the groove, the song basically sucks. One of the secrets of the song is the oodles of empty sonic space. That space is created by the distance between the clean riffing guitar and the trailing drums, and how Charlie comically hops to the front of the beat where Keith is and then falls way back, repeated every measure. How very far Charlie has allowed himself to trail becomes obvious when he hits the almost random double snare slap on the "and" of three and the "and" of four, instead of just the four. That "and" of four is actually into the next measure and Keith has already attacked.

The song also very much requires that the bass stay out of the way, being so understated as nearly to disappear. It's like watching Bill Wyman onstage, which you must admit is like watching paint dry. So I will take back one thing I said earlier. I know of one person capable of standing absolutely, stock still when Keith hits the opening chords of "Brown Sugar." The one person in the world who is best able to stay out of the way of anything Keith may do is his bass player. More about that in a moment, but to finish the previous thought before getting on to the next one, Keith mentions in his autobiography that this lagging behind the beat is Charlie's sense of humor, and that on given nights they even try to test one another's rhythmic limits, to see if one can screw up the other one. I'm sorry, but that's just way cool.

Paying the Bill: An Ode to Satisfaction

Now we come to the unhappy part of the story. As far as I can tell, Bill Wyman just wasn't destined for happiness and certainly not for satisfaction. (Holy cow. Just don't even think about it, okay? I know you know what I'm talking about.) Still, the crap that happened to Bill wasn't any worse than what the rest of The Stones got, but unlike them, it took the heart out of him, and really, it's not too clear his heart was ever really in it. But he was, ironically, the musical distributor of the joy in that rhythm section. Charlie was playful, but Bill, because the Keith-Charlie connection was so total, actually got to just play around.

He may have felt a little bit excluded or undervalued. Maybe all those women were so many proofs of his manhood. And I think Bill might have just belonged to slightly different time. His being significantly older than the rest of the band would have made it tough in the early days, I suspect. There is a very great difference between being twenty and being twenty-eight when you achieve stardom. It's sort of like why they draft kids between eighteen and twenty-one first off, for the wars. At that age, you can form the kids around the ideas they *have* to believe. But you'll never get someone who is twenty-eight to believe that death in battle is glorious, if he hasn't already bought in when he was younger. And maybe that was Bill's life as a Rolling Stone. I certainly don't know.

If Bill felt like a fifth wheel, I have to say, that's not the way I hear the music, so I must respectfully disagree. I think I do grasp what I hear (remembering I've been very wrong before . . .). But I'm a bass player too, so I'm pushing forward on this one. Bill had to do a very un-bass-playerly thing to succeed with The Stones. He had to resist the urge to play with Charlie. No drummer would be easier to play with than Charlie Watts, but somehow Bill understood what almost no other bass player would get, which is "hey, being tight and close with Charlie's kick drum will kill this energy." Bass players just instinctively want to hear that kick drum, and if not to match it, then at least to play off of it. But Charlie wasn't a kick-heavy player. Light right foot. He was and remains a snare and hi-hat guy. The kick is a time-keeper only. Perhaps it's because Charlie always wanted to be a jazz player, but there just isn't very much to work with in Charlie's kicks.

If you hear a Stones cover from a bar band and it lacks energy, it may be because of a heavy kick and a bass player who thinks he should match it. That's not how this music is played.

Bill had the amazing gift also of staying out of the way, rhythmically. He walked and wandered and he generally visited the root of the chord somewhere in every four to six beats, but Keith was pounding that, so it wasn't necessary. Bill has certainly produced two dozen bass fills that everyone hears and remembers, but his greatest contribution is the decision to use that thick, muddy, bass sound (common to many bassists of his generation) to bring the sound back around to what Keith had started but would never have time to finish (he's always already on to something else). It is what Whitehead calls the "satisfaction" of concrescence, the moment when what is being made culminates and becomes a contributor to what will come next.

So Bill often lags even behind Charlie, who is already lagging, and does so in a way that stretches out the sound even more, and Bill gets away with it because he brings the bar back around to where Keith had started it, making a thick, deep, four string memory out of a thin and twitchy five string jump. Bill uses the power of repetition to blur the point of entry from the point of exit of a musical idea. It all sounds very sloppy, and it is, but it works. So Bill never really played the bass rhythmically, as most bass players do (and are conventionally told they should do). His decisions on which notes to play are often more chordal or even melodic than rhythmic, interpreting themes, whether dark or erotic or playful that are suggested by Keith's riffs, and helping everyone see what was being suggested. This distributing of the goods is made possible by Charlie's mediation and synthesis, which is so complete as to offer a matrix for meaning and valuing the whole.

There are times, such as "Paint It Black," when the bass actually drives the backbeat, but that is the exception rather than the rule. More often, Bill is picking up on some little opening in the bar and messing around in there. The song "Miss You" is probably his masterpiece of simply fucking around in the interstices. So he waits to see how Charlie will synchronize Keith's energy and then spreads that around the room, as sound and as feel, and he does that without reinforcing the drums, creating a vague but highly tangible sonic atmosphere, sometimes playful, sometimes spare, sometimes bleak, sometimes brooding, sometimes outright dark. But it is the echo of the dying of your very own heartbeat.

What a Mess!

There was a development of this sound too, as Bill became more independent while also becoming a perfect master of his role in the rhythm section. The relation between the bass and the rhythm guitar in Stones history is like the way couples at first, when they are dating, finish each other's sentences with amazement and delight, but then after twenty-five years they can have a complete conversation without finishing any sentences at all. Bill's bass falls into an unconscious finishing of Keith's musical thoughts sort of like that. And as the years went by, the conversation between bass and guitar became so abbreviated that one could barely tell a conversation was happening. But it was still very musical.

Bill didn't write the bass line for "Shattered" but he played it for fifteen years. It's a menacing tangle of bottom end dissonance. It isn't made for the ear, it is made for the gonads and the solar plexus. It chases you down the street like a rabid dog. And the groove closes on itself in those lower (almost subsonic) ranges. Bill's job is to shut the door behind the band, to clear away the musical mess in a haze of bottom-shelf, down-on-the-floor-throwing-up-sick-drunk-head-spinning-I-can't-believe-I-did-that-again ooze. It works. But not since 1993. Ah well. Nobody gets to live forever.

And that brings us to the promise I made early on. What gets destroyed as we partake in the dreadful energy of rock? Well, ourselves, of course, in the form of our youth. Youth itself is sacrificed on the altar of rock and roll. You already know that, but it is time to look at it again. This is something like what Freud calls *thanatos*, the death wish that is being experienced beneath the organization of the energies. When you look for a tempo, you want the flow of death, but when you want to rock and roll, you want to stop your own heart every four beats and find a resurrection on the far side of the bar. And your chances of survival are pretty good, with some help from the right rhythm section, the masters of making the life force itself die a little at a time.

We can't live forever, but let's bring the whip down on the asses of the gods and see what happens.

3
Frenzy

We're always having something very funny happen when we start that number.

—MICK JAGGER, Altamont, December 6th, 1969

In mid-June 2011 the news was dominated by images of a surprising riot in Vancouver, following their hockey team's loss to the Boston team in the Stanley Cup finals.

I suppose most people normally think of Canadians as a pretty impassive lot, stoic in the face of disappointment, mild if not really meek. West Coast Canadians are, if anything, even more laid-back than their countrymen, so everyone was taken a bit off guard at the time. Sort of like some were in the second half of 1969, when the New Yorkers were actually able to behave themselves for a few days in August, but on the peace-love-dope West Coast, right across the Bay from hippie central, the crowd couldn't make it through a Stones concert without violence and death. The Dionysian frenzy? War? Rape? Murder? It's just a shot away, you know?

In this case, a photographer snapped a picture of a couple engaged in a passionate kiss while lying in the middle of the street, in the midst of the riot. The picture went viral. It was all quite soon over and forgotten, but the photograph captured our notice for a historical moment and it reminds us of something humans have known for as long as we have existed: There is a weird connection between the build-up of group emotion, and sex, and violence. That association has vexed us for a long time,

51

and to associate sex and violence, especially in a public setting, is still a good way to get yourself in trouble with the Man. Strangely, we can deal with violence and sex more easily when they're individualized and compartmentalized. What's up with this? And why is the build-up of group emotion so scary and so volatile?

Please Allow Me to Introduce Myself

Before we go any further, I need to make a confession. Brian Jones creeps me out, always has. He still has a weird sort of cult following of people who think he was the real genius, or that The Stones were no good without him, and so on. I certainly didn't know him and I really can't remember him at all (I was eight when he died), but I know that even on the fortieth anniversary of his death when the BBC interviewed Mick and Charlie, they couldn't come up with any kind words for Brian, and you could see them trying to. But no. He was a bad person. It isn't polite to speak ill of the dead, but Keith tells stories in his autobiography that leave people shaking their heads.

Brian was violent and cruel, and I fancy I can see that in his eyes when I study the old pictures. When I think of the embodiment of the negative energy the Sixties contained, I think of Brian Jones, and for my money, that's who Don McLean was really speaking of in the verse of "American Pie" about the disastrous Altamont concert in 1969. I know McLean said that the image in his mind was Mick Jagger, and that Brian had been dead almost four months when the concert happened, but to me, the figure "laughing with delight" at the conflagration of the world was Brian Jones.

If you are one of the Jones minions, please don't kill me. I'll recant everything if you'll just let me live. But I think the dark side of that groovy energy needs a face, and I think Brian is it, and so, what follows is a sort of meditation on what gets sacrificed on the altar of rock and roll, when the Dionysian frenzy turns ugly.

The Nature of My Game

No collection of folks, or even any individual, symbolizes for us more profoundly an S&D&R&R aestheticism than The Stones, and we all know that, at this late stage of history. But *why* did the Stones so reliably bring the Dionysian frenzy to the breaking point? To hear them tell it, you'd think they were more the victims of that craziness than catalyst or cause. That story isn't quite believable. The Stones may not have seen the frenzy coming, but they can't pretend to be innocent. I'm sure they never wanted anyone to be seriously hurt, and I think they were genuinely surprised at how thin the line was between a bacchanalia about pleasure and one about death.

If not in recent years, then certainly for their first twenty or so, going to a Stones concert could be, well, almost a sporting proposition (and that was part of the attraction), a little risky. You might come back preggers or even in a body bag, if you weren't careful. That includes the band themselves (on the body bag part—I'm supposing they aren't biologically right for the other). The frenzy phenomenon didn't wholly end, though, even when it did subside. You can find a vid up on YouTube where in 2005 a Pittsburgh crone attacks Keith Richards (for reasons unclear—she can't still want sex, but she certainly wants *something*), as he tries to get to his car.

Of the craze, Keith says that in the early days "what they were reacting to was being in this enclosed space with us— this illusion; me, Mick, Brian. The music might be the trigger, but the bullet, nobody knows what that is" (*Life*, p. 137). Still, I think there's something about the way the Stones have gone about crafting their personae and prosecuting their performance that taps into a deep (and disturbing) aspect of all human experience. I want to get at the bullet, if I can.

There are lots of *kinds* of crazy, so there's a very great difference between becoming schizoid, sociopathic, or individually manic, on the one hand (where I think Brian Jones belongs), and losing it with the crowd, or the mob, on the other (possibly this is the right category for the late Meredith Hunter, waving his pistol in the stage area at Altamont). Whatever takes hold when the Stones play brings people to do things in groups they wouldn't do alone, so it's more like the second kind of crazy. People don't suddenly become individually insane when Keith hits the first chord, but something happens to the crowd, for sure. It started with the girls. Keith describes it:

> The '50s chicks being brought up all very jolly hockey sticks, and then somewhere there seemed to be a moment when they just decided they wanted to let themselves go. The opportunity arose for them to do that, and who's going to stop them? It was all dripping with sexual lust, though they didn't know what to do about it. But suddenly you're on the end of it. It's a frenzy. Once it's out, it's an incredible force. You stood as much chance in a fucking river full of piranhas. They were beyond what they wanted to be. They'd lost themselves. These chicks were coming out there, bleeding, clothes torn off, pissed panties, and you took that for granted every night. That was the gig. (*Life*, p. 138)

That was the gig? Okay, he knows better than I would. But it doesn't seem like you could quite *book* that gig, you know? If that's the "sex" side of the Dionysian coin, what about the "violence" side?

Reading the Riot Act

The British parliament passed the real "Riot Act" back in 1714 to make it possible for them to use the death penalty on those who refused to disperse after the Act was read aloud. Rioting breaks out periodically among all sorts of people (however tame they seem), and for a lot of different reasons, some political, some religious, and even some *purely aesthetic*. Apparently, Igor Stravinsky's ballet *The Rite of Spring* provoked a purely aesthetic riot among the Paris highbrows at its debut in 1913. That must have been very strange. The crowd started booing the bassoon solo, early on, and even the police couldn't keep the peace after intermission. Stravinsky himself just fled. The fact that it was a pagan ballet is, well, not *entirely* unrelated to what I have to say here. What the dancers were doing, and the way the orchestra was playing, had a nasty effect on the apologists of conventional taste in that crowd. These are definitely the same folks whose grandchildren would tell you that rock and roll is the devil's music. (And so it is, but have a little sympathy and taste, okay?)

No matter what the reason, a lot of people find it upsetting when accepted standards of public behavior (aesthetic or moral) begin to be strained by collective human emotions. That's true at a soccer match just as it is at a Stones concert, but somehow, conventional people are willing to make some room in their tiny hearts for a good sports-brawl, even if people die, in ways they won't for what happens at a Stones show gone bad. In every case where this frothing mass emotion is released, there is this moment, I think, when it seems that all order has disappeared and we come face to face with, with . . . I don't know, whatever it is "we" are *without* that imposed order. We usually don't like what we see, or at least some people don't, and those of us who do aren't making any important decisions in the world. The revelers also have difficulty remembering what happened when it's all over. The riot doesn't have enough structure to hang a memory on.

The early Stones concerts in Britain were the scene of bedlam. I can barely imagine being there. There were girls screaming, and always a few angry rednecks calling our boys faggots, and before you know it, Keith kicks some guy in the face and it's lucky nobody is killed. Here is what he says, in part, about one such:

> Maybe if we'd been wearing our houndstooth jackets and looking like little dolls we wouldn't have outraged the males in the audience at the Wisbech Corn Exchange. . . . And a riot was started because the local yokels, the boys, couldn't stand the fact that all of their chicks were gawping and blowing themselves out about this bunch of fags, as far as they were concerned, from London. . . . That was a good riot, which we were lucky to escape from. (*Life*, p. 131)

More in a minute about this special sort of "fags." The point is that the riots at the Stones' shows were a little different from what surrounded the Beatles. It came to the point that almost every Stones concert led to some sort of disturbance that took a toll on property and persons.

The Riot Act wasn't actually repealed in Britain until 1973, though its last "public reading" was in 1919. But I'm guessing that at least a few among the British establishment might have been happy to dust it off and try it out in 1963–65—for the Stones, not the Beatles. With the Fab Four, one didn't get the same sense of impending danger. Beatlemania wasn't much different from the fuss over Sinatra and then Elvis. When The Stones showed up, somehow things turned darker and got ratcheted up a notch or two. So, on the one hand, The Stones *per se* do seem to make a difference in what happens. The scary tone of violence seems to form itself around the sounds and the whole atmosphere of The Stones. It isn't just female lust. It harbors violence.

A Little Help from Their Friends?

It's probably a good thing that our favorite fellows headed to the USA when they did. The UK needed a rest. On their first US tour, no one in America knew who The Stones were, so the girls didn't scream and the boys didn't see the need to take any swings at anybody—even in Texas, where a long-hair limey might get a pop on the snout just for crossing the state line. Only at the end of that tour, when manager Andrew Oldham placed some teeny-bopper plants among the New York audience, did the Americans get the idea that this was supposed to be a frenzy. So on the other hand (and there's always another hand), we can see it wasn't the music alone that was causing the riots, or even The Stones, *per se*. They needed a little help from their friends, a context and a clue to tell everybody this was a moment to abandon ordinary decorum.

As a final contrast, it's interesting to think of Led Zeppelin, which had the same dark and semi-satanic brooding, and the same sex, drugs, and so on, and even the same debt to the blues aesthetic and the deal at the cross-roads, but *not* the riots. It's true that Zeppelin missed the historical window by a couple of years, but apart from timing I see no reason why Zeppelin couldn't have ended up with the albatross of Altamont just as easily as The Stones. And surely Robert Plant had the needed testosterone to do what Mick did to the girls. So maybe it was just the times and not the Stones? We'll never know for sure. With that much said, there's no question at all that the Stones pushed us past the line between light and dark, when it comes to building up collective emotion. Their sex is androgynous and forbidden, their drugs kill, and their rock and roll . . . well, all I can say is I like it.

Gimme that Old Time Religion?

It isn't quite accurate to say that the collective frenzy has a "long history" because in fact, it's *older* than history. Stuff that old is a little bit tough to *know* about, so you're onto some slippery back roads of human thought when you decide to *think* about it—can't tell what people are *making up* from what *really happened*. It's like listening to a Republican administration. The vagaries of pre-history make it especially dicey for philosophers to discuss, since we never cared too much for facts anyway, and most respectable philosophers would tell you that there was *no* philosophy back then, just irrational failures of thinking. I disagree with that, and I'm not interested in being a respectable philosopher, but I agree it's pretty hard to say what philosophy amounts to back before writing was invented. Still, even respectable philosophers need only a little encouragement and they're off into their own land of the (conceptually) lost.

The problem of the frenzy showed up early on, even in philosophy, and it has re-appeared in turns from then to now, but we should deal with it more than we do. Socrates himself was an initiate of the "Eleusinian Mysteries," which involved fertility rites and perhaps some ritual orgies. There were no human sacrifices by that time in (recorded) Mediterranean history. But even at that, the early philosophers found the sex rituals and the crowd hysteria objectionable. Plato wrote about the problem of *eros* and how it makes human beings mad with passion, like when Keith said those girls were "beyond what they wanted to be." Plato wasn't much in favor of that sort of behavior, and he used his power as a writer to absolve his teacher Socrates of any real loss of rational control in the *Symposium*. Plato was pretty dedicated to downplaying Socrates's religious leanings (this frenzy was "religion" back then). We'll never know for sure if Socrates got his rocks off at the rites. So Plato sort of got what he wanted, I guess.

By the time people like Plato and Socrates lived, the fourth century B.C.E., the Dionysian festivals were coming into poor repute. It was a time of transition, and Plato definitely opposed the old ways of the flesh, and he didn't like The Rolling Stones (they were around back then, as I will explain, they just didn't have a record deal). Plato even claimed Socrates never got drunk, no matter how much wine you gave him. I actually know a woman who's like that, so I'm sure the phenomenon exists, but I just don't think that is the real Socrates. Plato also wrote about how certain kinds of music (such as blues and rock) ignite human desires and lead us to weakness and "effeminacy" (that's what it's called in the translations). Manliness and rationality in all circumstances were associated with self-restraint by Plato, and after he'd had his say, if you still did the old rites, you were just a wimp in the thrall of women. Plato didn't want people like that around and advocated banning their favorite music. In short: no Stones concert allowed in Plato's city. Plato wanted the women to be like men, not the other way around.

I've Been Around for a Long, Long Year

And that brings me back to my earlier point about The Stones being called "fags" by the angry male element in the audience. There is a story to be told about "the boys who serve the women" and "the boys who serve the men." Some might think the Stones serve the men, but I would beg to differ. You'll see. It looks like human civilization may be a lot older than we had long believed. Well, really there's no "may be" about it. Civilization just *is* a lot older, and people who think otherwise are kidding themselves. Recent discoveries in Asia Minor indicate that highly organized communal human life goes back to 10,000 B.C.E. (that's 7,500 years older than the pyramids, and 7000 years older than Stonehenge). Google the names "Gobekli Tepe" or "Nevali Çori" and see what you find.

The world of the "ancient" Greeks is, by comparison, only yesterday. We may have had civilization *before* 10,000 B.C.E., but we don't have evidence right now. It's a murky topic. After all, even by the most conservative estimate, there have been "modern humans" (in the biological sense of the word) for at least fifty thousand years, and perhaps much, much longer. It isn't reasonable to think the humans, with brains and hands and voices just like ours, would just hang fire on the savannah all that time. They had *big* brains. They got bored. They needed some entertainment. They started beating on things. What Charlie Watts does so well isn't that much different. (Is it just me, or does Charlie bear a resemblance to those fanciful models of Neanderthal man? You know the scientists now say that some Neanderthal DNA survived in us from cross-breeding, especially in northern Europe . . .)

Once you have the groove, you also have the dance—humans had excess energies and we were dedicated to getting that out of our system. One good way to do that is sex, but even that gets old after a while (for everyone except Bill Wyman). No one knows just how the dance and the music *became* the ritual, but it seems likely that the ritual involved sex from the outset. If it were not so, it would be hard to explain why it took so many centuries to discourage the fertility cults—I say discourage, since they weren't destroyed. There are still plenty of devotees of the degraded forms of these cults, in case you haven't noticed the existence of many thousands of "gentlemen's clubs," and a billion-dollar pornography industry. I'm not at all certain I would call the debauchery of the Stones tours a "degraded" version of those cults, but rather more of an upgraded resurgence.

The fertility cults also sometimes involved death, at least by the time we can document things. Whether sacrifice is an original impulse among humans we do not know, but the ritual practice of human and animal sacrifice is very, very old. Some authorities, following Freud, say it's a basic impulse and they find analogies even among the chimps these days. Others say it isn't so, but everybody agrees that humans and animals were sacrificed in the frenzy in many of the most ancient cultures. You'll be hard pressed to compartmentalize the sex and the death as you regress into more ancient and more primal versions of these rituals—and that may explain why we don't like to look at this and think of it.

Not knowing what to do with our extra energy leads us to be diabolically creative with our nimble hands and big old brains. A French thinker (widely read by philosophers, sometimes in secret) named Georges Bataille (1897–1962) named this extra energy "the accursed share" (or *la part maudite* if you're feeling fancy) and he also expounded in most uncomfortable clinical detail the proximity of death and sensual desire. He's a scary read. Go do it, by all means, but maybe not late at night when you're alone.

I'm in Need of Some Restraint

The story of Abraham and Isaac in Genesis is a classic account of how human sacrifice was gradually replaced with symbolic sacrifices. Human sacrifice in the part of Mesopotamia Abraham left (the city-state of Ur) was already extremely old; the area had been occupied by agrarian, communal humans for thousands of years, and the rituals of human sacrifice were deeply engrained in their public life. The religious system was more stable than we can imagine these days. It endured for centuries, probably millennia.

The religion was unremarkable in many ways, but offering up the first born was required (good thing they weren't requiring that in England, since Brian, Mick, and Keith would have had to go to the gods). Sacrificing the first-born was seen as an act of humility: one gives one's best and what one loves most, to one's god, and as a result, *all* of those alive in that society are second-born, or later. The practical reason to approve such a practice is that it curbs our over-weaning "pride of place." If everyone is second-born, or lower, no one has sole inheritance, and all the other problems that go with letting the first born live. The story of Abraham and Isaac shows how a substitution method called "redemption" could be used to replace the traditional way, so that pride is curbed and the first-born can be allowed to live.

So, things did eventually change. Not just the Hebrews, but the Egyptians and the Greeks also moved "beyond" human sacrifice, independently of the Hebrews, and long before Abraham in the case of the Egyptians. But it took hundreds if not thousands of years to squash the rite, and it still lingers today, associated with the Black Mass and enacted only an infrequent teenage rebellion, as an invigorating idea among the most forbidden of the outcast fringe groups. The Stones have played on that forbidden feeling, but mainly for its shock value, I think. They are devotees of the goddess, not of the Dark Prince.

It's hard for people today to grasp that sacrificing the first-born was once what ordinary people did from religious piety, and that the animal sacrifices in voodoo ought to be seen as a step *away* from that. Is animal sacrifice barbarous? It's hard to understand why people are troubled by the ritual sacrifice of a chicken but don't mind eating at KFC. Which of those two, in a just world, would *really* be more inhumane? I mean, be rational about this. Treating animals as if their lives had no value at all as against treating them as individually valuable enough for sacrifice to the gods? Maybe we haven't altogether *improved* our practical, moral sensibilities in the last couple of millennia.

I think Shirley Jackson's eerie short story "The Lottery" (maybe you had to read it in high school like I did) helps us grasp the idea of human sacrifice as it might be if it existed in the present. But in her version, the sacrificial victim is chosen by chance and is reluctant. There is evidence that among the Druids the "victim" *volunteered*, and it was a privilege to be so sacrificed. The stories of the early Christian martyrs have a lot of that same energy—read the unnerving diary of Perpetua if you doubt me.

Anyway, it is amazing what sorts of activities can be "normalized" with humans, and that includes human sacrifice. If Sarah Palin or Michele Bachmann lived back in that time, before Abraham, they'd be defending the sacrifices, because their type of conservative sensibility, about the importance of keeping traditions, along with their piety (which I think is genuine), has the same quality as the conventional worshipers in *any* age. Those gals would pretty much embrace, I'm confident, *whatever* the prevailing traditional norms were *whenever* they lived, and they would give up their own first born and condemn those who didn't if that was what their religion said. No mother wants to give up her child. But where the expectations and the practices of millennia demand it, it is done.

If Palin and Bachmann had grown up in the fertility cults of the Ba'als, even after Abraham's time, they'd also be doing the nasty with all the men at festival time just like *good girls* did back then. And it was very tough on young women who tried to choose between the traditional ways of the ancient Semitic races and the new and more modest ways of the Hebrews. If you aren't familiar with this dilemma, I suggest you read the Biblical book of Hosea. Hosea's wife Gomer was not a prostitute, she was raised in a fertility cult. God told Hosea (much to his distress) to *marry* her because he wanted His prophet to know exactly what it felt like to be the God of Israel, which kept backsliding into the fertility cults. So, if they lived in *that* later day (we're talking roughly the eighth century B.C.E.) maybe women like Bachmann and Palin would only do the seven veils in private, and only with their husbands (listening to the ancient equivalent of the Rolling Stones, on the other side of a screen). But unless you're a Southern Baptist, I think that much has been okay in almost any age.

Stole Many a Man's Soul and Faith

To give another example of a contemporary religious nut, the depiction of the Mayan human sacrifices in Mel Gibson's film *Apocalypto* is a horror in itself, but I must say, he makes no effort to understand the reasons any civilization might have for adopting the ritual. It's pretty ironic coming from the same guy who willed the world to watch the goriest depiction of human sacrifice in cinematic history (I mean *The Passion of the Christ*—a movie I'm betting Bachmann and Palin endorse, since it depicts *their* favored kind of human sacrifice).

Contemporary Christians (and me among them, conventional bloke that I am) still gobble up the God and drink his blood on Sundays and somehow fail to notice the analogy to cannibalism. (Of course, it's just a symbol unless you're Catholic, but *what* a symbol, folks.) If you must be a conventional bloke like me, I hope you'll try not to be an ignorant one—eating the god is about as time-honored as any tradition can possibly be, but it *isn't* the Jewish way; that's a *pagan* survival in Christianity, more of which shortly.

As frightening as they are, these life and death rituals have always addressed a profound human need. Perhaps we know now, in the last four thousand years or so, that this need can be (at least partly) fulfilled without the bloodshed. That "need" we name with the words "religious fervor," or what they used to call "enthusiasm." There is a reason the sports stadiums are full week after week, too. We desire a release of that fervor, a kind of build-up of group emotion directed at the gods, or God, or the Dallas Cowboys, or The Rolling Stones. There is a damn good reason the mainline Protestant churches are all in decline while every Sunday morning one can find enormous arenas filled with ignorant people who want to watch a preacher get possessed by the Holy Spirit while a chorus blares the same words over and over to loud-ass music. If he reminds you of Mick Jagger, well, is that really surprising?

The mainline churches tried to kill the build-up of group emotion in worship and it got very boring and people went elsewhere; in Europe, they went to see the soccer match, but in the US, they're still at church, plus the sports. And everybody everywhere went to the Stones concert. That is what humans always do and it's what they always have done, and

I dare to think it's what they always will do. We go where the action is.

The human race is not going to outgrow its desire for the transcendent experience of group emotion. The difference between a Stones concert and a Pentecostal revival is not huge, and there is nothing anyone can do to change that. But make no mistake, in this regard, the Christians are thoroughly pagan, and not pagan in the *civilized* way that the ancient Greeks and Romans were. Our times are closer to primitive cult than to civil religion, as practiced by elevated people like the Greeks and Romans. And the religious freaks have always been nurtured in the distant provinces of a civilization, remote places like Alaska, or the wild suburbs of Minneapolis.

Use All Your Well-learned Politesse

That brings us to the most ancient part of civilized human life where we have evidence, in places like Gobekli Tepe, and Google these too: Achelleion, Sitagroi, and Argissa Magoula. These aren't quite as old but pose the same puzzles. The debate over who these people were and how they lived will never end. We have no clear account of at least five thousand years of human civilization. That is about equal to the amount of time we *do* have in records for—the oldest writing is about 3000 B.C.E.

That's when "history" began, but there was definitely civilization of a highly complex sort *long* before there was writing. They had cities and politics and agriculture and markets and probably even rock and roll. I'm not kidding. Music, dance, and art came along way before writing, so if not practitioners of the oldest profession in the world, the Stones are certainly in the first five—along with the priests, politicians, and pimps (that's only one profession, if you go back far enough, or if you read between the lines in the present).

Some scholars believe that our civilized pre-history was, gasp, organized around the sense and vision of the *females* of the race. "Matriarchy" may not be quite the right word for it, since the idea that women "ruled" would be a very *manly* interpretation of what was going on. It might be truer to say that women were "civilized" and men had to be "managed"—and note that "man" is the operative location of all *man*agement. Back in the day, an otherwise sensible Swiss scholar named

Johann Jakob Bachofen (1815–1887) pretty much ruined his own life by suggesting that the evidence points to the existence of whole civilizations in which the Crone, the Mother, and the Maiden were the central figures of reverence—and of authority, such as it was. Bachofen was mainly ignored, but some took the trouble to mock him.

Frankly, I don't know whether the "civilization of the goddess" (as it was called by the archaeologist Marija Gimbutas) ever existed, and I don't need to know. What I'm sure of is that the stories of the orgiastic rites of the fertility cults that do survive point very clearly to a deep division that is still alive and well in our present civilization, a division between heavy-handed control (patriarchy), and whatever *opposes* that, which upsets the patriarchy and gets condemned and persecuted by the control freaks. Both The Beatles and The Stones tapped into that division, as had Elvis before them. Their prancing for the girls puts male insecurities on public display, but to be a man in a male-dominated civilization is to carry that division within yourself.

Bachofen had a young friend, none other than Friedrich Nietzsche, who became obsessed by this "division," which he called the Apollonian and the Dionysian energies. Nietzsche didn't care for the womanly aspects of the Dionysian, but he was fascinated by the way that the Dionysian energies kept popping up and breaking out into the frenzy. Apollonian energy is regimentation and order. Dionysian energy is the overflow of life energy, the accursed share. Every time the lovers of control get the upper hand, the cult of Dionysus springs up again, and like Keith said, there is just no stopping that energy. What happened in the 1960s has happened many, many times before. The Stones rode a wave of Dionysian energy that would not be bottled up by a heavy handed, patriarchal Cold War. But if loose lips sink ships, big lips offer a wagging tongue to the danger. The god that sacrifices himself *will* have his day. But long before this oscillation of Apollo and Dionysus, there was at least five thousand years of something else.

Mother's Little Helpers

There was a Cambridge scholar and philosopher named Jane Ellen Harrison (1850–1928) who wrote a whole bunch of books that trace the development of Greek religion from a swampy matriarchy up through the age of the Olympian gods that we all know, the age that Nietzsche talked about. The pivotal figure in her story was indeed Dionysus, the god of the vine, and yes, of the frenzy and the orgy, and he was the holy child of the Mother (the central manifestation of the goddess); the holy infant was the original man-child, the child hero, and the sacrificial victim at the rites, flayed and divided among the faithful.

If this sounds a little like the Christ story, well, you didn't really think the Christians made all that up, did you? They retold a very, very old story in a way that bridged a gap between Jews and pagans. Miss Harrison (as she was always called) ruffled more than a few Victorian feathers with her tales about the derivative (and religiously inferior) Christian version of Jesus and Mary. Like Mick Jagger, Miss Harrison is not without sympathy for the Christian story, she just sees it from a broader perspective—after all, the devilry itself is much older than Christianity. One of the things that has always impressed me about Mick Jagger is how wide his sense of history is and how very damn smart those lyrics are—not just to "Sympathy for the Devil," but in so many of the songs he wrote. He has a very keen intellect, sees things as they are, in my opinion.

And Mick knows, obviously, there is no reason to bother with being anti-Christian. You cannot successfully oppose the *kind* of story Christianity tells; it always just pops up again. It is the Dionysian story. The followers of Apollo hijacked it, as they always do, but it's the story of Dionysus. The Christian *version* of that story is a lot less objectionable than other versions we might have been saddled with. Nietzsche was right when he complained that Christianity is a puny, slave morality that renders the human race effeminate and opposes all that is mighty and virile in humans. That's exactly what I *like* about Christianity. I have always thought that slaves know more than their masters, and that over-weaning masculinity needs to be opposed with as much vigor as it takes to keep the boys from killing each other with all their stupid pointy toys.

Won't You Guess My Name?

Miss Harrison's main discovery about the Rolling Stones is in her book *Themis: A Study of the Social Origins of Greek*

Religion. The opening chapter is actually about Mick Jagger. One of his earliest songs is called the "Hymn of the Kouretes," where the island boys who serve the goddess strut around their golden child, Kouros (that was Mick's name back then), at the bidding of the goddess. The goddess likes it when the boys come to admire her perfect boy, and she gives the Maiden permission to lose it when they do. That was the gig. And that's how you book it. Ask your Mother.

Over several millennia, Mick had a lot of names. He was called Dendritis, and Nuktelios, and Isodaites, among other names, and later Bacchus, of course. It seemed he always had new albums and tours, but Mick finally surfaced in ancient Greece as Dionysus, and that was when he got the name we call him today. It takes Harrison over five hundred pages to tell the story of how Mick showed up to trouble Athens, but all her books are up on-line for free, so at least it won't cost you anything to read about it. Dionysus was eventually accepted among the Olympians, sort of like the irony of Mick Jagger becoming a Knight of the Realm. The appearance of Dionysus among the Greek gods was a real revolution, but that's a story for another time.

The story for today is about how Kouros and the Kouretes (that was the original name of the Rolling Stones) *behaved* themselves. They actually got along without too much strife back when they started out, but soon the males split off into those who like that kind of music and aren't bothered by an omnisexual, ecstatic orgy, and the males who saw that sort of behavior as weak and womanly. Those manly men didn't like being kept at the perimeter of the villages of women, and they started forming their Sour Grapes Clubs out in the woods and caves, and daring any of the girly-men to come and try their little fairy dances out where the real men are—the men who don't need women, the men who hate women for excluding them; the men who would beat women if they could get them behind a closed door; in short, the manly men. They want all the men to be like them.

But here's the thing. You really don't want to underestimate the girly-men. If you do, you may end up with Keith's boot in your face or his knife between your legs. Make no mistake, the girly-men are *men*. They are just as violent and just as dangerous. Eventually the Kouretes lived at the edge of the village and had to come and fetch Kouros to make a man of him, take him away from the women. If he didn't come with them, he was the enemy, the girly-man, the "fag." But he is irresistible isn't he?

Mick wouldn't go. Elvis went into the army, you know? That is how he became acceptable to the manly men. And didn't they love cutting off his hair? But Mick called the Kouretes to himself and kept them under his thumb. That's what Dionysus will do if you don't watch out. It really is Mick's band, as much as Keith and Charlie chafe at the suggestion. Yeah, he's no good without them, it's true, but that doesn't change the fact that She's the Boss, and Mick is her Golden Boy. No Mick, no Stones.

The story of the Dionysian frenzy is the story of the girly-men, and it isn't often well-told. But it is lived every day. So let me ask you a question: which group is *cooler*, the Beatles or the Stones? If you said the Beatles, you may not be a man at all, of either kind. The Beatles are cool, and they were girly men, but they aren't dangerous enough to be cooler than the Stones. And here's what I want you to think about for a minute. The Beatles pressed androgyny only just a bit (pretty mop-tops that they were), but as far as I can tell, they never went in drag (the closest they came was when John and Ringo borrowed their wives' coats for the rooftop concert in January of 1969, their last public performance). The Stones made a point of their femininity. Why do you suppose they did that? Let's think about it for a little bit.

"They're So Ugly It's Appealing"

This was a direct quote from a screaming teeny-bopper who was asked by a newsman outside a Stones concert in about 1965 why she liked The Stones so much. It's a fact. Those boys were just odd looking, every one of them. Big lips, square jaws, deep set eyes, pointy features—and they were all odd looking in almost the same way, except for Ian Stewart, who was sidelined from the band early because he didn't look like the rest of them (*Life*, p. 1 9). Ian Stewart looked like a *man*, was built like a man, and not a bad looking man at that. The others looked androgynous, like ugly, pretty, dirty things. One can barely recover from the picture they put on the cover of their single "Have You Seen Your Mother, Baby." The picture is so good it's disturbing. These guys set out to violate our gendered expecta-

tions. On purpose. These weren't just a bunch of guys who bent the rules, they were off-sides.

The complex psychology of the Dionysian libation bearers, at least in this patriarchal day and age, involves compensation for their effeminacy. That is how I would account for the blatant misogyny of the Stones lyrics. These days you have to keep the manly men, the Dick Cheneys and Donald Trumps of the world, and their cops and lawyers, at arm's length. So to do that, our girly Kouretes had to bite the womanly hand that fed them—or at least that's the way it had to *look* (it appears that only Brian Jones actually abused women). Back in the bad old days, back when the women got the orgies going and no cops existed to tell them it was immoral, guys like the Stones probably didn't need to be faux-macho. They just needed an invitation to the banquet. And boys like The Stones were always welcome (well, except for Brian). They were good toys to keep around. But that was *then*, and we weren't there.

Pleased to Meet You

So, now we're getting somewhere. According to me, it's The Father of All Pissing Contests (I mean the Cold War) that obliges good English boys like Keith and Mick (who don't hate women, they *love* women) to write songs like "Stupid Girl" and "Yesterday's Papers," and "Under My Thumb" and "That Girl

Belongs to Yesterday," and two dozen others that seem, if anything, outright hostile to women. Compare it with the message
in their song "Bitch," which might have been named "Under
Your Thumb." What is the message here?

If these guys are serving the goddess, they aren't quite doing
it in the limp-wristed, light-loafered way—and that, friends and
neighbors, might just be the key to everything: 1. The Stones
don't hate women, *this culture* hates women; and 2. the men
who call the servants of the goddess "fags" are the ones who
built and maintain that misogynistic culture. Even if it's impossible for a woman to win this struggle, it isn't exactly *easy* to be
a man who doesn't buy into all the patriarchal bullshit. But to
be secure enough in your (patriarchal) masculinity to challenge
the very *need* for women, and at the same time get all the girls
(see Bill Wyman's records in *Stone Alone*)? Is it possible that the
supposedly macho men are unmanned by this totally twisted
way the Stones present themselves? I think maybe so.

I also think that the Dionysian frenzy of the 1960s took a
dark turn at just the time when we could no longer absorb the
levels of testosterone being publicly exuded. We really needed
to find some way out of the cultural prison built by our mili-
tarism and fear (and these are different sides of the same coin).
Dionysus sprang up. There would have to be sacrifices on the
altar of Western manhood. As if the Summer of Love had not
already ended in a conflagration in Newark and Detroit
("love"? . . . my ass), the next year, 1968, was going to show the
true face of the world the manly men had built. By the end of
that awful year, over sixteen thousand American troops were
dead, along with probably a hundred thousand Vietnamese
(whose crime was wanting to govern themselves), and so were
Martin Luther King and Robert F. Kennedy. It wasn't possible
to ignore this any more. This was not about making pop records
anymore. This isn't *Sgt. Pepper's Lonely Hearts Club*, this is a
job for their Satanic Majesties. In the face of this melt-down,
the Beatles just quit. But the Stones looked the demon square
in the eye and guessed its name.

From Woodstock to Altamont

In the disastrous year of 1969, everything pretty much fell
apart. The one moment people remember was Woodstock, but

that wasn't the real Dionysian frenzy. That was basically a glorious and well-deserved vacation from the bullshit. The kids of New York (and Boston and Philly) had fought hard, and nobly, against the manly men. But the real thing, the genuine Dionysian frenzy was The Stones' prophetic tour of that year, ending at Altamont, and ending the Sixties. Everyone knew things would just get worse from there, but a corner had been turned, and unlike the others, the Stones would not fade away. The patriarchy doesn't give up all at once, but by December of 1969, it was on the run. Brian was gone and the Stones were reborn. I think he probably chose it. As Keith said right after his funeral, he wasn't going to live to see seventy anyway. He wasn't the kind of person who can. Empires fall too, and for about the same reasons.

I went to see the Maysles brothers' documentary *Gimme Shelter* when it was new. Before that I really had no notion of the early Stones phenomenon, being too young to grasp it until it was really over—although, like so many others my age, they, along with Springsteen, wrote the soundtrack to my own refusal of the patriarchy in the 1970s. But I have to thank my father for taking me to see that movie—rated GP in the antiquated system of the day, meaning I couldn't have seen it without a parent present. He didn't know what the movie was about beforehand, only that he had kids on the brink of teenage rebellion and The Rolling Stones were supposed to be cool, so get on board or get run over, you know?

The movie permanently formed my ideas about the Stones and the world. I think that if my pop (who was and is an apologist of the patriarchy if ever there was one), had known what we would *see* at that movie, he wouldn't have taken me and my sister. But it was the right thing to do, anyway. We lived in Memphis, one of the epicenters of the general disaster, and it had been a rough couple of years. Things were changing very fast. So he also bought me my first Beatles album, and my first Led Zeppelin album (I think that was mom's idea though).

To the parents among you, I think this is a good strategy for maintaining your influence over your kids, better than the advice you'll get from Sarah Palin or Michele Bachmann. It may be better to go even further; bring them their first doobie. Dionysus will have his day, and he *will* have his time with your kids and take his accursed share, sooner or later. If you love them, make a friend of Mick Jagger; it's the only way to protect them from Brian Jones. It's just a shot away, or just a kiss away. That's the gig, so you choose.

4

When Jumpin' Jack Flash Met Ziggy Stardust

David Bowie created the persona of the Thin White Duke by adjusting the character of Thomas Jerome Newton, which was the "Earth identity" of *The Man Who Fell to Earth*. That alien visitor was an adjusted Starman, which is who he was before he came to meet us and blew our minds.

The Starman in his turn was the leper Messiah, Ziggy making love with his ego and sucked up into his mind, and of course, Ziggy was Major Tom's return, altered by his existential crisis. After the Duke we have a run of aliens and misfits who pleased us, but by then we knew what to expect. Through the whole run, Mick Jagger was an unsatisfied Jumpin' Jack. He changed costumes and pranced outrageously, but he was always Mick and nothing other—and not just Mick but, more importantly, the lead singer of the Stones, which is about all the public will allow him to be.

It's well documented that between the advent of Ziggy and the time he put to bed the persona of the Thin White Duke, Bowie was, well, pretty close to being psychotic. He was apparently having difficulty in finding David beneath all the characters he played. One thing they all had in common was a lot of drugs. And somewhere in there, just before Ziggy died, he met Mick Jagger in the flesh, having known Mick's persona for many years already. Mick now claims he can't remember when he met David Bowie (see Jagger's "Tribute" to Bowie), but I think he does. Mick and David had boxed the London compass, keeping tabs on each other since Bowie's real breakthrough in 1972 with the rise of Ziggy. Before that Bowie would not have been so much as a blip on Mick's keen radar. Bowie was chugging in a fleet with Gary Glitter and Mark Bolan and a dozen other Jagger-wannabe's. Mick and his crew had pioneered and perfected the androgyny angle and there wasn't much they hadn't tried in costume and stage sets by 1971.

Mick was dismissive of the whole crew of imitators, and that was fair enough, but Bowie caught his discerning eye, in much the way Mick had caught Andy Warhol's eye a few years earlier. It takes one to know one, you might say. For the youth of America, 1967 was the Summer of Love, but for Jagger and Bowie, the magical interlude was 1973, and it lasted a full year. They were inseparable that year, and like the first dozen Disciples, they held all things in common, including wives, if one can believe what rock journalists and ex-wives say.

It ended, apparently, when Mick bragged to David that the Stones' next album cover art would be done by the new and fashionable Guy Peellaert. Bowie immediately hired the man for *Diamond Dogs* and beat the Stones to press by four months, and with one of the most outrageous covers in Rock history. Bowie claimed in an interview that Mick should have known better than to show him something new. By the time Peellaert's William Blake burlesque appeared on the cover of *It's Only Rock'n'Roll*, it was old news.

This was an interesting and problematic love affair, and instructive.

Street Fighting Men

Let's begin this story with a third party. Angie Bowie has had a good bit to say about this epoch, but I found a different source that is more philosophically interesting. I learned from Keith Richards's autobiography that (Sir) Mick Jagger envied David Bowie. That fact became a sort of embarrassment to Keith. Looking into it, I found that Keith had been harping on this point as early as 1980 (see Alan Cayson's book on Mick). Here's what Keith had to say in 2010:

> Mick got very big ideas. All lead singers do. It's a known affliction called LVS, lead vocalist syndrome. . . . If you combine LVS with a nonstop bombardment of flattery every waking moment over years and years, you can start to believe the incoming. . . . And even if you

don't completely believe it, you say, well, everybody else does—I'll roll with it. You forget that it's just part of the job. It's amazing how even quite sensible people like Mick Jagger could get carried away by it. Actually believe they were special. (*Life*, pp. 455–56)

It takes significant ego strength to disbelieve your own press, whether it's good or bad, but perhaps good press is harder to rise above since it feels like you don't *need* to rise above it. Bad press must be met with strength and perseverance by any who endure it, but everyone knows that. Not everyone knows about how praise can destroy a person's sense of perspective and, in the end, also a person's confidence.

The trouble is that whatever modicum of reality you hang onto, it isn't enough to help you take the true measure of either the flatterers or the critics, and those are the only two kinds of people yapping. Some of what they say is true, but how much and which parts? Of course, you *could* trust your oldest friends, but Mick had already discounted in advance anything Keith might tell him and had, in fact, lost respect for Keith, thinking the man simply a fool with a guitar, albeit, one he needed. If Mick underestimated Keith (and he did), he had been given plenty of reason to do so. Why should he be chained to this chump?

But over here was this bright, shiny, beautiful Bowie thing. Keith continues:

Mick had become uncertain, he had started second guessing his own talent—that seemed, ironically, to be at the root of the self-inflation. For many years through the 60s, Mick was incredibly charming and humorous. He was a natural. . . . Somewhere, though, he got unnatural. . . . He forgot his natural rhythm. . . . Whatever somebody else was doing was far more interesting to him than what he was doing. He even began to act as if he wanted to be someone else. Mick is quite competitive, and he started to get competitive about other bands. He watched what David Bowie was doing and wanted to do it. Bowie was a major, major attraction. Somebody had taken Mick on in the costume and bizarreness department. (p. 456)

Far be it from me to question, but I think Keith, so comfortable in his own skin and not feeling the pressure Mick had to deal with being out front, doesn't quite get Bowie and the *why* of this rivalry. What *Keith* saw was "Oh, someone wants to try to compete with you in wardrobe, Mick!" But Mick knew very well that more was going on. Bowie wasn't putting on costumes; he was creating art personas. Mick wanted to do that, or at least imagined he did. Keith finishes the rant thus:

> But the fact is, Mick could deliver ten times more than Bowie in just a T-shirt and a pair of jeans, singing "I'm a Man." Why would you want to be anyone else if you're Mick Jagger? Is being the greatest entertainer in show business not enough? He forgot that it was he who was new, who created and set the trends in the first place, for years. It's fascinating. I can't figure it out. It's almost as if Mick was aspiring to be Mick Jagger, chasing his own phantom. (p. 456)

How can Mick Jagger seriously envy anyone? But the rules of life include the one that says, *whoever* you are, you'll think someone else has it better. But this is more than that. This is about how to hold the top when you're at it. Fame is fleeting— fifteen minutes or so. You have to zig when the rest zag to hold the attention of the fickle public and Bowie was zigging like no one before him, and everyone but Keith Richards knew it.

Mick had to make sure not to zag, and that was his job, not Keith's. In a 1965 interview someone asked Jagger how long he expected to be doing what he was doing. He earnestly answered that he never imagined two years ago he'd still be doing it in the present, and then he surmised "maybe two more years." He was painfully aware of how quickly these things fade. It's easy for Keith to say after fifty years of success, "C'mon Mick, you're the man." It's fair for Mick to point at Bowie and answer "Only because I was paying attention while you, you were just speed-balling. . . and you're welcome, *Keith*."

So, Bowie and Jagger became intimates, for pleasure and for utility. But they weren't making common cause. Keep your friends close and your competitors closer, right? This involves not only sharing the same bed, but seeing whether you can dislodge the other guy's favorite lover. Christopher Anderson goes so far as to claim that Bowie himself, and not his wife Angie, was the inspiration for Jagger's song "Angie." There may have been love between Jagger and Bowie. The consensus of the rock rags is that there was almost assuredly sex. For the scandal sheet version of it, see Anderson's *Jagger Unauthorized*, pp. 86–91, or Wendy Leigh's *Bowie: The Biography*, Chapter 4.

But it may have been as much a street fight as a love fest.

God Knows I'm Good

It isn't easy to create ethics from an aesthetic, or a series of them. The woes of Oscar Wilde are certainly an instructive case, and the lesson is embodied in his masterpiece *The Picture of Dorian Gray*. Somewhere in some attic is a picture of Bowie that looks like Keith Richards. But he maintained his youth to the end, didn't he?

There are numerous philosophers who have issued stern and lengthy warnings about taking the aesthetic path in life, most famously in Søren Kierkegaard's *Either / Or*, Volume 1, which is the diary of a seducer. But most celebrity artists will not be vulnerable to such moralizing. Why, they will demand, should I not follow the lead of my senses and of what people want and demand of me? Is this not a kind of irresistible "imperative"?

The answer is made more difficult considering that if we had no bodily senses, no capacity for pleasure and pain, how could we ever learn right from wrong? We're animals following our natures. If that isn't the basis of right and wrong, then our Creator has a diabolical twist in fashioning us with such strong drives and then telling us that to be worthy before Him we must not act on them. What sort of morality is *that*, pray tell?

Thus, most who choose the aesthetic path to a moral life do not have any truck with the Western God. Buddhism or various Hindu disciplines are more popular, since the point is to be mindful of your spiritual development and aware of what's beyond your control, to learn compassion, and learn to resign the world. This ethic is easier to grasp from the standpoint of a celebrity artist.

Unfortunately, however, there's not enough guidance here for successful and deep relationships with other people, especially those who, shall we say, live mainly under the veil of Maya. Sometimes this word is translated as "illusion," but my scholar friends tell me that is a bad rendering. They then reject every other suggestion I make about how to translate it and inform me that I'll need to spend the rest of my life learning Sanskrit or Pali or some other language I could never master. You've probably had the same lecture from someone at some point. But I don't think Mick and David can learn it either, if I can't. That doesn't cut out their sense of a spiritual requirement of living that grows from what they do best—cultivate the senses (they are musicians, after all)—and reaches into the sorts of happiness and stable relationships and friendships they crave.

Bowie and Jagger were attracted to Buddhism and evidently variously practiced it. I think we can safely say that Jagger's 1971 conversion to Roman Catholicism was a phase. The danger with passing straight from an aesthetic, a style, a way of approaching pleasure and pain, and straight to spirituality is that the progress, whatever it may be, seems to carry very little in the way of social or political advice. Compassion, yes, but justice? Wisdom of the ages, yes, but aptitude in negotiating interpersonal conflicts? "This too shall pass" seems universally true but not so very practical.

Can't Help Thinking about Me

Is there something more out there that isn't just hackneyed claptrap about "To *have* a friend, *be* a friend" and other pop psychology crap? Yes. There is something worth considering, but it requires that we change our expectations about the relationship between *morality* and *ethics*. These two concepts are not "friends" to one another; they are something closer to mortal enemies, as I will explain. I don't endorse this view, but I find it very difficult to ignore, and very helpful in understanding what happens between people like Bowie and Jagger, with each other and with their intimates, in so far as they have intimates.

The distinction between morality and ethics goes back to Immanuel Kant (1724–1804) who grounded *morality* in "sensus communis," or common sense, that we carry with us on account of being a peculiar kind of sociable being who is *also* deeply unsocial; and, on the other side, *ethics* is the necessity of using our rational powers to recognize those rules and imperatives which conform our *wills* to our *duty*. This is just the sort of thing that led Bowie to write in his very first single with The Lower Third, that he had to leave home, head bowed in shame because he brought dishonor on the family name and the neighbors are talking, so he'll just start walking. This is a relentless wedding of morality and ethics that leaves him trembling in his bed every Sunday night after church. He hates it.

But morality and ethics, are actually fitted to one another, Kant claimed, and they encourage our "autonomy" as moral actors in the world. We give ourselves the moral law and conform, conform, conform. Sounds like Hell doesn't it? Kant also recognized the inevitability of conflict. He saw the conflicts, especially wars and the like, as engines of human moral progress, regrettable but needed, as our common sense gradually rises to the level of our rational understanding.

Don't Lean on Me Man

Simone de Beauvoir (1908–1986) thought this sort of view was, if you'll pardon my French, *merde*. She framed an alternative which casts some light on Bowie and Jagger—I don't say a flattering light, but it has the feel of authenticity. The ethic embraces ambiguity as its central idea—ethical life is not going to become perfectly clear for us when we don't pretend to others and to ourselves about what we really are and what we really want. The effects are pretty far-reaching. As she says, "the concrete consequences of existentialist ethics is the rejection of all previous justifications which might be drawn from the civilization, the age, and the culture; it is the rejection of every principle of authority" (*The Ethics of Ambiguity*, p. 14).

Rejecting every principle of authority seems like the opposite of ethics, but not in Beauvoir's world. Rather, such independence is a condition of living an ethical life. It was a thing back in the day. The paradox of human existence is this: the humans "know themselves to be the supreme end to which all action should be subordinated, but the exigencies of action force them to treat one another as instruments or obstacles, as means. The more widespread their mastery of the world, the more they find themselves crushed by uncontrollable forces" (p. 9). This well describes the dilemma of those who conquer the world aesthetically—the more they love you, the tighter is their grip on your inner being. The life of a celebrity artist is the opposite of free.

Beauvoir was herself a celebrity in the second half of her life. Her friends called her "*Castor*," which means "beaver." The public story is that she was always working. The private story is that the nickname had something to do with sex. But then, that's just people talking, right? She was a highly visible public figure (although "notorious" might be a better word than visible), and she knew a good deal about what that entails. Beauvoir's lifelong relationship with Jean-Paul Sartre posed a problem both to the world and to each of the persons so related. They had *cachet*, to be sure. They were cool intellectuals in a country that makes rock stars of philosophers. As far as I can remember, France hasn't contributed a single popular musician to the rock genre whose name could be recognized in the English-speaking world, but they gave us Foucault and Derrida, and if those aren't pop legends, along with Sartre and Beauvoir, no one is.

Beauvoir and Sartre were almost forty years ahead of Bowie and Jagger, but they did live to see glam rock—Sartre died in 1980 and Beauvoir in 1986. I don't think they noticed Bowie, but I'm fairly sure they would have taken note of the Rolling Stones. The Stones were hard to ignore, and they often lived in France. But Beauvoir and Sartre were breaking rules, and more sacred ones, long before Bowie and Jagger dreamed of androgyny and bisexuality. Beauvoir had a habit of seducing her young female students, and the younger the better, and then passing them to Sartre. She lost her teaching license in France for doing that, and *before* the Second World War at that—not the most open-minded time in history. If Angie and David had a *ménage à trois* on the night before their wedding, well, the Beaver and the Bug-eye were serially deflowering the *parents* of the generation that was seduced by the Bowies. Beaver and Bugs worked their whole lives to abolish the age of sexual consent in France.

A woman with credentials like this might have something interesting to tell us about the love and rivalry between Jagger and Bowie, especially since she had a similar struggle with the formidable Sartre, which could serve as a measuring rod (forgive the image) for almost any Bohemian intimacies. She says: "Man, Sartre tells us, is 'a being who makes himself a lack of being in order that there might be being' . . . his passion is not inflicted upon him from without. He chooses it. It is his very being and, as such, does not imply the idea of unhappiness" (p. 11).

That is a mouthful. It means that when you hollow yourself out in order to be what you have chosen, don't go making it someone else's problem. If you want to be ethical, own your freedom, accept your own choices and stop blaming the world for your inability to be satisfied. All of this cashes out in two ideas: "bad faith" is the condition of people who keep evading the absolute responsibility of their own choices; and "authenticity" is the condition of those who can own their own freedom, make themselves before others without guilt and without justifying anything to anyone. Such is Beauvoir's ambiguous world, and such is the world inhabited by the likes of Jagger and Bowie. The more powerful they were, the less the world could tell them what to do, and the less power the world had over them, the more raw and free was their encounter with one another. Neither was hollowed out for the world except as he had so chosen, and both knew it in the other.

Queen Bitch

In spring of 1973, and in the springtime of their year of passion, Jagger invited Bowie to the Stones concert in Newcastle, paid for the hotel, with the champagne, the roses, and all the implied control that goes with treating a new arrival on the doorstep of celebrity as your bitch. Bowie went, but not to be subjugated. Christopher Anderson tells the story thus:

> In the middle of "Jumpin' Jack Flash" Jagger noticed a sudden surge in the audience. Looking over his shoulder, he caught sight of Bowie hovering stage left, his trademark orange mane in clear view. Stagehands acted quickly to move Bowie out of sight, and all eyes were once again on Jagger. (p. 88, and see Clayson, p. 17)

That was when Jumpin' Jack Flash really met Ziggy Stardust. Bowie killed Ziggy and fired the Spiders from Mars two months later. It was unimaginable. Mick couldn't do that—as Bowie well knew. And that was when Mick began to speak openly about a solo album.

Philosophers are not journalists. I can't pretend to be a historian or a documenter and purveyor of facts at that level. I don't know these people and I don't know the people who know the people who know them. But how can we not find this relationship fascinating? Surely it means something philosophical from which we can all learn. I suspect that Mick's failure to extricate himself from the Rolling Stones is his great vexation.

Bowie fired his band. And he took on one persona after another. Mick is and always will be the lead singer for the Rolling Stones. He will not be a performance artist, he is to us an outrageous singer and, as Keith rightly notes, the greatest entertainer in the business—but there you have it: "entertainer." He is not an actor, a painter, an artist of any kind. He is, rather, the singer, and I mean *the* singer.

Is that enough? Keith thinks it should be. But Bowie was more, and quite a bit more than a singer. If he fell short of Andy Warhol as an art celebrity, well, he didn't fall short of anyone in rock music, as an artist. But as a performer, is he Jagger's equal? Never. No way. We may not know Jagger, but we know that *only* he is Jagger. For Bowie, we don't know him, but he is only as good as his next idea, or, in the present, his last idea: Lazarus.

The man defeated Jagger in the rivalry by making his death into a persona. That was authentically Bowie. Jagger had no recourse but bad faith. In his tribute to Bowie in *Rolling Stone* magazine, he represents Bowie as a junior colleague who copied him, the Great Mick Jagger, sometimes. Then Jagger expresses regret that they grew apart. Bowie had said something similar in a number of places. But they really *had to* grow apart.

Hell is other people, and they had caught a glimpse of the faker in one another, if not in themselves, and both were, well, they were much too fast to take that test.

5
Warm Impermanence

The embarrassing truth is that, back at the beginning, David Bowie wasn't into stuff we'd call cool nowadays. He had an odd affection for Anthony Newley and the sort of pop sound that dominated the late Fifties and early Sixties, and then he also had a dangerous flirtation with the Great Folk Scare. If you haven't ever checked to see where it all started, listen to "The Laughing Gnome" (1967)—it's unmistakably Bowie, but a strange ride.

For those of you who don't recognize the phrase "Great Folk Scare," it was the time when folk music almost became the dominant popular music in the US, but then we managed to avoid that (for the most part) thanks to doo-wop and the British Invasion, and also due to Bob Dylan's eventual boredom with acoustic guitars and banjos (praised and copied by Bowie in the Helm-like drums and Robertson-like guitar and Manuel-like piano in the song he wrote for Dylan). It was a close call for Bowie, and for us all.

But Bowie, well, he sort of liked that campy, silly stuff. He even became (gasp) a folk singer and songwriter, of the Donovan stripe. He also wanted to be like Dylan. (And don't we all?) But by the time Bowie penned that tribute to the Troubadour of Highway 61, the Scare had abated and the effect was very post-Newport. In fact Bowie never sounded or wrote much like Dylan apart from the one song. The point is: either way, it was really quite a stretch from folk pop to Ziggy Stardust and glam. It happened gradually, move by move.

How do you do that? And why? Part of it has to do with Bowie's peculiarities, of course, stuff no one else would have seen or done. But the journey has more to do with the Art World than you might think at first, and especially with Andy Warhol. That's what I want to talk about—the changes that led from David Jones, folksinger, to David Bowie, dominant among the creators of glam rock—and maybe to David Bowie, artist. We shall see.

The Philosophy of Art

In the second half of the twentieth century, Arthur Danto (1926–2013) was the most important philosopher of art in the world. There's a big difference between the "philosophy of art" and "art criticism," and neither one is the same thing as "aesthetics." Danto wrote in all three areas.

In art criticism he was among the foremost, and this is the activity of reviewing, comparing, adjudging, documenting, and organizing critical ideas about art. The audience is generally the interested public, but it includes artists and gallery owners and museum curators and anyone else who wants to consume or promote art. Good art criticism imparts information, judgments, and experiences of art to those who want to *read* about experiences of art. If the criticism is well written, the reader may have an aesthetic experience of the art of writing, but that isn't the primary aim of art criticism, according to most people. (I think art criticism should be art, but that leaves me in a small company.)

Aesthetics is the study of feeling and sensation and their relation both to the world and to perception, and even to knowledge. Art is often the featured subject matter of aesthetics because it is thought (and rightly so) that in the *experience* of art we find exemplary cases of how sensation becomes highly organized feeling, and then such feeling becomes not just perception but *heightened* perception. Art perks us up, makes us notice our senses and perceptive powers, goads us to refine them. (It's good to remember that perception involves the combining of *all* our senses into one experience of the world, including how it smells, looks, sounds, tastes and its tactile and kinesthetic character.)

Perceptions are created by our bodies, as a *synesthesia* of many physiological processes—and perception occurs just a bit later than the sensations that are received and processed by our bodies. What you are perceiving happened less than a quarter of a second ago, or so, but it's over before you perceive it. That's why humans cannot hit a baseball by perceiving it. They only see the ball leave the pitcher's hand and the spin and anticipate where it will be as it gets to them. There isn't time to perceive and then swing. It's the same with releasing a bowling ball or squeezing a trigger in target shooting. Aesthetics, as a discipline, is as much concerned with that sort of experience as with art.

Our senses are heightened in the presence of visual art, and of beauty (whether in nature or artifact), and of other sorts of highly organized stimulation, such as we find in music and painting and sculpture, prepared for the kinds of senses and feelings *we* have. We do not create art for non-humans. A symphony written entirely in tones below 16 Hz. would not be for humans, since we couldn't hear it—elephants, however, might enjoy such music quite a lot. The study of aesthetics could well include such a symphony, since it is not limited to merely human perception and sensation and feeling. And aesthetics does not have to study art at all. It just usually does.

Art, however, belongs to the human world exclusively, Danto believed. Even Bowie would not bother with a sub-sonic song for the elephants, all tones vibrating below 20 Hz. Of course, *someone* actually might have *tried* something like that (John Cage or Philip Glass), had anyone thought of it, but it would have been more for us to enjoy *the idea*, as a piece of art, than for elephants to enjoy the actual music. Philip Glass did take Bowie's compositions entitled "Low" and "Heroes" as the bases for his own Symphonies #1 and #4 respectively, but was this not Glass making art of what had been, perhaps, better described as "commodity" or, more sympathetically, as "song"? Was this not analogous to James Harvey and Andy Warhol— one designed the Brillo box, but the other created *Brillo Box*, the sculpture? One was known only as a commercial artist; the other was the greatest artist of the second half of the twentieth century.

And so we might note that "Subsonic Symphony (for Elephants)" is really not Bowie's domain. You can't sell such a thing, or its sequel, "Supersonic Symphony for Dogs," written entirely above 20 kHz. If Glass writes this stuff now, I should be credited—and given a Warhol *Brillo Box* as compensation. Even if I only had the *idea*.

Ideas can be art, Danto thought, so long as there is at least some *embodiment* of the idea, and assuming that there was some *meaning* thus embodied. Since my writing has embodiment (and that is how you can read it), it could be art, even if it probably isn't. On the other hand, if I only *imagined* this chapter, it couldn't be art. Embodied meaning is what art requires, Danto argued. It may require *more* than that, of course, but not less. Not everyone agrees with Danto, but I think he's right. And this definition of art belongs neither to aesthetics nor to art criticism, but to the *philosophy of art*.

The philosophy of art, apart from asking and answering the question "What is and is not art?" also pursues various other mysteries, such as why do humans create art? Does art exist in every culture? Is art essential to our humanness? Is there a universal art recognizable to all (such as music)? Is beauty indispensable to art? Is there sublime art? What is the "artwork" itself? Does the artwork involve the process of its creation or is it only the product? Does the artist's intention determine the meaning of a work of art?

There are hundreds of other questions and shades of questions connected to the philosophy of art, and this is what Arthur Danto did best. Danto had been an artist himself (his specialty was wood block prints, very nice ones) and also eventually he became a critic. But initially he was just a philosophy professor who happened to have a degree in art history as well. It can be a potent combination, if you're at the right place and time and if you seize the moment.

The Art World

There is a sort of social universe of people who care about art, and their motives are varied. Some produce it, some buy and sell it, some collect and display it, some regulate, promote, censor, lobby for or against it, and some just write and think and talk about art all the live long day. When we take this cross-section of civilization that is concerned with art, we have what Danto calls "the Art World." This is a highly interactive and dynamic cultural conglomerate; its edges are ragged and vague. Art trails off into commerce or kitsch, or commodity, or mere entertainment, or politics, or mere pastime, or hobby, or even religion, at its numerous edges.

At the center of the Art World are places like New York and Paris where large numbers of art people are concentrated and whose doings and makings are enviously noted by others in lesser locations. Where art serves some form of culture apart from itself, it's not "the Art World." Casual Bowie fans who have an album or two and who can tolerate an elevator-music version of "Rebel, Rebel," with an oboe carrying the Ronson guitar line, are not part of the Art World. It takes a willingness to aestheticize your life in order to fit in. This movable feast of culture called the Art World is of huge concern to serious Bowie fans, whether they realize it or not, for it's the Art World, in Danto's sense of that term, that *gave* us Bowie. Take your protein pills and put your helmet on, and I will explain.

Looks a Scream

Danto had something in common with Bowie, since both were pretty close to being obsessed with Andy Warhol, but in Danto's case, it wasn't just because he was a fan—in fact, at first he really *wasn't* a fan. But Danto became convinced that Warhol's vision and work had changed the world, irreversibly. Danto made the astonishing claim that Warhol's exhibit at the Stable Gallery in New York City in 1964 marked the *end* of art history. It was over. From the cave paintings of Lascaux, some 17,000 years ago up until April 1964, art had a history, and then, poof, Warhol ended it. Or perhaps it would be more honest to say that Danto ended it in Warhol's name.

Here's what happened. Danto went to the Warhol exhibit and saw the *Brillo Box* sculptures Warhol had made—and *make* them is what he *did*. Yes, they looked like ordinary Brillo boxes we could buy at the supermarket, but they were not. It was not like Marcel Duchamp placing a urinal in the art exhibit and calling it "Fountain." This was Warhol painstakingly constructing plywood boxes and creating the silkscreens to paint them, and then touching them up by hand after they were silkscreened, and installing them in a pyramid in the Stable Gallery as a sculpture.

We all know, by this late date, that Warhol was the progenitor of "pop art" and that a part of his aim was to hand us back in the form of art (with whatever glib critique it may imply) the images, colors, forms and figures that fill our overfilled lives and whose "art" we would not notice were it not for the activity of the artist in framing, repeating, installing, presenting, and otherwise calling attention to what we would normally ignore. Everyone also knows that he said "in the future everyone will be famous for fifteen minutes." This was not so much prophecy as simple observation carried to what it clearly portends. Time has tended to bear out the expectation in spirit if not in exact quantity.

In the process of ending art history—which he didn't know he was doing—Warhol achieved something that was to replace art: celebrity. The art he made was, after all, desirable, but that fact was mixed, inextricably, with the fact that it bore *his* name. Indeed. It was good, whatever *that* means. I sure wish I had one of those *Brillo Boxes* in *my* collection. I'd give my entire Bowie LP collection for one. Or for anything Warhol touched. Or anything he mass produced himself. Or anything he endorsed. I think I'm in good company here. *You* want a Warhol. You know you do. Don't pretend you don't. But the unintended consequence of this celebrity, on these terms, is that Warhol realized that his celebrity *was* the essence of his art, and he theorized it thus. If Andy wrote a book, the book was art because of Andy. If he made a movie, the movie was art because of Andy. If he took a walk, the walk was art because of Andy.

Andy even made art out of philosophy, with his book *The Philosophy of Andy Warhol (From A to B and Back Again)*. The book contains no philosophy to speak of; it is an autobiographical something or other—what? Mémoire? Not exactly. Aphoristic ejaculations? Well, there are many of those, and many blurted out opinions, but precious little philosophy— except that in calling it philosophy, Warhol exercises his considerable celebrity upon the meaning of that word.

And if Andy Warhol looked a scream, the look was art, as was the scream, because of Andy. I have read in several places that Warhol hated that line in Bowie's song because Warhol was self-conscious about his appearance. I have no idea what to believe in the piles of tripe written about either Warhol or Bowie, but every time I read that Warhol hated the song on account of that line, I smile. I *have* to. It's perfectly ridiculous to imagine that Andy Warhol cared how he looked *in that way*, that is, the normal vanity of normal people, leading to normal self-consciousness. Even if he said what was reported, it doesn't mean he actually felt that way. But maybe Andy did care about that.

Something prevented him from becoming Bowie's mentor. Maybe Bowie's song for Andy was too much too soon and contained an unforgivable faux pas. Great though Bowie became, he never approached Warhol's importance to the Art World (and I'll come back to this point). It may be a good thing that Bowie and Warhol were not close friends. It might have ruined them both, or at least Bowie. I doubt anything could have changed Andy apart from Andy.

Your Face Is a Mess

It was obvious to Bowie that Warhol, whether intentionally or not, had created an art form that could be picked up and built upon: the art of celebrity. It could be sold as art without being cheapened thereby. The key was continuous reinvention of your persona *as* artist, endowing upon whatever you do the status of artwork, or if not that, in the highest sense of "art," then at least artsy-cool. But to maintain such celebrity beyond fifteen minutes, the choices have to be just right—they have to be like Warhol's choices. There must be an artistic importance about the choices that drags the public up to and into what they wanted but didn't yet *know* they wanted. Part of the secret to making the public *desire* the work (or at least the new album) is that it carries the mystique of the artist's persona. But that alone would never be enough to bring the public along. The art also has to be, well, *good*.

Music never was Bowie's only artistic form of endeavor, but it was always his bread and butter. The stylings he took on, one after another were also art. He certainly never could have known that his different-sized pupils (the result of a fist fight with a friend over a girl) would be so important to him, but that was how we recognized the man through the ch-ch-ch-changes. "Is that Bowie?" Well, check the eyes. They're weird, you know? In a cool way. Still, the effort was more conscious and more Warhol-influenced than many folks realize.

After seeing a London production of Warhol's play *Pork* in 1971, Bowie hired the principal cast members, including

Cherry Vanilla, Wayne (now Jayne) County, Anthony Zanetta, and Leee Black Childers—all from Warhol's Factory—to create an image for him. The result was Ziggy Stardust, and in succeeding related personas—Aladdin Sane, the Diamond Dogs persona, the Man Who Fell to Earth, the Thin White Duke, and, moving from one creative crew to another, it went on to Lazarus, his final persona. If Bowie and Warhol had become closer friends, it's possible to conjecture that Bowie might not have been quite so independent. Warhol cast a huge shadow.

The End of Art

What Danto believed and wrote after visiting the Warhol exhibit in 1964 is that after *Brillo Box, anything* could be art, in principle at least. What Warhol had done was to inform us that the difference between art and non-art resides in what the Art World does *now*, in the present and for the future, *not* in what art history tells us. Art is no longer determined by a tradition or schools of painting or dance or architecture. Rather, it is the theories that are proffered and which dominate the Art World that provide us with Art. Since we will no longer be able to trace the history of movements in art by studying the characteristics of the art works, we shall have no further art history. What we have after April 1964 is an imperative to learn the theories uppermost in the Art World and then we can know what is and is not art.

Danto also expressed the opinion that art was only the first cultural form to come to the "end" of its history. He expected others, philosophy in particular, to come to a point where, for example, the Philosophy World determines what is and isn't philosophy, but Danto believed we were some ways short of that point. Art, however, has reached an end.

But the "end" is a sort of spiritualization, almost, of the forms that a cultural activity may take. It means that we're liberated from the strictures of the various stages we endured along the way, in which art must first be, say, classical and then romantic, and then realist and then impressionist and then cubist or pointillist or Dadaist, and so on, *rejecting* whatever it *had been* in order to become what it *will be* next. It is this historical dialectic Danto pronounced to be "at an end" in 1964. All of those stages are now available for the making of art, without the expectation that there must be a "next" in the way there was before 1964.

Art had, at the hand of Andy Warhol, rejoined the world of change and life and conversation and was now in the hands of those who make it, sell it, criticize it, exhibit it, buy it, even destroy it. We now see art's possibilities in Andy Warhol himself, Andy walking, Andy tired, Andy snoozing, and not being able to tell the silver screen from the artist. This is clearly not art history, whatever else it is. As audacious as Danto's pronouncement sounds, there is something to it, and it is something David Bowie understood, with or without any help from Danto (Bowie read a lot, and I'm betting he read Danto, but I don't know). In any case, the central insight of Bowie's song about Warhol reports an inability to distinguish Andy from his screen—this is as much his silkscreen as the surface upon which the films are projected, and any other surface you please.

Time May Change Me

It's not easy to distinguish the autobiography from the manufactured myth in Bowie's case, but the people who knew him insist there was no serious effort at misdirection on his part. He wasn't different from you or me—except that he got to have sex with whomever he pleased and, well, most of us don't—on that point, it's impossible to know what to believe, but if there wasn't just tons of sex, well, the storytellers sure say a lot of the same things. For one such see the biography by Wendy Leigh, called, appropriately enough, *Bowie: The Biography.*

The mystique and the masks are surely products of planning and intention, but not designed to keep us from learning who the man was. As he said at the end, in "Lazarus," his deathbed piece of performance art, "everybody knows me now." It's show biz, and that's about all it is. And it's all in good fun, even the part about dying at the end. Life's a warm impermanence, after all. Why waste energy trying to sell us a performer we aren't interested in—the *real* David Jones—when it's so much more fun, and more profitable, to imagine what *does* interest us, and sell us *that*?

It's easy to imagine it, but it isn't easy to do. Such a plan requires that the performer guess what would interest us when *we*, ourselves, don't know it yet. Do we want the man who sold the world? Well, we weren't sure. There came a moment of decision for Bowie, a moment when he decided to dive into an unknown water and try a hand at something that hadn't been done before—although we're familiar with it now. This is the celebrity whose persona shifts over and again to become a new artwork, and to enjoy another fifteen minutes of fame for going to the trouble to re-invent. Long before Hannah Montana morphed from Disney Sweetheart into the raunchiest pop singer in history, and long before Stefani Germanotta put on a dress made of raw meat, and even before Madonna became Marilyn Monroe, Bowie foresaw what it meant to trade in your person for a persona.

For some celebrities (Michael Jackson comes to mind), the psychological cost of reinventing yourself every five to seven years seems to be pretty high. It isn't easy for them to endure the isolation, whether self-imposed or a condition of their safety, and perhaps also the trials of "not being known" by anyone. Is it any wonder that Jackson could make common cause with Lisa Marie Presley? Jackson once complained that whether he told the truth or lied about himself made no difference, since people would believe what reporters said before they'd ever believe the man himself. For Bowie, however, it appears that his ego-strength (and I mean this in an entirely admiring and positive sense) was enough to keep him sufficiently grounded and creative and imagining and, if such a speculation is allowed, happy and well-balanced after about 1980, to all appearances.

How can someone so strange be so grounded? Well, Bowie wasn't strange. But he had strange fascinations. Tony Zanetti said that it was just about being adored, for Bowie. He was willing to be thought strange in exchange for that, and to keep changing if he could only guess what *we* wanted next. Was it Ziggy? Apparently it was. We didn't know it until we saw and heard it, but we definitely knew it then.

I Can't Trace Time

The song "Changes" documents Bowie's decision to adopt the life of shifting personas, while "Queen Bitch" and "Andy Warhol" from the same album explain where the momentum would come from, musical and artistic. The first verse of

"Changes" (and indeed of *Hunky Dory*) is a soliloquy, Hamlet-esque, filled with gnawing questions portending ominous answers—like fleas the size of rats feeding on rats the size of cats. What was I waiting for? What of all those dead end streets? How was I losing so much time? And what kind of success would taste sweet enough? And, by the way, what now—now that I'm so acutely aware the others don't see the faker, but neither can I?

"We" can't dwell on these things, we can't take that test, Bowie advises himself. We sweep all of it away in our changes, if we can face the strain. That includes the people who are no longer useful or inspiring to us—the band, the entourage, the business people, all quite dispensable. "We" have to become comfortable with the idea that we never really see ourselves as others do, and yet others won't know when we're faking. I can't trace time, but then again, neither can you. There's a space that we can fill with our imaginations, if we so choose. And we resolve to do it.

What brings Bowie to this pass? His first two albums (I'm thinking of *David Bowie* and of *Space Oddity* as the same album) had songs that occasionally betrayed moments of self-doubt, of self-reflection in the sense of self-undermining. These hesitancies had to be conquered. Somewhere between *The Man Who Sold the World* and *Hunky Dory*, Bowie became what Andy Warhol could not become—Bowie read the augurs and became whatever *we* wanted him to be. He painted, acted, wrote, strummed, pranced, sang, and transmogrified. Look out, rock'n' rollers, the folksinger has become self-aware. Indeed, he's out of this world. He'd like to come and see us but he thinks he'd blow our minds. When we had enjoyed and applauded Ziggy, Bowie retired him and became whatever we needed next.

But was it art? Performance art would be the easiest category to cover all the activities. By Danto's criteria, it certainly was embodied meaning. The Art World was a bit less enthusiastic about calling Bowie's creations art, however, and in Danto's world, they hold sway. Philip Glass was enthusiastic enough, and many artists bought their Bowie albums and listened, but in a way, that is exactly what you don't do with art.

An interesting fact is this: the popular world, filled with people like you and me, and with rock critics and the full weight of the recording industry, and people who shop at Wal-Mart, and people who definitely do not shop there, we all want the Art World to say of Bowie: "this was art, and this was an artist." They don't, however, treat Bowie as a performance artist, or indeed as an artist of any kind. Warhol is one of their darlings while Bowie is, well, a folksinger on cocaine and a magnificent showman, or something. He surpasses Elton John, sure, but not in a way that would turn anyone's head.

You Can't Trace Time

How, then, can we, the public, resist the urge to strangle the Art World? We want to say that Bowie was *better* than Warhol, don't we? But it also isn't true, is it? Bowie has endowed the world with priceless memorabilia. Warhol has given the world the art it will pay more for and hold to its breast more closely than anything Bowie ever did. I know you love Bowie. You're reading this chapter. But if I gave you a choice between, say, an original multi-track tape, a one-of-a-kind out-take from the *Diamond Dogs* sessions, or a *Brillo Box*, which would you take? Or if you don't like my example, choose whatever you would like from Bowie's *oeuvre*.

Here's the thing. That *Brillo Box* changed the world. The Bowie piece, whatever it may be, only showed the world how it had *already been changed*. After the *Brillo Box*, well, the days flow through my eyes, but still they seem the same. Give me the *Box* and accept my apologies, David. And I'll put on some music, your music, and admire my *Box*. Which music will I choose for my admiring? Well, dear reader, what would you recommend? Have you heard *Blackstar* yet? It's awesome. It's about being dead. I never realized I was interested in that until recently, but then, I can't trace time.

6
Magic Pages and Mythic Plants

The occult dabbling of Jimmy Page is well known, if not very well understood. Since Jimmy doesn't tell me (or anyone else) what's up with all that, it leaves us guessing—and oh how we love to guess. He doesn't talk about this stuff any more, so it is hard to know whether his much publicized dalliance with the devil was just a phase he went through, or whether it has more permanent meaning for him.

During Zeppelin's heyday, these dark doings were very much the engine of gossip. I was attracted to it (the gossip, not the occult) as a teenager, and yes, also disturbed—one of oh-so-many things that vexed the not-quite-children we all were. Like many of you, I played my copy of "Stairway to Heaven" backwards and yes, I heard "Here's to my sweet Satan." It's there. Mr. Plant can deny it 'til the cows get sacrificed, but I know what I'm hearing.

Maybe the whole point was to get us wondering and keep us talking, you know? Thinking back on it, maybe it was just a brilliant marketing ploy. Zep was horrified of being perceived as a "pop" band and they were intent on staying on the shadowy side of rock celebrity. I mean, these are the guys who compared the Rolling Stones to Bobby Goldsboro, since they were competing for time on the same airwaves, after all. This brings a groan from the real rockers. If ever a band had sympathy for the devil himself, it was the Stones, and here we have Robert Plant saying they're just namby-pamby. I don't think so, fellas. But that was pure posturing, and Plant knew it even at the time. We have enough historical distance now to know the difference between neighborhood trash talking and genuine judgment. Really, you can't diss a band, or a human being, more profoundly than with a comparison to Bobby Goldsboro. And besides, the Stones were "borrowing" from the Mississippi Delta well before Zeppelin had any similar notions.

It Makes Me Wonder

But, back to the deal at the crossroads (see "Nobody's Fault but Mine"): Was Page's self-presentation as a Devotee of the Dark just more marketing? If so, then it makes sense why Plant and Jones were always saying they didn't know much about what Page was doing—which was believable for Jones, but not so much for Plant. If Page was holding black mass (or some such) Plant would have known it—and Plant knew that we knew that he would know, which makes his disclaimers seem feigned. All a game? Let's entertain that idea for a moment.

By all accounts Jimmy Page was very much in control of the "idea of the band." He knew exactly what he wanted Zep to be, from the start, and Page was a brilliant strategist when it came to shaping the public perception of the band. So the cynical interpretation of Page's dealings in black magic is that it was nothing at all. He just muddied the waters around himself (and the band) to make them appear deep. (The true adept in this technique is Sting—toss in a couple of literary references and suddenly people think you're a genius.) Maybe Page aimed to attract rebellious, hedonistic teens to the image he was crafting, to set Zeppelin apart from the Stones, The Who, and their other "competitors." Being "bad boys" wasn't enough by 1970. Zeppelin was plenty bad, but that had all been done. They needed to be devilishly bad in order to get the upper hand on their bad boy competition. So they conjured an image of mystery and black magic (to go with the usual sex and drugs) and we bought it. Or at least, that's how the cynical story would go.

But I don't believe it. Even if Page understood that he could accomplish certain goals in publicity by making himself a man of mystery, using Plant to deflect and dismiss, and thereby intensify the intrigue, I also think that the reason the black magic strategy occurred to Page has to do with a certain path he was already following. Page and Plant were genuinely curious (in different ways), very smart and quite creative. They wanted to know things and understand things. In different ways, they valued the past and all that lay in the grit and the dust of history. If I'm wrong, Page should feel free to contradict me, when he reads this (in my dreams). I think the more reasonable story is that Page and Plant together went on parallel quests for their roots, and I have a theory about how and why it happened. I think that Page's predilections were magical while Plant's were mythical. Myth and magic are related but very different, as we shall see.

The Magic Runes Are Writ in Gold

Here's what I want to do, boys and girls (mainly boys, I'm sure; Zeppelin is something of an acquired taste for girls—at least if my long-ago girlfriends and long-time espoused are any barometer). I want to tell the tale of Page and Plant in a general way, using what everyone learns about myth and magic when we start looking into it, when we get beyond the particular version of myth and magic that drew us in. As we learn more, we move into a more general understanding of what magic really is and why myth is so pervasive in human history and in our present experience. When we've had a general look at myth and magic, it becomes clearer how and why Page moved toward, into, and through (black?) magic. But this is not an exposition on Aleister Crowley (1875 1947). Page found Crowley and became a fan, but it wasn't just a fascination with the life and views of a single practitioner. Rather, Page and Crowley had some things in common, like a fascination with magic, but more importantly, they shared a fascination with "will."

Not many philosophers write about magic. It doesn't often appear because most philosophers regard belief in magic as a quaint superstition that has been replaced by a more rational understanding of cause and effect. And philosophers have always been more concerned about present and future knowledge than about our ill-informed past. The past is the record of error, they think, but the future holds the prospect of progress in knowledge and wisdom. So one could say that there is a fairly stark difference between philosophy, as a practice, and the history of philosophy, which is the written record of what practicing philosophers have thought about over the millennia. Studying the history of philosophy is important for learning the practice, just as it is in art or religion or poetry or science, but the practice is not just the repetition of the history. No one would say that a historian of poetry is a poet, and so it is with philosophy, generally speaking. So most philosophers learn their history and then take stock of the present and future and set themselves to thinking. Other fans of philosophy may spend their lives studying, say, Plato or Aristotle, but these are simply scholars, unless they do more than explain to us what Plato or Aristotle thought, and when and why.

The Beads of Time Pass Slow

In the last two centuries, however, some philosophers (not just scholars) have become increasingly convinced that understanding our past is more crucial to understanding our present than we had previously suspected. These philosophers are called "historicists," and their numbers are ever on the rise. Some of the historicists are infamous, like Karl Marx, but most historicists work in the shadow (if not the shade) of the greater project of elaborating the triumph of science and scientific reasoning. Sometimes historicists like science and sometimes they don't, but all of them are interested in questions about roots and origins of ideas and culture. If science gives us knowledge, it's because we invented science, and long before we had science, we had a desire to control nature. The story of how we become better and better at controlling nature is the story of science, and before science there was, you guessed it, magic. Before there was history there was myth—the stories we tell ourselves about how we came to be the way we are. So, these two kinds of thinking, scientific and historical, are themselves the end results of magic and myth. The story of how magic becomes science and how myth becomes history is not just a tale of correcting our errors; it's about how we take a basic mode of human thinking and refine it until it becomes a more reliable tool for manipulating nature and understanding time.

Among the historicists, most do not worry about our distant past, the part that is shrouded in myth. But a few historicists have become interested in those questions and have expounded philosophies that take myth and magic into account. The most successful and famous of these philosophers was a fellow named Ernst Cassirer (1874–1945). Yes, those life dates make him Crowley's close contemporary. There were a lot of people interested in myth and magic belonging to that generation. It isn't an accident. You could well think of Cassirer as Dr. Jekyll to Crowley's Mr. Hyde. When I say "successful," what I mean is that Cassirer talked about magic and myth seriously and managed to remain respectable in the estimation of, well, everyone. Almost every other philosopher who has attempted to include myth and magic in a philosophy as something important, something that contributes in a positive way to our progress, has been bounced out of the company of respectable inquirers. The reason Cassirer has remained "legitimate" is that he wrote so many renowned books on science and math and history that no one was quite willing to dismiss him when he went on about myth and magic. But very few philosophers still study all that stuff. I'm not going to quote Cassirer much in what follows, or even explicitly mention him, but I want you to be alerted that most of what I have to say about magic and myth came from his books.

Your Head Is Humming, and It Won't Go

I will get to Cassirer's theories in a few minutes, but first I want to visit a few points about music and philosophy. Page and Plant never were philosophers, of course, nothing of the kind. A musician is a kind of practicing artist, as we all know. A musician who only plays and perfects music written by others is sort of like a scholar who only studies and explains the ideas of other people. It preserves culture, having many people who basically re-enact the past before our eyes—whether it's a string quartet playing Beethoven or a Zeppelin tribute band (or a philosophy teacher yacking on about Plato). All musicians begin this way—playing what others have written, training their bodies to do what has been done before, and then awaiting an experience of the thoughts that gave rise to that music, or accompany the playing of it, or which followed it. A part of understanding how a musician got the "idea" for this or that piece of music depends on enacting the music oneself. That's what makes your head hum. A music critic who cannot play or sing will never really "get it."

If you want to understand the blues, for example, you have to sit down and learn how to play them, and then think about how it feels to play that way, and then ask yourself how that kind of bodily expression symbolizes other experiences in life that a person might have. If re-enactment is all you ever do, you don't really "have the blues," but if you play well enough there's a genuine experience that you and your audience will share, sort of a remembrance of the possibility of the blues. It's an appreciation, not the true blues, but appreciation is very important. Another way to put it is that such a performance isn't magic, but it reminds us of the magic, or to put it in overly precise words, it is magical but not actual magic. Remember this point!

If You Listen Very Hard

I choose the example of blues for a reason, of course. Obviously, Page and Plant collaborated on an "appreciation" of this sort (and this is the kindest word one can employ for the practice of borrowing so liberally from one's colleagues). As Page said in *Guitar World* in 1998, "As a musician, I'm only a product of my influences." There's a John Lee Hooker–Willie Dixon–Howlin' Wolf–Lead Belly–Albert King–Blind Willie Johnson–Robert Johnson–Sonny Boy Williamson–Memphis Minnie thing going on here. We all know that Zep had to settle out of court more than once (most notoriously for "Whole Lotta Love" taken from Willie Dixon, without credit). Their cheery "appreciations" were regularly offered without credit or compensation to those who were being so richly "appreciated." Page said that "bluesmen borrowed from each other constantly and it's the same with jazz." The singer/songwriter Danny Dolinger put the point a little more acutely when he said "any songwriter who doesn't admit to being a thief is also a liar." So listen hard and you'll be able to call the tune.

There's the sense both of history and of re-enactment in Zeppelin's blues tributes, but it's a new plant that grows from old roots, the rhizome theory of musical originality. This is what makes Led Zeppelin a roots band, but it is a radical re-invention of the old plant that pops up into the sunlight here— or perhaps the plant is really a nightshade. In any case, the fruit has been desirable, and it doesn't taste like the blues. In the same way, a Plato scholar enacts an appreciation of Plato, along with his readers or the hearers of his lecture. If he sticks to explaining Plato, putting as little of himself into it as possible, it is philosophical but not quite philosophy. There's always a vital connection, but also a difference between the history of a symbolic form and its original enactment in the present. We can't quite repeat history and no ritual is perfect. Obviously, then, no two concerts are ever the same, and when we drop back in time from the concert to the rehearsals, to the arranging, and regress to the experience of creating the music and the lyrics to begin with, we will approach a widening gap between what has been and what will be.

Magic, for whatever else it does, arcs across the gap between what has been and what will be, and it does so by employing the means of what is, what exists in any present moment—the ideas, the materials, the will power. Magic is an art of bringing the will to bear on what is so as to connect what was to what will be. In short, magic is literally an art of timing. To time, to temporalize, actively, is to link past, present and future into an experience, and to will is to discern the element in those connections that is both causal in its power and not fully necessitated by the combination of circumstances. Where more than one thing can happen, "will" is a name we give to the cause of the thing that actually does happen.

If We All Call the Tune

In a very real sense, all serious musicians believe in magic. That's because they believe in the power of the will (whatever it is), when added to technique and repetition, to cause the future in ways that can amaze even the one who is doing the willing. It's not re-enactment. Speaking as a musician, and others will bear this out, countless times I have found myself playing things I have never heard before, never thought about, and upon realizing that such a moment was unfolding, I always try to stay out of the way so it will last. I'm willing what is happening (my part of it at least, since most often it happens with the whole band), and the willing is causing it, in some weird way, but it's not something I can fully understand with my intellect.

Everyone has experiences like this, but in musicians it becomes patterned, noticeable, and sought after. What musicians discover is that the will can be generalized, as can its power, its efficacy. In ordinary life we get accustomed to using our wills in very specific ways—I will that I should type the next word, and I do. It doesn't seem like magic because it's so mundane. Everyone expects his own will to have at least enough causal power to pull off simple, direct tasks, and to use present means to join past to future. If I will something a little less immediate—say, I decide to get myself a cup of coffee—a bunch of intervening acts lie between me and that end goal. I have to use my will to execute a whole series of equally mundane acts, all of which I understand pretty well, and in the end, I should succeed in getting my coffee. Hold on a second, I'm going to try it out. It's 6:30 in the morning, this piece is overdue, and I need a cup of coffee. I'll let you know whether this works. . . . . Okay, I'm back. It did work. No one would call it magic these days, but what I just did is pretty difficult to explain completely. Ask any philosopher or neuroscientist or physicist.

The example of stringing individual acts together, willing each act individually, so as to bring about a specific end is not the "generalizing of will" musicians experience. What I just did was fairly mechanical, without much spontaneity or creativity. I also didn't create any symbols in doing it, and as a result, there isn't a patterned energy left behind by my actions that can be re-used in the future. If I had left a symbol, there would be something surviving the process that could be used again by anyone who knows how to read the symbol. Remember that point too, if you would. A symbol is a repository of energy left behind from an activity of willing.

So the goal of getting coffee is general in the sense that it depends on a combination of intermediate actions, but as each action is done, the goal becomes more and more concrete, more within my mundane powers. It only seems magical when I lack the means to attain the end. On the other hand, if I sit here and attempt to will world peace, the means, the intermediate actions, are not within my power, and so my will fails to cause it. For all I know, there might be one thing I could do that would start a chain of events resulting in world peace, but I sort of doubt it. I would probably need a miracle—a suspension of natural order—to get that, not magic, which works with the natural order of things.

Sometimes All of Our Thoughts Are Misgiven

But what can my will cause? How powerful is it? Are some people's wills more powerful than others? Surely they are. Are there things we can learn that will enhance the causal power of our personal wills? Of course there are. That's why we learned to read and write. The command of language we have is proportional to the efficacy of our wills in social situations. And yet, even this doesn't strike us as "magic," right? Agreed. But it's still a source of some mystery as to how all this happens. If I should ever come to the (unwarranted) conclusion that scientific ideas of cause and effect can explain everything that occurs, including the workings of will, I will have ceased entirely to believe in magic. Let's hope that we never come to that point. Magic becomes science, increasingly, but as it does, it opens up larger questions about the efficacy of will that science does not explain.

Magic is safe for the foreseeable future, especially among musicians. The sort of experience that leads serious musicians to believe in magic is not the increased efficacy of the personal will that comes from learning, from practicing, from watching and hearing others play and repeating or varying their licks. That is "technique" and more like a practical science. In the case of Jimmy Page (and Clapton, and Beck, and so many others), Bert Weedon's *Play in a Day* guitar instruction book was not the source of the magic. Nor did the magic come from repeating and mastering Robert Johnson's licks. No, it's something bigger.

The magic happens when a musician is playing, under control, normally enough, and something in the moment detaches from his conscious intentions, he lets go, and no one thinks out or intends the combinations and movements that then occur—and no one could—but what happens also isn't an accident. Notes and finger movements start reeling out, almost of their own accord, but not quite. A musician hits a zone, a level in which what is happening is beyond his own understanding, and beyond his ordinary abilities, but not quite beyond his will. This can happen when he's playing alone, but it also happens when musicians are playing in groups, and, more astonishingly, sometimes it happens to two or three or all of them at the same time. Experienced musicians know what to do when this occurs: 1. get your mind out of the way and let it happen; 2. stay in the zone as long as you can; and 3. enjoy it because it won't last forever, but it might last for the rest of the evening.

The experience isn't magical, it is actual magic, in a sense to be explained. The difference is that the techniques involved co-operate with the present patterns and energies of existence (including the moods of audience and musicians, lighting, and acoustics), and all this co-operates with the past in ways that go beyond the mundane efficacy of the individual will (or even the "group will"). Forces and powers are co-operating that normally resist our wills, or are at least are normally unavailable for our use, but in these instances of "magic," the will has been general-ized in ways that tap into those forces. It happens. Ask any musi-cian. And that is the experience that makes music so addictive.

The Voices of Those Who Stand Looking

When magic happens, the musical instrument (including the voice) becomes a channel for generalizing will, extending its influence beyond the normal range. When groups of instru-ments are wielded by the right prestidigitators, in true concert, their efficacy grows beyond what any mechanical combination of wills can consciously intend or even understand. Chanting is a good, primitive example of the compounding of will that occurs in groups, but so is singing hymns in church. In the same way that three violins played slightly out of tune will tend to draw one another into proper tune as an effect (in indi-vidual reality, each remains out of tune), the combination of many voices brings about efficacious effects that are not reducible to the individual, isolated events that compose the general pattern. This "experience" (of the whole being greater than the sum of the parts) occurs in all kinds of group settings, but the point is that it is not mere ritual, not simple re-enact-ment, not magical, but actual magic.

It isn't hard to understand how Jimmy Page got addicted to this experience of magic, along with so many other things—back then, his was an addiction-prone personality. The predilections of musicians for drugs are fairly well docu-mented, and indeed, one can see how altering the state of one's consciousness might make it easier to get one's thinking out of the way so that the larger forces can take over. Thinking, reflec-tion, and conscious willing all get in the way of this experience. Drugs work, sometimes and for some people. So does alcohol. Anything that tends to unweave and loosen the edges of consciousness may create avenues by which peripheral possibilities for action come into greater efficacy. We begin to act without the mediation of thought. And we may like it too.

Musicians come in all kinds, just like normal people, and Jimmy Page is a recognizable type—a Type A musician. He's smart, creative, talented, and very much in control. Every successful rock band has at least one musician of this type, sometimes more. But Page knows that control of the "small" variety is the enemy of big magic, so, like all Type A's who also want to experience magic, he is at war within himself: the part that insists upon precision, discipline, exactness (the session player, the middle-class Anglican), is against the side that wants magic, the Jimmy Page of Led Zeppelin (most nights). If the will can get Session Jimmy to take a hiatus and let Zeppelin Jimmy come out and play, then maybe the drugs do the trick. I'm not defending it; I'm just saying it makes sense to me.

The Dark Lord Rides in Force Tonight

Yet, Page is the sort of person who wants to know why there is magic sometimes and not other times. Because he's so Type A, he also wants control over it, to be able to make it happen, to extend the power of his will until all the obstacles that lie between him and the experience are under his power. It's not surprising that such a person would be drawn to the likes of Aleister Crowley, who had a similar sort of personality. Reading Crowley's ideas about "true will" would resonate with anyone who wanted to know how and why, especially for the purposes of control. We could psychoanalyze Jimmy if we wanted to, but I see no point in that. Everyone has insecurities and unfulfilled desires, and just about everyone is looking to extend his or her will and gain control over things that threaten or please us. Most of us are pretty obsessive when it comes to matters we really care about. And when we reach the limits of our personal influence, nearly all of us begin to strategize about how to get wider circumstances to co-operate with our plans. In short, we'll resort to magic of some sort or another.

And here—I hope my family and colleagues won't be shocked—I will confess that I think the broad philosophical outline of Crowley's thought is probably defensible. We philosophers pay too little attention to those human powers that lie below the level of intellect and understanding, and the will, whatever it is, is among those powers. The simple fact of our experience is: the will has efficacy in the world, it originates in something like desire, and it is not just a mechanical series of individual actions strung together for the achievement of ends. Will exists in a general form that can draw people (and perhaps also other natural forces) into co-operation. In short, if by "magic" we mean "efficacious generalized will operating beyond the reach of intellectual and scientific explanation," then magic exists. Page is no more superstitious than you are. He was just more curious than most people about how to get this strange phenomenon working and under his control. Whether he still is I don't know.

To Bring the Balance Back

There are other types of musicians who just aren't vexed by the issue of controlling the magic. In fact, most musicians accept the affordances of magic as gifts, unearned, unmerited, and always to be enjoyed. They don't spend their days wondering how to master the magic or arrange their generalized wills. Instead, they just show up at rehearsal or a gig in a hopeful frame of mind and wait to see if anything happens. If enough time goes by with no magic, they'll find another group of musicians or change the style of music they play, or even quit for a while. But Page isn't like this. He's driven. There is something of Faust in his lust for magical control. Jones and Bonham weren't like this, however. Apparently, everyone knew from the first rehearsal that Zeppelin was going to be magic. The first song they ever played was "Train Kept a-Rollin'." Jones said that Jimmy "counted it out and the room just exploded. There were lots of silly grins and 'oh yeah man, this is it.' It was pretty bloody obvious from the first number that it was going to work."[3] In short, it was magic. Real magic, not just magical.

One last point about magic before we move on to myth: The legends are true. Over time, dabbling with magic will drain you of the life force. It has a (more or less) natural explanation. If you constantly use your own body as the conduit for the organization of efficacious energies that are beyond your ability to understand, the delicate balance is disrupted between your power of understanding (and rational life) and the efficacy of your own desire (which is growing all the time as you indulge

it). Your behavior will become erratic because your understanding has been locked in the basement to keep it out of the
way of the magic. In time, this disruption of the balance
between desire and reflection will affect your judgment, and
you will not know what is and is not within the scope of your
will. You will make bad choices. You will begin to lose it. A few
years of this and you'll look about like Jimmy Page did in 1977,
completely drained of the organized energies that sustain life.
I hope you survive, and I am glad he did.

Don't Be Alarmed Now

You wouldn't know it from the way I've been going on about it,
but magic isn't very important in the grand scheme of things.
It's a collection of techniques for connecting the past to the
future by means of resources (including ideas and materials)
that exist in the present. But the mechanical ways in which
past and future are connected by the present are much more
pervasive than the magic. Our wills are not very strong in comparison to natural laws, as in physics, as you may have noticed.
Involving no obvious share of will, natural causes are also easier to predict. Even our magical experience falls short of magic,
which is to say that it involves mainly setting our efficacious
wills to the task of closely repeating what has existed in the
past while largely ignoring whatever novelty and creative possibilities the present situation contains. It is more like mecha-
nism than magic. We play our music not in the moment, but
just as we rehearsed it. Magic is rare, and it is also fleeting—
unless it leaves a symbol.

I said earlier that a symbol concentrates a vital pattern of
energy that can be re-used, liberated in any present moment
from its physical cocoon and revitalized by the efficacy of the
will. That sounds so mystical, but it's quite mundane. Let me
prove it. Do something for me, would ya? Just raise your right
hand and circle your index finger in the air, like the gesture
meaning "whoop-de-doo," or "so what?" I'll wait while you do it.
Go ahead.

Okay, are you done? Look, if you actually did it, you just
proved my point. I wrote some words on my computer, it was
3:23 P.M., Central Standard Time, January 31st, 2017. At whatever time and day and year it is where you are (Hell, I might

even be dead by now), you released the pattern of energy I created at some point in the past. In the meantime, the energy pattern, and its efficacy, just sort of sat around in various places inside a bunch of copies of *Metaphysical Graffiti*, that don't even exist yet as I'm writing this. There's an extra sort of mystery, beyond magic, that is involved in the way that symbols (including words) can somehow store energies and efficaciousness, and how those symbols actually can preserve and carry forward not only the causal history of their making (in this case, all the printing and distribution processes) but also the concentrated will of the symbolizer (in this case, that would be me). Anyone who symbolizes, and that would be all of us, not only believes in magic, practically speaking, but also believes that the past, dead as it may be, remains active in the present and affects the future.

The Piper's Calling You to Join Him

The belief in magic is just one of thousands of manifestations of "mythic consciousness," which provided the basis of human civilization. Mythic consciousness is still very much with us, then, and it shows up most tangibly when we "believe" what symbols tell us. In the broad domain of our mythic consciousness, the world is not composed of atoms and chemicals, but of wills. Knowing that dead people communicate their wills to us all the time is a pretty clear example. I mean, I get a clear picture of what Bonzo's will was (what he wanted all of us to hear and feel) every time I put on a recording (which is a symbol) of his solo on "Moby Dick."

When we recognize that we can re-vitalize the will of the dead, we also realize that we cannot be certain that the natural features of our world are not symbols too, living manifestations of the will of some other being whose language and symbols are difficult for us to recognize. If you have even the least doubt that there may exist, right now, in the present, symbols created by a will or a power that is non-human, then mythic consciousness is operative in your life and self-understanding. Myth does not mean "falsehood," it means that the past is connected to the present for us by a symbolizing power we don't fully understand. That power is somehow concentrated in certain kinds of physical existences that can be ordered in ways that make it possible for others to release some of their efficacy at later times.

Sometimes Words Have Two Meanings

Robert Plant works at the level of myth in a much more conscious way than most people. That's because he's a lyricist who likes to emphasize that mysterious symbolic vitality in some of the lyrics he writes. Plant has a marked tendency to draw upon archetypal images. These are symbols that take in, concentrate, and intensify the causal efficacy of many less powerful symbols. Just as a collection of wills can create magic that is beyond the power of an individual will, some symbols can concentrate the meaning and vitality of many unconnected symbols. Plant did this with poetry, but it is well worth remarking that Jimmy Page was a talented visual artist (he didn't spend eighteen months in art school for nothing), and those amazing covers to the LZ albums were usually his design concepts.

The point is that Page was no simple magician, he is himself a fine creator of powerful, archetypal symbols. I'm pretty happy to have the original "functioning" covers for *Led Zeppelin III* and *Physical Graffiti*. Yet, the driving force behind the use of poetic lyrical symbols was really Plant. The manipulation of words is a gentler magic than the manipulation of current public perception (Page's Faustian need). But lyrics have a magic all their own that can complement the more aggressive living magic of concert and recording and press.

It was Plant who brought the bucolic Welsh countryside into the creative process of the group. Literally, Plant supplied the plants, the herbs and roots, for Page's magic spells. These came in the form of setting, of the connection to nature, and the affection for simplicity and health, and the poetry of light over darkness. Plant has often been described as a hippie, a sort of "Summer of Love" refugee, a bit of sunshine to complement Page's nighttime prowlings. One sometimes wishes that Pink Floyd had a member like Plant. The "hippie" thing may be more image than reality, but I think it's got a basis in fact because I can discern its results. The music is almost always darker than the lyrics. It is surprising how much peace, love and understanding, even anti-war sentiment, is present in the lyrics themselves. There's an especially heavy dose of "love," as we all know—all kinds of love, done in every conceivable way with almost any candidate. Here's a point where Page and Plant seem to agree: eros. On the other hand, any male who has ever been between twenty and twenty-nine years old can see how likely this point of agreement is.

I have to confess here that I hardly ever paid attention to the lyrics of Led Zeppelin's songs before I began writing this chapter. There are a few exceptions, like "Stairway to Heaven," but mainly, I did what most people do. I would pick up a few lines here and there, as they emerged from the music into articulateness, but I had no idea what Plant was on about, really. I knew there were lots of archetypes in the lyrics, but I also knew that he was more intent upon making his voice the fourth instrument in the band. It wasn't about the lyrics, it was about the way the whole thing sounded and felt, and Plant knew that very well. In other words, even in studio recordings, the mythic had to be subordinate to the magic. And yet, the lyrics still had to be good. There needed to be depth and organization and concentrated power in the symbols, and there was.

Plant's lyrics are not great poetry by any stretch, but they're pretty good symbolizations. What I mean is that when the lyrics are read, and considered in relation to the musical feelings, they usually enhance one's overall sense of the whole. Knowing the lyrics does not disappoint the listener. The group all contributed to the lyrics, but I think it's fair to say that, since Plant was in charge of their final delivery, he was also in charge of their final form. Once in a while the group would indulge its love of archetypes. We see it in songs like "The Battle of Evermore," and "Kashmir," and "Achilles' Last Stand." Even a pop song (sorry fellows, you were a pop band too, and you know it[4]) like "All My Love" was almost entirely written in archetypes. Even in the bluesy tunes, images and archetypes from Celtic, Indian, Nordic, and even Christian mythology would surface.

Our mythic consciousness, for whatever else it is, leads us to expect our symbols to bear meaning. It's nothing short of the physical graffiti we leave behind, knowing it is a time capsule. To organize the physical world into symbols represents a commitment to the transmission of meaning across eons of time, and that is why the ones who do it with a sense of purpose, like

Plant does, can rightly claim "this is a song of hope," in introducing "Stairway to Heaven." Another way of putting the point is that there is no science without magic and there is no history without myth. "Science" is a word we use when we are ignoring our own faith in the greater meaning of the natural world and seeking, like a bunch of sadists, its unconditional submission to our all-encompassing wills. "Magic" is a word we might use when we are being a little more humble and less domineering. Similarly, "history" is a word we employ when we are pretending to know the past as past, and ignoring the mediation and power of the symbols by which it is freed into our present understanding. "Myth" is a word we might use when we are being a little more conscious of our dependence upon processes we don't fully understand.

As We Wind on Down the Road

So, philosophers emerge from the history of philosophy, scientists from the history of science, and musicians from the history of music. In trying to burst out of the past and into the present and future, a crisis point will always arrive, a place where the artist or thinker will ask what he or she really has to say, something that is original, something that hasn't been said before, something that involves great risk. The risk is in creating symbols. It's risky because repeating what the "great ones" have done will always garner praise, when it is performed even marginally well. But to attempt something new is to risk failure, criticism, obscurity, shame, to make oneself vulnerable to derisive laughter, ridicule. So they made up four symbols for Page, Jones, Bonham, and Plant. Some people have laughed at and ridiculed and scoffed when the group said that the name of the album just is those four symbols. I am not one of them. I'm no longer a troubled adolescent, but I still think the album is magic.

7
The Kids Aren't Alright

Mods, Teddy Boys, and Hooligans

The Who was a Performance Art Troupe. I only recently learned that. It hadn't occurred to me until I read Pete Townshend's autobiography. I list them in the top five rock bands of all time—we all know the list, even when we disagree on the order. Mine goes Stones, Beatles, Who, Zeppelin, Floyd. Each band occupied a logical slice of the cultural pie, consciously worked out by the young marketing geniuses who pimped these bands to an unsuspecting world (the likes of Brian Epstein, Andrew Loog Oldham, and, for The Who, Kit Lambert and Chris Stamp). I was too young to grasp the differences in the 1960s; it was all rock and roll to me, which meant very cool. By the time I achieved refined sensibilities, the scene had changed, so I never really "got it" until recently, Pete's autobiography.

Pete says that these bands were fashioned after the groups kids had fallen into at school. (Maybe *their* schools; mine looked a bit different.) The Who was supposed to represent "the Mods," while The Beatles cornered the "Teddy Boy" market, and The Stones were hooligans, speaking for ne'er-do-wells of all stripes. There was only so much space in the domain of cool. When The Who began, categories for spacey art rock (Pink Floyd) and driving acid blues (Led Zeppelin) had not been imagined. Besides, that was musical space, not kid-space. Eventually kids would mark out their space with their concert t-shirts, but that was later.

Pete changed his tune on this assessment, in his history of The Who, allowing that *they* went for the Teddy Boy thing before discovering the Mod thing. All the same to us. I'm pretty sure Herman's Hermits was some version of Teddy Boys, and The Animals were some version of Mods, and The Kinks were some version of hooligans, but what would we Yanks know about it? And changing the story is Pete's stock in trade, anyway. You have to look between the lines if you want the truth. Or you could just ask Roger Daltrey and get the soft version. The *hard* truth isn't his specialty.

Art School

Lurking in the background of the entire British Invasion were two constants: American roots music, and the "Art School," that peculiar British hybrid of the trade school and the high-brow art institute. From Art School, Townshend had some difficulty deciding whether to be a musician or a sculptor, so he followed both paths until one crowded out the other. Hailing from a family of professional musicians, Pete's choice now seems inevitable. But in the early 1960s, he was being exposed to the collision of high art and popular culture. Andy Warhol definitely made his dent on the island. Pete now says "I didn't learn much about art at art school, but I did learn a lot about playing guitar" (*The Who: Fifty Years*, p. 51).

That isn't how he told the story in his autobiography (see chapter 5). He was exposed to a lot of cutting-edge thinking about art during art school, and especially fascinated by "artistic auto-destruction," which is what I was witnessing as a kid when The Who was on television. My father grunted sounds of disapproval: "Why would anyone broadcast such a display?" the grunts meant. I distinctly remember Keith Moon kicking over his drums at the end of "My Generation," and even then, I thought to myself, "Wow, I'll bet that's expensive. I wish I had some drums. I wouldn't kick them over." My father hated it, so I liked it. I begged for the drums (me and twenty million other kids). I got a damned trumpet. But hey, that's where John Entwistle started too. Served him well in various operatic scores that were on the horizon.

It's deflating to learn, lo these many years later, that all that thrashing about on TV was supposedly not anger, but art, consciously planned as both a gimmick and an aesthetic state-ment. These kids weren't poor and they had nothing much to complain about in England, and they knew it—the kids were alright (at that point). *They* didn't have to go to Viet Nam. They were playing around, trying to get famous and make lots of money. Oh, yeah, and there were girls. They wanted girls. This seems forgivable, given the hormones and their ages. It's hard to imagine becoming so famous so young and behaving respon-sibly when it comes to basic desires. They were boys, and you know what they will be.

Still, I don't think there was *no* anger. Pete was angry all the time back then. He narrates a story about how his grand-mother once put her head in the door and yelled at Pete and John to "turn that bloody row down." In response, Pete threw his amplifier at the wall, saying "fuck off," but *feeling* very calm, he claims. Entwistle's reply was "great." Now, I don't know about you, but I have never thrown anything at a wall, least of all a valuable piece of equipment. And I never used the f-word with my grandmother *present*, let alone directed *at* her. And Pete pushed Abbie Hoffman off the stage at Woodstock. His displays of temper are infamous. No, Pete was angry in general, at the world, and I think I know why. Stay tuned.

The one thing the kids were serious about, apart from all that sex, was "art," and to them, American R&B and rock music was the greatest art of all. For The Who, it was less about Howlin' Wolf and Blind Willie Dixon, and more about Bill Haley and Elvis, but when you're in England back then, you sort of have to *imagine* what the American kids are really doing. The Stones were shocked to learn that American kids didn't know who the bluesmen were. The British brats all thought we were having more fun than we really were, a point proven when they showed up on our shores and discovered we liked *them* better than Frankie Valli and that Elvis was passé (temporarily).

Like The Stones and The Beatles and so many other English bands, The Who couldn't really *play* R&B or rock properly, and in botching the effort, they all created an entirely new sound that American kids lapped up like retriever pups in a room full of cat vomit. We had no idea this music was recycled (and we loved their accents and attitudes). The difference between a Mod and a Teddy Boy was utterly lost on us, but at least we did notice that

The Rolling Stones lacked manners. The way the Brits were conceiving of themselves was very different from what we heard and saw. If you read the early interviews with the various British bands, their confusion about the US is pretty clear.

True Lies

Reading Townshend's account of this time is like entering a hall of mirrors unexpectedly: All the images are familiar, but they appear stretched and twisted and back-lit. And it's hard to find the doorways. Then, there is the credibility gap created by Pete himself, claiming to traverse the Sixties and Seventies without serious drug use or addictions, or even much in the way of sexual adventures, only to fall through every one of those funhouse trap doors in the Eighties and Nineties. I was surprised by his perspective and by his story. I didn't believe his book and I don't believe it still. Something's not alright here, least of all Pete as a kid.

In the history of philosophy there have been a number of notorious autobiographies. In fact, a philosopher is credited with creating a form of autobiography we call "The Confession." St. Augustine of Hippo was a fourth-century Christian bishop in North Africa, and his *Confessions* started the "tell-all" genre. It is now regarded as both a literary classic and one of the most important books in the history of philosophy. But whether it's "true" is another matter. Some people think Augustine created an allegory of himself, exaggerating his youthful sins to lend drama to his later conversion. Such lies are told for the sake of a higher truth. Hold on to that point, if you would. It will come back later.

Autobiographies are written for many reasons, but the confession seems to be one of the most popular. It's definitely Pete Townshend's purpose in *Who I Am*. Why do people want to do that? Absolution? Perhaps that's part of it. But can the *public* absolve a person for misspent time, for private deeds of cruelty, for stupid mistakes, for tragic decisions? Seems far-fetched. Are they securing a legacy? Manipulating permanent perception? Surely that is a factor too, and that is definitely on Pete's mind. These still don't quite add up to the "confession," though.

What, then, is the exhibitionist urge to put one's sins on display for the greedy consumption of everybody and his brother?

I want to talk about Augustine and also a notorious philosopher whose sins were, shall we say, scarlet: Jean-Jacques Rousseau. I choose the latter because Townshend oscillates between being first the one and then the other in his offering, and he drags his band through the muck in like fashion, sometimes torturing them, sometimes torturing himself. But Daltrey? Well, he's closer to the messianic than the sadistic.

My Love Is Vengeance

Augustine wrote his confessions for a more elevated purpose than most. It was his Christian "testimony," for one thing, all about his conversion experiences. The ostensive aim is to convert the reader. But it is *really* a philosophy book. One problem the Christians had encountered and struggled with was whether the teachings of Jesus could be treated as a "philosophy." The first generation of his followers came down hard on the "nay" side of that question. Christianity is not a philosophy, on the one hand, and it is not magic, on the other.

In John's Gospel (12:20 ff), the disciple Philip comes to Jesus while they are wandering around Jerusalem, with a few thousand of their closest friends. It must've looked like Woodstock (and we know how much Pete, and Peter, *loved* that sort of thing). Philip tells Jesus that there are *some Greeks* there who want to talk to him. Knowing that the Greeks want to know about the immortality of the soul, Jesus gently skips the formalities, and proceeds to the heart of the matter. You have to die to live forever, he says. Since Philip will not understand, Jesus asks God to have a word with the misguided man directly from the clouds. The message was, to put it mildly, "this stuff is not philosophy." To those who heard God's voice, it sounded like heavy metal thunder, a little like John Kay, with a vengeance. And then Jesus threw his guitar into the crowd. (But the disciples went to get it back.)

But philosophy, being basic to the human condition, is not so easily eradicated. By Jesus's time, everybody in the world spoke Greek and everybody read Plato and Aristotle, basically because it's really good stuff. The early Christians weren't willing just to toss philosophy, like an annoying guitar, into the crowd. So they didn't. They divided themselves into two factions, Aristotle's Christian followers in Antioch, Paul's stronghold, and Plato's followers in Alexandria, which was the Las Vegas of the Greek world (but it had evolved over four centuries into a great center of learning, as Las Vegas surely will . . .). These two groups of Christians proceeded to throw flaming projectiles at one another for the next seven hundred years until finally the Muslim Caliphate relieved them of their worries by destroying both. It was high time.

Augustine landed, like young Tommy Walker, in the middle of the mess, the greatest meltdown in world history, the decline of the Roman Empire, which was the World War II of the ancient world, except in slo-mo. In the first generation following the creation of the book we now call the Bible, Augustine was the right man at the right place to reconcile Christian religion with philosophy. People wanted some hope, so Augustine taught them deaf, dumb, and blind faith. His *Confessions* was the popular book he wrote for the educated masses (the world had not yet fallen into the illiteracy and darkness that would characterize the Middle Ages), although everyone was now reading Latin rather than Greek. That was a good thing because it provided an opportunity to translate all the scattered "holy" writings into one uniform language. So Augustine's *Confession* is as much about bringing Christianity to philosophical respectability as about telling the story of Augustine's misspent youth and eventual humbling before God. Most people think Augustine managed the task quite well.

Tommy

Some people say *Tommy* is sacrilegious. I don't agree. It isn't exactly *orthodox*, but that's not the same. I think *Tommy* is a lot like Augustine's confessions, twentieth-century style. The trouble in the messy fourth century was that people were just too sophisticated to believe anything about gods and magic. They needed hope. It was one awful war after another and their politicians were dishonest and the world they worked so hard to build was unraveling. Augustine explained to them that belief was about being free—most people say that Augustine *invented* the idea of free will for a world surrounded by cynics and stoics and egoists and power-mongers. Something similar in the twentieth century, except that after a couple of World Wars, it's religion people can't buy.

I don't see how *Tommy* is all that different. In a disillusioned world, here comes Roger Daltrey, deaf, dumb, blind, but very good at intuition. He transforms the holiday (holy day) camps into utopian communes where people can learn to be free by playing pinball by intuition. Christianity succeeded as a commercial venture as well. Every year I get a notice from my church informing me of how much I have contributed and containing the legally required disclaimer that in return I have received, and I quote, "intangible spiritual benefits only." This is the essence of the message in *Tommy*—looking at him, I see the millions, gazing at him, we feel the heat, and listening to him we get opinions and excitement at his feet. Intangible spiritual benefits, no?

Roger Daltrey came into his own playing this figure. He had been searching for his place in the band, in the world. Pete said that adapting the persona of Tommy to performances on stage, during that time, consummated the "marriage" of the band. Now everyone had a clear role. "With this change, the band was at last complete," Pete said. Now we understood how to see Roger—the working class messiah, abused, misused, damaged, but free. He was blind but now he sees, and the new boss is not the same as the old boss. If he's not the messiah in a traditional sense, he is something like we imagine when we read the confessions of the saints. In a very real sense, Augustine's *Confessions* is the *Tommy* of the fourth century.

But here we begin to touch on the real problem, because Saint Monica, Augustine's mother, is *no* Ann-Margret, even if Augustine's father (sort of) *is* Oliver Reed. And let's begin with Oliver before we land in baked beans. It is widely known that Keith Moon and Oliver Reed were huge drinking buddies. No one could drink quite like they could. The fact that the real Oliver survived nineteen years longer than Keith has to be chalked up to genetics and a strong constitution. Alcohol dogged Pete Townshend's existence from all sides for as long as he could remember. That "our savior's" Mum and Dad are murderers who assuage their guilt with alcohol isn't surprising. That Oliver Reed plays the role is convenience as well as type casting. Pete knew a fit when he saw it. After all, Reed killed the hooker with the heart of gold in *Oliver!* Now that's the sort of father who figures in a confession *worth reading*.

Baked Beans

And then, there's the baked beans. Well, first it's suds, then beans, then chocolate: all things decadent, spewing forth from the television screen broken by, yes, a bottle of champagne. Later, just before she loses all control and pushes Tommy through the mirror (where he sees himself but *not* her), Mum first threatens to break the mirror with a bottle of vodka. In the nightmare world in which Oliver Reed murders your mother's lover so he can be, well, your father, and your drunken, over-sexed whore of a mother is Ann-Margret grinding on a bolster pillow, *and* your perverse pedophilic Uncle Ernie is Keith Moon, *and* your sadistic Cousin Kevin is Paul Nicholas who, at that time, was famous for playing . . . wait for it . . . Jesus in *Jesus Christ Superstar* (I kid you not. Pete cast Jesus as a sadist, and no doubt enjoyed that little twist) . . . *this* is Tommy's world. It is also Pete Townshend's real-life hall of mirrors, and if you can find the doors, you might know what it's like to be the bad man behind those blue eyes.

It comes as no surprise that this story is his autobiography made into art. But he really had to have Roger to embody it for him. Pete can't play Pete. How much Roger knew about all this ugliness is anyone's guess, but I will register my own hunch. I think Roger knew everything. I think he might be the one person who ever really felt Pete's need and in a very adult and responsible way, drew healthy boundaries and then, within those limits, did what he could for his tortured friend. From about 1980 (Keith Moon's death) until 1995, Townshend was drinking three bottles of brandy a day, and chasing it with cognac. Roger wasn't. As he puts it "I wasn't a goody-goody; I dabbled in the natural,' says Roger. But I was in a band with three alcoholics and someone had to be straight. They were three lunatics." It isn't an accident that even in the early Seventies, Pete was seeing Roger as a savior of sorts. And when it comes to telling the stories, I'm sorry, but I believe Roger. You have to swim through a lot of baked beans and alcohol to get to the bottom of Pete's mess. As Roger says, "I love Pete to bits. He's incredibly complex; bordering on madness. But when he is creative, some of the music he makes is incredible and we've been together for fifty years; we're like brothers."[1]

The Bargain

Once you cross a line, it's hard to go back. You said it; it's now on record. Augustine attracted readers with salacious stories of wine, women and song, and then, like soup at the Salvation Army, your enjoyment costs you a tedious sermon. But hey, why not the soup without the sermon? When you create a whole new literary form, you can't control what others do with it. After the Saint of Hippo, the cat was out of the bag and meowing for all it was worth. Naughty bits told everywhere, and without the Salt Lake City ending? You bet. And philosophers would not exactly be the main purveyors of smut, but they did their part, as we'll see.

I hadn't followed The Who since the early 1980s. I saw them on the 1980 tour (July 10th, to be exact—ain't Wikipedia a wonder?), with Kenny Jones on drums. It was a sort of consummation with me, and for some reason they were out of my system. I didn't like the music any less, but somehow (unlike the Stones), the Eighties weren't made for The Who and Keith Moon wasn't made for Eighties. But they looked great, sounded fantastic, hadn't lost a thing, apart from Keith (although that was an irreparable loss). But after that concert, I admit I lost track of the third best band in the history of rock music. I think a lot of people left the Sixties and Seventies behind at about that point. We all just moved on into Lauper-land. It was a fair bargain, or at least the best we could get.

So I wasn't aware of the ups and downs in the last thirty years. I noticed when Entwistle died and thought to myself "shame, great bass player," but then resumed napping. So the second half of the Townshend autobiography was mostly news to me, I am ashamed to admit. I was unaware that Pete had undertaken a bunch of major compositions and I did not realize that he saw himself primarily as a "composer" (as opposed to a songwriter and/or performer). I can see that I have a lot of

---

[1] See: <www.dailymail.co.uk/tvshowbiz/article- 014979/Roger-Daltrey-reveals-attitudes-marriage-vows-far-straightforward.html#ixzz4MiLsaNKM>, accessed October 10th 2016.

listening to do beyond my old LPs, and I look forward to that assignment. On the other hand, if these compositions were regarded as genuinely important by the cultural powers, I would know about them (and so would you). I'm guessing Pete was shooting blanks, so to speak.

Do You Think It's Alright . . . ?

Again, I admit I wasn't keeping up with the kids, so I also didn't know about Pete's crash and burn, and his public shaming over a brief encounter with child porn. More on those things later. But once in a while I would see a picture of Roger Daltrey on a magazine cover or an ET short, and think to myself "he can't possibly look that good." But the comings and goings of the older Teddy Boys and Mods didn't seem to matter, somehow, or at least, not like the Stones did. Bad manners wear well, when practiced with panache, and are quite different from childish fits, for which Pete was infamous. The artsy outlook is adaptable, but I think we can all agree that David Bowie dominated that cultural space in the world of popular music. There was room for angsty singer-songwriters, and Pete probably could have moved in there if he wanted, but eventually Paul Simon reclaimed it. Pete decided to become a great composer. There is a tiny cultural space for that, but Pete didn't have the right credentials to go there. Instead he became a latter day Salieri of sorts. I am sure that aficionados are following his every move. One assumes that Salieri had his following as well, but he was no Mozart.

Then came Pete's tell-all. Like many, I had some catching up to do. But instead, I pulled out all the old records and listened through. Yes, it was all still great. From the time of the release of *Tommy* as a movie, I loudly and annoyingly defended the idea that The Who brought a musical seriousness and credibility to the rock genre that no other group could have achieved. This claim is patently false, of course. There couldn't be less than ten other rock bands that could do everything The Who did, and then some—the early Genesis, Yes, and ELP come to mind. The grand ambition of the rock opera, coupled with the film version, might even have been within the range of Elton John or Billy Joel. But their prog-rocking came slightly later and built on what The Who had done (with a little help from the show-tunes revolts of Webber and Rice, and Ragni/ Rado/MacDermot). Townshend's autobiographical narrative (however dubious) seems to confirm my annoying judgments about the band.

I also had no idea that he was on the cutting edge of so many technical advances in recording and sound effects (at least, according to him). I am not in a position to question him, but I also don't quite believe him. If Daltrey says "Pete did all this stuff," then I would believe it. You will say I don't like Pete Townshend. Not so. I think I like him better than he likes himself. Townshend depicts himself (persuasively) as a self-absorbed, now apologetic, hopeless narcissist who has reasons, but no excuses, apart from an artistic temperament, for his persistent weakness of will and fabled childish behavior.

Les Enfants Terribles

There was a great philosopher who was so much like Pete that it seems too close to be an accident. Jean-Jacques Rousseau was the terrible child of the eighteenth century, hero and anti-hero all at once, of the Enlightenment. Like Pete, J-J was passed around as he grew up to various relatives, none of whom seemed to have much understanding of what to do with a genius. Like Pete, J-J's origins were bourgeois and dysfunctional, and like Pete he showed a tendency to rebelliousness from the start. Like Pete, J-J became an aesthete who brought trouble behind him everywhere he went. Like Pete, J-J was a scientific tinkerer, and good enough at it to have done it for a living, if had wished.

Like Pete, he wrote operas, still often performed to this day, and not just because J-J became such a famous philosopher. They are performed because they are good. It makes one wonder what will become of Pete's body of operatic work. I think some of it may survive for a while, at least. But for 50 years? That's mighty hard to foresee. But Rousseau was a musical innovator. He created his own system of musical notation to replace the cumbersome notation that we still use—but Rousseau's system looks like an awful lot of rock and jazz charts I have seen, and heck, you can get an app for it.

The parallels go deeper, however. Rousseau had the devil's own time maintaining human relationships. He would grow paranoid and had difficulty in trusting people. He continually said things that scandalized people and got him in trouble. Unlike Pete, however, J-J was very political, and so his paranoia was sometimes justified. People actually were trying to kill him. *There* is a monster Pete never had to face. But there is reason to look at J-J is his *Confessions*, five hundred pages of pleading his case before the judgment of posterity, a gambit for absolution and understanding for his mistakes and episodic misbehavior, with elaborate explanations thereof—too elaborate, if you know what I mean. A bit contrived for my taste. His confessions were published only after he died, but he was giving private readings of them to selected groups for years ahead of that, damaging the reputations of some living and many recently dead people. The police eventually interdicted his readings at the demand of one person whose reputation was suffering.

Indeed, this is a fair description of Pete's autobiography. One almost senses that he is asking the world to forgive him, in the name of art, his many transgressions, for the sake of the art he gave us. This is a latter-day Oscar Wilde with a five-hundred-page *De Profundis*. In Rousseau's day, the tell-all was a new idea (again)—specifically, it was Rousseau's idea. But today we're pretty hard to shock. Still, the reputations of Moon and Entwistle (or what little was left of their reputations) are pretty much trashed by Townshend. Daltrey comes off as a saint by comparison. But then, Daltrey *was*, by comparison (the bar was low), and besides, he's still above ground and if need be, can afford lawyers.

The convenient thing about being important enough to write a major autobiography is that you can *choose* which specifics to condemn in yourself, and perhaps draw attention away from even greater faults. Rousseau pioneered this territory, leaving some of his listeners in tears at how honest he had been regarding his faults and flaws. Townshend is clearly worried about his historical legacy and is also busily doctoring the mythology. He wants to be seen as the Mozart of our age and is sure to associate his name with the necessary classical lights, and to create a myth of his childhood, complete with mystical experiences of heavenly music. Bosh. *But* . . .

A Very Naughty Boy

Pete does not know that he had a sort of twin: that same fellow from Geneva who scandalized all of Europe with his traipsing and cavorting. Unlike Pete, J-J changed the world beyond mere popular culture (although he was certainly the darling of the decadent). J-J had the gift of philosophy along with literary and poetical and scientific gifts. Rousseau's political ideas were formative in the minds of the framers of the United States.

Like Pete, J-J often bit the hands that fed him, but in addition to many childish fits, Rousseau found a way to be downright dangerous. He was hailed as the harbinger, even as the very intellectual father, of the French Revolution. He had attacked the overly cultivated manners of the power elite and had suggested that it was *civilization* that led to human corruption.

Meanwhile Rousseau practiced, well, human vice of every imaginable sort. By comparison, Pete Townshend was (almost) a good family man. I hope that Pete's kids forgive him, but Rousseau's never got the chance. He persuaded his babymama (whom he never married) to leave them all at the foundling homes. Rousseau would coax money from wealthy widows and keepers of salons. They wanted more from him than just a good intellectual conversation and a tune on the pianoforte. So Rousseau spread his *joi de vivre*, so to speak, in many *petites morts* around the Continent, not forsaking England itself in the effort. For all we know, Pete may be a descendant. It would explain some things if he were.

We can see between the lines in Rousseau's airing of the dirty laundry that he was introduced too early to the world of adult sex, and of the more stringent type. He frankly admits that he liked nothing quite so well as to be spanked. His governess, Mademoiselle Lambercier, would spank little J-J when he was bad. He liked it. She quit doing it, once she realized he was getting his jollies, and that left him sad. Rousseau wrote many years later:

> This behavior of an unmarried woman of thirty who is the only one who knows her motive appears noteworthy to me. Another thing that is almost as noteworthy is the date. This took place in 1721 and I was not yet nine. I do not know the reason for this precocious sensuality;

perhaps the reading of novels accelerated it; what I do know is that it had an influence on the rest of my life, on my tastes, on my morals, on my behavior. I see the thread of all that; it is useful to follow its track; but how can I mark it down on these sheets without soiling them?

But J-J finds a way. I am picturing Ann-Margret, frankly. Only *she* knows her motives. His next remarks are, I think, the most telling ones:

> This first emotion of the senses impressed itself so much upon my memory that, when it began to warm up my imagination after several years, it was always under the form that had produced it, when the sight of young and beautiful persons made me uneasy, the effect of it was always to set them to work on an idea, and to make so many Mademoiselle Lamberciers out of them. The obstinacy with which these images returned on the slightest occasion, the ardor with which they inflamed my blood, the extravagant acts I was brought to by the desire to see them realized, were not the strangest things that happened in me.[2]

In other words, things got weirder still, but we'll leave that for the historians and psychoanalysts. Rousseau just couldn't seem to control this *thing* that was set loose in him by these early experiences. It followed him into maturity (he was over fifty when he wrote this), and it seems always on the verge of being evoked by circumstance. *That* was the wellspring of his creativity. He had to do something with that energy.

And here, I suggest, you have the origins of Captain and Mrs. Walker, of Uncle Ernie, of Cousin Kevin, of the Acid Queen, and of Tommy himself. I have always felt that *Quadrophenia* was macho compensation: a portrait of the artist as a young punk. Pete was never that boy. He tipped his hand in *Tommy*. His youth is about sex and death and the edges of human experience —and about freedom and vision through art. The difference between Pete and J-J is that the latter put his finger on the problem: memory, and what it does to us. At the very least it makes us crazy, and at its worst, well, you get images and sounds that can free the millions through your confession. But these visions of freedom never freed J-J. And they never freed Pete.

---

[2] These passages are from the fragments of the *Confessions*. See Rousseau, *The Confessions and Correspondence*, p. 590.

Apologia Pro Vita Sua

The music was enough, Peter. Your sins aren't scarlet—they aren't even pink, for Christ's sake. Have you noticed what your peers were doing? You're a choirboy with a bad attitude. We knew that the day you showed up on Ed Sullivan. It's what we like about you. You don't have to defend yourself. What if, in a moment of weakness, you clicked the wrong button on the Russian kiddy porn site? What if you thought about it for a thousand nights before you did it? C'mon Pete. Not one soul you've moved with your art is different from you, even if the particulars vary. You faced the hardness too soon, and the redemption was aesthetic. You were a kid. It's alright not to be alright.

See Me, Feel Me

I don't know whether that book is a tell-all scandal sheet, because I'm not sure what might be missing, but there are plenty of juicy bits about everyone, *except Roger Daltrey*. Unlike Townshend's other bandmates, if Roger ever strayed from the straight and narrow, that tale awaits another storyteller. As with Rousseau, the dead come in for a bit edgier treatment, and one assumes they won't object. But the living fare better, with the sole exception of Pete himself. The old saying is that one ought not speak ill of the dead, but in the world of tell-all autobiography, the converse holds. But one is at least in charge of one's own self-condemnation.

Among the other tabloid nuggets, Pete confesses that Mick Jagger is the only man he "ever wanted to f**k," and is frank about his own infidelities, infatuations, intoxications, and infrequent incarcerations. But somehow, it feels contrived. Maybe I'm still pissed off about the auto-destruction ruse, but I can't help wondering whether all this embarrassing self-revelation is not leading us away from still deeper secrets.

And here we come to the motive force behind Townshend's life, as he claims to understand it. Pete believes he was probably sexually abused as a young boy, but perhaps has blocked it from his memory. Surely no one can forget Keith Moon's disturbing performance as the pedophile Uncle Ernie. Keith seemed fearless, to me, as a kid watching that—my father took me to see *Tommy* during the first theater run, in spite of his grunts of disapproval. He also took me to see *Gimme Shelter* and *Serpico* too. And he bought me *Led Zeppelin IV* (on the advice of a friend my own age). I'm beginning to think Dad understood more than I allowed. But there I was, a boy, being totally creeped out by Uncle Ernie and thinking to myself, "Why would he let himself be perceived this way?" The "he" is Keith Moon, the rock and roll god who kicked over the drums. The question has stuck with me. But here is the answer. I would bet my boots that Keith Moon wasn't abused as a boy. He doesn't get that this is *real*.

No One Knows What It's Like

Townshend is indeed an artist and writer of a high order, and he knows as well as anyone that the gun appearing in the first act must go off in the third. He weaves his whole story in such a way as to make it completely convincing, when at the end of the book, he finally offers his full public defense regarding his 2004 arrest for visiting the child pornography website. I don't know the truth, of course, but if I were a writer, and I had something that dark to defend myself from, I would know enough to build the defense in from the start.

No one still alive can dispute Townshend's version of early childhood events. All the main characters are dead. I can see what Pete *wants* us all to believe, and even if it is true that he has a weakness along these pedophilic lines, either *because* he was abused as a child or even if he wasn't, his lifelong preoccupation with abused young boys is manifest in his *oeuvre*. Examine Rousseau's little discourse on the surprising power of memory over the forms of desire. Perhaps Pete understands himself better than he can afford to tell us, but there is no question this 2004 episode humbled the man, and set him to worrying that his work would be tainted, perhaps buried, by the scandal.

Such newfound humility may account for the almost complete absence of negative judgment regarding Pete's bandmates (even the dead ones), family, rock and roll rivals, and dishonest business managers in his book. Yet, we all know that Townshend has been a take-no-prisoners verbal pugilist his entire adult life. One might have expected an autobiography reflecting in literature the trail of human destruction he created for those forty years. But now, by this adjustment of mythology, Pete loves everyone and hopes they will love him.

Something smells here. The gentleman doth protest too much. Pete Townshend emphatically *does not* love everyone, and I think the thing that convinces me of this is that the audio version of his book (which he reads himself, very credibly), omits the acknowledgment of his ex-wife, Karen, to whom he was married for some twenty-six years. The physical book contains a paragraph of that nature, but it's missing from the audio book. The *edit* on the audio version is actually audible where this paragraph was cut out.

Mind you, in Peter Townshend we are talking about one of the premier recording engineers and producers of the twentieth century and *he leaves an audible edit* of his autobiography *where the acknowledgment of his ex-wife should have been.* A lifetime of overdubs and the man couldn't have smoothed this edit out? What's up with that, Pete? I await the honest version of your story in which you either *successfully* manipulate us all or tell the *whole truth*, since either one would be the same, in effect. I just hate being lied to, and at the very least, Pete is framing the truth so consciously that it becomes a dialectic of hagiography made credible by calculated self-abuse. The effect is not believable. I am recommending a book for you, Pete. The *Confessions* by Jean-Jacques Rousseau.

Gazing at You, Listening to You

Suspicions aside, the Townshend autobiography is an incredible book, in both senses of that word. Everyone should read it, not just Who fans, not just rock fans, not just curious gawkers, *everyone*. The story Townshend tells so ably encompasses the zenith (and its lurid decadence) enjoyed by the generation that inherited all the ill-gotten gains of high Colonialism and its Neronic decline. It is the time of Caligula in the civilization of the English-speaking peoples. If I could bequeath only one book to civilizations of the distant future to characterize that fall of Empire, this would be the book. The reason is that Townshend's perspective, whether he knows it or not, epitomizes everything for which we should be condemned by the future, along with everything for which we might claim the right to redemption. Yes, the baby boomers wasted, destroyed, even raped the world they inherited. But what else were the kids gonna do? There were no worlds left to conquer. But it feels pretty hollow, like there's a hole in the bottom of our being.

8

It's All Dark: The Eclipse of the Damaged Brain

All that You Love

Being has a hole in it. And the hole is your very self. Like many of you, I learned that tidbit of information before I was really ready for it. We feel like an orifice. That doesn't have to be bad news, but it can be and often is. It gets pretty dark down in there, and there is madness and death in the hole, but joy and hope originate from that same "absence." I wish I had understood the brighter side of it when I was younger.

But I was listening to Pink Floyd. I don't know if it would be apt to say I "loved" the music, or even really "liked" it. Somehow that doesn't capture the relationship. One can say "Pink Floyd is awesome," or "cool," but "I love Pink Floyd" seems almost perverse. We are in awe of this music, we respect it, we appreciate it, but it has not been made for love or fondness or affection. It's about black holes and dark sides and shadows; it's about hanging on in somewhat noisy desperation, but the noise has to be closely arranged for the maximum effect.

All that You Do

I can only put this in personal terms, but I think you've probably had experiences like mine too, and that they are surely still with you just as they are with me. With few resources for resisting the maximum effect, and no comprehension at all, at age twenty-one, I once listened to "Brain Damage" about forty times in a row, jerking the needle up as the first chord of

131

"Eclipse" slid in and setting it back; the last time I let the record play through to "Eclipse," mainly because I was too far gone to set the needle back by then. I did this repetitive exercise not because I really wanted to hear the song forty times, but because right then I didn't know what else to do. Staring at the album cover on the coffee table, in the sort of dim light that is so conducive to exploring the outskirts of consciousness, enhanced by whatever mind-altering substances I had on hand, anaesthetized, alone, and, frankly, heart-broken (the way one sometimes is, and can only be, at twenty-one). And I kept repeating to myself "this is impossible," with an intensity that only someone that age can gather. Which is to say, I actually meant it.

Many of you have been to this place, in your own way. Somewhere in the course of it, I came to the edge of the conscious world, as if a door opened in the psyche, and I peered through it, saw that I was, well, nothing to write home about; nothing before I was born, nothing after I die, and therefore nothing now. The darkness, the sheer nothingness of the void, the warm terror that is so far beyond worldly fear, and the sudden understanding that I did not have to choose the narrow path of my familiar habits of consciousness—all of this, and more, was behind the door that opened, somehow, through the music. I realized that holding my own little mind together, in the conventional and expected ways, was an effort I made every day, usually without noticing how much work it takes. And I also realized I didn't have to do that, that being sane and acceptable was actually a choice, not a requirement.

Like you, I have friends who stepped through that door; some came back and some never did. In my own case, I closed the door, quit the drugs, turned off the music (for many years) and went back to school. I mean, how can you have any pudding if you don't eat your meat? The music that had gotten me through the 1970s and into the early 1980s came to be associated with the scary door that opened, and so I turned off not just Pink Floyd, but also Yes and Led Zeppelin. It should have been clear enough, but I wasn't sure which music was the Mephistopheles opening the door, responsible for the visitation of the void. I have since come to understand that Zeppelin was not much more than a respectable roots band, that Yes always dwelt in the light. Pink Floyd was the problem. Well, no. I was the problem; Pink Floyd was the musical mirror I stood before in the dark and said "bloody Mary" forty times, until she finally showed up.

Years of gradual revelation about how consciousness works, and how it applies to my own history has cleared some of the murk. I don't understand it all, not by any means, but let me take you through a part I think I do get, if you want to go. It might be cool, although I doubt you'll "love it." I think you should cue up "Brain Damage" and "Eclipse" and listen to them now. This isn't a requirement, but it will help us occupy the same headspace. I also want you to avoid looking at the album cover for the moment.

All that You Touch, See, Taste, Feel

If you pay close attention to your own experience, it may dawn on you that your consciousness is always restlessly looking for something to fasten on to, and then when it does find something, it is never quite satisfied with whatever it has. At any given moment, your body is being pelted with sights and smells and feels and even tastes (yes, you taste even when you're not eating—for example, right now, I really want to brush my teeth—never mind why). In all that sensory confusion, you are paying attention only to a small part of what's available for your attention. When your eyes are open and the light is good, chances are that you will pay the most attention to what you are seeing, and then you will voluntarily put the rest of your senses into a supporting role.

Favoring your power of sight is perfectly voluntary on your part, and you can alter the weight you give to any of your senses at any given time. But the visual stuff is so much more interesting and powerful to your momentary consciousness— draws your attention so much more seductively—that you may need to close your eyes or dim the lights before any of the other senses can be in command for very long. This is the reason we don't listen to Pink Floyd in bright light. To do so is simply wrong. We want the ears to be in charge, and we want the sound to tell us what the light means. We want the ears to tell all the other senses what everything means. And that can be done. Pink Floyd is not background music. It demands center stage. With sufficient openness and also discipline, we can even have sounds drive the meaning of all the other senses and even our interior feelings and emotions.

But here is something that may not have occurred to you. There's such a thing as an aural or auditory "image," as distinct from a visual image. I am not talking about the visual images that may be inspired by sounds, those dancing color patterns, or the memories of places we have seen, or various album covers, that spring into consciousness when our eyes are closed. I mean the auditory image itself, the way we experience the music so that the sounds make sense, have a pattern and an order that we can understand. You can have an "image" of sounds. Try this: Imagine the melody to "Money" in your head right now. You may also be visualizing David Gilmour singing it, but leave that aside. Just imagine the song. What is going on in your head is not made of sound waves, and it is not visual. You sort of "hear" the song in your head, right? You know you aren't actually hearing it, but somehow it is there. That is an auditory "image," because you are imagining it. It is very different from a visual image.

The same is true of all our senses; they all give birth to images of different sorts. You can imagine what a fresh cut lawn smells like, and a rotting corpse, and cookies baking, without actually smelling these things. That is your olfactory imagination, and the result of the effort at imagining produces images. And you "can just taste" those cookies before you eat them, can't you? We often use our power of making tasty images when cooking, especially when choosing combinations of spices. So remember, not all images are visual pictures.

All You Create

Visual images are spatial. When we are conscious of visual images, they have a top, a bottom, a left, a right, a depth, and an imagined distance from us—these are all spatial dimensions. Follow me in a little experiment. Do not look at the album cover, but picture before your mind the cover of *Dark Side of the Moon*. You know it well, the prism enveloped by blackness, the ray of light on one side, the refracted spectrum on the other. You know approximately where in the field of black to situate the prism, you know roughly which direction the tip of the prism points.

But are you altogether certain? Is the prism off to one side by just a little? Is the prism a pyramid or just a triangle? Is it tilted just a bit? This is all about spatial order. Are you sure about which side has the ray of light and which side is the refracted spectrum? Try imagining it both ways and see if you can decide which is "correct." So long as you are trying to re-create in imagination the album cover you have seen so many times, you will be working with a kind of consciousness that is really visual memory, but you also will experience a certain freedom to alter and vary the image right now; yes, you are trying to re-create it, but in truth, you are creating it, which is the only way you can actually remember anything. The image is yours to alter as you wish, and there is no right and wrong about how you imagine it unless you choose to judge your image against another one (which you don't have to do).

Some philosophers call this power to create images the "spontaneity" of consciousness. That sounds more sophisticated than saying "wow, man, the image just appears from nothing," but that's what "spontaneity" basically means: the immediate presence of whatever is present to consciousness. As you spontaneously make a visual image, you can move the image around, trying it now one way, now another. But the point is that you can situate the visual image in your mind spatially in most any way you choose, play around with it, invert the prism, change the colors of the spectrum, and so on. That is what I mean by spatial order in visual images. There are also limits to what you can do with a visual image—for example, you cannot simultaneously imagine the prism as both a flat triangle and as a pyramid; you can, at most, alternate between them. So not only is there spatial order, but there are rules or laws (and limits) that apply to the act of imagining visual images. These are mainly geometrical rules, by the way, because geometry is the general structure of space.[1]

---

[1] Here's something fun to do with your brain that your math teacher never taught you. First, take some drugs. Now, imagine a point. Now make it move in one direction. It becomes a line. Now, make the whole line move in one direction. It becomes a plane. Now make the whole plane move. It becomes a solid (it has three dimensions). You are using your imagination to multiply dimensions. You can go beyond three dimensions if you really, really work at it, or if the drugs are good enough.

Auditory images exist in time in about the same way that visual images exist in space. That is, instead of up and down and left and right, you have mainly "before" and "after" when it comes to imagined sounds. Imagining what someone said or a melody takes you some time, whereas visual images seem to appear instantaneously. Both are spontaneous, but obviously "spontaneity" isn't the same thing as "instantaneity" (I made up that word, but I sort of like it). There are limits and rules with auditory images also. If I ask you to imagine the melody of "Money," you just cannot do it all at once. The melody takes time to imagine; within a certain range, you can speed it up or slow it down in your imagination, but you cannot collapse it into one instant or extend it to an hour (for one time through the musical phrase). If you try to make the image all at once, the song just disappears; if you try to extend it too long, other images intervene before you can finish it. And imagined time does not follow the same rules as physical time. You can imagine a melody, without distorting it, much more rapidly than you can physically create it singing it out loud. It would be cool to learn whether there is some sort of ratio of imagined time to physical time. No one has figured out a way to measure that, but there is some kind of relationship I'm sure. Anyway, the point is, we find the laws that apply to auditory images in the way time is structured (always with a past, a present, and a future).

All that Is Now, Gone, to Come

Most people are not trained to work with auditory images in the way we all habitually mess around with visual ones, but musicians learn to do this with auditory images—they have to learn it. They may not know how to explain it, but music unfolds over time, and that allows them some freedom and variation and creativity in the way they are remembering and anticipating what is in the music. To create music, to work with it at all, requires that one be able to, in imagination, arrange and re-arrange experiences in time. Musicians all know that temporal arrangement is the basic pattern of order in a piece of music—the "groove" of the piece (see Chapter 2). Choices of notes and chords come later and are built on the timeframe.

To give you an example of some features of this kind of temporal "order" (and it has many, many features): Sing to yourself in your imagination (hell, do it out loud if you want to) the opening line of "Brain Damage." You are singing "The lunatic is on the grass" (and I know you will say "grahhss," whether you are British or not). You may also be picturing your favorite image of a madman on your front lawn (for me it always starts out as Charles Manson, whose picture frightened me as a boy, and he's definitely coming for me, not walking away or sitting still), but that is visual imagery. I want to draw your attention to the fact that, as you complete the line you are singing, you now want to pause for a bit and then repeat it. You have an urge to do that, and it will be a strong urge. Interestingly, it is easier to stop yourself from repeating it out loud than to stop yourself from repeating the auditory image. Our control of our bodies is quite a bit easier than commanding our own consciousness. Consciousness is suggestible, but hard to control.

If you imagined the first line of "Brain Damage" (and you did, because I have you in my power), you will probably repeat it even if I tell you not to (so much for my delusions of omnipotence). If you sang it out loud, you will repeat it silently in your imagination, even if you don't sing it again. Why? "Well," you will answer "that's how the song goes." And I will say "that is precisely my point." The auditory image lives in these urges that tie the past (your memory and previous experience) to the future (your next experience), and in an orderly way—you know how the song goes, you learned it, and you remember it. If anyone starts you down that time-path, you will project into the immediate future the temporal sequence you learned, and you'll just take off down that path (like a friggin' lunatic). You almost can't help yourself.

I assure you, Gilmour and Waters are well aware of this little feature of consciousness. In writing the lyrics, Waters didn't have to repeat that first line at the beginning of each verse.[2] In writing the music, Gilmour didn't have to repeat the same melody when the words were repeated. So why did they do it? In a sense, every child knows the answer. Repetition is, perhaps, the most powerful weapon in a musician's arsenal for controlling your consciousness. By means of repetition, a musician can rob you of almost all of your freedom. Your desires and

---

[2] I guess Waters was actually the last person who really had a choice about that.

your next act of consciousness can be controlled by getting you to fix your will upon only a single possibility for the future. If you doubt for a single second that Waters and Gilmour are doing this on purpose, I invite you to sing "Us and Them" in your head. You are doing it because I suggested it, and now I know you are so totally echoing yourself. I want to point out that "Us and Them" comes right before "Brain Damage" on the album. You honestly think this isn't a conscious set-up? The boys know what they're doing. It is a gentle kind of brain damage.

A repeated line is the most quickly learned in any song. You probably sang the repeated lines in "Brain Damage" the very first time you heard the song. I know I did. We were shown the time-pattern with the opening verse, and then shown the slight variations—he's in the hall, they're in the hall, he's in my head, dammit, he's in my head—and then, tacitly, seductively, Waters sort of said "now boys and girls, repeat after me." And we do it. We almost can't help it. And once we have co-operated, he has us where he wants us. We're nearly compelled to listen to the next line to find out what the lunatic will do. Off down the path we go. The lyricist is quite powerful in terms of getting us going, but now he can't stop us, so he loses his power once he uses it—Waters is a bee who stung you, but the stinger is gone, and with it the bee. Of course Waters is a whole hive. Repeated melodies are also powerful, but not as much as repeated words. But when you repeat both words and melody, as in "Brain Damage," the power becomes hypnotic.

There's a lot to be said about auditory images. I haven't even scraped the surface, but if you understand that these images work with your memories, your expectations, your desires, and most importantly, your will, well, you know most of what you need to know about why you eventually opened the door to your soul and took the trip into the void (or at least I think I know why I did). That trip is about how past experience and present desire make the future—sort of, make the future before it happens, as an image we project and then live our way into—and music is probably the single most powerful way to penetrate a person's regular "defenses" against, well, mind-control, and take him where he didn't quite intend to go. Music penetrates every pore of the body, moves the body and consciousness wherever it will, and endows those who create it with an incredible power.

Everything Under the Sun Is in Tune

Fortunately, it's difficult to make music well, and those who do learn to make it well are themselves even more susceptible to its power than those who simply listen. Waters and Gilmour may have you in their control, but they are more had by what they are doing than you are. The music itself takes the musicians where they didn't intend to go. So there is a cosmic balance in music, because only those who are most deeply moved by it are able to create it, and being so deeply controlled by it themselves, they have little energy left for using it to control others. Usually. Instead, they generally make music to express, please and, paradoxically, free themselves (from everything except the music), first from the inside out, and then from the outside in.

What I mean by this is that in a musician, the music first exists inside, as a kind of urge for release, and that urge then manifests itself as bodily movements (exercising the vocal chords or moving the fingers on a fret-board). That is inside-out. After that, the music is generated as sound waves, and finally re-absorbed into the body (mainly the ears) as heard sound. That is outside in. When the cycle is completed, there is a kind of fulfillment of release.

But while playing, there is a short lag-time between the onset of the urge and the re-absorption as intelligible sound (even after our ears hear it, it takes a little time for it to be processed by the brain). To keep the music going, a musician has to generate new urges and act on them while absorbing the results of previous urges. Thus, from the inside, a musician is always at least a little bit ahead of what his body is hearing, while from the outside, he is a little behind himself. When playing music, your whole existence, physical, conscious, emotional, gets extended in time, and more extended depending on how far ahead of yourself you can get with the urges, while still retaining the meaning of the sound coming in. This is a total rush, by the way, when the loop gets going and the durational lapse is expanded successfully. Of course, if a musician fails, gets too far ahead, the whole loop snaps back into the immediate present, and he's likely played a wrong note and is staring stupidly at his fret-board. That never happens to Gilmour, of course . . .

The result of this temporal self-extension is the creation of a traveling time-loop that can expand our awareness of "now" to a few more seconds than in a normal act of waking consciousness. In ordinary activities, "now" probably lasts a couple of seconds at most, as the last conscious act perishes and the next act is anticipated. "Now" for a musician can last up to eight or ten seconds, depending upon how and what he is playing. When improvising in a band with others, the musician gets a maximally expanded "now." Playing something thoroughly rehearsed and memorized tends to shrink the effect to something that is fairly mechanical, and expanded in time only for as long as it takes for the urge to become a sound that is heard (which isn't very long). Having an expanded now is an attractive experience, and in the expanded interval, a door is opened, a trap-door in time itself, through which the musician escapes. What the door is like and where it leads depends on both the musician and the music itself.

That is why musicians play mainly for themselves, and only secondarily for those who listen. And that is why musicians are themselves among the most devoted music fans. Practicing music is not as much a discipline as a pleasure, even an addiction to temporal escape, for those who can find the trap-door in time. Gilmour and Waters know many such doors. Perhaps too many. They are almost too good at what they do.

Heaven help the world if some truly great musician (not our heroes in PF) were ever detached enough to use the music he creates to work his will solely upon others, for it turns out that a musician can, with talent and practice, funnel you through the trap door he chooses and eject you into whatever place he wants you to go—if you let him, and, as we already saw with the "repetition strategy," it is pretty hard to stop him if he knows how to do it. Our heroes know this bit of magic. And there are dozens of other strategies besides repetition. Prime among these is getting you to create for yourself the images, under the domination of the auditory time pattern (of memory and anticipation), but including, especially, the visual images as a supporting cast; this is crucial to making good music. Waters needs you to see the lunatic almost as much as he needs you to repeat the line. One type of image reinforces the other. Your body is laid open by the presence of the sound, and then re-organized temporally by its pulses and repetitions and movements, and then you start seeing things in your head that make the music seem like more than just sound. It's a limited kind of time-travel. So you use your own energy to create visual images (your own version of Charlie Manson), and work with the music, actively, to find a temporal expansion that is sort of analogous to the one the musician experiences. You generate successive urges of your own and then experience the images you create. But, make no mistake, your experiences are quite different from the musician's. The musician exerts a level of control over the character of the time-expansion that the listener does not.

All that You Beg, Borrow, or Steal

So you can create different kinds of images with your body, not just visual ones. When your ears are in the driver's seat, the other kinds of images your body is creating—all the way from the way the couch feels against your backside to the visual picture of the lunatic in your hall—will swirl and change with the music. All of this activity plays on your own powers of attention. Attention is weird. It's like a vortex. At every moment your attention casts about for something to focus on, and as soon as some enticing possibility presents itself in any of your modes of awareness, you zero in on it, like going down a space-time wormhole, and for a split second, everything else just disappears.

This act of "appropriation," in which your consciousness begs, borrows or steals something from the perceived world for its own private party, happens so quickly that it is easy to miss what is happening (unless you have, er, umm, slowed the process down with some sort of, umm, chemical enhancement, which I do not condone, of course). But what happens in that split second when you "attend" to something is that you get sucked into a vortex, like a descending spiral in time, and at the end of the slide, an "object" appears. Then, all the rest of your sensory information returns as the background against which the object of attention stands out. The reason you could not resist repeating the line from "Brain Damage" is that it drew your attention down a wormhole, and at the end of the time-slide, there was the same damn line again. So you said it in your head. This is like a carnival funhouse in time, and you could easily cross the line over to infinity—or perhaps listen to the whole song forty times in a row, if you're dumb enough to try that.

This whole sequence of events we call the song "Brain Damage"—the lyrics, the tempo, the melody, the amazing surge when the drums kick in, the climactic line that gave the album its name—all of this can become the extended and complex object of your attention. Once the sequence starts, it seems almost as if it completes itself, and almost against your will (which is why it is difficult to turn off any good song in the middle, or, what is much more unusual, it is hard to turn off *Dark Side of the Moon* anywhere in the album—the whole album is one long experience).

To get a sense of this level of control, consider this: If you are listening to "Brain Damage," you just yearn for those drums to kick in even before they do, don't you? That's why Nick Mason and the boys made you wait an extra, excruciatingly sweet, swell of four beats for each drum entrance—just for the simple value of anticipation. Good musicians know all about building tension and release in your little brain. Do you not want to raise your arms and make drum motions in the air, as if to help Nick find those same drums in the same order just one more time? Do your lips not move spontaneously with the sound of Roger's voice so as to make a date for a future lunar rendezvous (with Syd or whomever you expect to meet there)? Do you not release yourself in combined despair and defiance, in a lofty bitterness at a stupid world that cannot understand?

Alright, step out of the vortex—Jesus, I'm falling into a trance just writing about this shit. And now I can't get that damned song out of my head (maybe I found the lunatic). Try something else, now: Release your attention for a moment, and just think of nothing in particular (and here, the chemicals can also help, which I still do not condone). Try to think of nothing. You will find that there is a certain restless feeling inside you. Your consciousness is squirting all over the place, begging for an "object," something to focus on, anything. And if you close your eyes just to deny yourself any visual information, your brain will start borrowing visual images from your memory, and you'll be hard-pressed to make it stop. But let's try to stop this for a moment if we can. There are a few ways to do it. The easiest way to make it stop is just to give in and think of something in particular, just one thing. That object won't last long, but at least it is more satisfactory than dealing with the perpetual motion machine of your attention deprived of an object.

All that You Say

There is a way to train and discipline your brain to be more orderly: imagine just one word over and over. This is why they teach you a "mantra" for meditation in many Eastern religions. Repetition of a single word or very short phrase can bring your attention into focus. One is taught to repeat the word every second or two at first, while attention is in its usual frenetic condition, and then slow the frequency as calm sets in. The regular wandering of attention is brought gradually under your control. It is like calming your own private little Jack Russell Terrier by quietly saying "good dog" until he stops bouncing off the walls.

It's a dicey idea to calm your attention by saying the equivalent of "bad dog" to yourself. Some mantras can be pretty destructive. From personal experience, I can report that hundreds of repetitions of "this is impossible" over forty repetitions of "Brain Damage" make for an unwise plan. Don't do that. If you think that which word-images you choose to dwell on in your imagination doesn't affect you, I would gladly convince you otherwise. And since I'm being so solicitous of your well-being at the moment, I also do no not advise you to use any Pink Floyd lyric as a mantra, for reasons that will soon become clear.

There are others ways, however, to set your attention at rest, or to "unify attention," we might say. For example, if you turn up the music loud enough, you can make all that restless inner activity subordinate to the simple act of hearing. You can listen to music like a mantra that comes in from the outside world instead of an auditory image you create for yourself in your imagination. When you do that, you are using your power of sense perception to overwhelm your other two main types of consciousness, imagining and thinking (or cogitation or conception). Imagining is the kind of consciousness we have been talking about before, with the images; conceiving is what you do when you work with concepts (which is why they call them concepts, I guess), like doing math in your head for instance. You might imagine the numbers, as visual images, but an image of "2 + 2 = 4" is different from carrying out the conceptual operation of addition. You can confirm that if I ask you to add 17 and 27 in your head. Picturing the numbers doesn't give you the answer. You have to think to get the answer. If the music is loud enough, it may be pretty tough to do even that much math. The point is that you perceive, in addition to conceiving and imagining, and it is hard to do more than one at a time. Your brain, however damaged, makes fast transitions among them, though, so you might feel like you can think, imagine, and perceive all at once. In a sense you are doing all three much of the time, it's a question of which one has your attention, which is only one of them.

Whereas meditation, which is a kind of imagining, creates a type of internal and voluntary control (when imagining masters perceiving and conceiving), perceptual sensory overload begets a certain external and involuntary control of your mental processes. In the first case, one gives the inner life, the inner dynamic, an upper hand by depriving the body of movement, the ears of sound, the eyes of light. That is, the outer world is subjugated to the inner power of the will, and your wandering attention is set on auto-pilot by the repetition of the mantra. It may not surprise you that this process, reducing everything to your own free will, makes you feel powerful. Unfortunately, you can't do very much while attempting it, except perhaps become enlightened.

When you use the over-stimulation of the senses to silence the inner life, giving your perceiving body and your soul to whatever external stimulation is the most powerful, you can't hear yourself think at all, and your imagination gets scattered or enslaved. It is not surprising that you are at your least powerful, and least able to feel the freedom of your own will, when you use the outer perceptual world to squash the inner one. Your attention is at the mercy of whatever you are perceiving, and the acts of imagination you undertake are barely voluntary. In the case of music, to use the inimitable words of Waters, "all that you touch, all that you see, all that you taste, all that you feel . . ." comes under the sway of . . . of what? All that you hear, of course. In all the obvious lyrical choices in "Eclipse," that word "hear" is conspicuously missing. No way is this an accident. Roger knows what you are and are not doing when you have his voice in your ears.

Everyone You Fight

There is a reason why the American government uses loud heavy metal music to torture the people it claims are our enemies. It isn't because they like Metallica. Rather, Metallica weakens the will, if you hate the music, or after a while it does that even if you like it. Ironically, the same music seems to strengthen the will of the soldiers who are pumping themselves up to kill, but that isn't really what is happening. The music actually cancels their sense of freedom not to do what they are doing, anaesthetizes their emotions, cancels their imaginations, and turns them into killing machines. And that is what they want, given what they are being ordered to do. The soldier's will doesn't disappear, but it is set upon one task only, the fight. It's curious to consider whether such a reduced will is "stronger" than a free one. Is the person who employs his free will not to strike back when provoked stronger or weaker than the person who cannot stop himself? The "detainees" at Guantanamo Bay often pray to resist the Metallica—this is a fairly powerful self-assertion of the priority of the inner life over the physical body. For some of them, perhaps it works. I hope it does.

In any case, I think you will see why the government doesn't choose Pink Floyd to torture people. They want co-operative, docile prisoners, not insanely detached ones who don't care whether they live or die. And if I were a soldier, I think I might choose Pink Floyd for battle if I wanted help in letting myself be killed, rather than help to survive. It is clear that the music itself, whatever one chooses, carries a total message about how to be . . . or not to be, if that is the question. And for Pink Floyd, that is certainly the question. I would not be surprised if this is among the most frequently chosen suicide music.

So the point is that perception can squelch imagination and conceptual thought, but either of the other two can also trump its rivals, under the right conditions. So you have these three main choices about how to be, if you choose to be at all: imagine, perceive, think. It's like your own private game of rock, paper, scissors. Clearly perception is your rock, conception is your scissors, and imagination is your paper. But I never understood how "paper covers rock" was really a victory. I mean, rocks can shred paper as easily as they shatter scissors, right? Metallica is "rock" music, and I don't think or imagine very much when I hear it. Perhaps "paper covers rock" depends on what is written on the paper. If it's the lyrics to "Eclipse" with a little prism against a black background, be careful. The rock is still under the paper, and it's waiting there to blunt your scissors if you try to think too much about the words.

All You Distrust

It is not an accident that those who follow Floyd also follow a common pattern. We turn down the lights and we turn up the volume. We turn it up until the inner world has no choice but to follow wherever the music may lead. *Dark Side of the Moon* is one of the greatest collaborative works of art of the twentieth century. Part of the reason is that it forms an aesthetic whole, a total experience that puts us in a place of externally induced inner silence for forty-three minutes, a sort of comfortable numbness. There are many artworks that can accomplish the same end of creating a "whole experience," from Beethoven symphonies to Tarantino movies, which can hold us affixed to something external for long periods of time. Not all such experiences have the same effect. Some really get us going, but Pink Floyd does the opposite. It mellows us or paralyzes us.

All such experiences have external control, perception over imagination and thought, but clearly the external control is only one facet of the work of art. We can also silence our inner lives for hours on end watching television, and there is nothing "great" about that. Yet, the vortex of attention is exploited by artists of all sorts, good ones and bad ones, in order, presumably, to show us something meaningful or beautiful or perhaps even educational or profitable. Artists use a thousand devices to get our attention, and then we expect some pay-off for having given ourselves over to their external control—for having trusted them with not only our time and our senses, but with our free will. We make ourselves vulnerable to artists when we allow them to take control of us, to offer their creations as possible objects of our attention. This is a way of opening the doorway to the soul, and hoping that something worthwhile will come through it. And some of us want the trap-door as well, those of us who truly live for aesthetic experiences (that includes every good musician and many music fans).

In a sense, I would say that a chef more than a musician is the ultimate artist in this way, because not only does a chef convince us to give away our time, our attention, and our senses, but in this case we actually consent to put the artwork into our bodies and have it become a part of our own physical being. This is an astonishing act of trust, when you think about it. But the music we hear and the sights we see become part of our bodies and part of our memories also. There is no going back once you have seen or heard something—you cannot "unsee" or "unhear" it (remember that the next time you pass by an automobile accident, or have the urge to say "I hate you" to someone you love).

When it comes to experiencing artworks, we reserve a special level of attention, and with it a heightened level of vulnerability to what we will experience, and so there is a special kind of trust involved. For that reason, music requires us to expose ourselves. Do you trust Gilmour and Waters? Would you want your daughter to date them? Yet, we are so very vulnerable and they are so very seductively good. Yes, we trust them. What can we say? We like living dangerously, don't we? What if the dam breaks open many years too soon, like, when we're twenty-one?

Everyone You Meet

In what I have said up to now, I have been drawing on a theory by the French philosopher Jean-Paul Sartre (1908–1980), so you should probably meet him. He's dead of course, so you'll have to settle for meeting his theory. But I don't want to weigh you down with a bunch of crap that would be boring, and yet, I do need to be a little more explicit about what is going down here.

Nearly everything I have been doing to your head is called "phenomenology," which is a pretty sassy method of doing philosophy. There are different ways of doing phenomenology, and some of them are, well, a trip. Sartre frankly makes my head explode with dark forebodings, takes my thoughts where they didn't intend to go, sort of the way Pink Floyd takes my imagination through unforeseen trap-doors. This is not to say that Sartre is cooler than Pink Floyd, but I have a feeling the boys in the band may have read some Sartre along the way. I'm not fishing for a compliment, but if you kind of dig what's been happening up to now, you could check out some of the books I've been using. Here is the obligatory footnote.[3]

I can't tell you much about Sartre here, but I can give you a sense of the dude. He was a hero of the French resistance in World War II, a controversial radical all his life, and he could really write. They gave him a Nobel Prize for literature, but he told the Swedish Academy to stick their prize where the sun doesn't . . . race around to come up your behind, if you get my drift. I admit I think it is kind of groovy to turn down a Nobel Prize. I mean, I would accept the prize, and I have nothing against the Swedish Academy, but it takes some serious balls to say "your prize is bullshit" when it's that prize. I repeat, I would take it, in case any members of the Academy are reading this . . . I haven't earned it, but I don't want to lose my shot just in case the Academy likes PF.

I brought this up before, but now I'm back to it. Sartre said (and I think he was right) that when we form an image, whether visual or auditory or olfactory or kinesthetic or some combination, we simultaneously "believe" something about the image we form. You can't form an image without believing something. I think that is damned interesting—I finally understand why I clapped my hands when Tinker Bell was dying in Peter Pan. I do believe in faeries, I do, I do. At least I did. You clapped your hands too, asshole, so stop trying to be so grave about everything just to seem so all-fired laid back. You didn't kill Tinker Bell. I'll bet Syd Barrett didn't clap. So Sartre calls this belief thing the "positional act" of consciousness. In a sense, we "believe" an image into existence. But before we get to what we believe, I need to tell you something kind of freaky.

Sartre thinks that images are not something in your consciousness, the images *are* your consciousness. When you pay

---

[3] Primarily I am using Sartre's *The Psychology of Imagination*. This was first published (in French of course) in 1940, and a lot of stuff has been learned about how the brain creates images since then, but I think the core of Sartre's theory is still intact. Also check out *Imagination: A Psychological Critique*. This is far less exciting and was written three years earlier when Sartre was figuring out what was wrong with everyone else's theories. For a really wild ride see Sartre's novel *Nausea*, which is frankly a lot like listening to *Wish You Were Here*, and the protagonist, Roquentin, reminds me of that dude who is on fire on the cover.

attention to something, steal a piece of the world for yourself, it isn't the thing outside your body (like a tree or a Pink Floyd song on the sound system) that has your attention, it is your own imaginative activity you are paying attention to. This isn't hard to understand when you think about it. Trees are made of, like, cellulose and water. When you see a tree (that is, perceive it), it's not as if actual cellulose is flying through the air and entering your body. "No," you say, "light is entering the body." Yes, but not the same light that's over there bouncing off the cellulose. The little photons are communicating with each other and sending a certain wave-particle pattern your way, and it affects your body, but the light isn't exactly entering your body either; it has to be changed. Your body turns the energy in the photons into nerve impulses and electrochemical reactions. Your image (apparently) comes from those reactions, not directly from cellulose or light.

The same is true for sound. You are not hearing the record or the CD or even the band at the Pink Floyd show. Sound waves are getting turned into electrochemical reactions by your body. But here is where things get freaky. How the hell, pray tell, do a bunch of electrochemical reactions inside your body create an image that refers to just that song, or just that tree? They're just ordered reactions, and they are yours, not the world's. And they may serve to generate the image, but the image you are paying attention to is not made of electro-chemicals—at least its meaning is not, and I see no reason to think the image itself is "made of" those. Even if it is, you don't have to study body chemistry to understand your images, so I don't see how it helps anything to say that my visual tree image is made of such and such a reaction, while my auditory image of the PF show is made of this other reaction, and so on. I mean, BFD.

When I say Pink Floyd is spacey, I'm not trying to say "I prefer this collection of electro-chemical reactions to the ones I call KC and the Sunshine Band." There is a lot more to images than electro-chemical body processes. It has been a bit of a mystery among philosophers for quite a while as to how the images in my consciousness have meaning and reference to things like trees and rock bands, to which they have only the vaguest similarity in physical structure. So how do the images do that?

Sartre thinks it doesn't make much difference, ultimately, how we answer that question, since our answer can only be probable at best. But there is something we can know with absolute certainty, he claims: that we are paying attention, in every case, to the image, directly, not to the tree or the band. In fact the image just is our consciousness. Screw the perceived object, we'll never know exactly what it is, and we don't really care about it. We want our daisy-chain of images, and as long as we get them, we can pretty much tell the cold cruel world to go piss off. And Sartre says we can know everything there is to know about the images we make because, well, we made them. There isn't one thing in your image, even of a perceived object outside you, that you didn't put into it yourself.

The down side of this is that you can't learn anything you didn't already know from an image. The up side is that you can be certain about the image itself. That isn't much of a victory in the land of knowledge (I mean, so what? We do know what we know, at least when we know it well enough to create it), but it is your very own creation. Your images are your special gift to yourself that no one else can give you (never mind that you stole them from the world). You might as well be proud of your little images, since no one else will be, and they contain all you know (which isn't very much or very interesting in the grand scheme of things, as Waters and Gilmour constantly remind us).

All that You Give

So let's say you and I are listening to *Dark Side of the Moon*, with the lights low and the volume high. In one sense, we're listening to the "same" album, even though the sound waves hitting your ear drums are not precisely the same individual waves that are hitting mine. I'm over here and you're over there. The waves have the same form, almost. I mean, the acoustics may be better where you are sitting, worse where I am sitting (because you stole the best seat, which makes you an asshole in my book), and the shape of the room affects the sound waves. But even if the sound waves were utterly indistinguishable, you and I would still be hearing different music, even if we are stealing from the same sonic cookie jar.

Let me make it more concrete. I happen to be a musician, and let's say for argument's sake that you're not (because I want to feel superior to you, to punish you for taking the seat I wanted, and I'm writing this and you're merely reading it, so

I get to decide). When I listen to "Brain Damage," I attend to all kinds of things you probably don't even notice. (Now imagine the spooky laughter from "Brain Damage"; I'm doing that.) We bring different histories into the room, different sets of expectations about music, different levels of physical sensitivity, and different powers of imagination. Okay, your images may be better in some ways, but I prefer my own auditory images.

So when my body and my consciousness go to work on the music, I give myself auditory images of a sort that are certainly different from those you give yourself, and they may even be radically different. And we can both vary the ways we make the images, even in the presence of the "same" sound waves. I can approach "Brain Damage" in a spirit of resignation, if I want to; then, with an act of will, I can move to a feeling of strong resolve not to let the bastards rearrange me till I'm sane. When I shift from one way of giving myself the images to the other, the auditory image I am creating for myself shifts accordingly.

I also hear the bass line first and foremost because I happen to be a bass player, and I can construct my image of the total sound from that starting point, and I usually do (although not with Pink Floyd because the bass lines are boring and monotonous, but that is intentional on their part, of course). So perhaps I start from the keyboard sounds and work my way out in constructing the aural image. If you are not a musician, you may not have these options for building your own aural image, but you may have other choices that I do not have (and would not want of course). We both have habits in the way we make our images, but we also have options—spontaneity again, freedom.

All You Destroy

So what? Well, here is the key to how Pink Floyd took me, and probably you, through the trap-door and out into the abyss. In order to construct your imaginative consciousness, you have to, in Sartre's terms annihilate the world of perception. So all those sounds hitting your ears are getting whacked, and your body is substituting a different electrochemical type of order for the sonic order. Now, electrochemical reactions work differently from sound waves. This difference is far more complicated than the reduction of sound waves to electrical impulses like your telephone does. The point is that you use the stuff going on inside your own body as an "analogue" to what's going on in the perceptual world, to use Sartre's word.

That's right. Your body is a sort of short-delay analogue playback unit. It does not take long to convert perceptual energies into the stuff you make your consciousness with, but it isn't instantaneous. There is a slight delay.

And do you know what is happening during that delay? You are annihilating the perceptual world. Perceptual energies are like the specimens that crime labs have to destroy in order to analyze them. You can't really use photons and sound waves without destroying them in the process. You destroy what you are physically hearing in order to imagine it just afterwards, and you are paying attention not to the stuff you hear, but to the stuff you created to replace the stuff you heard.

Nobody knows what consciousness is "made of" although it seems to be some sort of subtle arrangement of energies that, as far as we know, only exists on the back of electrochemical brain and nerve activity. But that energy is so very subtle and so highly ordered that it might even be subject to quantum weirdness—for example, consciousness might be able to travel more quickly than the speed of light, and might affect things in the universe without any measurable space-time relation. There's no good evidence for saying consciousness is just physical energy, in the way we currently understand the word "physical," only that as far as we know, it doesn't occur without physical energy. Maybe it can, but we don't have any convincing evidence that it does.

But here is the point: your body is a weapon of mass destruction, and the stuff it is hell bent on destroying is all the types of stuff you perceive. It's like a massive invasion of the body-snatchers, as you suck up Pink Floyd sounds and turn them into, well, some very subtle stuff that you then pay attention to. And there is not one thing you pay attention to that you didn't snatch, destroy, and substitute.

While Sartre was ticking away the hours that make up a dull day, he wondered about something that never would have occurred to me. He asked himself, "well, Jean-Paul [this is how he addressed himself when he was thinking], how do we carry out this act of annihilation? Is it just one way, or are there several?" Damned if he didn't come up with an answer, which is part of the reason he got famous enough to turn down a Nobel Prize. This is how he puts it:

The image also includes an act of belief, or a positional act. The act can assume four forms and no more: (1) it can posit the object as non-existent, (2) or as absent, (3) or as existing elsewhere; it can also (4) "neutralize" itself, that is, not posit its object as existing.[4]

This is fairly tricky, but it's the whole key to the Pink Floyd trap-door. One of the bizarre things about images is that the perceptual object does not have to be present for you to make one. You can hear "Brain Damage" without the sound waves, basically because you have heard the song before and you carried out the required destruction, and made the substitute, and you still have the substitute, implanted in your body-memory. If you haven't heard the song, you cannot imagine it. But having heard it once, the image pattern you gave yourself then is all yours. The more you repeat the action of destroying and substituting, the easier it is to recreate it when the song is not playing.

So the destruction of the perceptual energies needs to happen at least once, but—and pay close attention here because things are about to get even creepier—after that your imagination can do the work of bringing the image up with any perceptual information at all, even just the energies inside your living body, which you also perceive. Once you have the pattern, you can make the image of the song out of anything you happen to be perceiving. That's because the song you paid attention to was never "the song," itself, but your own imaginative creation, done in the presence of the song. You are a very resourceful little cuss, if I do say myself, using your own digestive processes, for example, as material for singing Pink Floyd songs in your head. All that you eat . . . can become Pink Floyd songs.

The constant in all this is that you are still destroying stuff in order to make other stuff to pay attention to. And you can destroy it in exactly four ways, Sartre says. I am not sure I buy the claim that there are exactly and only four ways to demolish my perceptual experience, but we won't go into that. Sartre was smarter than I am and certainly smarter than you are, reading your Pink Floyd book with your oh-so-damaged brain cells, so we'll just trust him for now. What are these four destructive acts in which you are constantly engaged? Let me move by concrete example.

---

[4] Sartre, *The Psychology of Imagination*, p. 16. I added the numbering.

The Sun Is Eclipsed by the Moon

First, turn the page back and look at the "four possibilities" again from the Sartre quote. You are not listening to "Brain Damage" at the moment, but now imagine it anyway. The sound waves are not here, but the song exists, right? So it isn't annihilation number (1). You are not saying to yourself "this doesn't exist." We will return in a minute to number (1).

So is the song just absent (2), or is it definitely elsewhere right now (3)? What do you believe about it when you imagine it? The song is almost surely playing somewhere right now (that must be weird for the boys in the band, to know that somewhere on Earth all the songs on *Dark Side of the Moon* are probably playing, 24/7/365). But that wasn't relevant to you when you formed your belief about it just now. You weren't thinking about that. It wasn't number (3) when you made the image, although now it may be (3), since I suggested that you think about the song as perpetually playing elsewhere. But that is not what you believed a minute ago when you gave yourself the image.

As far as we can tell, you have to believe one of the four Sartre gives us, and only one, in order to imagine something. Imagination will not occur unless you believe something, and it is your belief, your "positional act" that annihilates the perceptual stuff and substitutes the image. So in this case, a good candidate is that you "believed" the song simply to be absent, which is to say it could be present, but just doesn't happen to be. So you annihilated, let's say, your digestive energies and the light in the room (you need some stuff to annihilate, but anything will do) in the mode of "absent."

In the case of a song that exists in many, many recorded examples, this is an obvious way to do it. It's just contingently absent, I believe, and in so believing, I orient myself negatively in the world, and take a shredder to my perceptions, and make the auditory image of the song. But in the case of making an image of a loved one who is alive (as far as you know), but not present at the moment, in order to think of her, you will annihilate your perceptions (perhaps, say, the pain in your left big toe, and the way the room smells) in the mode of number (3): "I believe her to be somewhere else," and presto, an image of your darling (with only a trace of foot odor left over; maybe you should have used other material for this precious image).

As you can quickly see, there is a world of difference between imagining a loved one who is believed to be elsewhere, number (3), and imaging a loved one who is dead—doesn't exist, number (1). You will not want to imagine a loved one whom you hope is alive (although you don't really know) in mode (1). That would disturb you. Allowing yourself to believe your beloved is dead in order to imagine her is dangerous stuff, and you will be superstitious about doing it. And you will choose number (2), absent, when she is in another room, and number (3), elsewhere, when she is far enough away as to require some time to bring her to your presence. Number (1) is, then, dangerous and disturbing. You only use number (1) when you are cornered. Most people prefer number (3), elsewhere, for their chosen belief about even the dead (whether elsewhere is heaven or hell seems to depend upon other judgments). But number (1) is quite a commitment, and commitment is scary.

Number (4) is odd. It is the mode we use when we need to believe something, but we can't decide whether it is (1), (2), or (3), and we still want the image. Sometimes when I hear a melody in my head, I don't know whether I have made it up myself or heard it somewhere else. Obviously it isn't number (1), since the damned thing exists in my head, and potentially in the air if I hum it out loud. But whether it is merely absent or elsewhere, I can't decide, so I let go for a moment and believe it in the neutral mode, which is kind of a meta-mode or a meta-belief; it gives me some place to hang out while I shuffle through the other three ways of destroying and replacing my perceptual world with something I find more interesting. Then I can have my image and eat it too, so to speak.

Okay, you're almost to the end, but you may not want to read further. Once you have, you won't ever be able to unthink the thought you're about to have. Don't say I didn't warn you, which is more courtesy than Gilmour and Waters showed to me. Here is the trap door.

Sartre said freedom is the most terrible thing we all face, because in the face of it we cannot escape responsibility for what we are. You are actually completely free to choose what to believe about not only the images you create in the absence of the object you are imagining, like the song "Brain Damage" that isn't playing at the moment. You can, if you choose, nullify, in any of the four modes, the objects that are present in your perception. You can believe that something right in front of you doesn't really exist, or is absent even though it seems present, or is elsewhere even though it seems to be here.

So let's say you are feeling really detached from your loved one. She can be sitting right in front of you, and you can still make her absent, elsewhere, or even non-existent—in other words, dead to you. People do this to each other all the time. It is this act that, when done from an attitude of cruelty, makes murder and slavery, and rape possible. You pretty much have to negate another person who is right in front of you, and do so selfishly and in defiance of your own perceptions, and self-satisfied with your own imagined substitution, in order to behave so monstrously. Or you may just subtly negate that other person, because she is gay, or black, or poor, or anything else you happen smugly to think justifies your little triumph over her. You say, "to me, you are absent," or "you might as well be elsewhere, because you are to me," or, "to me you don't exist at all, you are nothing."

But Pink Floyd doesn't do this and doesn't teach this and doesn't approve of it. Some music does, but not Pink Floyd. Because our heroes discovered that, when something is right in front of us, the beloved and anyone and anything, we can still refuse to believe any of these three negations, and just detach ourselves from any commitment about their existence at all. Perhaps you now see where this is going. We may say "I just don't have to decide about you, my love—whether you're absent, or elsewhere, or nothing at all; I am neutral about you."

There are many other committed but subtle attitudes we can adopt when we annihilate the presence of those we love and replace them with whatever we may desire or wish or will. Many of these annihilations are utterly benevolent—to see, for example, not the person your true love is, but who she most ardently wants to be, who she is trying to become. That requires a benevolent negation of her faults—not the ones that bother us, but the ones that bother her about herself. To imagine our loved ones in this way is a kind of encouragement, a kind of unselfish gift. These benevolent ways of imagining others are all quite familiar and concrete.

But Pink Floyd makes almost no use of these familiar attitudes of annihilation, in either their benevolent or the malevolent forms. They wish us neither ill nor well. It is not so much that they miss us, or love us, or hate us. Instead they use the neutral, uncommitted mode, number (4), to show us two rather disturbing things: (1) that it doesn't really matter which attitude or type of belief you choose, because as long as you have the option of neutrality, all the others really amount to the same thing; (2) the person you most destroy in annihilating your world is not others, it's yourself. You are condemned to destroy the world and yourself, and only free in how you choose to do it. You are still responsible for your choice no matter how you try to wriggle out of it, so why bother to choose?

There is no "better" or "more authentic" way to destroy yourself and create an illusion to believe in. And it makes no difference whether you see yourself as not really existing at all, as absent for a time, or as displaced; in the end you cannot really escape neutrality except by lying to yourself. The lunatic is in your head and he's not you, and no one else is you either. I didn't want to become aware of this "neutral" option, at twenty-one or now, and the only safety one can find is to flee into the three conventional modes of annihilation, and to try to use them benevolently. It may be a lie, but it's a useful one. Neutrality is very, very dangerous.

Isn't it amazing that music can be created that draws you, entirely without malice, inexorably, but by your own act of believing, straight into the abyss of meaninglessness? Now go listen to "Brain Damage" again and pay attention to what it really does to you. It neutralizes you, all the way down into the nothing that you are.

But it's your turn now. The sun is coming up and I've been dwelling in darkness long enough. I'm going to have a cigarette and a cup of coffee and see what images I can make from those. See you on the dark side of the moon, if I want to.

---

[5] I want to thank my friends, Jan Olof Bengtsson and Cory Powell for conversations that helped me think through this stuff and improve it.

B SIDE

Born in the
USA

9
A Touch of Grey: Gratefully Dead?

Tuning Up

DALE: Jerry had a diabetic coma, he came close to dying a couple of times and the Dead Heads were like "oh no, he's not gonna die." When he did die, I wasn't expecting anything like that, I'd just seen him. And I figured they'd go on, and even when he died I figured, well, what are they gonna do? Are they gonna go on? Where are the Dead Heads gonna go?

ROBBIE: They were adrift for a while I do believe.

CORY: I never saw the Grateful Dead . . . I always wished I'd lived in the Sixties, it's pretty much the best you're gonna see, even going to see a pseudo-Grateful Dead show. . . . But really the kids that do that, no matter what machine is making money off that, they're gonna find somewhere that they can go and gather, and be together, and do what it is they do and experiment and socialize.

ROBBIE: There were a lot of hangers-out, you know, back in the day, like now, only more so. Some of them had indeterminate functions, if you know what I'm saying.

Live Dead

So here's the thing. I couldn't help being intrigued when, after a stint as The Other Ones, the band started touring again as just The Dead. No longer Grateful? Jerry was gone (and Pigpen, and Keith, and Brent). It set me to thinking when

161

Jerry died. It set a lot of us to thinking, even those who normally don't, and even a few who no longer can. I saw some of my Deadhead friends who hadn't had a thought in years suddenly entertain one, handling ideas like those gorillas handled that Samsonite luggage on the old TV commercial (poor Samson, after Delilah and that haircut, and the jawbone and all those Philistines, now he's reduced to a proper adjective for ugly plastic luggage, but I digress[1]). So I had friends who were way past thinking, even primate thoughts, so they just had to whistle through their teeth and spit. Something was over. The shoe was on the hand that fits, and that's all there really was to it, as the poet said.[2]

But I'm not much of a poet. I want to think about this. Hopefully I'm not past doing that much. I read a lot of shit about death and life after it, and it occurs to me that if you want proof of life after death, look around you. Most of the people you know, among the "living," are probably good evidence that life after death really happens. There was this story about the Buddha. A woman whose child died makes a long journey to seek out the Enlightened One. On finding him she throws herself at his feet, "Master my child is dead. I have heard that you have the power to bring the dead back to life. I beg of you, please restore my child." The Buddha looks upon her with compassion. "I will restore your child to you, but first you must do something for me." The mother says she will do anything. "Return to your village and bring back to me a person who has never known pain like yours." The mother quickly agrees and rushes off toward her village. A disciple says "Master, when she returns, will you really restore her child?" The Buddha says, "she will not return."

And there you have it, the First Noble Truth: Life sucks. It truly blows. Not just a little bit either. You want life after death? Well, let me put it this way: if that woman came knocking on your door, would you be joining her for the return trip? If so, just wait. Just mark time and have a fatty. Your time is coming. And,

---

[1] What seems like a digression in music can become your main riff.

[2] The poet is Robert Hunter, of course. I hope he won't mind my weave of his lyrics with what I have to say. Apparently Jerry Garcia wrote the line in "A Touch of Grey" that said "Light a candle, curse the glare." One is tempted to see Hunter and Garcia together as one poet.

as the poet said, "you will get by, you will survive"—until you don't. The poet's other half didn't. He's gone. Sort of.

Sound Check

Robbie: We used to hire bass players if they got a new Jazz Bass and a Fender amp, it's like "You're in, it doesn't matter, you're in, baby."

Cory: There's that unwritten rule—do it to the grave.

The Epistemic Bassist

Philosophers have "epistemic principles." They like fancy words for simple things to make them sound smart. The first epistemic principle was invented by the first father whose four-year-old kid discovered the meaning of the word "why." After about six patient answers to the repeated question "why," he said to the seventh "because I say so." Presto, epistemic principle: I know what I know because I just know it. Philosophers have managed to turn this simple answer into a formula they call "justified true belief," and they have some explanations of it that are longer than any jam by the Dead, but it comes down to a single riff in the end. "Because I say so . . . and I'm so very smart and you're so very stoned." I need a principle for my little creation here, and I don't like "justified true belief," so I will state my own, without the nuances: I trust Phil. Not because he shares a name with a disciple and a groundhog. Not because his name means "brotherly love." I trust Phil because he plays the bass, and he is very smart.

Now there are lots of types of "smart." There is the visceral smart of Pigpen, just somehow knows what to play, can make up lyrics on the spot; there is Jerry's utterly frenetic genius, which defies description; there is Billy's and Mickey's grinding groove; Bobby's way of matching the chords to the groove with razor thin response time. These are all kinds of smart, and not just in music. If you look around you, you'll find co-workers and classmates who do the same things in their lives that these fellows have done on stage.

Then there is Phil. Phil sees the Whole. Nay, Phil creates the Whole from its parts. It's a fact that bass players are the true masters of the whole sound. They have to be both musically and rhythmically astute, but most of all they have to hear what everyone else is doing and weave it into one sound. Bass players share a secret fellowship, a sort of *gnosis* peculiar to their breed, a kind of smart that is hard for others to recognize or understand: the art of the whole sound. Bass players don't actually believe in musical epistemology, they are practitioners of musical metaphysics. More on metaphysics later.

The story of Phil's induction into the band is a case in point, how the bass player creates the whole sound. In 1965, The Warlocks were a hot band, but the guy on bass could not cut it, as Jerry said to Phil "we have to tell him what notes to play." Jerry continued "I know you're a musician—you can pick up this instrument so easy" (Phil Lesh, *Searching for the Sound: My Life with the Grateful Dead*, p. 46). What Jerry knew (and Jerry knew so many things) was that Phil heard the whole, grasped it, understood it. The fact that Phil had never touched a bass guitar was irrelevant. Like Jerry, I know a bass player when I see one too, whether he actually plays bass or not. It isn't as mystical as it sounds. It's a way of seeing and a way of hearing the world—in relation. It isn't hard to recognize if you know what to look for.

Phil writes a book like he plays, like a bass player. A linear narrative adapted to the whole that it will finally become. There are controversies about many events in the career of The Dead, but even if everything else reported by others is sincere and true from its own perspective, in all disputed matters you should still trust Phil. He knows enough to remain silent where nothing ought to be said, just as he knows what notes not to play. And he knows how to say what he does say in the warm light of the Whole. So Phil is my epistemic principle because he is the maker of Dead metaphysics. I know what I know because I hear it with my own ears, but most of all, because Phil says so. If you don't trust Phil, go read another essay. This one will just piss you off. But I have two more reasons for trusting Phil. I'll save those for later.

First Set: Acoustic

DALE: Death is final to me. . . . It's a very nice thought, and hope, that there's a reward at the end of everything. Gives you something to look forward to, something to keep you in a straight line. . . . But I think that we created God. It gives us somebody to blame, somebody to go to when we're in despair and hurt.

ROBBIE: I have the more Buddhist view, that the ego is in fact demolished, that your sense of self, there's no such thing once the big black nothingness comes, so you're not aware of it. There's nothing to fear other than cashing out too soon, the effect it might have on those left behind. I do think that the universal spirit well, where all souls conglomerate and are regenerated. . . . there's no energy created or wasted, it just changes, that holds true throughout all known creation. They say that the human body at the instant of death, lightens by twenty-one grams, I don't know, but possibly that's the spirit essence. All religions have some basis like that. But I do think that modern ethics and morality have been devised over time by man to help control man, because man is only this far above the animal. Man is a dangerous creature because now he's got technology, but barely has control of his bestial instinct. That's why we see the world is in the shape it's in today.

CORY: I wouldn't mind reincarnation. I don't want to remember being me exactly, but I wouldn't mind living again having some sort of sense of the way I was. To learn from my past and be an old soul, I would like that. . . . It's a damned romantic idea.

ROBBIE: Still, when I go to bed at night I say an Our Father, because it's expedient. The jury is completely out as far as I'm concerned on religion.

DALE: I haven't been to confession in a long time, not looking forward to that. I have had many pure thoughts today, though.

Immortality: **Not that Cool**

Philosophers, real people, and probably gorillas with luggage, have been wondering about whether we really die when we die for as long as there has been luggage (which predates Samson, and even Nimrod, but maybe not all the "mighty men of old"[3]). When Pigpen died in 1973, Jerry said "That mother-

---

[3] And there is some totally wild shit in Genesis 6. I can't resist; I tried and failed. You have to check this out, Genesis 6:1–4: "When men began to multiply on the face of the land and daughters were born to them, the sons of God saw that the daughters of men were so fair. And they took as their wives any

fucker—now he knows" (Lesh, *Searching for the Sound*, p. 213). Socrates, who looked a lot like Jerry, was condemned to death for riffing with the boys when the rich folks were trying to sleep (or some other trumped up charge), and so if you can picture this, there he is, sitting around with a couple of those guys, Simias and Cebes, and those two are bitching and whining about his impending demise. The dialogue Plato wrote about this is called *Phaedo*, nevermind why. And they are freaked out that Socrates is there with them today, but tomorrow he won't be, so they discuss all the theories people have about whether we survive death in some way or another.

There are reincarnation theories and immortal soul theories and what not, but it kind of comes down to whether there is something eternal about us, some essence-of-you that pre-exists your earthly life and that's why it has a shot at post-existing it. I know this is kind of strange, but go with me for a minute here.

You're sitting there thinking, "Well, sure, I didn't always exist, but I'm sort of hoping I always will from now on." And Socrates is saying "you are so screwed, dude, if you're thinking that." Any idiot can see that if you got created at some point, and that's all you are, the stuff that got created, you are going to be in a world of hurt trying to convince yourself that lasts forever. I mean, let's say you think you started when your parents did the nasty (I know you don't want to think about that—man, I hope you don't—I mean, I don't even want to think about your parents doing it, let alone think about you thinking about that;

---

they chose. Then the LORD said, 'My Spirit shall not abide in man forever, for he is flesh: his days shall be 120 years.' The Nephilim were on the earth in those days, and also afterward, when the sons of God came in to the daughters of men and they bore children to them. These were the mighty men who were of old, the men of renown." I don't know what was going on here, but anyone can see that this is about the limits of our time on earth, and that works with what I'm saying in this essay. You've got a situation where the "sons of God" are getting it on with "the daughters of men" because they are such righteous babes, and it's looking like the Summer of Love or Woodstock around there, all to the music of a band called The Nephilim, and nobody even knows who they were. I wonder why I've never heard a sermon about Genesis 6. Let this little piece of prose be my sermon on Genesis 6. We'll see if anyone answers the altar call. Didn't the Nephilim play Woodstock? Or the Grateful Nephilim? CSN&Y: Crosby, Stills, Nephilim and Young? I honestly can't remember.

just chill for a minute, this is going somewhere, I swear). So, you were nowhere at all before that unthinkable night when they did dirty deed, right? And so, what, pray tell, do you think is going to outlast the final passage of protoplasm to dust? Do you honestly think your folks getting their (much younger) rocks off is of eternal significance? Did they create your soul? Do they have such power? Do you? Come on. You just won the Sperm & Egg State Lottery. No, dude, you're going to have to come up with an answer as to where you were before the nasty night, or you're toast in the long run. If your folks created your soul, or if you don't have one, you're history when you die. That's Socrates's point to his friends with the funny names (better than "Pigpen" though).

So let's say you think God created you. I know you don't think that, because if you did, you'd be reading *Mel Gibson's Passion and Philosophy* instead of sex, drugs, and the philosophy of rock. But I'm hoping there's just one person who reads this and seriously believes God created him or her, all special-like. (I am going to so totally fuck with your head if you think that.) So let's say, just for shits and giggles, God did it, God created your soul. So, that means God foresaw your entire pathetic existence—you, and me, and Pigpen, and Jerry, and that woman who never came back to collect on the Buddha's promise, and her child. I'm stealing a lick from a philosopher named David Hume here (see Hume, *Dialogues Concerning Natural Religion*. You've got two big problems at least, and my bottom dollar is riding on the odds that you can't solve them.

First, how much do you trust this God? If He couldn't do any better for you than what you've got now and what you're looking forward to from here, which is nothing less than the deaths of many you hold dear followed by your own, probably in great pain, despair and misery, and then the eventual destruction of all you hold dear, then either it's all a fairly cruel joke or this God of yours just can't do any better. I mean, how do you know He wouldn't pop you right back out of existence just as easy as He popped you in? Or maybe sustaining your existence just isn't a serious priority for Him, or maybe He's too busy or having a bad hair day? How do you know? Phil can't help you with this; he's just the bass player. I trust Phil, but God has some explaining to do.

Second, let's say your God exists outside of time, in eternity, whatever that is. How is an eternal being going to create something that exists in time, like your skinny ass? I mean, if you really existed in His mind from the beginning, and you always will exist in His mind, what are you doing down here? Wasn't it good enough to Be in eternity, as one of God's ideas (if not one of his better ones—I mean Gandhi and Mother Teresa and Jesus and Buddha were pretty good ideas God had, but you're not in the top ten-thousand, if you don't mind my pointing it out)? Wouldn't it be better to hang there, at God's eternal pad, than to be sent on a very bad beer run without enough money to get yourself back with the goods? Welcome to your life. This is the beer run. So are you being punished? Tested? I'm paraphrasing Hume here but the point is easy enough. Either your sorry existence among the living calls God's motives into question (in which case your immortality is looking pretty shaky, since you can't trust Him), or God can't do much better than to bring you into the universe whenever the planets align and your parents co-operate, and even then He may not be able to hold onto you forever, for all you know. This is what philosophers call "the problem of evil," and what I just laid on you is called an "inconsistent triad." Here it is in "philosophese."

Not all of the following can be simultaneously true:

1. God is all-powerful.

2. God is perfectly good.

3. Evil exists.

Take your pick, but at most you can have two of these. They might all be wrong, but for my money, door number three is pretty hard to resist. I've seen what's behind door number three. So have you, or you will soon enough. That was Buddha's point about Life sucking. It may be part of the reason he doesn't talk about God. It's also part of the reason he didn't think it would be all that good if you live forever, and what's even sadder is for you to deceive yourself into thinking you want that, immortal life. Buddha says that you really don't want to develop a case of the immortality munchies, because that sort of hankering could get your ass reincarnated, and then you're stuck here all over again. The Enlightened One called this the cycles of "samsara," not to be confused with Samsonite, although they really aren't that different. Think of samsara as bad luggage, sort of an ugly yellow color, and your whole essence is inside the luggage, and there are gorillas tossing you around, and then they finally wreck the suitcase and you get out. Then you stupidly think: "Wish I had another piece of luggage to get into." And the wish is all that even holds you in existence. Just say no, dude. This is a very bad trip. And like an idiot, you keep on wishing, and then you get into another piece of Samsonite, and you do it over and over because you just can't learn your lesson. That's the immortality munchies, and if you didn't already have a raging case of them, you wouldn't be here now. And unlike the baggage handlers at O'Hare, the gorillas never go on strike.[4] That's Buddha's Second Noble Truth, which is called the Cycles of Samsara, or in my terms, the Samsonite Scenario.

Phil talks about how Billy used to get the munchies. They'd be on their way home from a gig and Billy would "drum irrepressibly on my shoulder as he sat behind me in Jerry's car, while chanting 'Red Rab-bit, Red Rab-bit!' the name of an Automat-style food kiosk we'd always hit . . ." (Lesh, *Searching for the Sound*, p. 60). I see no serious problem with the actual munchies. It's such a small part of the bigger problem, but a lot of Buddhists decide to try fasting just to make sure things don't get out of hand with the Red Rabbit thing. But Buddha liked to eat well enough, so go on to the automat and don't worry about that.

So you've got two of the wisest people who ever lived, Socrates and Buddha, telling you that death is a release from your Samsonite Scenario, something to be welcomed, not dreaded, and their advice is "okay, you're free, so don't screw it up and come back." But that's not quite Phil's advice, and I trust Phil. Socrates and Buddha didn't play the bass.

---

[4] I wonder how the baggage handlers' union felt about that old Samsonite commercial with the gorillas. I also wonder how Diane Fosse felt about it. I admit that I bought the luggage, but I got it used at a garage sale. There was nothing inside. That would have made the Buddha happy. But gorillas are going to be harmed in this essay. I love and respect and revere gorillas, I prefer them to human company, so please don't rag on me for the way I'm going to use them as a metaphor. It's just a metaphor, okay?

Second Set: Twin Lead Guitars

CORY: Ever since the whole thing began, people have been trying to describe it, trying to communicate what it is that's in their head, and nobody can do it. People have been trying and people will continue to try . . . to describe the Dead experience, to describe the way they feel, how it is that Brent's keyboards sounded that night, and exactly what it is, you know man . . . people try, and part of it is that they're too fucked up, part of it is that you can't grasp it.

ROBBIE: There's a certain level of mysticism to grounding in electronics. If you read a paper by the RANE Company on grounding, even those guys who are very good at what they do, have posited that there is some element of mysticism to ground problems and ground looping, you know, once again, Phil was an electronic music academic in his younger years . . . the sixty-cycle hum, it's found sound. Since we all went almost all digital, the nasty sixty-cycle hum is greatly reduced, but it comes out of old guitar amps a lot.

CORY: My sixty-cycle hum would be the past, it always comes back. Sometimes it comes back as a physical thing or a person who has an idea or something that they require you to address or absolve yourself for, and probably my fear of the present and the future becoming the past would be my sixty-cycle hum. And what I make out of it is that while I'm busy thinking about that and worrying about it, other stuff happens and the next thing becomes and occurs and it takes over just like that. . . . Karma, I don't think it's this thing that if you do something to me, that something is going to happen to you, because something or somebody knows that you did something to me and needs to happen to you. I think it's just a name for something that already was happening, because people notice whenever they feel bad about doing something, and something comes back to them very soon after that, well, karma got me there.

ROBBIE: Why do these old guys, like horrible dictators who collaborated with the Nazis or the Vichy government in France, and somehow they live to be ninety, but they go to their deaths shaking in their boots, 'cause they be worried. I often imagine those guys, like wow, that'd be scary. They never admitted it, but they know deep in their hearts that they were complicit in the deaths of, say, a lot of Jewish children or Argentinean dissenters or whatever. I believe there's a special place in hell for them.

An Everlasting Jam

So in case you are getting seriously bummed out, hold on. You may be grateful yet. In the Western world, we haven't really been able to heed the Buddha's advice. It is just so engrained in us that we must personally be of eternal significance that we keep trying to find ways around the Samsonite Scenario. So along comes this little dude named Immanuel Kant (1724–1804) and he is way smart. He figured out that you can't really know whether you have a soul that lives forever, but you can't quite help thinking you do. It's more than a suspicion in the back of your mind, it's something that if you don't think it might be true, you can't very well think about anything else. So you go on thinking you are Immortal, whether you want to or not. And you also think about two other things. Kant puts "God" and "Freedom" in the same three-piece jam band with "Immortality," that he calls The Postulates.[5] God is the drummer, Freedom plays lead, and Immortality is on bass, of course. And Kant is going to use Buddha's law of karma for some new and different advice.

Buddha's Third Noble Truth is the Law of Karma. This often gets expressed as the law of cause and effect, but that isn't quite right. Cause and effect is just something like, if you drink like Pigpen, don't be surprised when your liver gives out. That's not Buddha's point. It would be closer to say "what goes around comes around," but not necessarily in the ways you expect or understand. For Kant, while he doesn't use these exact words, karma comes down to the problem of "finitude," which means not knowing what you absolutely need to know in order to do things right. You don't know there's a God, you don't know if you are really free, and you don't know if your life has everlasting significance, but if you don't believe these things, life isn't really worth living. But life is worth living, and it doesn't have to totally suck. That's how The Postulates get their start.

---

[5] The two main works I am drawing on are Kant's *Critique of Practical Reason* and *The Groundwork of the Metaphysics of Morals*. This is not light reading, but it may be worth the effort.

Kant's point is that there should be a very cool band like that, even if there isn't one. I'll leave the drums and lead aside and just give you the bass line.

So why, Kant asks, would you think you want to live forever? Why is that so all-fired important to you? The answer is not "Well, life is pretty good, so I don't want it to end." Kant says that's not really it at all. When you are on the right path—and believe me, for Kant and for Buddha, the "right path" is the noble eight-fold path (which is Buddha's Fourth Noble Truth—it just has eight parts, more like Motown octet with back-up singers than a jam trio), when you're on it, you want to keep on doing what you're doing. It's the zone. It's a jam you don't ever want to end, because, just like Phil, you're learning how to play the bass as you're playing it. Here is what that's like, in Phil's words:

> After playing a wrong note, for instance, I would quickly resolve it to a proper note—but then I took to repeating my mistakes (a simple matter, since the music was built out of repeating modules or strophes [read, "Samsara"]) in order to resolve them differently each time. I soon began to see the dissonances caused by wrong notes, or right notes in the wrong place, as opportunities rather than liabilities—new ways to create tension and release, the lifeblood of music. (Lesh, *Searching for the Sound*, p. 53)

You don't need to get all worked up over the monotony of "repeating modules" if you see them as opportunities for creativity rather than as a drone of one damn life after another. The West has always looked to creativity for solace in the face of death. But here is Kant's point: once you figure out what Phil knows, you won't have any reason to want the music to end. You may suck at the bass now, but you will want to keep perfecting your technique, your understanding, and most of all, contributing your own bass line to God's sweet groove and Freedom's screaming lead. But for all the world it looks like the music is going to end and someone will have to pay the piper. So in your imagination you say, "no, I will play on forever, and I don't care if I ever get paid." That's Kant's bass line. You live as if it will never end. And hey, maybe it won't. Can't ever be sure.

Drum Solo

DALE: If I lived forever, I'd outlive all my friends, I'd outlive all my family members, I'd be waiting for the end. I don't think I would want to live forever, although I'm not in a hurry to die. We always want to go a little bit further, we don't want to end it and we hope that it won't, you know, I wouldn't want to, really, outlive my children. . . . It's very hard to let go. . . . The house isn't there anymore, that I grew up in, my folks, the people who raised me, all of that is gone. . . . I'd like to be very old when I go, that's what I want to die of, old age . . . Do I look for despair, do I look for hope? Sometimes the lights all shining on me, and other times I can barely see. I will get by, I will survive. . . Despite the despair you have to look forward and you have to keep going, you don't give up, or I don't. I can't just lay and wallow in sorrow and misery. It's always gonna be there and it's gonna bounce back around. . . . But you can't give up and you've gotta keep going. . . . there are other people who depend on me, and it's not just me. . . .

Four-String Metaphysics

So how does it work, I mean, how do you make up a bass line that doesn't suck? The first thing you have to remember is that it's not all about you, it's about other people too. Phil describes it like this:

> During the [Acid] Test itself [at the Fillmore West], the acoustic space of the hall was finely sculptured and very dense—it was very much a sonic "landscape," [this is your life, your chance to create] with solid objects here, open spaces there, paths of least resistance (for sound). One could wander from an area dominated by the Thunder Machine, traversing a space populated by disembodied voices carrying on so many simultaneous conversations (almost like being in Neal [Cassady]'s head) to a space in front of the stage where the music was pretty obviously being played by the band. However, the so-called nonmusical sounds from the other regions would come stealing in, sometimes masking the music being played. (*Searching for the Sound*, pp. 70–71)

That's your life, in a nutshell and seen as a whole, a serious Acid Test. You'll want to avoid the Thunder Machine most of the time, but it's always there, so you might as well get used to it. Your band is the people you know and live with and create with. The question is whether you're going to recognize the opportunities and do something worth doing amidst all the confusion. Phil goes on:

> These experiences set off some interesting trains of thought for me: Why couldn't noise, or speech, or sounds that weren't made up of a series of harmonics be part of musical thought, musical discourse, especially if used rhythmically? We had already begun experimenting with feedback . . . and one of our favorite tricks became fading down to a sixty-cycle hum (normally the bane of a musician's existence) and using that as our fundamental tone to generate harmonic music.

So Phil is saying, take a look at what you might have overlooked, even something you despise, and create around it—for example, death is a pretty atrocious sixty-cycle hum. Phil finishes the thought with a flourish:

> The main event at the Fillmore, however, was the manifestation of the group mind in a large crowd. For the first time, the physical, luminous, and sonic spaces were unified—the dancers moving, the musical sound breathing, the lights pulsing—as one being, limited only by the inscrutable laws of probability. At the end, after eternities of ecstatic ego loss, a voice was heard asking, "Who's in charge here?" (*Searching for the Sound*, p. 71)

Of course, it was a cop (not the Thunder Machine) who asked the question that brought ecstasy (which means getting outside yourself) to an end for this manifestation of the group mind— and the cops don't mean to be cosmic gorillas, but that's sort of their job. The gorillas always show up, say "get back in your own suitcase" and it's no big deal. They can bring time back to eternity, but they can't take eternity away from those who have been to that place. I mean, you were out of your suitcase, and with all the others who were out of theirs, and the gorillas can't take that away from you. And this is the second reason I trust Phil. He understands the relationship between space, time, light, eternity, mind, and body, all in terms of creative opportunities and the group mind. We enact these opportunities by acting together well, and we have to make up the rules as we go, before we can really even learn what they are (or what they were).

But there's a catch. Phil is not riffing to the same beat as I. Kant and The Postulates. The Postulates are not very open to creativity. They are at the mercy of whatever groove God lays down, and they stay inside the established harmonics, and inside their luggage. The Postulates don't like mistakes, and they don't see them as opportunities to make up new relationships. Mistakes are just bad (m'kay?) as far as they can see, and they are awfully afraid of dissonance. So they have lots of rules about how to play the God, Freedom and Immortality minuet and trio. The main rule is called the "Categorical Imperative," which says that you have to think of each and every act of yours as a sort of "law of action," and you have to be able to desire that each action could be a universal law, and if any dissonance (contradiction) shows up anywhere, you shouldn't do what you are doing. There isn't a lot of room for individual creativity when such rules are laid down, not much room for context and nuance, and so the group mind becomes more like the Borg than like the Acid Test. Phil doesn't do gigs with I. Kant and The Postulates—they look more like the gorillas than brothers and sisters.

I. Kant and The Postulates have had a lot of commercial success, plenty of platinum recordings, they get played on Fox News and all the Clear Channel stations. But every record has the same beat, and that beat numbs the senses after a while. As the poet said,

> I see you've got your list out, say your piece and get out
> Guess I get the gist of it, but it's alright
> Sorry that you feel that way, the only thing there is to say
> Every silver lining's got a touch of grey

Third Set: Getting a Little Looser

DALE: I'm not sure how many other people I've influenced in my life. I have children, and without me, they wouldn't exist, so that might . . . I'd like to think He had something, if there is a God. I haven't discovered a cure for cancer, or I haven't done any great thing in my life. I'm sure there's times, if He's up there. He shakes His head, but life is very valuable, all life, to me, and IF he created me, damned good idea.

CORY: I'm at a point with people and animals that I have to draw the line, so as not to allow myself to be taken advantage of.

ROBBIE: Getting your energy ripped off, that's what we used to call that.

DALE: Did I think Jerry was a God? Did I worship Jerry? Uh, yes, he was someone to follow, although we didn't know exactly what we were following. When he died, we were hoping that either Phil or Bobby or somebody would take the reins and we would have someone else to lead us.

ROBBIE: That's what the Dead were about all along, is metamorphosis, rebirth and resurrection . . . ultimately it was always about the spirit of the music.

Of Monkeys and Engineers, or Guerilla Gorillas

So how do you get around the gorillas? The first thing you have to accept is that God may be the ultimate gorilla—maybe not, but maybe so. You just can't be sure, but if you're going to make your life something beautiful, something worth living and dying for, you'll need to develop an understanding with God. If He wants to play in your band, He will have to listen to everybody and try to adjust His groove to how the whole sound—and light and space and bodies—are all gyrating. He is invited to the Acid Test, but only if He plays well with others. If He wants to be a gorilla and start smiting the Samsonite all over the place, well, we'll have to become guerilla gorillas. There is a way to beat God at His own game. And Phil knows how to do it, which is the final reason I trust him.

There was another philosopher named Alfred North Whitehead (1862–1947) who is pretty much on the same page as Phil.[6] Whitehead said, there is something even God doesn't

---

[6] I say Whitehead is on the same page as Phil, but he wrote philosophy like Jerry played guitar. Most people don't get it, but for those who do, it's an amazing cosmic jam. The book I'm drawing from is Whitehead's longest jam, *Process and Reality* (New York: Macmillan, 1929) which is a strange trip and thanks for all the fish, if you get my drift. Pick it up and don't worry if you don't understand it, just sit back and take it in. It's interesting. In 1978 a pair of well-meaning scholars named Donald Sherburne and David Ray Griffin did a "corrected edition" of *Process and Reality*, which is sort of like going

know, which is what it's like to have just your perspective on the whole cosmos. Sure, God knows what it's like to be you, and everybody else, but God doesn't know what it's like to be just you, and nobody else. That's your hook line, your signature lick, that's your advantage. It may not seem like much, but think about this: if there is something that it is like to be just you, then there is something about being just you that even God can't contribute to the Acid Test without you. God needs you, and maybe more than you need God. That's why your skinny ass is here. Whitehead calls this your "self-creativity." Whitehead thinks God can't get free of the gorillas Himself, and He is trying like hell to get a little help from His friends, which is why He creates them. So maybe you're not one of His better ideas. But you're certainly not His worst idea—I mean surely Hitler was the worst idea God ever had. Jerry was an excellent idea, and you might be a pretty good idea, all things considered. It sort of depends on what you do. What God needs, apparently, according to Whitehead, is a guerilla army of co-creators, so that the cosmos can have a serious Rave, and the gorillas eventually give up.

The real gorillas are evil and chaos, and they suck because they are trying to unmake everything we are making. They have an easier time of screwing everything up when we stay in our luggage. It seems like they do a lot of damage, but they can't win. The reason is that they can't unmake anything unless we make it first. The gorillas are reactive because they can't be proactive. And here is Whitehead's ace in the hole: Even if they tear down everything you made, they can't ever undo the fact that you made it. When we make music, even God can't unmake it—it happened, and even if God could erase every trace of what we made, He would still remember that we made it. If He willed Himself to forget us and our music, He would remember willing that. Whitehead calls this the "objective immortality of the past." It just means that whatever has once been done, always will have been done, and whatever value those jams had, that value affects everything that comes

---

back through a live recording of the Grateful Dead and electronically correcting all their mistakes—which would not be a wise thing to do. The new edition is very clean, but if you want the original recording of Whitehead, you need to find an old copy, before 1978.

after it in some way, and even God can't undo it. Of course, there really isn't any reason to think God would want to undo it, and there are lots of reasons to think that God is doing all that can be done to help us make up the coolest shit. But even if God is the ultimate gorilla, He's gonna have to reckon with your bass line—forever.

Unscheduled Jam

CORY: Sometimes I think that heaven or hell is not only in your mind, but it's simultaneous with life. If you feel that you're doing good, and you're doing everything in your power to be what you believe is right and do what you believe is right, you have high, clear mental stability there, and you feel good about yourself and it's just heaven. However, if you're this seedy, awful, nasty mother-fucker . . . or even if you're just an asshole, you go around raining on people every day . . . all it takes is one person to cross your path in the wrong way, and set you off, and then you're going to be cross with the next person you see too, and that might ruin their day, and they might ruin the next person's day, and that will come back to you because maybe you might ruin somebody's day that comes back around to you that very same day, and this person is pissed off at you because of something that somebody else did, because of something that somebody else did because of something that you did.

Gratitude

When Phil plays the bass, he is acting, and even God can't undo what he's doing. I. Kant and The Postulates can bitch about the mistakes if they want, but they can't fix them. Might as well learn to see the beauty in dissonance as moan and weep over what can't be changed. Kant and his band are so uptight about what God might think of them that they miss out on their own lives, and that is ungrateful. God needs more than our best guess about His ultimate rules. He needs us to grow, to try things, and most of all to learn gratitude for the chance to add a line to the Acid Test.

I know that Phil knows this, because he learned it from Jerry, among others. Here's how Phil describes Jerry's life, as a whole:

His many gifts, his delight in life, and his gusto for experience were balanced by an endearing humility of spirit and an almost obsessive refusal to take himself seriously . . . he never failed to deftly skewer ballooning egos. It was the warmth of his heart that just pulled everybody in. Even though, like most of us, he didn't suffer fools gladly, there was room there for just about every-damn-body. (*Searching for the Sound*, p. 320)

The gorillas can't get you here. You don't need any Samsonite, and you don't even have to trust God that it all works out for the best. You got to play in the band, and nobody can take that away from you. The word I was looking for, the one that started me thinking, I found when Phil describes when he almost died himself. Recovering from his liver transplant, Phil says:

It all comes home to me when, midway through my first week of recovery, Jill wheels me outside the hospital front door to see a stunning sunset. I break down completely in a flood of gratitude; deep down inside, I haven't been sure if I'd see anything so beautiful ever again. I now know the simple joys of being alive—breathing, seeing, hearing—are infinitely precious, and I'll never take them for granted again. (*Searching for the Sound*, p. 330)

This is no "paint by number morning sky," as the poet said, this is the genuine article. That was the word I was wondering about: gratitude, as in grateful, as in Grateful Dead. I am pretty sure that some people never learn gratitude. I hope to God I'm not one of them, but I trust Phil because my epistemic principle says, in its final formulation: "Know gratitude when you see it." Jerry and Pigpen and the others may be gone, but their Gratitude lives. Now it makes sense to me why the fellows dropped "Grateful" from the name. We are all Dead already, we were born dead. But we aren't screwed, because the part that is really up to us is the gratitude, and some of us get that and some of us don't. When you help somebody get that who doesn't already get it, you are kicking the ass of every gorilla. The ones who get it make beautiful things, and they don't bother to blame God when it doesn't seem to last. The beautiful things do last. No gorilla can take that sunset away from Phil, even if "the rent is in arrears and the dog has not been fed in years," as the poet said. And, my friend, no asshole can take the bass out of your hands, as long as you don't let him. Play your riff, right now, and the cosmos will just have to deal with it. That's my riff at least.[7]

Encore

ROBBIE: All the notes are still out there. The Dead would agree with that.[8]

---

[7] I want to thank my wise friend Danny Dolinger for teaching me that genuine gratitude is just as hard to learn as compassion, and my parents for buying me that Dan Electro bass guitar when I was twelve, even though they knew I would use it to play that god-awful rock and roll.

[8] I wanted to improvise a chapter, find a riff and take it all the way home. without knowing where it would lead. So I wrote this whole chapter and left spaces for others to improvise. And these are a couple of guys from the band I play in, Cory Powell and Dale Groves, plus another guy I wish I played with, Robbie Stokes. I wanted a conversational jam with people who really had the right Head for the Dead, and I wanted them from different generations, different stages on the path, you know? So my young friend Cory, he was twenty-two and played lead guitar in our group, the Bone Dry River Band. He learned to play by listening to Jerry. He has a young body, but an old soul. Dale is the BDRB drummer. We call him Teaser—nevermind why (use your imagination). Like me, Dale has a touch of grey, but only a touch, and he has followed the Dead since 1980, going to over 140 shows. He's been through plenty and has come out grateful and still with the rhythm in him. Robbie Stokes is a fantastic musician who collaborated with the Dead and Mickey Hart and about everybody else at some point. Check him out at www.robcoaudio.com. Robbie was in his late fifties when I wrote this and he still looks a fraction of his years. I'm lucky to be able to call him up and get that close to the Dead themselves. So I gathered all three of them at The Mix Cafe/Alchemy Sound in Carterville, Illinois, on February 19th, 2007. Jon Pluskota recorded our conversation. The dialogue you see in this essay is from that night, which I ran like a jam session.

10
An Everlasting Kiss: The Seduction of Wendy

Bruce Springsteen's female characters are composites of women we all know, archetypes—but they all seem to be boxed in and smothered, by parents, by conventional expectations, by working class economics, by their own fears. The message to one and all that Bruce brings them is "together we can break this trap." Especially prominent among the objects of his desire is "Mary," who shows up in about ten songs. But Sandy, Linda, Rosalita, and their many sisters, all receive this message: you can be rescued from your disapproving parents and uninspiring jobs. Even if you aren't so young anymore, you will be taken away to a place where love will be wild and real, to the river, to thunder road, or at least the boardwalk. It's a sort of fairy tale. And that's the point.

Dreams and Visions

Many of us not only grew up with Springsteen, we grew up on Springsteen. He has always had an almost magical power over those who were in the frightening transition between childhood and adulthood, the time when we are on the threshold of responsibility, when we are old enough to see what became of our parents and young enough to believe that it need not happen to us. And Bruce knows a secret about us. We may be growing up, but secretly we still want someone to read to us in bed at night, to fill our imaginations with possibilities and hopes. To remain on the path we are following results in broken backs, broken wills, and broken hearts. We see it in our parents.

This moment of awakening is a doorway, or more likely, a window, and Bruce appears there at bedtime telling us stories about places we haven't been and things we haven't done, but still might go and do if we don't wait too long. Yet, we are too cool for the same old fairy tales—now we need more than just directions to Highway 9, we want suicide machines to take us there, because the crocodile that swallowed the clock is turning us all into pirates. It's a death trap. We need to flip a Never Bird to that whole dying town on our way to, well, wherever we're going—second star on the right and straight on until morning. So I think Bruce is a rebel with a cause, and the cause is keeping the dreams and visions alive, and not quite growing up—at least not if that means killing off the madness in his soul.

Bruce is Peter Pan. And he knows it. That is why he sings his most passionate seduction song to Wendy. Some people will have forgotten, and younger ones would not know, that NBC did a famous live broadcast of the play version of *Peter Pan* in 1960, starring Mary Martin as Peter, and it was so popular and beloved that it was repeated (with much publicity) in 1963, 1966, and notably, 1973, about the same time Springsteen was writing "Born to Run." Kids of Bruce's generation grew up with the play on television, as well as with the 1953 Walt Disney animated movie version.

One thing that has always been fascinating about Peter Pan is that tantalizing relationship between Peter and Wendy. If you have never read J.M. Barrie's classic book, but have settled for just the stage version or the many movies based on it, there is probably something about Peter Pan that you don't know: the play may be about Peter, but the book is about Wendy. (The play was first produced in 1904, but Barrie did not write it into a full book until 1911.) It begins with Wendy and ends with her, describing a girl who has an issue with her mother, Mrs. Darling. Mrs. Darling's position as the center of attention is threatened by Wendy's birth. As Barrie describes Mrs. Darling:

> She was a lovely lady, with a romantic mind and such a sweet mocking mouth. Her romantic mind was like the tiny boxes, one within the other, that come from the puzzling East, however many you discover there is always one more; and her sweet mocking mouth had one kiss

on it that Wendy could never get, though there it was, perfectly con-
spicuous in the right-hand corner. (p. 7)[1]

You'll want to pay attention to that kiss, the one Wendy
can't get from her mother. It's important. Barrie makes it clear
that Mr. Darling can't get the kiss either, and eventually he for-
gets about it or pretends it isn't there. But Wendy sees it and
she wants it. Mrs. Darling doesn't know it, but by withholding
the kiss she is creating Peter Pan in Wendy's imagination, and
the more she strives to control Wendy's "dreams and visions,"
the stronger Peter becomes. Here is what Mrs. Darling does to
Wendy:

> Mrs. Darling first heard of Peter when she was tidying up her chil-
> dren's minds. It is the nightly custom of every good mother after her
> children are asleep to rummage in their minds and put things straight
> for next morning, repacking into their proper places the many articles
> that have wandered during the day. If you could keep awake (but of
> course you can't) you would see your own mother doing this, and you
> would find it very interesting to watch her. It is quite like tidying up
> drawers. You would see her on her knees, I expect, lingering humor-
> ously over some of your contents, wondering where on earth you had
> picked this thing up, making discoveries sweet and not so sweet,
> pressing this to her cheek as if it were as nice as a kitten, and hur-
> riedly stowing that out of sight. When you wake in the morning, the
> naughtiness and evil passions with which you went to bed have been
> folded up small and placed at the bottom of your mind and on the top,
> beautifully aired, are spread out your prettier thoughts, ready for you
> to put on. (p. 9)

Is this a children's story? I suppose that if the (aptly named)
Brothers Grimm are telling children's stories, so is J.M. Barrie.
But this is dark stuff, the sort of thing that could keep Freud
busy for a lifetime. Even from watching the sanitized play or
the movies of Peter Pan we can tell that the children aren't
happy, that they want to escape, to fly away, but we are never
told precisely why. Taking a gander at what Barrie says above,

---

[1] Peter Pan is available free on-line from the Guttenberg Project:
http://www.gutenberg.org/catalog/world/readfile?fk_files=34649&pageno=6.
All my quotes from the book are taken from this source.

it becomes a little clearer. If Bruce wants to "guard" Wendy's "dreams and visions," I think I know why she needs a guardian. Maybe we all do.

Barrie enters the darkest corridors of childhood, parenthood, and adolescent struggle, and in that place he finds the character Wendy. Scholars agree that while the name "Wendy" can nowadays be a diminutive for "Gwendolyn," it appears that J.M. Barrie simply made up the name "Wendy." There were no "Wendys" before Peter Pan, even if there's a Wendy's on every third street corner now, serving up gigantic slabs of beef tallow to clog our arteries and dull our minds. But Barrie's Wendy is all women—as they wish to be, not as they must be to satisfy a world that will brand them as tramps if they don't comb their hair in the rearview mirror. But Bruce can see that Wendy doesn't want to be one of those girls, she is different—the object of his passion, the mother of lost boys, the May Queen who returns to Neverland in spring to clean the winter's mess.

Falling for Wendy

Every boy who has so much as a sliver of imagination falls in love with Wendy as soon as he first hears the story of Peter Pan. Those boys who have a romantic turn of mind never get over it. Bruce never got over it. I can tell. Neither did I. That is why "Born to Run" affected me (and millions like me) so profoundly.

The mansions of glory and suicide machines may have drawn in the boys on the football team and the ones in shop class, but the romantics demurred until the first line of the second verse: "Wendy let me in, I wanna be your friend." He's singing to Wendy, we all gasped. "Let me in?" we asked. "Where?" But romantics all know, and Bruce knows that we know: Let me in the nursery window. Peter Pan appears at the window, and he can't come in unless Wendy opens it. And Wendy always does, because that is what Wendy really wants.

This is all quite conscious on Bruce's part. He didn't pull the name "Wendy" randomly from a hat or ask to be "let in" just because it was cold outside. He knows who he's after. And as I imagine it, Bruce must have asked himself "who is the girl every romantic boy wants to steal . . . no, not steal, she has to choose it . . . to liberate?" That girl has had many names:

Persephone, Helen of Troy, Rapunzel, Juliet, Becky Thatcher, and for boys of the twentieth century, her name is Wendy. We have always loved her and we always will.

I think all the boys, including those destined to be gay, fall for Wendy (even if a few just want to be Wendy, which is fine by me and Bruce). Most of us recover, which is to say, we eventually grow up. But while we're still boys, rescuing Wendy is our very calling. Sometimes she is trapped in Kansas on her aunt and uncle's farm, until a cyclone takes her to Oz. But the Tin Man and the Scarecrow and the Cowardly Lion, those romantic dreamers, all love her, whether in Kansas or Oz. Sometimes she lives on the bluffs above the Mississippi River in Missouri and is lost in Injun Joe's cave. Sometimes Wendy is the Pretty Woman trapped in a life of prostitution until Richard Gere shows up to bring her the fairy tale. But sometimes Wendy is stuck in a toxic, rusting hole in New Jersey. For every Wendy there is a Peter Pan. Sometimes he's made of tin, sometimes he arrives in a big black limousine, and sometimes he's just a scared and lonely rider. What is always true of every Peter Pan is that he hasn't really grown up, and he doesn't plan to do so. He's the man-child, the *puer aeternus*, as C.G. Jung called him, the eternal son. He leads with his heart, not his head, and he deals with the fallout of doing so, regardless of the cost. The lost boy loves Wendy and only Wendy—well, it might be more accurate to say that he loves every Wendy.

For you girls reading this (and I do mean girls, since I'm not attempting to address the woman in you), I am well aware that your perspective is being left out of this. To this complaint I have only two things to say. First, I'm a boy, so I can't easily pretend to understand how Bruce's song affects you. Second, I have something else for you to read. I recommend Hope Edelman's essay on losing her virginity to Bruce Springsteen's music called "Bruce Springsteen and the Story of Us."[2]

And here we come to a point that bears some investigation. If it were just me, I'd be too embarrassed to proceed with this, but over and over I hear from men and women across generations that this damnable song, "Born to Run," reaches down into a place inside of us, grips the vitals of our souls, and tugs

---

[2] In *Racing in the Street: The Bruce Springsteen Reader*, edited by June Skinner Sawyers (New York: Penguin, 2004), pp. 196–210.

until it loosens the scar tissue and frees an almost uncontrollable pent-up passion. We yearn and pine for something that seems lost, we want out, we want it back, whatever it is. Finally, as the words fail, as the music reaches a screaming crescendo and then falls down in a chromatic scale that touches every single note and into a vortex of anarchy (that is where Wendy is, at the bottom of that musical hole), Bruce counts off and we learn that the highway is jammed with broken heroes, just like us, on a "last chance power drive"—and I don't know in my intellect what that is, but my heart knows, and I don't care if I lose my mind, I'm headed there, with Wendy, and if it costs me my very life I'll die with her on the street in an everlasting kiss. And somehow, at the moment we feel it, this doesn't even sound stupid.

It may seem anti-climactic, but when I recover my full-grown wits, I would like to know, frankly, how does Bruce do that to me—and to half the people I know or ever knew? And why do I pity the boys who don't see it, who don't share it? Don't they love Wendy? Cynical, pathetic bastards. Bean counters. Senators and sons of senators. They have no imagination. They don't believe in fairies. Screw them.

The Wild and the Innocent

Most philosophers are uncomfortable with discussing imagination—they discuss it, but they don't like it much. It has been thought to be just the opposite of "reason," and philosophers like reason. Imagination is unruly, it deceives us, it likes to play tricks on us, and it doesn't want to be pinned down to just one orderly way of doing things. Thus, it is not surprising that most philosophers in the Western world have, since the days of Plato, belittled and condemned imagination—most, but not all.

Robert Pirsig's lonely rider in *Zen and the Art of Motorcycle Maintenance* discovers, with great effort, this same conspiracy to kill imagination, and while it may cost the rider his sanity, he resolves not to give in to the pressure to "grow up" and be rational. Pirsig's narrator's alter ego, Phaedrus, is overwrought to say the least, but it isn't a bad idea to read this character as Peter Pan, and the lonely rider as a grown up Peter Pan trying to remember what his younger self once knew.

For a small handful of devoted ponderers, the power to create images before our minds has seemed like the grandest and finest mystery of all. They admit that imagination is the servant of our emotions and passions (it's hard to argue with that), and they readily confess that in serving these fiery masters, imagination also further inflames them. But, some of them have countered: given that we humans are such emotional and passionate beings, it seems strange to neglect the topic, or to demote the powers of consciousness which spring from and serve our passions to the level of mere annoyances and obstacles to the "serious" work of the mind.

Perhaps the most notorious defender of imagination was an Italian philosopher named Giambattista Vico (1668–1744). Most professional philosophers have heard of him, but only the most intrepid among them will dare to study his ideas. Studying Vico could cost you your sanity. His masterwork, *The New Science* (1744) is one of the wildest rides you could ever take.[3] This is the philosophical equivalent of a moonshot. Why?

Vico was a fairly ordinary and respectable philosopher until he became (dangerously) curious about the origin of human law. Being a thorough sort of inquirer, he dug around in ancient books until one day it occurred to him that he couldn't really escape the conclusion that law—and religion, and science, and just about everything else—comes from myth, and the bad news is that we made up the myths. This can be troubling to the sorts of people who want "truth" and "knowledge" and "morality" to be something more than just our collective imagination. But Vico was fearless. Twenty years of study followed this disturbing realization before he discovered the "master key" of his new science: what he called the "imaginative universal." You know this idea by a different and more familiar name, the "archetype." The notion is so much a part of our parlance and culture today that you may not have realized that someone somewhere along the way had to come up with this idea. Vico was the guy who first saw it and named it. People thought he was crazy. Many still think that.

---

[3] I don't advise you to take this ride alone. There is a nice English translation of *The New Science* by Thomas G. Bergin and Max H. Fisch, but I recommend that you first consult a slightly tamer guidebook. Get Donald Phillip Verene's *Vico's Science of Imagination*. Think of it as a safety net when you're walking the wire.

What did Vico discover? It's so simple that it is hard to believe the idea wasn't obvious all along. But it wasn't, not to grown up minds. From the time of Plato, people on the Western side of the world had been working without surcease to discredit myth and to prove that reason was the legitimate root of all human knowledge—even God was rational, they said. God didn't imagine the world into existence, He spat out mathematical formulas, and here we all are. These laborers were so successful that the Western world finally forgot that there was ever an important constructive connection between myth and reason, even though the connection was plain to see in Plato's own works. When they demoted myth to the status of falsehood and lies, they made human imagination the liar. In short, we all forgot the childhood of the human race and tried to pretend that reason was its own self-sufficient creator. But Vico was determined to help us remember our childhood.

He argued that imagination has a logic all its own, more basic and far richer than what we call "logic" today. When we think, Vico said, our operating platform is made of these "imaginative universals." You can't think at all without them, but you can't grasp them with reason; you have to grasp them in the way that you understand fables and fairy tales. It sounds wild to an adult, but any innocent child can do it, as Vico pointed out.

Darkness on the Edge of Town

There are lots of examples of imaginative universals—every myth is packed with them, but let me isolate just one imaginative universal to help you along. Vico says that in mythic imagination, a city is actually an altar to the gods. Cities are not *like* altars, they *are* altars. We create cities as altars, and the whole idea of a city comes back to that. If you dig deep enough, you'll just see it. But let me offer a few analogies to help you.

Traditional villages of indigenous people are organized around certain crucial places. They have a heart, which is usually marked with a consecrated totemic symbol. In modern cities, the area is called "downtown." As for the totemic symbol, I happen to live along the Mississippi, and it is pretty difficult to miss the Arch as one approaches St. Louis, or the Pyramid as one approaches Memphis. What the hell are those? They don't always put them downtown, but these totemic symbols still mark the meaning of the place, its heart. There is a giant statue of Vulcan in Birmingham, and a giant Jesus overlooking Rio de Janeiro, a huge obelisk in downtown Buenos Aires, and the Eiffel Tower in Paris, a Space Needle in Seattle and another in San Antonio, and even Mary of the Mountain overlooking Butte, Montana. Washington D.C. is simply nothing but totemic symbols. In Atlantic City, it's the Boardwalk, where Madame Marie used to tell fortunes better than the cops.

Traditional villages have a place where decisions are made, a place where the elders meet. It is the "head" of the village. In modern cities, that is city hall. It may be downtown, it may be somewhere else, but this is the place where the decision-makers are supposed to consult the wisdom of the ages. This is where the "law" is kept. It is like the chancel area in a church or synagogue or mosque where the sacred writing is kept. The sacred writing of a city is its law and its history. That's why you expect to find statues and portraits of past leaders throughout the place—these are the ancestors, and wherever we keep their images or their possessions, we do so because we know we cannot forget the ancestors without also forgetting the law.

Traditional villages have places, usually a dark place on the edge of town, where the dead are buried. We still consecrate the ground and fill it with symbols, creating a "necropolis," a "city of the dead" that mirrors in form and structure the city of the living, with its own heart, head, and sacred writing.[4] And finally, traditional villages all have a place where the refuse of collective human life is deposited—archaeologists love digging around these places. In modern cities, this is called the dump. It may be the necessities of communal living that determine the need for such places, but it is the human imagination that separates and sanctifies them as the proper altar to the gods. Your house is organized in a similar fashion, a microcosm of the city, an altar within an altar.

---

[4] If you're saying to yourself "wait a minute, the old cemetery is downtown," you are showing your lack of historical sense. We don't do things that way, and you know it. The cemetery *was* on the edge of town, until later the town grew up around it, which is why the houses around the cemetery are newer than the cemetery. It's true that the burial ground is often the churchyard itself. This requires a longer story than I can tell here, but it's an interesting one for another time.

If your city lacks a consecrated heart, or if it doesn't properly respect its own law, or its ancestors, or if it treats itself as though it were simply one huge dump, the sacred order is upset. The city is an altar, and you don't want to defile it. The child in you already knows this. The grown-up will have to remember it, which is hard. But remembering this piece of poetic wisdom is the only way you'll ever really know why we want our cities to be beautiful and prosperous and orderly and safe and bustling with life—such cities make the gods happy when they are. This is also why we want a winning sports team; it proves the favor of the gods upon our city. And you already know this. But if you treat your city like we have treated, say, Newark or Camden, you soil not only your own nest, but you defile your altar to the gods. Don't be surprised if the sports teams can't win. This is part of the reason Bruce's songs about the hopelessness of the dying city and the desire to find a better place strike us so deeply. We simply know that to live in a death trap is a suicide rap. We have to get out while we're young.

Obviously Wendy is also an imaginative universal, as is Peter Pan, and Captain Hook, and the Crocodile who swallowed the clock, and Neverland itself. There are many thousands of imaginative universals, all of them deep and rich in imaginative content. Poets, like Bruce Springsteen, write with them. These images can morph and change into infinitely many forms, but when they have been packaged well, we grasp them—not with our rational minds, but with our memories. Vico says that memory is imagination, and it is far more important than rational thinking. Vico also points out that the education of children deeply depends on these mythic stories and their archetypal characters. He says that if we fail to teach our children the fables of the race when their imaginations are strong, in childhood, they will have nothing to think about as their imaginations wane in adulthood. I fear that northern New Jersey has a lot of people whose parents didn't tell them stories, or more likely, the leaders and the wealthy people of these dying towns just don't believe in fairies.

But it is also pretty hard to listen to Vico. He seems like a hopeless romantic man-child who taps at the window of the mind's nursery, not a serious scientist of thought. And his (ironically titled) *New Science* reads like a description of Neverland.

The pirates don't like it. Before you get all indignant about this, consider at least one of their arguments.

Captain Hook

René Descartes (1596–1650) was probably the most unrelenting critic of imagination who ever lived; he was ingenious, and he looked just like Captain Hook. He had lots of very impressive rational arguments, but one was especially effective at proving that there was a great difference between thinking about something and imagining it.[5] He instructed us to think about a figure with exactly a thousand sides of equal length. He called this a "chiliagon." There's nothing unclear about this concept, and it would be easy to verify, mathematically or empirically, whether any given object in our senses or our minds was or was not a chiliagon. You could, for instance, ploddingly count the sides, but the best way is to measure just one side, multiply by 1000, compare the result with the area of the entire figure (arrived at by another precise formula), and thereby determine whether the figure has exactly one thousand sides. The object in your senses will perfectly match the concept in your mind.

But now, try to imagine a chiliagon. You quickly discover that you sort of can't do it. You can imagine a figure with a lot of sides, but you can't tell whether it has exactly a thousand, or maybe 999 or 1,001, or just a lot. Why, Descartes wants to know, can't you get a determinate and clear idea with your imagination, when you can do it so easily with your reasoning? There must be a difference between imagination and reasoning, he concludes, and you would do well to trust your reasoning, your "thinking" and not your imaginings, at least if you want knowledge. And Captain Hook wants knowledge.

Famously, Descartes then insisted that "I think, therefore I am," is the safest bit of knowledge anyone can have. And this is pretty much the opposite of "I imagine, therefore I am." This is very convincing. It is so clever that it pitilessly turns children into pirates. It is so convincing that it seems to deal a near fatal blow to Peter Pan, while Descartes and the rest of the pirates

---

[5] This comes from Descartes's "Sixth Meditation," in *Meditations on First Philosophy*.

capture Wendy and condemn us all to a life of running from the crocodile. Western philosophy grew up, and growing up means counting and measuring everything until imagination simply dies, the light goes out and no one claps for Tinker Bell. Such are the leading men of Newark, and maybe your hometown too, and maybe your nation. Bruce shows us the situation in "Born to Run" and a hundred other songs. And that's where Wendy is being held by the pirates.

The Crocodile

If we want to rescue Wendy, we have to find the flaw in Captain Hook's plan. There always is one. Descartes's argument, for all its ingenuity, cannot explain the origin of reason. In the world he lived in, the seventeenth century, people were happy to believe that God gave us reason when He created us. That was their favorite fairy tale, and they believed it so hard that it seemed like they hadn't even made it up. Reason didn't have a worldly origin, only a divine one, they said over and over. They weren't entirely wrong, but inside their cold-blooded logic was a ticking time-bomb.

Vico told us that if we didn't pay attention to history, we would have no account of reason and how we became rational. Reason, he insisted, also came from myth, and developed over time. In fact, he said, reason is a "modification" of the mind. You know how to modify a car? Well, it's like that with the mind, it just takes longer in the shop. You can't buy an after market package for modifying the mind, you have to weld each part from raw materials—you even have to mine and refine the metals yourself, first the Iron, then the Bronze, then the steel. It's a long story, as long as history itself, but the short version can be seen in this point: you can imagine without reasoning, but you can't reason without imagining. At the very least you have to remember the chiliagon long enough to think about it, and memory is not a kind of reasoning, it's a kind of imagination—which is why it is so unreliable and variable from one person to the next. And Descartes did not discover his argument about the chiliagon using reason, he made it up—that is, he imagined it before he could put it into logical and mathematical order. Vico did what he could, but people believed Descartes anyway.

Yet, as the human race "grew up," it kept encountering more and more evidence that the world was very old, that many civilizations had existed for thousands of years and had gotten on quite well on the strength of fairy tales. And then they finally noticed that their own civilization was based on myths too, like Adam and Eve. There was mist on the beach of reason. Soon there came terrible fights between pirates and lost boys when the romantic poets showed up in the late eighteenth century. The lost boys took down a lot of pirates, but they didn't get Captain Hook. Then about 1859 Charlie Darwin came screaming down the boulevard. He was driving a hemi-powered drone called *The Origin of Species*, with a crocodile riding shotgun, spouting a new fairy tale about the human race that the pirates couldn't live with and couldn't live without. The tale was told in a way they couldn't resist, full of facts and figures and slimy creatures that crawled out of Greasy Lake and took over Jungleland. Crocodiles, are very old, you know. They haven't evolved in any serious way since the Triassic (that's about 220 million years ago). Crocs don't evolve because they don't need to—a perfect predator, a time machine you never have to wind up. For them, the Energizer Bunny isn't even much of a snack. That's a pretty scary clock.

Charlie and the crocodile said humans weren't always rational, that our race has a natural history, that our myths came long before our reasonings, and that time is very real. Vico had warned us, but pirates are very proud and they never listen. Now they're in a hell of a fix, and Wendy is up for grabs. That's when Bruce comes in the window.

The Kiss

And so what about that everlasting kiss? In Barrie's final chapter, "When Wendy Grew Up," Mrs. Darling is adopting lost boys and sending them off to school, but Peter wants nothing to do with that. He perches in the nursery window and listens to Mrs. Darling's plea that he be adopted also. He doesn't budge, but Wendy can't stand to see him go away. This is the moment when Bruce sings his song to Wendy. Peter says that she should come with him:

> "Well, then, come with me to the little house."
> "May I, mummy?" [Wendy says to Mrs. Darling.]

"Certainly not. I have got you home again, and I mean to keep you."

"But he does so need a mother."

"So do you, my love."

"Oh, all right," Peter said, as if he had asked her from politeness merely; but Mrs. Darling saw his mouth twitch, and she made this handsome offer: to let Wendy go to him for a week every year to do his spring cleaning. Wendy would have preferred a more permanent arrangement; and it seemed to her that spring would be long in coming; but this promise sent Peter away quite gay again. He had no sense of time, and was so full of adventures that all I have told you about him is only a halfpenny-worth of them. I suppose it was because Wendy knew this that her last words to him were these rather plaintive ones:

"You won't forget me, Peter, will you, before spring cleaning time comes?"

Of course Peter promised; and then he flew away. He took Mrs. Darling's kiss with him. The kiss that had been for no one else, Peter took quite easily. Funny. But she seemed satisfied. (pp. 124–25)

I'm not saying Bruce read Peter Pan and consciously noticed the importance of the kiss, but whether it was from study or simply a powerful imagination, Bruce built the kiss into the climax of his most passionate song. Anyone can see that the song is about the everlasting kiss, and about being willing to die for it. In the moment that our lonely rider offers that everlasting kiss to Wendy, he teaches her to fly, to find Neverland, the place with no time where the kiss can last forever, and in that embrace is both death and life.

This is no chaste offer. Wendy will have to wrap her legs around the velvet rims and strap her hands across the engines. (What sorts of rims are made of velvet anyway? I want to see those rims, Bruce. Get back to me on this, will you?) The price of that deal the rider offers is nothing short of motherhood. But in motherhood is the everlasting cycle of life and death. Wendy has to grow up. But Peter does not. He's always losing his shadow. His is not the curse, and every Wendy knows that. It isn't fair; it's just the way things are. But we can live with the sadness. The madness of love is worth it.

And where did the lonely rider get this catastrophic kiss? He took it from Wendy's mother, quite easily. And how did he manage that? Barrie helps us out a little bit. When Peter first appears, Mrs. Darling is asleep by the fire in her children's nursery, dreaming. It is she, not Wendy, who first sees Peter Pan. This is what Barrie says:

> The dream by itself would have been a trifle, but while she was dreaming the window of the nursery blew open, and a boy did drop on the floor. He was accompanied by a strange light, no bigger than your fist, which darted about the room like a living thing and I think it must have been this light that wakened Mrs. Darling.
>
> She started up with a cry, and saw the boy, and somehow she knew at once that he was Peter Pan. If you or I or Wendy had been there we should have seen that he was very like Mrs. Darling's kiss. He was a lovely boy, clad in skeleton leaves and the juices that ooze out of trees but the most entrancing thing about him was that he had all his first teeth. When he saw she was a grown-up, he gnashed the little pearls at her. (p. 12)

I have to ask you now to use your imaginations. Remember, the city is an altar. Peter Pan is the kiss. Barrie understands this, and so does Bruce, and so do you, when your insides catch fire at the climactic line in "Born to Run." But I have to ask you to make one more imaginative connection. Mrs. Darling is Wendy, when she grew up. It is complicated and a little scary, but Barrie helps us cope with it. On the night when Peter steals her children, this is the scene in the nursery:

> Then Mrs. Darling had come in, wearing her white evening-gown. She had dressed early because Wendy so loved to see her in her evening-gown, with the necklace George had given her. She was wearing Wendy's bracelet on her arm; she had asked for the loan of it. Wendy loved to lend her bracelet to her mother. (p. 14)

The suggestion of a loving and symbolic bond between the father, the mother, and the daughter is reassuring. And in spite of the threat Peter poses to her happiness, "Mrs. Darling never upbraided Peter; there was something in the right-hand corner of her mouth that wanted her not to call Peter names" (p. 14).

It's easy to forget that the entirety of "Born to Run" is one side of a single conversation with Wendy. What a stroke of poetic genius. Bruce rewrote the seduction of Wendy by Peter Pan in language we could all remember, from childhood. Our lonely rider is trying to make Wendy believe that he has the kiss, no, that he is the kiss. And he isn't lying. She is hesitating. Who can blame her? It's crazy. In the song, we never get her answer. But we already know the answer. She will go with him for a time and then she will grow up. And he won't. But the kiss will last forever, and she always will have been, and always will be Wendy. And by the way, I think that the strangely enchanting glockenspiel in "Born to Run" is Tinker Bell, and I think Bruce did that on purpose. But what can I say? I believe in fairies. If you don't, I am quite content to let the crocodile have you.

11

Blinded by the Subterranean Homesick Muse: The Poet as Virtuous and Virtuoso

Bruce Springsteen is a poet, a very good one. But poets and philosophers have been on bad terms in the Western world for at least 2,500 years. In the *Republic*, Plato refers to the quarrel between poets and philosophers as "ancient," so it may be a lot older, but if Plato didn't start the fire, he has certainly been stoking it for the last two and a half millennia.

Why? Well, Plato declared poets to be a pack of liars and excluded them from his ideal city, the city to be ruled by a philosopher king. Plato thought that poets cannot be trusted because they say just anything they damn well please, and they say it so prettily that the mass of people believes them. And you just can't expect the masses to choose the True over what seems Beautiful, and, having chosen what pleases their fancy, they'll also claim it's the truth. That's why many religious people today (not all) like to believe in the Bible. It pleases them to do so and it makes them feel like they know something divine. And people are, by and large, both gullible and frightened of the unknown—I don't exempt myself from this, of course.

In Plato's day, people treated the epics of Homer the way today's fundamentalists treat the Bible. And on that account, Plato had a low opinion of the intelligence and judgment of ordinary people; the Greeks called them the *hoi polloi*, the teeming and chattering unwashed masses.

In ancient Athens the trouble was all these damned poets going around with their clever words, invoking various Muses as their guides, to sanction their authority, and then telling

scandalous stories about the behavior of the gods. These stories make the gods seem less admirable—and less moral—
than ordinary human beings. It was sort of like watching the
celestial divines take turns on the *Jerry Springer Show*. The
behavior of the God of Abraham in the Bible is a close parallel.[1] And the people ate it up. In our day, it's television invoking corporate sponsors and then depicting our leaders as,
well, people who seem less admirable than we are ourselves.
And we eat it up. The more things change, the more they stay
the same. What can be done? Plato suggested that any city or
community that wishes to keep its own soul from rotting simply has to ban such people.

He also explained why the poets lie—it's because they don't
really see the truth. They think they do, but they believe the
world of the senses is reality, matter in motion, and so they use
their imaginations (which depend on the senses), instead of the
power of reason, to create their songs. Their words become a
verbal copy of the physical world, and when these words are
nicely arranged, people recognize their own sensory and emotional experiences in them, and they are pleased, or angered, or
saddened—or (and here's the point) they feel whatever the
poets want them to feel. Because the people feel it strongly,
they only see what the poets want them to see. That would be
fine, Plato thought, if poets knew anything, but they don't—
they make things up, and with the encouragement of applause,
poets become convinced that they are speaking the truth, even
though they really know they're making it up.

I'm sure that more than a few readers here have noticed
what a problem television is, especially to uncritical people.
The mass audience sees an image on CNN or Fox News, and
they forget about the corporate powers that sponsor those
images, and also edit and select and manufacture them—to

---

[1] I wonder how many people know that the Bible is simply filled with
poetry. Pick up a Bible. Now turn to Genesis 3:14, where God is pronouncing
the curses on the serpent, the man, the woman, and the earth. You'll notice
that the indentations and line breaks are different here. That usually means
you're reading poetry. God's curse is a poem. Now thumb through the book.
You'll see this pattern a lot. Almost the whole book of Isaiah and about half of
Jeremiah, for example, are written in verse. The New Testament has less
poetry, but it is not exempt. See Revelation, Chapters 18 and 19, for a couple
of long poems.

serve a number of interests, mainly financial. But the TV viewer thinks he has a truth, because he thinks he saw something with his own eyes. What's actually happening is that the images seen stir feelings in the viewer, and the feelings then dictate the opinions a viewer forms about the images he has seen. In time, he sees only what accords with the habits of feeling that have developed while watching the canned images. Springsteen adapts an old maxim to this situation when he says "believe none of what you hear, and less of what you see" in the song "Magic."

How many of us would be tempted, if made king, simply to ban the TVs? Or perhaps many others among us would seek to control the images ourselves for some higher purpose? We don't want to serve ourselves or control others, we just don't want them to be misled, right? Well, Plato isn't interested in controlling the poets either. He suggests that we offer them a laurel and invite them to go to a different city, one that is already corrupt, to ply their trade. Plato is sort of a "Poetry NIMBY."

I may sound sympathetic to Plato up to this point. I like Plato as well as the next philosopher, but on this matter I am not in sympathy with him. I think he's a dangerous elitist, and I don't like people who think better of themselves and their own abilities than those of their fellows. Blame it on my working-class family origins, or call it a democratic disposition, or call it plain common sense. I can't stand elitists. Psychologically speaking, poetry is a threat to philosophy because philosophers want their own stories about "reason" and "truth" to be believed, but they don't tell the stories well enough to bring applause from the masses, let alone conviction. And so, while people pay good poets a lot of money to sing their songs, they ignore the "truths" of philosophy, and they think of philosophers as daft and unaccountable dreamers. That pisses off the philosophers. Philosophers, in general, secretly harbor the conceit that they'd all be better leaders than the ones chosen by the people.[2] There

---

[2] For an example, take a look at Stanley Rosen's essay "The Quarrel between Philosophy and Poetry," in *The Quarrel Between Philosophy and Poetry: Studies in Ancient Thought*. Rosen belongs to a school of philosophers called the "Straussians," who are students and followers of a Plato scholar named Leo Strauss (1899–1973). This bunch is elitist in the extreme, and to my thinking, a collection of crypto-totalitarians.

are a lot of crypto-totalitarian personalities studying philosophy, and Plato is their leader. Be extremely wary of anyone who
likes Plato too much. That person really wants to be obeyed,
not argued with.

So what of it? I want to see whether I can, as a chastened
philosopher (whose cats won't even obey him), invite the poets
back into the city and see what they know—about Beauty,
about Goodness, and about Truth. I have a feeling that poets do
know something more than the world of the senses, and I think
we should begin the reconciliation by examining their Muses—
the deliverers of the Beauty, Goodness and Truth that the poets
"know." We might as well start with the scariest and most
potent poets alive.

A Grudge Match

There's a certain type of song that only the virtuoso poet-song-
writer can pull off. It may even seem to be a genre unto itself.
Some examples everyone knows are Don McLean's "American
Pie," Bob Dylan's "Subterranean Homesick Blues" and of course,
Bruce Springsteen's "Blinded by the Light." There are certainly
others by lesser-known virtuoso songwriters, such as "When I
Go" by Dave Carter, and "The Bishop and the Ghost of the
Nazarene" by Jonathan Byrd, and "Stained Glass" by Danny
Schmidt.[3] Astonishing, impossible songs! The songs I mention
here are all in the domain of white-boy folk music, but other
styles of music have their own close equivalents. I'm not speaking of the merely clever poetizing of the better then average
song-writerly song, I am speaking of the completely over-the-
top, testosterone-laden, swashbuckling wordsmithery that only
a young man (or a man with a young Muse) would even dare to
attempt. This is a sowing of lyrical wild oats in the far-flung
back forty of the human imagination, and only the chosen few
reap a harvest there. That field, when plowed, is dangerous to
the soul and the mind, a place on the edge of sanity itself.

There are numerous studies by people, both amateurs and
professionals, who spend their precious energies trying to puzzle

---

[3] Do yourself a favor. Google these songs. Don't just read the words, listen
to them, and add these three songwriters to your iTunes inventory. I'm not
kidding. You don't know what you're missing.

out all the references and allusions in these songs, and I'm not saying that is a total waste of time. It can be fun, but it's mainly beside the point. What is this sort of swaggering of the poets?

As far as I know, the song genre doesn't have a contemporary name (I'll try to name it before the end of this chapter), but this type of song has been around for a very long time, longer than recorded history. The ancient Greeks apparently called it "dithyramb," although that name is not Greek and came into their language from some mysterious place beyond history. In the days of Plato, the dithyramb was a kind of ecstatic song sung to the god of wine, Dionysus. But Dionysus was a late arrival in the Greek pantheon, a young god as gods go, and the dithyramb is much older than he is. It was originally sung to the goddess, not a god.

In the dithyramb, the singers would face off against one another and have poetizing contests. It probably looked like a scene from *Eight Mile*. It's still alive. But men have apparently been doing this sort of song for a long time—for about as long as there have been women. And that may be a great part of the point. We will get to that. Some men have a gift for the spontaneous demands of the contest, but most men can't do it at all. The contest is one way that, among poets, the men can be separated from the boys, the virtuosos from the merely virtuous. If you'll excuse the image (and it is the first of many you'll have to excuse), the dithyramb is a poetic licking contest, and the guy with the trickiest tongue wins.

And how do poets know who wins? In a sense, everyone just knows, when it's over, and it's like a poetry slam in which the audience decides, but pushing it off on the audience only defers the deeper question. Grant that the audience just knows who won; how? This is not a rational process of developing criteria and measuring each contestant against some objective standard. In truth, the poets are comparing Muses, and they are not saying "I love my Muse more than you love yours," they are saying the converse: "my Muse loves me more than yours loves you, and I can prove it, you pantywaist . . . watch this":

> . . . Madman drummer bummers and Indians in the summer with a teenage diplomat, in the dumps with the mumps as the adolescent pumps his head into his hat . . .

It may seem juvenile, but I have to propose a grudge-match: Dylan and Springsteen. Whom do the Muses love the most? Picture Bob and Bruce, in concert, at The Meadowlands. We are all in a circle, no lyric sheets allowed. Oh, and Weird Al Yankovic is the Master of Ceremonies.

The Tenth Muse

A Pause. The reader of a feminist bent may already have had more than enough of all this boyishness. Yes, yes, I know. We all talk too much and say too little—as Gertrude once put it to a long-winded man, "more matter, less art." But you like Springsteen, right? And you can tolerate (or perhaps secretly enjoy?) his constant objectifications and eroticizations and romanticizations of the "fairer sex"? If you really don't want to be put on a pedestal and sung to by an impassioned man, why don't you listen to (and read about) someone else? I think you do want that, and that you do want to be adored, and you do want a man who would die for you—or at least a woman who would, which is why you also like the Indigo Girls. Amy Ray is Bruce Springsteen in drag, or vice versa, because when erotic desire gets that intense, frankly, it doesn't matter who is doing whom.

I think that is why Plato (who was something akin to gay) called Sappho, the poetess from Lesbos (who was either a lesbian, or not, or poly-amorous and omni-sexual, or not, depending upon which expert you ask and when, and what sort of mood you're in when you hear the answer . . .), anyway, Plato called Sappho the "Tenth Muse." We will spend some time on the other nine Muses shortly, but for now, be aware that Plato didn't say this because Sappho was a woman, he said it because she was so very good at poetry that it seemed divine to him (if not sufficiently divine to win her a place in his ideal city). In the ancient world, the idea that a woman should be poetic came as no surprise at all—it was expected. In the world before history, everyone understood that women can do directly what men can do only derivatively—whether that is creating words or creating babies, both of which were seen as pretty magical back then (and still are by anyone with any sense).

The simple point is that when a woman could do the poetizing thing, this was regarded as entirely natural. Of course women have the power of the word. That's why they ruled the whole world for about ten thousand years before recorded history.[4] What is surprising, to the ancients, is when a man can do anything creative at all. And then as now, no real man would be stupid enough to take credit for the achievement—he credits the woman who loves him, his inspiration, his Muse. None of this happens without the blessing and power of the woman in charge, and the man receives the words as a gift, just as he receives children. All the Muses are female. How absurd would it be to have a male Muse? But feminine authority, creativity, and generosity do not begin or end with just the Muses.

For example, Socrates wasn't called the wisest man in Athens because some dude told him so. It was a woman, the Oracle at Delphi—and she added an interesting left-handed compliment. If Socrates was wise, it was because he recognized the full extent of his personal ignorance. Just the sort of thing I hear from the women in my life, minus the part about being wise. Socrates took that oracular observation as a blessing anyway. Only once did he become so full of himself as to claim he really knew anything, and the only thing he claimed to know was love—eros. He had reason to regret having said that afterwards, but that's another story.[5]

So if you my dear feminist would rather throw away the key to your chastity belt than entrust it to a man, I can't blame you.

---

[4] Since the middle of the nineteenth century, archaeologists have increasingly been unable to avoid the conclusion that human civilization is about ten thousand years older than recorded history. The archaeological record also increasingly indicates a widespread likelihood that women were the leaders of these complex civilizations. To learn about this, I recommend that you begin with the writings of the Swiss classicist Johann Jakob Bachofen (1815–1887), and move from there to the Cambridge classicist Jane Ellen Harrison (1850–1928). Their writings are easily available. The best recent writer is, in my opinion, the Lithuanian archaeologist Marija Gimbutas (1921–1994), who was a better archeologist than an interpreter of what she found, but she is still a very responsible interpreter. Unfortunately, there is a lot of total crap out there about this "pre-history," like Riane Eisler's popular book *The Chalice and the Blade*. She has the audacity to call the careful, qualified language of responsible scholars "quaint," but Riane, sweetie, it is that careful language that separates women like Harrison and Gimbutas from girls like you.

[5] If you are intrigued, I told the story in my own way in "Chef, Socrates, and the Sage of Love," in *South Park and Philosophy: Bigger, Longer, and More Penetrating*, edited by Richard Hanley.

Men are pigs. But we're all pigs for you, baby, and I'll need to ask you to read a different chapter. But I will grant you one thing for sure: the idea that there are only nine Muses, with just one Mother, is definitely a male invention. Men get nervous when too many women start generating too much of that delectable energy, and when men get nervous, they start counting things. "Nine of you and no more!" said Herodotus. In truth there are infinitely many Muses, as many as there are actual women and possible women. Please don't be too harsh with us when we are frightened. If you only understood what you do to us, it would scare you too.

The Early Rounds: History, Tragedy, Comedy, and the Stars

You'll have to wait for the main event between Dylan and Springsteen while we warm up. How did it come to this, the battle royal between the two titans of the white-man dithyramb?

Well, in the early eliminations we saw some able poets. For example, in the eastern semi-finals, Michael Stipe did "The End of the World as We Know It," and Billy Joel sang "We Didn't Start the Fire," but the audience knew that these were not the purest and most powerful deliverances of the Muses. Still, Stipe and Joel made it to the semis by backing up their poetic claims with "Fall on Me" and "Only the Good Die Young," which are pretty impressive pieces of rhyme, if not quite the pinnacle. But their weakness is exposed when we consider that it is not so difficult to turn actual history into rhyme. Any able wordsmith can do it. The Muse of history is Clio, and she isn't the Queen Mother of the Muses. The problem with history is that, well, it's over. Her songs, the ones she inspires without help from other Muses, may serve as a clever record of past experience, but they don't burst into the future. The Muses together do not only sing of what was, they sing of what is and will be again. To make it into the finals, the offering must transcend the past, and that is why Billy and Michael were eliminated in the Urban White-boy Division.

And they were eliminated by Paul Simon, when he did "Sound of Silence." He had set them up for the take-down with "Fifty Ways to Leave Your Lover." But when Simon came up against Springsteen in the regional finals, he pulled out his best, "You Can Call Me Al": "A man walks down the street, says 'why am I short of attention? Got a short little span of attention and oh my nights are so long' . . ." It was good, but Bruce won by a nose with "Spirit in the Night": "We'll pick up Hazy Davy and Killer Joe / And I'll take you out to where the gypsy angels go / They're built like light and they dance like spirits in the night . . ." Clearly a whole gathering of Muses, no?

Paul Simon's primary Muse is named Melpomene, the Muse of tragedy. If you think about it you'll see that the vast majority of Paul's lovely words depend on the sense of tragedy and loss—even when he is chipper enough to be singing about the color film in his Nikon camera, he still just worries that his mother will take it away from him. Bruce is not so limited. Your mother is not going to take your film, Paul. Chill. It makes me wonder if the "mother and child reunion," the one that was "only a motion away," actually ever occurred. Paul left us all hanging on the outcome. Maybe Mama Pajama just spit on the ground and sent the boy to the house of detention. Paul has issues, but he's a grand poet. I am not sure he wants to be loved by his Muse. He seems to be doing straight time in her house of detention, and she's a Nun with a big ruler for his hands. Where's the radical priest when you need him?

Bruce, on the other hand, shows that he has the favor of Clio in songs such as "Youngstown" and "Nebraska," and he is on better than formal terms with Melpomene in songs like "Streets of Philadelphia" and "Reno." Yes, history and tragedy are there, and they are not cruel nuns. They like Bruce and he likes them. The audience just knows.

But speaking of Melpomene, word has it that Robert Johnson and Muddy Waters are scheduled for the finals in the Delta Blues Division down at the crossroads in Mississippi; the Devil himself is making the calls there, since they have both already cashed in their mortal chips. And it's down to Jimmie Rogers and A.P. Carter in the Dead Hillbilly Division, but there are rumors that Carter lifted some of his lines from his kinfolk, and then someone's daddy came looking for him with a shotgun. Hank Williams and some Honky Tonk Angels (hopefully not too many for a pinhead) are the judges in that one.

When it comes to blues and country and hillbilly music, this is a collaborative effort between Melpomene and Thalia, the Muse of comedy and nature poetry. Bruce leaves the nature poetry to John Denver and other wimps who change their names,[6] but he does do comedy. Bruce doesn't write "ha-ha" funny songs, but he does write songs made from funny stories, and his favorite comic trope is irony.[7] A good example of Thalia's efforts with Bruce would be "57 Channels (And Nothin' On)," in which Bruce also calls on the help of Urania, the Muse of the celestial sky. In that tune he buys a satellite dish, points it at the stars, and "A message came back from the great beyond / There's 57 channels and nothing on." He finally shoots the TV, a tribute to Elvis. You'll find simply countless lines about the sky, the stars, the sun and moon, and the "great beyond" in Springsteen's poetry. He and Urania are pretty tight, and Bruce doesn't like the way "the Giants of Science spend their days and nights" trying to control her skies and count everything (see "Santa Ana" from *Tracks* if that bit of lyric evades your memory).

Sam Houston's Ghost

However those contests may unfold in the great beyond, what we will have at the Meadowlands is a truly impressive contest for the (temporarily) living. But this is like the Super Bowl—you have to endure a lot of commentary before kick-off, but the game will be worth it. Probably. Never trust a philosopher.

This may come as a surprise, but maybe not. Texas has its very own Muse, and all songwriters have to pay homage to her. It's true that whatever Texans can't buy they will simply steal, whether it's oil, culture, Iraq, or Texas itself, and their Muse is no different. They stole their Muse from Mexico, but the Mexicans had already stolen her from the Spanish, and the Spanish stole her from the eastern Mediterranean in the Middle Ages. Her name is Calliope, the very one who crashes to the ground in "Blinded by the Light." Calliope is a big woman, pear shaped, fertile, Texas-sized; she likes gravy and greasy bar-b-cue and she ain't satisfied with a short poem or a little

---

[6] I suppose you're all well aware that Bob Dylan's name used to be "Zimmerman."

[7] If you want to hear the purest deliverance of Thalia in the "ha-ha" category, download "Title of the Song" by the group Da Vinci's Notebook, from their album *The Life and Times of Mike Fanning*.

tally-whacker (that's what they call it in Texas, in polite company). That is why Townes Van Zandt couldn't write a short song. He was from Texas. I don't know about his tally-whacker, but I do know that Calliope liked him better than he liked her—she wouldn't leave him alone, couldn't get enough of him. Townes was supposed to face Steve Earle in the finals of the Drunk and Drugged Cowboys Division of our contest, but he died. Calliope crushed his skinny ass. Steve Earle wasn't willing to let the thing go, so he has been trying to die ever since then, just so he can get his match. Some people, especially Right-wing politicians and the corporate powers of Nashville's Music Row, wish Steve well in his quest for the other side. But I don't. I like him right where he is, and Townes can wait.[8]

All of Calliope's boys know that they stole her from Mexico (see "Pancho and Lefty" from Townes's catalogue), and they'll tell you so if you ask them. Bruce learned the story. He had to. He kept on singing about Spanish girls (definitely an obsession of his) until one day the big ole woman said "you have to write about Texas, that's where I live; and as for your little ditty about Go-cart Mozart, I don't care for it; I was not sneezing and wheezing when you tripped me, and I am not a silicone sister, these are real . . . so you owe me." Bruce gave her an epic, "Galveston Bay," and then told the story of her kidnapping in "Santa Ana." Penance done. Bruce has always been a good, pious Catholic.[9]

---

[8] Actually, the event really did occur, sort of. Check out the CD Steve Earle, Townes Van Zandt, Guy Clark: *Together at the Bluebird Cafe*. It sounded like Steve and Townes were so very intoxicated that night that they could barely perform at all, but it is such an amazing gathering of true Texas poets that it is worth a listen. Guy Clark was, as far as I could tell, more or less sober, but it's not like he was unfamiliar with the rule requiring strong drink. Nobody won that night, however, because Calliope didn't show up at all—the Muses have a pact, ever since the whole Dixie Chicks debacle: they don't cross the city line in Nashville any more, although they will visit some of the more depressing towns on the outskirts. As Guy Clark wryly observed, alluding to Townes Van Zandt as "William Butler Yeats in jeans": "There ain't no money in poetry / That's what sets the poet free / And I've had all the freedom I can stand." (See Clark's "Cold Dog Soup.")

[9] A certain type of Catholic, that is—Springsteen calls himself "lapsed," but as Stan Friedman notes in a review, although Springsteen's "words certainly are not scripture, many of us have used their dense layers of meaning to help reflect on our own faith. No one should be surprised. Springsteen's theology has been the subject of numerous magazine articles, books, and even

Canadian Border Five Miles from Here

There are some pretty poets north of the border. Leonard Cohen won the Shivering Canucks Division, when Gordon Lightfoot made the supreme mistake of singing "Wreck of the *Edmund Fitzgerald*" in the final round. The audience fell asleep, and anyone could see that this wasn't Clio's best work. Cohen had advanced to the finals with a victory over Joni Mitchell (the Canadians are so damned egalitarian that they let women into these things). But Cohen got to go first, and proved the better woman by singing (or attempting to sing, which was about all he could ever do, but that never stopped Dylan either) "Joan of Arc." In that astonishing procession of lyric, Cohen actually has the audacity to depict the fire, yes, the fire, as Joan's amorous suitor. The fire stalks her all of her (short) life and then "marries" her at the stake, and consummates that desire by consuming her body—and with some coaxing, she wants it. Holy shit! That is what I said the first time I heard the song. Love'll do that to you if you aren't careful. The "Joan" reference wasn't lost on Joni, and she decided to forfeit. Discretion is the better part of valor. Good call Joni. Leonard was always a little bit unstable.

Then Cohen clinched the deal over Lightfoot in the finals with "Hallelujah," which I know you've heard. This is an impossible song, but it isn't the same sort of song as "Blinded by the Light." It's a hymn. Cohen worked with all the Muses, and it's a good thing Springsteen didn't have to compete with him (due to the immigration restrictions the Canadian government, adopted in 2002 to keep all thinking Americans from over-crowding Toronto in search of safety and genuine civil liberties). But Leonard's favorite Muses were Erato and Polyhymnia. Erato, as you might guess, gives her boys erotic poetry and marriage songs. "Joan of Arc" is principally hers. Polyhymnia, as you might also guess, is responsible for hymns—sacred song of all kinds, and she worked together with Erato on Cohen's "Hallelujah."

---

seminars. Churches work his songs into their liturgies. Biblical allusions populate all his albums, with some cuts being influenced by authors such as Flannery O'Connor." Springsteen is indeed a Flannery O'Connor sort of Catholic. And Friedman's entire review of *Magic* is very perceptive, and right on the money in my view. See it at
http://www.christianitytoday.com/music/glimpses/2007/magic.html.

Bruce knows Erato and Polyhymnia very well indeed, as any Springsteen fan can attest. Religious imagery shows up in almost every Springsteen song, and when he gets religious, it's almost always about some woman. One of my favorites is "I'll Work for Your Love," from the album *Magic*, in which Bruce takes the Ecstasy of Saint Theresa and turns it into a seduction song for a bar maid who catches his eye. "I watch the bones in your back like the stations of the cross," says he. This tune may be the best collaboration of Erato and Polyhymnia since "Hallelujah," but with the added help of Thalia. Where Cohen's song is so over-the-top that it borders on giving way to simultaneous joy and despair (if that is even possible, which I wouldn't have believed until I heard the song), Springsteen's tune displays ironic wit—he surely snickers at himself as he says "I watch your hands smooth the front of your blouse and seven drops of blood fall."[10] It's too much; it's funny.

Dancing in the Light

We are down to just two Muses now, so the *pièce de résistance* can't be far away. Their names are Euterpe and Terpsichore. They are performing Muses, the ones who descend on the performers and the audience and create the magic in the music (that's Euterpe's part) and the ecstatic dance (that's Terpsichore's part). The contest is not just about the words, it's also about the delivery, the energy, the communication between the poet and the crowd. Some artists specialize in just this part of the poetic process—performing other people's songs and doing it so well as to enchant us all. Undoubtedly, in recent times, the darling of Terpsichore and Euterpe was Elvis Presley. He wasn't much of a songwriter (he didn't suck, it just wasn't his gift). When Elvis sang and danced, we all wanted him, women and men. There wasn't a dry seat in the house. How can one man possess that much erotic energy? Euterpe and Terpsichore wore Elvis out, and us too.

---

[10] Stan Friedman thinks this may be a veiled reference to Leviticus 16:19. That looks right to me, and is reinforced by an earlier verse: "The dust of civilizations . . . Slip off of your fingers / And come driftin' down like rain." See Friedman's review cited above. I don't know what Bruce reads, but he certainly once read the Bible and the Lives of the Saints. It's all over his music.

Plato held such poets in special contempt. The Greeks had a name for poets who performed other people's songs: "rhapsodes." In contrast to the poets who create their own poems, who are simply deceived about whether they know anything, the rhapsode just sits around cultivating his own vanity, and hasn't the moral fiber to realize that he's just a wanna-be. Plato wrote a whole dialogue about the pretensions of the rhapsodes, called *Ion* (that's the rhapsode's name, and he was sort of the Elvis Presley, or more likely the Michael Bolton, of ancient Athens). Plato was hell-bent on making this type of poet look as bad as possible, so he depicts Ion as a total fool and a hopeless poser who really wants to be a military leader, but hasn't either the courage or the knowledge to do anything except act. It sort of reminds me of Ronald Reagan's service in the Second World War—and as President.

Obviously Terpsichore and Euterpe also love Bruce. They have given him a sense of the power of performance that exceeds most of the rhapsodes, if not quite coming up to the level of Elvis. And Bruce is no rhapsode, he's a real poet. Of particular note for our purposes is that Terpsichore and Euterpe have a very uneven relationship with Dylan. More often than not audiences come away from a Dylan show disappointed. I have never heard anyone say that about a Springsteen concert. Dylan does not love or respect his audience, and he does not want to be loved by the Muses of performance, although sometimes they take hold of him whether he wants to be taken or not. Clearly Dylan knows these Muses, but he's a ragged clown, and while the reels of rhyme may be skipping, Dylan himself is standing stark still, hiding under a hat, behind dark glasses, chasing shadows, just like he said. I wouldn't pay it any mind.[11] Meanwhile Bruce is dancing in the light, and not too badly for a white boy (even the Muses can't wholly counteract the genetic stiffness of a northern European heritage—which is why I have come to question whether Elvis was really white), and he's dancing with Courtney Cox, who looks like the embodiment of Terpsichore to me. What a babe.

---

[11] I am not alluding to the infamous "booing" incident at Newport when Bob pulled out the electric guitar. Not only is that all blown out of proportion, but Bob was right. Folk music had become maudlin. It was definitely time for a little electricity.

The Poetic Virtue

You can see that the fightin' words are starting up at the Meadowlands. Both Dylan and Springsteen are virtuosos. They are, at least some of the time, loved by all of the Muses. That is what makes a poet a virtuoso. But that isn't enough. What makes a poet virtuous? The words "virtuous" and "virtuoso" obviously come from the same root. It's the Latin "virtutem," which means moral strength, manliness, potency, excellence. The word "virile" comes from the same root, "vir," which means both a man and a hero. "Virtuouso" comes into English from Italian as the man possessing the greatest skill, especially in music. I don't suppose I have to point out that the word "music" comes from "muse," but I just did anyway. This "virtue" is literally a certain relationship between a potent man and his Muses.

The virtuous poet is something akin to chivalrous in his response to the Muses. He loves and yearns for them, he would die for them willingly, and he sees them everywhere and in everything. I say this is akin to chivalry, and not chivalry itself, because the yearning isn't chaste—not in the least. The virtuous poet is an amorous type, and nothing is off limits—he wants all the Muses at once, if he can persuade them—a *ménage à neuf* (*dix*, if you include the poetic member, but every poet has a dix, while only the best can get a neuf—sort of gives a new sense the line "I can't get eneuf of your love . . ."). And indeed, that neuftette is what creates songs of the sort we find in "Blinded by the Light" and "Subterranean Homesick Blues." And that is the name I'm proposing for this sort of song—the *Ménage à Neuf*. It's a special kind of song, needless to say.

How does it come about? Obviously I'm just guessing. I have never written any such song. The best my imagination can come up with is this: imagine a bar, the poet's meat market. It's simply packed with young men on the make. But there are exactly nine women. You already know their names. Now, in such a bar, the odds of going home with just one of them are not high, even for a pretty smooth talker. They are not coy, not chaste; they want to go home with someone in this joint, but they are picky. You'll have to do better than "do you come here often?" or "your place or mine?" if you want any company tonight. I am way out of my league. I'll be lucky even to get my face slapped. And these women are all very different. Clio is bookish, Urania is pretty spacey, Calliope just ordered an extra helping of gravy, Terpsichore won't sit still, and Euterpe keeps trying to sing with the band. It's bedlam in here.

Now imagine some young buck strolls in and he leaves with all of them, while the rest of us have to settle for Rosie Palm and her Five Sisters (at least for tonight—we'll be back).[12] On a night like that, dressed to the nines and for the nine, you could get blinded by the light, because this affair isn't done in the darkness. Or you could go seriously subterranean, because all these women, even Urania, come from underground, Gaia's cave, and they're always homesick. What can a poet say to woo them all? What impossible pick-up line can he invent? I mean all of these women are beautiful—well, there are eight beautiful babes and one big ol' mama from Texas who will be a lot of fun in the sack.

There is a secret to it. The poet asks their Mother. She owns this bar, and it's only by her good graces that any aspiring poet even gains entrance. You see, poets don't just make up their words—they "remember" them. The Mother of the Muses is named Mnemosyne. In English we still use (or misuse) her name when we speak of "mnemonic devices," meaning memory aids. Her name means "memory," of course, and if there is a single master key to the poetic art, it is the art of memory. And my clue that this must be what's going on is that the song that flows from the Ménage à Neuf is so devilishly hard to remember. It doesn't follow chronology or history, it is so replete with extra rhymes and metrical tricks that if you want to learn such a song, even as a second rate rhapsode, you'll have to spend days and weeks on it. And Springsteen and Dylan not only learned such songs, they wrote them. All nine Muses will go home with a poet if and only if he knows how to woo their Mother—to cultivate memory. And I don't mean simply his personal memory. The poet has to tap into the collective memory of the human race, and to see in it all the configurations of the present and the future, what was, is, and will be again.

It requires a gift, but the gift is worthless without the discipline to use it, to become worthy of it. The two things the

---

[12] If you don't know what I'm talking about, listen to the tune Jackson Browne put on his live album *Running on Empty*, called "Rosie." If you still don't understand the nature of this lament, I can't help you.

virtuous poet knows are: (1) that his creations are not his own, that he must approach them with gratitude and humility, because they can be taken from him at any time; and (2) that if he doesn't work with his own memory and the memory of the race, he will never create anything worthwhile. The virtuous poet is grounded and disciplined, appreciative and humble to his Muses, if not toward the rest of us. That is why all good poets read widely, and among the things they study most intently are the lyrics and musical moves of their fellow songwriters.

You Can't Tell the Players without a Program

The main event is here. A hush falls over the Meadowlands. A young poet who expects to be a contender announces his arrival on the public scene with a piece of almost impossible poetry, a Ménage à Neuf, as proof that he has gotten the permission of Mnemosyne to enter the contest. And he saves that gift for the finals. Dylan has a lot of great bits, but he knows which song is his true Ménage à Neuf. He was so brash as to have Allen Ginsberg and Bob Neuwirth write out some of the poster-boards and stand behind him at a distance as he flipped them to the ground in the video for "Subterranean Homesick Blues"—the whole idea of a music video was quite possibly his creation. Those poster-boards are the very gauntlet. And Springsteen is there to pick it up. The winner gets to call Woody Guthrie his daddy.

Dylan doesn't think any white man's Muses love him more. These "niners" (I am tired of typing the whole French phrase, so we'll call these songs "niners" for short) are punctuated with astonishing internal rhymes—where the poet of ordinary virtue settles for a nice rhyme or partial rhyme at the end of the line, Dylan says:

> Get sick, get well, hang around a ink well
> Ring bell, hard to tell if anything is goin' to sell
> Try hard, get barred, get back, write Braille
> Get jailed, jump bail, join the army, if you fail.

The audience says "oooh." And Bruce answers:

And some fleshpot mascot was tied into a lover's knot with a whatnot
in her hand
Now young Scott with a slingshot finally found a tender spot and
throws his lover in the sand
And some bloodshot forget-me-not whispers daddy's within earshot
save the buckshot turn up the band.

Very fancy. Dylan edges ahead by a nose for economy and meter
on the "internal rhyme" round. All poets know that using fewer
words is better, and resorting to proper names for an internal
rhyme is a sign of weakness. Now Bruce goes first:

Some silicone sister with her manager's mister told me I got what it
takes
She said I'll turn you on sonny, to something strong if you play that
song with the funky break.

In this round we add alliteration to internal rhyme. Bob impatiently answers:

Maggie comes fleet foot, face full of black soot
Talkin' that the heat put, plants in the bed but
The phone's tapped anyway, Maggie says that many say
They must bust in early May, orders from the D.A.

Note that he uses the proper name for meter, not rhyme. But
this one has internal rhyme, alliteration, assonance, consonance. Notice how he gradually transformed the rhyme from
"foot" to "but" by interposing "soot" and "put." Masterful. Bob is
trying to cut the contest short—skip ahead to the heavy stuff.
"Top that, asshole," he seems to say. Bruce says:

Some brimstone baritone anti-cyclone rolling stone preacher from the
east
He says: "Dethrone the dictaphone, hit it in its funny bone, that's
where they expect it least"
And some new-mown chaperone, standin' in the corner all alone
watchin' the young girls dance
And some fresh-sown moonstone was messin' with his frozen zone to
remind him of the feeling of romance.

And the whole audience knows Bruce is referring to Bob as the moonstone, and he is suggesting that Bob will be courting Rosie Palm tonight while Bruce goes home with all the choice trim. So Thalia really likes the part about the funny bone, and she always liked Bruce better than Bob anyway, and Terpsichore didn't fail to notice the part about the young girls dancing, which Bob can't do. So together they hatch a plan. Clearly this was going to be stand-off, a stalemate, a draw. Dylan is the more accomplished poet, but Bruce has the heart. He's a scrapper. Don McLean's people are off sulking in a coffee-house, singing Roy Orbison songs, but at the Meadowlands the crowd could only say "ooooh," and look from Bob to Bruce, Bruce to Bob, and it just didn't look like anyone was going to give an inch.

You know their stories. Year after year, song after song, the Muses kept delivering the goods to both Bob and Bruce. But time has told the story. After about fifteen years, something happened to Dylan. The Muses left. The songs started looking lame. It became undeniable when Dylan thought he had been born again. For heaven's sake Bob, you were chosen in utero for a special life. Why don't you just appreciate it?

Things were looking a little rough for Bruce too, during the days of *Lucky Town* and *Human Touch*, but he never lost his faith, like Dylan did. In 1995, with *The Ghost of Tom Joad*, it was clear to those who were listening that Bruce's Muses were all still with him, even if that was one of Melpomene's albums—and they still are. Most critics think that Dylan's "dip" in the eighties and nineties was serious, but his new songs from *Time Out of Mind* (1997) to *Tempest* (2012) were excellent. The Nobel Prize people agree, it seems. In sales his comeback wasn't rewarded with quite the world reception one might have expected, although The Prize will surely improve world sales. But Bruce's popularity and sales never slipped. On the world stage he grew from 1975 until now. The critics and the fans continue to gobble up the goods. *High Hopes* (2014) rose quickly to number one in ten countries, and only one studio album failed to chart at number one in the US since 1995— the acoustic Seeger Sessions, which went to number three. Dylan has nothing comparable and has been far less prolific. Nobel Prize vs. prolific creativity, with ever growing sales and world acclaim. Undecidable.

Back at the Meadowlands, Thalia and Terpsichore have whispered something in the ear of our emcee, Weird Al Yankovic (Thalia plays in the sandbox with him sometimes, as you know): "Al, sweetie, we want you to prance right out between Bruce and Bob, and this is what we want you to say, and be sure to say it just like Bob would." Al doesn't need to be told twice:

> Rise to vote, sir
> Do geese see God?
> "Do nine men interpret?" "Nine men," I nod
> Rats live on no evil star
> Won't lovers revolt now?
> Race fast, safe car
> Pa's a sap
> Ma is as selfless as I am
> May a moody baby doom a yam? . . .

And he goes on and on like that, ending with the poetically impossible:

> Go hang a salami, I'm a lasagna hog

. . . all to the tune of "Subterranean Homesick Blues." You might overlook it at first, but study those lyrics very closely. The whole song is written in palindromes—the same backwards as forwards. Weird Al named the song, well, what else? "Bob." Who's the ragged clown now, Bob? The crowd at the Meadowlands gets the point. Bob doesn't know what he's talking about. No wonder the Muses left him to his own right hand for twenty years. He treated them poorly and they got tired of it. Taken down and bested by a geek, the Clown Prince of Pop. Anybody can do that trick, Bobby, even Weird Al.[14] You just take yourself so seriously. Have a little fun for

---

[14] I was at an Arlo Guthrie show once, in Oklahoma, and he was telling tales on Dylan. Among many very funny stories he had, one was about a "vacation" he had taken with Dylan and some third songwriter—I think it was Ian Tyson—and they all rented a cabin off in the woods upstate to write songs. Arlo compared it to fishing for songs, and complained that he had been fishing downstream from Dylan all his life, and the trouble is that Dylan catches them all, and he never even throws the little ones back. And Arlo actually

god's sake! And probably Bob has a small tally-whacker and never wrote a kind word about Texas. But pride goeth before the Fall, and I don't think Bruce ever gave in to pride. I'll bet a fiddle of gold that Bruce is a sensitive lover and would never do a quickie with a Muse (or two). Just my suspicion, but I'd wager. But there is a reason why, today, Bruce's voice is regarded as a moral guide, while Dylan wields no moral authority at all. Just a good songwriter, and one too proud to go to Sweden and claim his prize. Yes, pride is an issue here.

That leaves only one thread hanging. Why are the philosophers so peevish about the poets? It's simple. There is no Muse for philosophy; it's boring, and the philosophers are just jealous, and they don't stand a chance in that oh-so-excellent bar. But I could also point out that Plato started as a poet, a pretty good one, apparently. But not the best. And his ego wouldn't take it, and we've all been paying the price ever since. Plato was just a philosophy geek, and I suppose he's had his revenge, but I won't be booking any flights to his city. I'd rather go to Asbury Park.

can call Woody Guthrie "daddy." I share this anecdote because I have been hard on Dylan here, and it must be obvious to all of you psychologist types that I know good and well he's the best. Writing tribute songs in the basic style of "Subterranean Homesick Blues" has become something of a sport among his admirers. I recommend that you check out Dave Carter's "Don't Tread on Me," and Jonathan Byrd's "Cocaine Kid." Tonight was just Bruce's night, and he had the home field advantage. Across the East River, the story would have been otherwise. The audience really does matter.

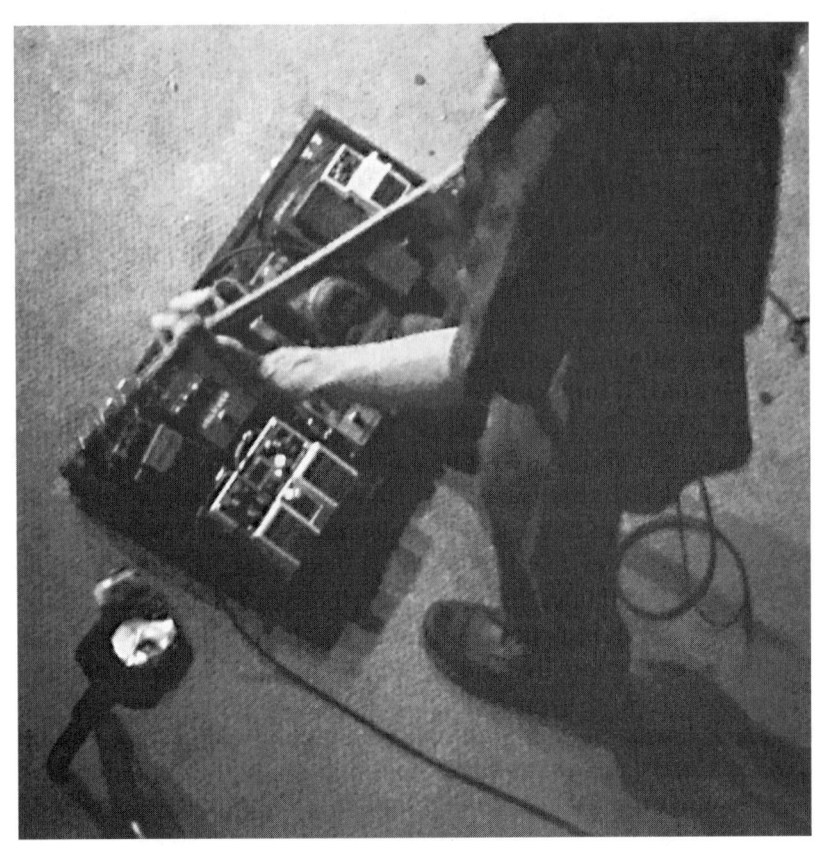

12

Prophets and Profits: Poets, Preachers, and Pragmatists

Perhaps this is the issue that frightens the prophets. A people may be dying without being aware of it; a people may be able to survive, yet refuse to make use of their ability.

—ABRAHAM JOSHUA HESCHEL, *The Prophets*

I have always thought there was something beyond the usual going on in Bruce Springsteen's music, and I was reaching for a word to describe it. Clearly he is a poet, but the forms and subject matter point to something beyond poetry. Clearly Springsteen is not a philosopher; he does not fill his free time studying Aristotle and formulating clear ideas about knowledge, being, and the good life. Yet, here is someone who can ask "what if the things you do to survive kills the things you love?"—someone who observes that the power of fear can "take your God-filled soul" and "leave you with devils and dust." I was tempted by the word "prophet" to describe him, and I was not the first. Is there something prophetic about Springsteen's approach to music? What is a prophet anyway?

The question led me to the philosopher who has spoken more about prophecy in recent years than any other. It seems that each generation gets one such philosopher, and not much more than one. In the present it is Cornel West, philosopher, orator, public intellectual, lay preacher, and Hollywood film actor—West had a small role as "Councillor West" in all three *Matrix* movies. West loves music—George Clinton, John Coltrane, Miles Davis, and yes, Bruce Springsteen, whom he has called a prophet. As philosophers go, West is much quicker to credit the crucial role played by popular music in culture than almost any philosopher in Western history. So here's someone who speaks reverently of popular music and culture, and spends the rest of his time talking about prophecy and hope. It is logical to consult West on what has been bugging me about Springsteen.

Taking a look at what West says about prophets, prophetic thinking, prophetic action, I began to think that this was indeed the right word for describing a voice like Springsteen's— and I want to make it clear that Springsteen is not the only figure who bugs me in this regard. Paul Simon, for example, seems to be cut from similar cloth. But there are precious few who really occupy this company. West says that four things go into prophetic thinking. Let's look at them.

Four Chords and a Cloud of Dust

The first element is "discernment," by which West means that a prophetic figure has a "nuanced historical sense," remaining "attuned [yes, attuned] to the ambiguous legacies and hybrid cultures in history." And so attuned, the prophet is able to "keep track at any social moment of who is bearing most of the social cost." This really is one of Springsteen's strong suits. From "The Ghost of Tom Joad," to "Born in the USA," to "My Hometown," to "Wrecking Ball," Springsteen is engaged in a continuous act of prophetic discernment and tracking who is carrying the social cost. He never backs down, and he is never wrong.

The second element for West is what he calls "human connection," by which he means placing great emphasis upon empathy, where empathy is understood as "the capacity to get in contact with the anxieties and frustrations of others."[1] This also seems apt in considering Springsteen. He writes in the first person, boldly, constantly, and describes conditions and burdens that simply never were his own—a homeless worker, an ex-con trying to go straight, a Reno hooker, a gay man dying of AIDS. I very much doubt that Bruce ever camped by the railroad tracks with "no home, no job, no peace, no rest," but I certainly feel that he knows what it is like, and I don't doubt him

---

[1] Cornel West, *Beyond Eurocentrism and Multiculturalism, Volume 1: Prophetic Thought in Postmodern Times*, p. 5.

when he says "wherever somebody's struggling to be free, look in their eyes Mom, and you'll see me." On the other hand, I have never endured such a situation either. Yet, those who have been through the ordeals he describes are the very bedrock of Springsteen's public. He sees and feels their lives, and gives it back to them not only as art, but as truth. This is the power of empathy, and the result of the effort is human connection, "never losing the humanity of others," as West puts it.

The third element in West's scheme is what he calls "tracking hypocrisy," but doing so in a "self-critical" rather than "self-righteous mode." West continues that the prophet accents "boldly and defiantly the gap between principles and practice, between promise and performance, between rhetoric and reality." Of many choices, I think of Springsteen's song "Your Own Worst Enemy," which says "the times, they got too clear, so you removed all the mirrors." Assuming the moral high ground so as to call out the hypocrisy of others is a slippery business. It invites people to take pot-shots at the messenger. Springsteen has always shielded himself by trying to remain down to earth, unpretentious, humble, grateful to his audience, and prepared to admit his own faults. As West says, we have to recognize that "we are often complicit with the very thing we are criticizing" (p. 6). The constancy of Bruce's effort at humility over five decades has given him unusual moral authority in the eyes of the public. Where Paul Simon often gave in to cynicism, Bruce just keeps coming back and speaking truth to power, and one of those truths could be summarized as saying to such people the moral equivalent of "you power brokers and pundits think that ordinary people don't see you for what you are, but they do."

For West, the final element in someone prophetic is hope. West says that "to talk about human hope is to engage in an audacious attempt to galvanize and energize, to inspire and invigorate world weary people." Sounds like a fair description of a Springsteen concert. The seats fill with people whose jobs "leave them uninspired," and Bruce and several of his dearest friends take them into the living room on E Street and talk about a train that carries saints, sinners, losers, winners, whores, gamblers, lost souls, souls departed, kings and fools, and on that train "faith will be rewarded . . . hear the steel wheels singing, bells of freedom ringin'." I can't think of a modern troubadour who can show us so much despair and human misery without taking away our hope, our shot at freeing ourselves.

Rising and Falling

Springsteen, quite possibly more than any other figure in the English-speaking world, embodies all four of the elements West combines to make a prophet. And there is so much more. This is not a songwriter who offers a few prophetic moments, it comes album after album, concert after concert, a drumbeat of prophecy as steady as Max Weinberg's right foot. Bruce even boldly ventures to tell us the future:

> Now there's a fire down below
> But it's comin' up here
> So leave everything you know . . .
> There's bodies hanging in the trees
> This is what will be, this is what will be.

I'm not sure what the prediction is, but it isn't good news. And as I consider the lyrics of "The Rising," I find the label "prophet" tempting indeed:

> Wearing the cross of my calling . . .
> Spirits above and behind me
> Faces gone, black eyes burning bright
> May their precious blood forever bind me
> Lord as I stand before your fiery light.

This is a New York City fireman bravely facing his end and dreaming of the resurrection. Who but a prophet dares to discern the historic moment of 9/11, to write the words in first person of one who perishes, who audaciously finds hope in the blackness, and tells us of a rising? I am sorely tempted, but somehow I just know something is missing here. This is powerful stuff, the best we have, but it is not quite prophecy.

Pragmatists, Poets, and Preachers

Sometimes philosophers have silly arguments, sometimes they don't. One argument they've been having for about twenty years (you decide if it's silly) is the future and direction and meaning of the philosophical school called "pragmatism." I would tell you what pragmatism is, if I could, but it turns out that this is what people are arguing about. It's somewhat easier to say what pragmatism *was*, but all participants in the argument seem to agree that it doesn't ultimately matter, since none of them is willing to be bound by some strictly historical sense of the term.

There are lots of people arguing over the term and its meaning, but the three main choices seem to have been Richard Rorty, Cornel West, and Hilary Putnam. They all agree that pragmatism is supposed to be practical in some way, but beyond that, they don't have so much in common.

Rorty and Putnam are disadvantaged in the debate, being no longer with us. And since Rorty didn't believe in God, we can assume that if he was correct, he is out of the debate; and if he was wrong, he is out of the debate for a different reason. But he has many supporters who, we may assume, are not exactly praying for him, but they still read his books and speak his lingo. Rorty, calling himself a pragmatist, spent nearly thirty years trying to convince everyone that philosophy was not much use, and that the real hope for democratic civilization lay with the work of poets. Poets create words and whole vocabularies; they sort of go fishing for the future and bring back a stringer of fresh marks and noises, the fish of the future, providing the rest of us with linguistic sustenance. Because so much depends on language (everything does, according to Rorty), a great deal of weight is given to those who make the words (or find them, or reel them in, or whatever it is they do). Today's poetic metaphors become tomorrow's literal truths and common sense, Rorty says. Let's call this "poetic pragmatism."

If poetic pragmatism is like fishing for the future, the ocean that such poets set out upon is one of possibilities for living, for thinking, for being. And if the poet is the one who braves this sea and brings back a hold of fishy words, those words are cleaned, cooked and consumed first by the masses (from the semi-literate dockworker to the college graduate, who is also sometimes semi-literate). The political leaders eventually digest the innards, and the philosophers then sit around discussing the discarded bones. At least, that is Rorty's story, as abridged.

On the other hand, Cornel West says that pragmatism should be prophetic. By this he means that not just poets, but philosophers (and others) should speak to the masses, make their own contributions to the market-place of words, use philosophy to change and improve society. Such philosophers sort of preach their moral message and pitch their preaching to the sonic tastes of the masses, especially those members of society whose voices are not heard by the powerful. In a sense, the "prophetic" part of West's pragmatism has to do with one special aspect of prophecy: the tradition of excoriating those who ignore and mistreat the needy from motives of greed and self-satisfied power. The prophetic pragmatist goes fishing with the poet, reels in a few of his own, and shares the responsibility for cleaning and cooking them, making the powerful digest the guts, and then discussing the bones with the philosophers, but not too much of the last. All this activity keeps a body busy. As I said, West calls this "prophetic pragmatism," but I will call it "preachy pragmatism," for reasons that will be clear shortly.

Then there's Hilary Putnam. He was a nice man. He didn't think philosophers should wax poetic or sermonic. He thought philosophers contribute "reasonableness" to any discussion of human problems, unpretentiously, humbly, but assertively. His philosophers can ride on the fishing boat, even cast a line in the water, but in the end, he is saying "don't underestimate the need for a well-ordered and productive discussion of the bones." This is why he never could win the debate. He might even be right, but it doesn't matter because this is not going to capture anyone's imagination, except bone collectors', no matter how well he made the case. We can call his kind of approach "sober pragmatism," but the consumers of philosophy usually want a little wine with their meal. In the public mind, the contest is between poets and preachers. Teetotalers need to find themselves a good meeting with the friends of Bill W.

A Pop Quiz

The debate over pragmatism has been raging for more than a quarter of a century. West is ahead, as measured by books sold, movies and CDs made and consumed. Rorty has a strong enclave in the academies. Putnam has a good AA meeting going for people who are trying to shed their addiction to analytic philosophy, one day at a time. But all pragmatists insist on something practical, and that a philosophy has to pass the test of "experience." I want to run such a test. The true poets of the present culture are not those who publish highbrow verse and teach in English departments; they are the songwriters. And among these, any number might be identified as poets of the type Rorty praises—the creators of vocabularies that inspire the mass imagination, and whose lyrics suggest possibilities for living. But in order to test Rorty's vision against West's we need someone who is also at least arguably prophetic—takes up the cause of the dispossessed, the outcast; someone who speaks truth to power, identifies the sins of greed and the consequences. In short, we need a poet who has found a way to preach, and has achieved the ear of the public.

This requirement narrows the choices. In fact, beyond Bob Dylan and Bruce Springsteen, I can't think of anyone at all in the present. Dylan has preachy songs, but there is no consistency of worldview or message. Where Dylan created a persona, Springsteen revealed himself as a person—or at least, that's how it feels. To his public, Springsteen is what he seems to be, in the sense that he never attempted to shroud his origins or his perspective in a myth. Springsteen is the better test case. (Some people will mention Steve Earle in this company. I actually agree that he might be an even better test case, but he simply does not command the public's attention in the same ways or at the same level.)

But here we encounter a serious problem. Rorty knew almost nothing about poetry, apart from what he happened to like. West knows a bit more about prophecy, but his perspective on it neither is nor claims to be deeply informed. For him, the idea of prophecy derives from contemporary sources—Reinhold Niebuhr's call for a prophetic Christianity in the 1930s, Martin Luther King's oratory and leadership in the Civil Rights movement, various Christian Marxist voices. It would be handy to know something a little more thorough about both prophecy and poetry—where they come from and how they have been inherited in the Western world.

Prophets Proper

I needed someone who could tell me more about prophets. Enter Abraham Joshua Heschel (1907–1972). Heschel probably

knew more about the prophets than any person in the twentieth century. But among the many things he said and wrote, he
took some trouble to distinguish poets from prophets. The confusion of poet and prophet goes as far back as human history,
partly because both are clearly moved by a spirit of some kind,
be it a Muse or a divinity; partly because prophets do not hesitate to write in verse, and both bring words to the masses; and
partly because prophets and poets often share such a broad
range of social and religious concerns. We've seen above how a
voice like Springsteen's addresses this shared territory, and in
much the way West requires. Heschel calls this "the profound
kinship of prophetic and poetic imagination."[2]

The confusion of poet and prophet is understandable. As
Heschel reminds us, Ezekiel complained that he was to the people "like one who sings love songs with a beautiful voice and
plays well on an instrument, for they hear what [I say], but
they will not do it" (*The Prophets*, p. 387; Ezekiel 33:32). No one
feels obliged to do what Springsteen tells them to do, no matter how well he sings it or plays the guitar. At least in this
respect, he isn't different from Ezekiel. Furthermore, Heschel,
in what may be the most notorious and controversial part of his
account, compares the "call" or "appointment" of the prophet to
an act of seduction of the prophet by God (pp. 113–15). Most
people don't think of God as a seducer, or worse, a rapist, as
Heschel contends. The relationship of the poet to the Muse is
often described as the seduction of the poet by the Muse, but
not as rape.

But according to Heschel, there are some deep and crucial
differences between poets and prophets, and we should not
underestimate their importance. First, what the poet calls
"inspiration," the prophet calls "revelation." While the poet is
grateful for the words, the prophet often receives them with
dread. And the poet doesn't know what power inspires the
words, but the prophet knows exactly Whose message he is to
bring. And while the poet wants the job, the prophet doesn't.
There's no profit in being a prophet. The image of rape, used in
Jeremiah 20:7, indicates, according to Heschel, the "sense of
being ravished or carried away by violence, of yielding to over-

---

[2] Abraham Joshua Heschel, *The Prophets* (New York: Harper and Row,
1962), p. 268.

powering force against one's will. The prophet feels both the attraction and coercion of God, the appeal and the pressure, the charm and the stress" (p. 114).

Fishing with Bruce and Jonah

I mentioned the fishing trip. This is a good place to take an imaginary one. Many of you will recall the story of Jonah, but you may be fuzzy on the details. God shows up and tells Jonah to drop everything and go to Nineveh and "cry out against it, for their wickedness has come up against me" (Jonah 1:2). Let me translate. God shows up in Asbury Park and tells Bruce to go to New York City and stand on a street corner and cry out against its wickedness. What is the response? Jonah heads for Tarshish. Let me translate. Bruce heads for Nebraska.

You know what happens next. Bruce catches a flight for Omaha and God starts doing a Buddy Holly re-run with the weather, and Bruce confesses to the passengers and crew that he's the problem. So they hand him a parachute and push him out over Lake Erie. Miraculously, Bruce is caught in the net of the last solvent fishing boat in the upper Midwest, spends three days in the hold with the rest of the fish, does some serious praying and repenting, and gets spat out in Buffalo. Seeing the error of his ways, he hitches a ride to Manhattan, stands on the corner of Broadway and 42nd Street, and explains in tones an octave too high that if the people of Sin City don't repent in forty days, God is going to make New York look like, well, like it did on September 11th, 2001. But, in this case, the good people of New York believe Bruce, repent in sackcloth and ashes, and God relents. No September 11th. Yet, Bruce is not happy about this. He feels like a fool and goes off to F. Scott Fitzgerald's fabled Ash Heap and pouts (until God tells him not to be such a pansy).

This is all pretty hard to picture; a fable. But the key feature of it is the call, the appointment—the seduction and coercion. Prophets resist their calling because it isn't good news. It means a life of ridicule and rejection, a life on the profitless margin of acceptability. And this is true even if the people actually repent—which they usually don't. As Heschel puts it, "the mission [the prophet] performs is distasteful to him and repugnant to others; no reward is promised him and no reward could temper its bitterness" (p. 18). The prophet is afforded no life of his own, no leisure to work on a dream, and no escape from a town that rips the bones from his back. The prophet knows exactly Who has put him where he is, and it isn't a welcome Muse. For the same reason, poets don't usually profess to grasp the full meaning of their own words, but according to Heschel, prophets definitely do (p. 388).

"Honey, Let's Invite the Prophet to Dinner"

When people think of prophets in the abstract, or from the pages of books, they often seem to think it would be nice to have such people around these days, what with all the greed and wickedness and idolatry abounding. Upon serious consideration, the truth is otherwise. It is hard to have a dinner party with a prophet, you don't want one in your neighborhood—and especially not in your church or synagogue or mosque. They may wear animal skins, marry prostitutes, and name their children things like "Not-pitied" and "Not-my-people" (*The Prophets*, pp. 52–53; Hosea 1:6–9). Springsteen named his kids Evan, Jessica, and Sam. If you're thinking you'd like to have the Springsteen family over for dinner, it is because Bruce isn't a prophet.

Prophets have what we would call, in today's favored psychobabble, "boundary issues." No matter what you've done, it isn't good enough, and prophets don't hesitate to inform you of it. As Heschel points out, prophets exaggerate our sins and aren't known for being especially realistic about things (p. 14). You think you've done okay in this life? Bruce might agree, but Hosea and Amos and Jeremiah aren't impressed, with you or Bruce. The boundary issue is clearest when it comes to matters of religion—what Rorty calls the great "conversation stopper." Now poets may speak of religion, indeed, they often do, and so much poetry draws upon religious imagery and religious sensibilities that it is not easy to imagine poetry without them. But even John Milton and William Blake stop short of prefacing their poetry with the phrase "Thus says the Lord . . ." (p. 389). You want to talk about a conversation stopper. What would even Cornel West do with a prophetic pragmatist who begins his speech with "Thus says the Lord"—especially when the rest of the message is likely to be very, very bad news?

Give Me the Bad News First

We looked at Springsteen's response to 9/11 in "The Rising." It admittedly seems like something a prophet might or would say. But something's missing. Let us drop back to the issue of Viet Nam for a moment before we examine the more recent wound to the American psyche.

Heschel points out that "a tribal god was petitioned to slay the tribe's enemies because he was conceived as the god of that tribe and not the god of the enemies. When the Roman armies were defeated in battle, the people, indignant, did not hesitate to wreck the images of the gods" (p. 12). We have never, in the USA, hesitated to petition our God to help us defeat our enemies, even when we fought one another. But in Viet Nam, we lost the war. Why did no one blame God for failing us? Why would we not wreck the sanctuaries of church and synagogue and mosque to show our displeasure with a God who had not brought us victory? Most of us (not I, not Bruce, but most of us) were certainly convinced that the enemy was godless, that our struggle was divinely sanctioned, and that our victory would be a victory for truth, justice, and freedom. But perhaps we, and Springsteen, know that the relevant God is not a tribal god, and does not condone violence—Martin Luther King and Abraham Joshua Heschel, had certainly made the point.

But there's more. As Heschel says:

> The prophets of Israel proclaim that the enemy may be God's instrument in history. The God of Israel calls the archenemy of his people "Assyria, the rod of My anger" (Isaiah 10:5) . . . "Nebuchadnezzar, the king of Babylon, My servant" whom I will bring 'against this land and its inhabitants' (Jeremiah 25:9; 27:6; 43:10). Instead of cursing the enemy, the prophets condemn their own nation. (*The Prophets*, p. 12)

I can recall many people, including Springsteen and King condemning the US government for the foolish adventure in violence that was Viet Nam, but I cannot recall them or anyone else saying Viet Nam was the rod of God's anger, or Ho Chi Minh was God's servant, giving the United States exactly what it had earned by acting as though the commandments of its God were mere suggestions. I can easily, in my own prophetic mode, believe that the US deserved exactly what it got, but our more recent behavior in Iraq and elsewhere suggests that we haven't yet learned our lessons about greed, empire, violence, lies, and the misuse of God for the debased ends of idolaters who pretend to sanctity.

But here's a question worth considering. What would happen to Springsteen if he were to have written a song depicting the 9/11 hijackers as instruments of our own God sent to take down our towers of Babel and our monuments to greed, and depicting Osama bin Laden as the servant of our own God, giving us exactly what we had earned, in our greed and faithlessness? Yet, Isaiah and Jeremiah were saying something comparable to this in their time. And when you think about it, Springsteen would have had a stronger case, since Bin Laden, unlike the kings of Assyria, professes to worship the same God we claim as ours. And indeed, the worse news is that, between the two of them, Bin Laden's language is closer to the language of the prophets than Springsteen's. I can hardly imagine a less comfortable observation, but I think it is wise to be chastened by it, and to use the words "prophet" and "prophetic" with greater care than we typically do. I will point out that Bin Laden was not a prophet for the US, for the prophet comes from within the people, and is never himself the instrument of violence. But if Springsteen were to say the very things Bin Laden said, that would be pretty close to the language of prophecy as employed by Amos, Hosea, Jeremiah, and Isaiah.

And the Good News Second

But here's a more comforting thought. "The Rising" is not prophecy, but it is lamentation. The greatest lamentations in Western history were written by a prophet, Jeremiah. This is a more productive point of overlap, a place where the poet and the prophet may console one another, for the prophet does not want his warnings to be fulfilled any more than the poet or the philosopher wants it. I wonder if Springsteen might be willing to sing:

> How lonely sits the city
> That was once full of people!
> How like a widow she has become,
> She that was great among nations . . .

She took no thought of her future;
Her downfall was appalling,
With none to comfort her.
"Oh Lord, look at my affliction,
For the enemy has triumphed!"
(Lamentations 1:1, 1:9)

But there are no prophets now who, like Jeremiah, have seen the warnings fulfilled. The United States stands, at least for the present. There are only poets and pragmatists and politicians and people with feelings of foreboding. And even if a prophet should appear, God forbid, we should remember that sometimes God withholds the Mighty Hand of Justice. I do not think the United States deserves a better end than did Israel and Judah, and I do not think our current president is morally better than Ahab. But Ahab and the children of Israel tolerated Elijah. The George W. Bush administration wouldn't even tolerate Ambassador Joseph Wilson, and he wasn't exactly saying the terrorists were God's servants, or calling the President a faithless and adulterous idolater. The United States has indeed earned a worse punishment than Israel and Judah, war by war, torture by torture, conquest by conquest. Ill-gotten gain abounds, but God is, as Heschel put it, anthropopathic—God has human-like feelings, and the prophets tell us what they are. God, if there is one, surely understands our weakness, and why, against the advice of conscience and our betters, we have insisted upon a King and an empire. Heschel and Cornel West and Bruce Springsteen have done all they can do to enlighten us. Now it's up to the rest of us. The question is open, and God's furious judgment, while it has been well-earned, is not yet pronounced. Surely a prophet will appear to warn us before that happens, and looking around, I see none. But if Donald Trump isn't Ahab, I don't know who is. May he find his Elijah, and soon.

13

The Long Decline

A Cautionary Word

Before we go further, I need you to understand and agree to the following: I am not responsible for what may happen to you if you overdose on Neil Young. I have seen some results in the past that deter me from excess, on this point. I have friends who probably won't ever come back from abuse of this unpredictable substance. So, small doses, okay? And not too many close together. The same goes for every risky kind of recreation, of course. I know that you know, but I wanted to remind you.

Now, I also need you to know that just as Danica Patrick is a *professional* race car driver and Hillary Clinton is a *professional* politician, I am a *professional* philosopher. I don't like that word, but it's correct. For a living I spend my days with baffling books. People *pay* me to tell them what those books mean. Good work if you can get it. I do not recommend that you launch off into an activity of this kind all at once or on your own. I also don't recommend you try what Hillary and Danica do, for rather different reasons.

Philosophical puzzling takes training, because you need distance from potentially dangerous stuff you will read, and you must learn how to take in a baffling book in a *safe* situation, with friends around in case things start to go bad. And there can be flashbacks, even years later.

With that said, Neil Young has written not one but two books, and they *are* baffling. I will now do my job, to the best of my ability. Do not try this at home.

Hippie Dreams?

Neil Young got off weed a few years ago and simultaneously discovered that he's manic. Or at least *now* he is. He says he hasn't written a song since he gave up the ganja, but he *did* spill the entire remaining contents of his damaged memory into a computer. Someone was willing to print it, and charge money for it. My money. Then they did it *again*. And I ponied up, *again*.

I don't regret the "investment," if that's what it was. I learned things I never expected to know (or cared to). For example, did you know that a 1959 Lincoln Continental can *almost* go fifty miles with a battery weighing more than the chassis? (This is when it isn't blowing up or burning to a crisp.) Bet you didn't know that. But Neil ended his second book with "Lincvolt" as the hero. He devoted about fifty pages to it in the first book, when you add them up. He may have something here. I admit I want a Lincvolt. So do you. Let's get there later.

And did you know that there's a metaphysics of model trains which used to be in Neil's head, but now occupies another fifty pages (or more) of that first book? Actually, that's a pretty cool theory too, but no room for it here.[1] I'm beginning to think the dude is just crazy enough to have stuff right. You lose your mind, then you see the world as it really is. Now, I have to say that the idea for this essay you're reading now emerged from the cover of Neil's second book—not the cover art or title, but the following: "New York Times Bestseller Neil Young." And then on the back, the hype is all about Neil Young the "author." Neil ironically admits to coming from a line of real authors, doesn't feel like he can afford to be anything but ironic about "authorship."

Neil worried that his second book "was going to get serious and obsessive," which (he admits) happened with the first one. Jesus, did it ever. On the other hand, Neil's *Hippie Dream*, which is a "book" in only the loosest sense of that word, *was* a bestseller. That first "book" does contain some of the bio-trivia you would expect, written in the idiom of a (crazy smart) man

---

[1] This may seem hard to believe, but there is a full technical, philosophical treatment of Neil Young's metaphysics in my co-authored (with Gary Herstein) book *The Quantum of Explanation*, Chapter 7. So if you really must know . . .

who barely finished high school, half a century ago. I think Neil certainly read many books during his life. But I doubt that he remembers them, and I am confident he wasn't paying attention to *how* they were written. So, his first book is more like a montage than a narrative. That analogy does a disservice to montages, though. They make *some* sense, after all.

But the second book really is a montage and is *intended to be*. It has some organization, topically, and *could* be called a book. But the reason to buy the second book is Neil's illustrations. There are about fifty sketches and watercolors of cars Neil did himself, and they are very good. He has a genuine talent for illustration, it seems to me (my eye is untrained). I think he could make a living at it. But this is about "books," what they are, and what they mean, and how to tell.

Writing *Hippie Dream*, Neil carried around his laptop for a few months and typed whatever popped into his head with only a modicum of awareness that people would need to be able to understand it at some point. Sure, he knew we might want the details of his life from his perspective, but you'd think there would be some accommodation for the standard processes of thinking and comprehending. Mostly he was just trying to *not* smoke dope. But the poor, curious souls like us must *pay* for their curiosity. Dearly.

Buried in his ramblings, like raisins in a bowl of oatmeal, are just the sorts of morsels that we were looking for, and the proportion of raisins to oatmeal roughly mirrors the proportion of good songs to crappy ones he has written (about three dozen plumpers in a catalog approaching a thousand). But, when Neil is on, *he's on*. The autobiography has moments. So does the memoire, *Special Deluxe* that followed. When Neil is *not on*, well, it's best to change the channel. Then it occurred to me, this difficult-to-follow-narrative is how Neil wrote songs too. It's sort of a challenge to get the meaning, and sometimes not quite possible.

Philosophy and Literature

These two fields have a dicey history. Philosophy is often practiced as a kind of literature. You are reading such an exercise. Philosophy doesn't have to be written down, of course, but since it often is, it must on occasion conform to the canons of literature, whether it likes them or not.

Philosophers probably should strive to write well. They usually make no effort. They should be grammatical at a minimum. That is a strain and a constraint they ill appreciate. Being clear is a value among some philosophers, but no sage wants to be limited by clarity, if something profound is being said. If any piece of written philosophy starts looking too well written, it is voted off the island. It's "mere" literature. The main reason Proust and Twain and Vonnegut aren't "philosophers" is that they knew how to write.

This situation gives literary critics the right to rag on philosophers for writing badly. Such sages may be a bit clearer than, say, Neil Young's writing, but they are generally less worth reading. Literary critics have not failed to point this out. They are nothing if not dutiful on this point.

On the other hand, once and a while a philosopher comes along who can really write. Plato was one such, and Marcus Aurelius another. It does happen. In recent history, they gave the Nobel Prize for literature to Henri Bergson, who only wrote philosophy, and also to Jean-Paul Sartre, who wrote all kinds of stuff, but he turned it down. (Sartre didn't accept and refuse to go get it, like Dylan, he *declined* the award itself.[2]) Worthy of such recognition also was William James (a philosopher who wrote like a novelist) and his brother Henry (a novelist who wrote like a philosopher). The Nobel committee basically apologized to Henry James, after his death, for not giving him the prize. I assume he was past caring by then.

On the Other Hand

Literary people are notoriously bad at systematic, purely logical thinking of the sort philosophers must master. They are better at dialectic than at metaphysics and logic, but they cannot match philosophers in dialectic. Narrative, image, symbol, metaphor—these things trip philosophers while the lit people toss them as freely as major league baseball players turn their routine double plays. But ask a lit person a serious question about meaning, and you get an ever-shifting ontology of God knows what, a slew of vociferous opinions that even God couldn't pin down.

---

[2] See his statement: <www.nybooks.com/articles/1964/12/17/sartre-on-the-nobel-prize>.

Most scholars of literature learn just enough philosophy to learn what they happen to like and then repeat the tired phrases they half understand for their whole careers. Lacking the genuine command of philosophy they become doctrinaire and dogmatic, and not a little bit frightened that they will be uncovered as charlatans and posers. The professional philosophers do not do this. They don't care what the lit people say. They quietly disrespect lit people as pseudo-intellectuals and pass on to their more boring (but ontologically precise) conversations.

It takes a philosopher twenty to fifty pages to say what a good writer says in a paragraph. It takes a literary critic an infinite number of sentences to say nothing at all (with rare exceptions). It takes a great writer exactly the right number of words to say exactly what needs saying. These will be neither philosophers nor literary scholars.

All My Words Come Back to Me

So Neil Young's manuscript meanders, madly and maddeningly, in a middling manner. If there is a plot, it might be called *Hippie's Progress*. Neil is surely some sort of pilgrim, Blind River to the Golden State. There's a confessional tone and absolutely no effort from Neil to get revenge on anyone for anything, even Ronnie Van Zant. ("I heard old Neil put her down . . .") Neil just grants (the late) Ronnie the point and explicitly regrets having written "Southern Man."

Part of me wishes Ronnie had lived to see that. Part of me is glad Ronnie didn't grow old and become like Charlie Daniels and Ted Nugent, and that he never had to see *Duck Dynasty*. Sometimes it's just better to die young. He'd rather see the sky fall than see Michigan and Alabama more alike than different. But come to think of it, there's an awful lot of Alabama blood coursing through the veins of Michiganders, after that Great Migration. Well, anyway, Neil leaves Ronnie in possession of the field. And the same may be said for almost everyone Neil ever disagreed with.

We also get the backstory of a number of Neil's hits in *Waging Heavy Peace*. For example, "Long May You Run" is about a hearse aptly named Mortimer Hearseburg, Mort for short. The details are in the follow-up book. "Old Man" is not about Neil's father, but since his dad always believed it was (beautiful sentiment that it is), Neil never disabused the parent. And so on. But you have to dig around for this stuff. No index. He brings up a song, gets distracted (trains, cars, women), finishes the story fifty pages later. He doesn't claim always to know what his songs mean.

I once played in a band with a fellow who got very mad at me for telling him that Van Morrison's "Into the Mystic" was about an actual river in Boston, and a sailor coming home. He didn't know there *was* such a river. He wanted the song to be about the mysticism of falling in love, and that is what even Wikipedia and Van Morrison himself still claims, these days. But it's false. Read the words. When I told my bandmate what it was about, he said, angrily "never, ever tell me something like that again." I didn't. I get it. Sometimes our imaginings are better than the truth.

If you're at all like my bandmate, and if you find Neil Young's lyrics philosophical and profound, you should avoid Neil's literary efforts. By Neil's accounting, there's a lot less to these songs than meets the mind, upon hearing them. Don't get me wrong, I think Neil is a brilliant songwriter and a very smart person. But he'll take the mystery and joy out of those songs for ya. Still, who says that songs have to mean what the writer says they mean? "Puff the Magic Dragon" *is* about smoking weed, *even if* that was never in the minds of Yarrow and Lipton. The same is true of "Into the Mystic." It doesn't matter what Morrison thinks he was saying. Artists don't get to control the meanings of their artworks, exclusively. And it's a good thing.

The Death of the Author

For thirty years or so, literary critics and philosophers of literature and art have been arguing about the issue of "artists' intentions." The extreme views are, on one side, that the artist's intention just *is* the work's meaning, and nothing more. No one actually believes that—whether it be a song, a book, a poem, or a painting.

Most people expect our common sense about such things to have some standing. If you create a sculpture that looks like a giant phallus, and everyone says it looks like that, it doesn't matter how much you protest. You sculpted a dick. You say it's a giant bamboo shoot? Okay. The work certainly does mean what the artist intended it to mean, if it has been created with any competence. But it may mean more than that, or it may fail to capture what the artist intended for any variety of reasons. Your bamboo shoot looks like a dick. Sorry. Still, most people will want to start their interpretations with a question like "What was he trying to say, here?" And they will give the artist's intentions pride of place in interpretation. That is common sense.

On the other side, some philosophers of art claim that the artist's intentions have no value at all in determining the meaning of an artwork. They say the artwork is an autonomous form that can be passed from interpreter to interpreter without shedding any of its meaning and the full meaning of the work is in the work, when we learn to grasp its *form*. This is called "formalism." Its most notorious advocate was I.A. Richards (1893–1979), and there were some notable Americans (most with Oxbridge educations), such as John Crowe Ransom (1888–1974), Cleanth Brooks (1906–1994) and Robert Penn Warren (1905–1989).

Such interpreters don't consider the artist's biography, cultural background, economic need, or any other historical factors to be determinative of the meaning of an artwork. The autonomy of the excellent work of art means what it means in virtue of its formal elements; this is, they say, the whole meaning of the work. These people are fuddy-duddies, arch-conservatives of a stripe, but usually are very smart. Robin Williams's character, "Mr. Keating," in *Dead Poets Society* mocks these people for "measuring poetry."

At the other extreme, there are theorists who say there is *no* enduring form in the artwork, and no fixed meaning; rather, it is the uncontrollable *surplus* of meanings that eventually undermine our efforts to "fix" the meaning of an artwork by using a point of reference, or an anchor, outside of the work. The artist can't do it and neither can the philosopher, and neither can your grandmother, or Joe Schmo, or the President, or God. They call this failed anchor a "transcendental signified" and they like to attack its presumptions, and those of anyone who drops that anchor.

These people are called "post-modernists," or sometimes "deconstructionists." They are hard to satisfy. They don't even agree with themselves, let alone with each other, and on principle. They're usually terrible writers and, some will say, intentionally obscure. Every sentence contains a host of qualifications, and even the qualifications are qualified, mostly by being retracted. The most notorious practitioner of this approach to theory was Jacques Derrida (1930–2004). These people are more fun to drink with than the formalists, but you don't want to loan them money. They can interpret away the conditions of any transaction that depends on language, especially written language, and money just is a problematic surplus of meaning to them.

If you don't already know, I regret to inform you that common sense is hard to find among academics. These people can't change a flat tire and most can't find their own asses with both hands. I think this was widely known already, but I'm confirming it, from within the din and chatter. When it comes to discussions of the meaning of art, well, there hasn't been a smidgeon of sanity for a long time. It isn't the fault of *today's* professors. That discussion went gaga (or more precisely, dada) during the First World War and was downhill from there. Today's academics are complicit, as carriers of the infection that keeps killing common sense, but they all caught it honestly, congenitally so to speak, from their teachers, in the womb of graduate school, back to dada days.

It is a good thing Neil Young doesn't really see his music as art. It would make less sense than it does, and sometimes it comes pretty close to making no sense at all. I don't think of him as the savior of common sense, but at least he knows what quarters of the intellectual city to avoid. He spends his days with engineers and tinkerers and inventors and musicians— not the most stable crowd, granted, but more sensible than academics and artists, by light years.

Neil *does* see his songs as having meaning, but doesn't believe he really controls *what* they mean. As far as I can tell, he just vomits out songs, sort of, without concern about whether they are any good, and leaves their ultimate meaning and popularity to others. There are exceptions, like "Ohio," when Neil got pissed off about Kent State. I'm fairly sure he exerted control over the meaning there, including the threats of revenge against the government. I wonder if there wasn't discussion in the halls of power of deporting Neil for that song. I guess they had other fish to fry, what, with a war to lose and an office building to break into to make sure George McGovern wasn't hiding any dirty secrets.

"Ohio" aside, for the most part Neil blurs and slurs the past and the present and the future until it all runs together like, well, "like a watercolor in the rain," to borrow one of Al Stewart's better lines. The vagueness in Neil's songs, and sometimes their outright incoherence (for instance "Down by the River," but hold that thought—it may make more sense than it seems to), invites us to interpret them for ourselves. That's Neil's take on things too.

But is it art? Surely some of it is, right? Lots of people say his writing is art. Let's look at a couple of ripe candidates for art and try our hand at "formal criticism" and "deconstruction," see whether Neil Young deserves a Nobel Prize, like Bob Dylan. Shall we? I am choosing two artworks from the same album, *Everybody Knows This Is Nowhere*, which, in itself, is a snazzy bit of word-play on the emptiness of trying to gain knowledge through meaning.

To be a good theorist, you need to eliminate as many independent variables as possible. We all had to learn that along the way, although this surely ain't science. But we are inquirers, on a quest for meaning, so let us take ourselves seriously, even if no one else does. No one ever accused formalists or postmodernists of failing to take themselves (over-)seriously.

Formalists don't care about context, but for post-modernists, context is the whole ball of wax, the very key to what is *un*said or *can't be said*, or some such crap). Nevertheless, let's eliminate variables: These two songs are from the same time period, recorded by the same musicians, written the same day, in fact, with similar themes. Thus, it doesn't matter which drugs were involved, since it was the same drugs, more or less, depending on what time it was. It doesn't matter about Neil's development as an artist, if he developed at all, because this is a slice of the same time. If he got better later, or worse, it doesn't change what we will say about these two songs. The same moment in history, in culture, and the same spaces—LA, one home studio, same rented equipment, same producers, these can all be treated as constants available in the context. There are more constants, and they are revelatory, but let's not get ahead of ourselves.

Formalist critics don't care about any of these historico-biographico-culturo-factoids. These are not needed and don't matter at all, so they claim. The work stands for itself and its full meaning is in its form. But I still worry about common sense, so I'm playing it safe and eliminating independent variables anyway. (I may have my own aims in mind.) For formalists, I will note that both are *songs*, belonging to the great tradition of lyric poetry. Both use *words* exclusively (no other sub-articulate human sounds). There is no neologism. Both use the tropes of double entendre and innuendo. Both are written for the ear more than the eye. Both have simple and regular meter ("Cowgirl in the Sand" is trochaic, "Cinnamon Girl" is anapestic). Both have semi-regular rhyme schemes, with "Cowgirl" tending to couplets and "Cinnamon Girl" to cinquain. Both are about "girls" and male sexual desire, and both take the full life-span as the relevant temporal spread for love.

First I will offer a sample of formalist literary analysis and critique of "Cowgirl in the Sand." Then I'll do a post-modern critique and analysis of "Cinnamon Girl." Mind you, I don't really buy this stuff, and I warned you not to try this at home. But Neil Young is an "author" now, and we must do what we must do. After the exercise (it's fun when you aren't self-serious), I promise, we'll really get to the bottom of things. I will reveal the true meanings of the songs. You won't ever have to wonder about it again. And if you're like my old bandmate who didn't know the Mystic was a river, well, you'll also hate me.

Cowgirl in the Sand

It might seem that this weird song is a fine candidate for post-modern treatment, especially since it makes no apparent sense. But that is all the more reason to *refuse* to look at it that way. The formalists insist that every "great" work of art is intelligible based on its form alone, but also *creates* a new form that gives a rule to subsequent art. After Michelangelo, for example, art is never the same and must deal with his achievement in some way. Even rejecting his forms is an artistic statement.

The same might be said for Frank Lloyd Wright in American architecture. Just about every residential street in the US is populated by houses that either borrowed his ideas or stand out because they rejected those ideas. Degraded versions of Wright's forms are everywhere. The same may be said of public buildings, decorative features of almost any interior space you walk into, design elements in dishes and furniture, and the list goes on. Wright was a one-man rule maker for subsequent history. Formalists love this stuff.

It's easier to see Bob Dylan as holding that place in the history of songwriting than Neil Young, but there's room for more than just the top tier of form-creators in our cosmos of art. If Bob Dylan is the Jackson Pollock of North American song-poets, Neil young is more like the Jasper Johns. No, Neil wouldn't be Neil without Bob, but Neil decidedly isn't Bob and might have a form or two up his own sleeve. We certainly know how to recognize a "Neil Young type of song" when we hear it. So the forms are there.

Formalists refuse to separate *what* is said from *how* it is said. In a good poem, they insist, these are part of the same form, and the form is not only the key to the meaning, it *is* the meaning. Now, one central problem posed by "Cowgirl in the Sand," for a formalist, is whether the song is about one girl or three. This is much discussed by rock critics and popular culture fandom. "Oooh, how mysterious, I think it's one girl, three names for one girl." "Nah man, what have you been smoking? Dude is remembering three different girls and they *all* got away." And so that discussion goes until late in the night, reaching no resolution. But a formalist will serenely point out that there *is* a definite solution to that problem—or, if there is not, then the artwork is inferior (or the critic is a ninny). Let us assume the artwork isn't to blame.

How do we decide such a question, three girls or one, based on form alone? Remember, we don't care what Neil was thinking, and we don't care when he lived, and we don't care what his life experiences were. We look for clues within the work, exclusively. What, then, does a formalist see? Hmmm.

Well, for the stanzas, the poet chooses the heroic couplet for his meter and rhyme. Clearly a nod to Chaucer and the traditional power of the couplet. The couplet is interrupted by a rhyme triplet in the refrain, that dissolves the meter and becomes almost free verse, pinned in at the last moment by rhyme—name, same, and deferred, game. This dissolution of the metric structure joined with deferred perfect rhymes converges on the word "woman" in the final line of the refrain. It says *the* woman in you. Thus, it is one woman, but in the mode of the universal woman, the womanness or womanhood that is everywoman. Unity does prevail, at the universal level. Even if it were three individual women, they are one woman, in the highest sense.

Yet, we may go further. The refrain is repeated *without* alteration, *three times*. Thus, it is one woman in particular that is meant. The music provides a clue here. The song is over ten minutes long, while the lyrics are minimal. There are long instrumental remonstrances between verses, but not between the verses and the refrains. Time is passing, the mind has gone below the level of articulation during these musical passages. Life is being lived. Otherwise the music would not be *part of the song*. That just isn't true.

Thus, we have no choice apart from treating the verses as episodes in a particular relationship, each beginning formulaically with a greeting, a name, and a question. The three questions that comprise the second line of each stanza constitute a new poetic form—about command, about decay, about appearances, successively. These questions correspond to the question in the second line of the refrain, about identity: "is it the same?" he asks. Is love that powerful? The poem draws us into this question about the power of love and then releases us into a maze of questions. The one question that lingers quite beyond the structure of couplets and questions is the question "Can I stay?"

The answer to that is yes and no. Yes, you can endure, while the song endures. No, you may not endure if it means expecting places to matter and be commanded. Is *love* command, or decay, or appearance? Briefly, yes, it is those and only those. This is one woman, one game, one life.

As a formalist, I might criticize the poem for its deep cynicism about love, but I also might go the other way, praising its tragic sensibility and recognition of play in the midst of command, decay, and mere appearance. It's not like formalists all agree about what is good, let alone what is great. Having your interpretation prevail in the UFC of lit crit tends to depend on how prestigious your universities are, in the great academic rat race of, well, command, decay, and mere appearance. Notice that for formalists, analysis precedes critique.

Total Bullshit

This is total bullshit. Granted, it's all true of the poem/song, but formalists have no concern at all about whether the author thought about these kinds of things in writing. The proof is in the poem itself. I am only pretending to be a formalist, but this thing says *what* I said it says, and it says it *how* I said it says it. No denying it. On a side note, there is a difference between *total* bullshit and *complete* bullshit. I'll explain that after I sling some more bullshit.

Cinnamon Girl

A warning: post-modernists like long, unclear, obscure sentences. There is even an award for the worst sentence of the year.[3] I will provide one: The post-modernists like to speak in paradoxes and cryptic rhetorical questions, the answers to which are not obvious to anyone, but all must pretend they are (never actually giving the answers, of course, since no one knows what they are and everyone is afraid of looking like they don't know), and never, under any circumstances, allowing some incipient category of totalizing discourse to dominate the act of reading. That is why the reading offered here is not of a poem, or a song, or a recording, or a commodity. We have before us a "text" and that's all. For the post-modernist the analysis *is* the critique. It is mere pretense to treat them as separate.

This text, nominally "Cinnamon Girl," is either vacuous or brilliant, or both. As post-modernist critics, we must expose, blunt, block, even deny the totalizing pall cast by the transcendental signified. The presence of it in the text leads us to look for the meaning in a presupposed location beyond the text. In "Cinnamon Girl," the transcendental signified is the "girl." We are tempted to ask "Who is she?" But there is no "girl," wandering around Mexico or South Central LA who is "holding down" the meaning of this text by being "the" girl it was "about." Even if she existed, the text is hardly capable of being tied down to her or by her in any stable sense. So, releasing forever the illusion that there is a sixty-something cinnamon girl somewhere in the world who ensures us that the text has meaning, we look instead to other characteristics of the text and we read *closely*.

It is important to remember that this verbal production that someone called "Cinnamon Girl" (who knows if Neil Young

---

[3] <www.denisdutton.com/language_crimes.htm>.

really wrote it, and what difference would it make if he didn't?) is therefore and in the first place *not* an artwork. It is a production of discursive practices that accompany and set boundaries upon an age, and every discourse that aims at a "signified" beyond the text also contains the seeds of its own undoing. The immanent limits of the text are thus part of the text. What lies at those limits is *not said*, and beyond those which *can't be said* and are also part of the meaning.

Look, then, at what is *not* said, at the pregnant silences wherever they are suggestive. We shall identify patterns of movement within the text that betray its unthought meanings and show its edges and spurs and fractures.

[A pause. Post-modernists are maddeningly slow at actually saying anything, and once they've said it, they take it back. To do this right would take seventeen more pages that say no more than I have already said, so I'm gonna speed this up a few notches because it's driving me nuts.]

For example, why is the cinnamon "girl" not a *woman*? Is she a juvenile, or perhaps infantilized by the patriarchal background conditions of poetizing in a world of rock boys and their testosterone? Or is this a matter of racism? Is cinnamon a euphemism for Latina? Mestiza? African American? Cinnamon does mix well with brown sugar, after all.

And now, *now*, we have a point of entry for a deconstruction of the song, or more properly, the text. The key to this interpretation is in the way we spread girls all over everything, like butter and sugar and spice and everything nice. It is neither race nor gender per se, but the combination of racialized gender that presents to us the very pliability, the spreadability of that girl that "Neil Young" pointedly *fails* to mention in his lyrics. But were she not so, the text simply could not be presented this way. We want to spread that girl across the rest of *our* lives, nevermind her life. No woman of the dominant class could be so spread, but that cinnamon girl will be a girl for the rest of her life, spice for the other and always thus *othered*.

In fact the othering of the cinnamon girl, and its erasure in her spreading, is a condition for her very desirability. Note that the text indicates that we want to live with the "girl" with no mention at all of what it means for her to be stuck with that apologist of othering, that purveyor of over-weaning male desire, that rapist and enslaver of all that enters his gaze, that colonizer of all that evades his gaze. This monster gives himself away at the margins of the text and disgust is not too strong a reaction to those who see what he would do to this girl and any other such "girl" who captures his momentary fancy. He makes of himself a pedophile, it matters not whether she is "of age." because *for him* she must be a "girl," *and* in the end, whether she is really of a mixed race is irrelevant so long as he can construct her according to his categories. That is more important than whether she fills out her tax forms with one race or another. His aim is to spread her, temporally across a domain of othering oppression and to bind her in that position while he savors his own self-deceptions.

Complete Bullshit

Now, this is complete bullshit. The difference between "complete bullshit" and "total bullshit" is important. Complete bullshit is self-sufficient but also self-enclosed. It doesn't tend to spread. It is like a cowchip for the intellectual elite. You can pick it up in one piece and sail it through the air, and even if it lands hard it doesn't spread very far and eventually disappears into the ground it came from.

But "total bullshit" is different. It spreads, totalizes, impersonalizes, reduces, dehumanizes, and is the tool of totalitarians and fascists. It turns everything it touches to shit. It's like that feedlot on I-40 near Amarillo. It ruins the ground, the water, and the air, and then you end up eating a little of it at every McDonald's. Before you know it, everyone is shitting it into the common sewage, and the treatment plant is getting old and eventually you get intellectual cholera. The lovers of standalone form are haters of everything genuinely human, messy as it is. Their bullshit makes the pomo cowchips look like good fertilizer. Just don't step in a fresh one and you're golden.

The vast majority of contemporary literary criticism is complete bullshit. Everyone is sick of having to step around it, especially those self-loathing academics who do it because they never learned anything else—there have been two full generations now of literary critics trained in complete bullshit. They rarely bother to read literature any more. They just read theory. It's all they know. They are harmless and irrelevant. Like philosophers.

I think that maybe the Swedish Academy gave Bob Dylan the prize because he never over-interpreted his poetry. He was content to be the Testosterone Kid. Fuck anybody who doesn't like his stuff, but especially fuck those who *do*. Idiots. Shows how stupid they are. *Of course* they gave him the "Prize." They cared about *the prize*. They wanted *it* to have a future. How good could it be, if they didn't give it to Dylan? (Or so he might think in the privacy of his thought.)

Neil Young is *not* thinking that, in spite of the praise heaped on him by the purveyors of complete bullshit. It wouldn't be easy to say what he *is* thinking, especially for him, but it isn't "people should respect me if they want to respect themselves." It's more like: "I want to live with the cinnamon girl, yeah, I could be happy the rest of my life with the cinnamon girl." And there isn't much more to it than that, unless I miss my guess. He is a manchild.

Not that anyone should care what I think, but I find his perspective more touching, kind, gentle even, than his reputation seems to indicate. Of course, if I were writing *my* autobiography, I think I might be able to convey a similar impression, contrary to fact. And I don't know Neil Young, so I don't know the facts. Well, I do know some facts, and that brings me to the promised revelation of the true meanings of those two songs.

Down by the River

The formalists and the pomo critics are opposed by the traditional approach to literary criticism, which is called the "historical-biographical" style. In this tradition, the critic seeks to learn about the author (what he or she read, who the teachers were, who the influences were, how the style developed, the sources of plots and thematic elements), about the time period (what was happening, what was known, what the trends and pressures and rewards were, and so forth), and also studying what the artist or writer said about the piece, before, during and after its completion. This is close to common sense and even if it doesn't fully determine the meaning of a work of art, surely it offers some part of its meaning.

The meaning of a song can change long after it is written. For example, the Elton John–Bernie Taupin song "Candle in the Wind" spent its first twenty-four years being about Marilyn

Monroe, but became a song about Princess Diana for the next twenty years, becoming, by some accounts, the biggest selling single of all time. In like manner, Neil Young has felt perfectly free to interpret his songs in numerous (often incompatible) ways over the decades. The historical-biographical interpreter cares about this, but it's never the whole story.

And sometimes, once in a great while, just knowing one fact about the making of an artwork answers the main questions— but first we have to *ask* the right questions. That's more than half the ball game. In this case, I already asked it: who is the "girl"? You'll say, "wait a cotton pickin' minute, now, that's the question you asked about the cowgirl (and Ruby and the dream-woman) and about the cinnamon girl." Right you are. And now I ask it again. Who got shot at the river?

Answer: the cowgirl and the cinnamon girl. It's all "one girl" in the deepest sense of the word. The relevant fact, missed by totalizing formalists and suspicious pomo chip-slingers is this: Neil wrote all three songs in one day *and* he had a fever of 103. That was one hell of a day in the life of a songwriter. He was basically delirious. And in the course of a few hours he wrote three songs that music critics list among the greatest in rock history. She was one girl not because Neil only imagined one girl, or only intended one girl, or might have said it was one girl, or might have been obsessed with some one girl that day. This isn't a reach for a transcendental signified, and it isn't a belly flop into forms of poetry and music.

It's about the nature of *time*. To be one finite human being in Topanga that day, deliriously scribbling three sets of lyrics and eking out three grooves that bring them to life doesn't leave room for full development of three different characters. Even if the imaginative visitations of these "girls" wore different visages, all of them were his baby, all of them were life partners, and all of them had some kind of ambiguous power over him. He killed the girl finally because she could send him away forever. The "girl" was the fever itself. It was with him through the time he had, and it helped him write the songs. The same can be said about whatever drugs were at work that day, and about everything else that went into those songs. All of it was the "girl." She is the form of the song and she is the context and she is the dialogical partner of a fevered brain, and she is that brain too.

The meanings of these songs, then, are tied to one another and to a sick day in Topanga Canyon. There is no point in ignoring or denying this. It has to be a part of any sane interpretation of the meanings of these songs and there's no point in talking about one without examining all three. It would be like reading one of *The Lord of the Rings* volumes and trying to talk about Frodo on that basis alone. Common sense requires what I am insisting on, and you can't get to this conclusion without doing a little history and biography and trying to hold the independent variables at bay.

Long May You Run

My personal bullshit alarm is honed by years of experience with backbiting academics and the mindless babbling of literary critics. I *am* cynical, I promise. I don't think my grand revelation is bullshit. I admire Neil Young as a songwriter and I love his singing voice. I also think he's an interestingly half-crazy brilliant person. I wonder what a conversation with him would be like, and whether I could follow it.

Neil seems quite sincere in his public willingness to accept most of the blame for all wrongs and to claim very little of the credit for his enduring failures and successes. His books don't inspire us to wish to become part of his life, but they ring true. He comes off as boyish, changeable yet sweet, and harmless until he doesn't get what he wants. Then he tends to walk away rather than rage about how things are. He changes the cast of characters in his life every decade or so. We all know someone like that, even if Neil Young is one of a kind.

The subtitle of the first book should probably have been the title and vice-versa. By quite a long stretch, the hippie dreaminess outpaces the peaceability. Neil is the standard Canadian contradiction: a commonsense libertarian socialist—it's a combination we can't seem to strike in the lower forty-eight. I can't help wondering if we combined the populations of Hawaii and Alaska, would we not have Canadians? Libertarian socialists?

Still, Neil has been in the US for a very long time, even if he strongly identifies with his Canadian roots. No one can doubt his sincere concern for the environment, but as an example of his embedded paradoxes, consider the following argument that he makes: The reason we need *luxury* solar-electric cars is that people *want* their luxury cars and will support, of their own volition, an environmentally sound plan so long as they don't have to sacrifice anything they really want. This seems true, and more likely to succeed than any plan to raise people's consciousness. People will drive environmentally sound cars if the cars have all the *cachet* of the 1959 Lincoln Continental. They truly will. Neil wants to use his celebrity to bring attention to the environment, but in a way that has a shot at working. That is common sense.

Neil's "books" are not for everyone, but both make great bathroom reading since the chapters are short but not too short, if you know what I mean. As far as I can tell, it makes no difference at all in what order you read them. Seriously, start anywhere, read some parts again, skip other parts. That's how Neil did it, I would bet. So why shouldn't you? Just try to catch that shift on the long decline.

14

Emptiness in Harmony

This isn't exactly an essay. It's several vignettes that trace connected themes in and through the music and the life of Paul Simon, more or less chronologically. When you finish the first vignette, you're going to think I don't like Paul Simon. That isn't true. I would have to reckon him my favorite songwriter. I like his music better than the Rolling Stones or David Bowie or the Beatles, and like Bruce Springsteen, he hasn't lost a thing by the passage of time and still writes great music. He can do some things Springsteen doesn't really try—like writing Broadway musicals and movies and acting and comedy. So keep reading beyond the first episode below. You'll see.

As a body of work, Paul Simon's creative contribution to the world is far superior to Bob Dylan's, if for no other reason than because of its reach beyond youthful, swashbuckling poetry and through life and into old age. The volume of excellent work is so much greater than Dylan's that it doesn't matter whether Dylan's ten best songs are in some way "better" than any of Paul Simon's. We're talking about rarified company here. One thing I will *try* to minimize in the vignettes that follow is the ever-present temptation to compare Paul Simon with Dylan.

Simon's aesthetic range and reach are immense. In thinking about his music, I have been driven to use aesthetic ideas from all over the world. There really always was something cosmopolitan and yet rooted about his musical curiosity. He was the first among the American songwriters to go to the territories beyond our borders where the interesting music was being made, to listen, to collaborate, to come home with new sounds and rhythms. His odyssey has been ours as well. And he has made all the mistakes we would have made. But he is dauntless. Here are some thoughts about his work.

Therapy for the Self-Conscious Genius

Artists must be punished. So says our twisted culture. Better still, they must punish themselves. A happy artist is no artist at all, we insist. Among all the artists, especially in the world of the macho twentieth century, the men must be violent, the women desperate, and everyone suicidal. It gets really interesting for us when artists pair up, like Jackson Pollock and Lee Krasner, Diego Rivera and Frida Kahlo, Ted Hughes and Sylvia Plath, maybe Richard Burton and Elizabeth Taylor (I never thought they were *acting* in *Who's Afraid of Virginia Woolf?* just a normal evening at home with Dick and Liz.) Are they really "artists"? With all that Shakespearean carrying on, yes, surely that must be art.

But what of Paul Simon? That perpetually unhappy man?

We especially love it when artists are all screwed up and put it on display. We demand that too. That's how we make sure they're the real thing. When we elevate ("escalate"?) movie actors, or, yes, folksingers and pop musicians, to makers of "fine art" the paradox becomes sharp. This isn't fine art. It would be more honest to admit that we went gaga for it when we were young and now want to feel it wasn't vacuous. And we project our bad conscience about liking fluffy stuff onto our celebrities until they hollow themselves out for us. They want to be taken seriously, as artists, so they do it. And round the circle goes.

There's good news and bad news. Good news: what these poor kids create really *is* art. Bad news: it isn't "fine art," as we and these sufferers would have it be. Indeed, there is no such thing in any healthy culture. Such is the argument of popular philosopher Crispin Sartwell (1958–). I agree. "Art for art's sake" isn't art in the richest sense. It doesn't grow from what we are. It is vomited from the depths of what we are not but *would be* if we could.

Over the centuries in the Western world, we came to identify this excrescence with "beauty." As a symptom, Sartwell quotes Théophile Gauthier: "Only those things that are altogether useless can be truly beautiful; anything that is useful is ugly, for it is the expression of some need, and the needs of man are base and disgusting" (*The Art of Living*, p. 68). Having thus placed beauty on the throne, we later turned against beauty in the twentieth century, as Arthur Danto (1924–2013) documented in his classic work *The Abuse of Beauty*. After all, what do *we* know?

This self-negation, this life-denying activity we call fine art in the West, in the last 250 years, is the fruit of a cult: the cult of genius. It dates back to Johann Wolfgang von Goethe. In his twenties, he wrote a semi-autobiographical novel called *The Sorrows of Young Werther*, about a listless, silly young man who makes sketches of rustic life and writes bad poetry. He falls in love with an equally shallow young woman who is bethrothed to another, perfectly decent man. They pointlessly carry on until Werther can take no more of not having his beloved. So he kills himself, botching the effort, so it takes him a while to die. The novel has obvious formal flaws and weaknesses, but the young Europeans couldn't get enough of it. They identified the hero with Goethe himself and everybody started imitating him. A bunch of frustrated boys killed themselves for love. It was ridiculous and awful. It was popular fiction gone south. This was 1774 and following decades.

Goethe soon hated the book. But people called him a "genius," and the word was transformed. It once meant a spirit of creativity that inspires someone for a time, as in "Rembrandt had the genius of painting," or "Handel had the genius of music." Ethereal spirits that alight upon a person and deliver a very special ability. But now, after 1774, "Mozart *is a* genius," or "Goethe *is a* genius." Hence, the nauseating rise of self-conscious "geniuses," a whole generation of willful poets and artists thinking themselves misunderstood and under-appreciated by the dull masses who cannot fathom their artistic depths.

So, I admit I don't believe in "genius," or in artists who simply must suffer for the sake of the gifts they bring. This is the flotsam of a sick civilization. Sartwell rightly points out that only in the Western world, and only in recent centuries, has *anyone* ever had the notion that artists are different from the rest of us and that they are hard to fathom. It's basically crap we tell ourselves. Why?

An Island Never Cries

It's a rare terrible line from Paul Simon. He wrote "I Am a Rock" before he was famous. He wrote "A Hazy Shade of Winter" after he was famous. Both use the same poetic trick. Most of the lyrics could be true of anyone, but there's a line or two in each song where Paul pushes out the *non*-geniuses, reminding us that *he* is suffering in ways that *only* the genius can grasp. These are references to himself as the poet—he has *his* poetry to protect him, and *his* memory skips while looking over manuscripts of *his* unpublished rhyme. I don't know about you, but I don't really get to deal with my ennui by writing poetry (not since I was a teenager) or by poring over my own unpublished poetry manuscripts, or, indeed even arriving in a strange town to find people waiting for "a poet and a one-man band" (to foreshadow the next vignette). Not my life. Not yours either. It's only about Paul.

So Paul draws us into the song with lines about common experiences, only to remind us that *he's* the misunderstood genius and *we* don't understand how awful it is. He positioned himself as a prophet-poet from the onset of the folk era. His biographer Peter Ames Carlin collects enough brash and grating boasts and dismissals from Paul's lips to ensure that no one would want to have been hanging around him during that time. Surely it *is* hard to be the artist and genius in a time when everyone demands that such folks must suffer for their art. On the other hand, how bad is the problem? Especially after you make your first few millions? Seems to me you could just relax. And after all, you're a very fine poet. Enjoy it, huh?

But not if you *believe* the illusion you created. Life becomes the task of extending the illusion, wrapping it in an enigma, and perhaps being too busy (like Dylan—oh hell, I said I wouldn't do that) to go and collect your Nobel Prize. I'll bet Simon would have gone to get the prize. He accepted the call to give the prestigious Ellman Lectures at Emory, and didn't mind one bit hobnobbing with the literary elite. He was always pretty clear about being an intellectual from an intellectual family, and is comfortable in such a setting. No group is more intent upon being in charge of who gets called a "genius."

Wouldn't it be better to use our "genius" for the benefit of others? Humble artists who don't pose as geniuses, but whose work *merits* the judgment, get little attention. You sort of have to sell yourself as a genius in order to be called one. But the little people who merely do great work must surely live happier lives. When The Bangles recorded "Hazy Shade of Winter," they left out the "misunderstood poet" part, and *regarde ça*, the song was now about anyone at all who needs hope. Not about misunderstood geniuses whining at their loneliness. Nice edit.

Zen and the Art of Dilettantish Maintenance

A Zen moment. Sometimes, unexpectedly, we see straight through the mundane and into the pure existence of the possibilities that surround it. Somehow, the moment vanishes and its pure being is just there, empty of all you thought it was, but full of nothing else. It isn't exactly a revelation, or an epiphany, or a visitation. It's an aperture, the arrival of the already. Or something like that. It has happened to you. It's not a bad thing, but not exactly good.

I'm no adept in any kind of Eastern philosophy, let alone the subtle field of Japanese aesthetics. But I am fascinated by it. All of it. My guide on this foray into Zen and Paul Simon's music is, as I have indicated, Crispin Sartwell, someone whose writing and thinking I admire a good deal. He gets into all kinds of trouble and then always gets out of it again. Look him up. Sartwell knows way more about Zen than I do, but I think neither of us lives a Zen life. Still, the world may forgive a hopeless dilettante who confesses his ineptitude in advance. Even Goethe said "the dilettante" is what he wanted to be. Well, then, damn the torpedoes.

There is emptiness in everything. Here are some examples: the absence of what *was* but is no more; the spectral presence of what *wasn't* but might have been; the fleeting is-ness of what *is* but soon won't be anymore; the haunting intuition of what *isn't* surrounding what is; the excruciating quasi-availability of what *will be* but isn't yet; the tragic barrier between what *could be* but won't be. All empty. Each feels different, by legions, but all feel like a nothing pervading something. When we see or hear or feel ourselves, or someone else, or something else, as being surrounded and permeated by all these emptinesses, the uncanny *sense it makes* takes us from behind, from a blind spot in our process of existing. Hard to describe, but common enough.

Sartwell tells the story of the two great Japanese tea-masters Rikyū and his teacher Jōō. It's the sixteenth century and no people ever took tea quite as seriously as these people at this time. The teacher and student are invited to a tea ceremony, and walk together through the marketplace to get there. Jōō notices a vase for sale, one especially suited for his own tea ceremonies, but, not being rude, Jōō doesn't stop to buy the vase, nor makes any remark about it. After all, to arrive at someone's house for tea with a vase in hand is to arrive with a gift for the host. And to remark to one's student about the desirability of an object is to place an obligation on that student to obtain it, as a gift for the master. Not appropriate.

The following morning, Jōō sends his servant to purchase the vase, but alas, it is already sold. At that moment, Jōō receives an invitation for tea that day with Rikyū, who wants to show him a newly purchased vase. Surmising what has happened, Jōō arrives and there is the vase, holding exactly two tsubaki flowers (camellias), like two friends, adorning the table. The vase had been in perfect condition, but now was damaged. Inquiring, Jōō learns that Rikyū has chipped an ear off the vase with a small hammer. Jōō says:

> It is strange that you have chipped an ear off that vase. From the moment I saw the vase yesterday, I have been fascinated by it, and kept thinking that I would use it at my tea ceremony, but only after breaking off an ear. So, before I came this morning I planned to carry out a scheme. Thinking it wouldn't be very interesting to chip off an ear after discussing the matter with you at the end of the ceremony, I had planned to break off an ear myself at the recess or some such time. (*The Art of Living*, p. 40)

And so saying, Jōō produces a small hammer from his pocket. There is a lot here, in this Zen moment. The teacher does have the "authority" to chip this vase, and Rikyū knows that Jōō knows that Rikyū saw Jōō notice the vase and bought it from under his nose, but now Rikyū has saved Jōō the trouble of making the vase "imperfect" ("wabi-sabi" in Japanese).

Why damage the vase at all? Because a vase missing an ear draws from us a sense of its vulnerability, of its relation to a past and a future that includes and exhibits its incomplete-ness, and through *noticing* that missing ear, *we* become mind-ful of the emptiness that the vase *is*, and that surrounds everything. The flowers may be fresh, but they are dying in the vase. We must be mindful of the present. Death is in it.

Socrates said that doing philosophy is practicing for death. He would know, since Athens ordered him to drink the hem-lock. Rikyū was also ordered much later to commit ritual sui-cide by his wealthy patron (not Jōō). As was customary on the occasion of hara-kiri, Rikyū made up a poem as his last act, an ode to his dagger. In a way, that act was already included in the chipping of the vase, the plucking of the flowers, and every other significant act, done in mindfulness. Zen moments aren't always primarily about death, but they always include it. Death, especially your own, is something you want to get right, and that requires mindfulness.

In that frame of mind, I revisited one of my favorite songs, Paul Simon's "Homeward Bound." But now I had new questions. In my mind's eye, I always saw the endless streams of smokes and magazines, and movies and factories, and the strangers' faces. And that railway station. I always saw Paul, and some-times with Artie Garfunkel, as the lonely figures, the poet, the one man band, like flowers in that vase, I now see. I never saw *myself* in the song. *I* wasn't far from home, after all. As I said above, it's a poor me song, but Paul constructs it so as to get us to see him and not ourselves in that lonely place. I felt compas-sion. Paul longed for home. I would too, were I he. But I was quite wrong to envision the song this way, I now understand.

New questions, mindful ones: what is really *missing* from that meaningless stream of days away from home? Well, back there, back home, back *in the past*, when music played, that was home. And the music plays there still. Without Paul. Home. So if I'm that singer, my present thought flies from this gloom and foreign land . . . where? Where my love *lies* waiting. *Silently*. What? Is she asleep? Something is not right here. There is an ear missing from this vase. I only just noticed it. So I asked my class (they are reading Sartwell and listening to Paul Simon with me): "*Why* is she silent?" A pause. My student Eric says "she's dead." I answer: "What else could it be?" (He just bought my vase, I think.) Another pause. "That's why she is lying silently, isn't it?" My student Alexis says, "I wasn't ready for that." Well, we never are, unless we are truly mindful, and that isn't how I live.

I have just taken this class through a tea ceremony of sorts. I have been (ritually) changing the strings on my favorite guitar while conducting this class—I can't serve tea, I realized. I'm no good at it. It takes years of practice. So how do I communicate ritual and mindfulness at the same time? Over four decades I have made a complex and fluid ritual of changing guitar strings. That ritual can be shared, in a way, with others. My life is not so much ritualized. I'm an improviser. So I'm no Rikyū of changing strings; I actually dislike doing it. Yet, I have seen Amy Ray, of the Indigo Girls, back before they were famous, change a guitar string in forty-five seconds *while* continuing to sing, to Emily Saliers' playing, and without missing a word, smiling. That's more like Rikyū changing guitar strings.

Another new question for the class: Why does "Paul" (I indicate scare quotes with my fingers in the universal gesture for quote marks) only *wish* he was going home? Why not just do it? My old answer was: "Well, he's in England, and home is New York, and it's far away, and he has to make a living, and he has to keep his promises." Is that right, now that we have understood the truth about his love? No. The class got and provided the answer. Now I want *you*, dear reader, to *see* the chipped ear in this poem, that missing piece. *His love is dead*. "Home" is where *she* is, and *she* isn't *anywhere*. Our singer *wishes* he was dead. Home. With her. This song is about grief and contemplating suicide. "Paul" has decided not to commit suicide. He has chosen to endure. The rest of his life. But now he can't find his music any more. It's wherever *she* is. That's why his words now echo in all their mediocre meaninglessness, in the wells of silence, one might say. They really always did. Emptiness in harmony. One looks for comfort, no?

Here is a bit of comfort. The song may have started out autobiographically, but there was no death in Paul Simon's life during that time to place him in this situation. He really hadn't experienced death at that time. The song is contrived, in a benign way, like Rikyū's invitation to his teacher. But he *is* a songwriter, after all. This isn't always just about Paul. It's about anyone. Since that time, when Paul was young, he has lost plenty of people he loved, especially his father, and if Peter Carlin is to be believed, *that* loss was the hardest of Paul's life.

And now Carrie Fisher. It's *already* in his song about home. This isn't about when you actually happen to experience this kind of grief, it's about being alive and seeing that it is already there, in the form of emptiness, and the only question is the harmony.

It's wise to go ahead and knock an ear off that vase *now*, or write that song about the death of your loved one *now*. Contrived? Hardly. At least, not more than life itself. The already always arrives.

The Moon and the Mayflower

In a wearied voice the singer confesses his need for some rest. His melody comes from a Bach chorale. But our singer was a notable presence in the Great Folk Scare, and he probably heard the melody in a 1965 recording by some fellow New Yorkers, named Yarrow, Stookey, and Travers. No one ever accused Paul Simon of being lazy when it comes to scraping up a stray sound and making it his own. They've accused him of the opposite vice often enough. I mentioned my songwriter friend who said "Any songwriter who doesn't admit to being a thief is also a liar." The same has to be said for artists in general, including writers of books on rock music and philosophy. We all see, we borrow, we transform, we put our names on it. I want artists to get paid, but I never bought the raw, capitalist version of copyrights and permissions. I believe in the folk process. Artists have always struggled to get paid. Even Aristotle talks about it (see *Nicomachean Ethics*, 1164a16).

But when it comes to assembling a new song, it pays to be something of a scholar. Paul Simon certainly is. That dreary little ditty called "American Tune" has a lot going on. Surely Paul heard "Because All Men Are Brothers" in '65, and learned that it was a melody Bach had used in several of his works. Back in 1973, when he wrote "American Tune," you couldn't just Google this stuff. You had to go to the library. It is pretty likely Paul stumbled on the English translation of the Bach chorale. Heck, it's in every Protestant hymnal, and the Catholics have a different translation from the original Latin in their hymnal.

I see signs of both versions in Paul's "American Tune." Paul went further, too, and found that the tune came from an old German love song, "Mein G'müth ist mir verwirret," ("My Mind Is So Confused"), which is the source Bach pilfered. I know

Paul took the time to get this translated (maybe he translated it himself). His lines about needing rest and being confused come from the German version. The lines about being battered and abused come from the English versions of the Latin poem Bach had translated into German for his chorale (maybe he translated it himself).

I think the first two verses of Paul's song are from the point of view of the Statue of Liberty, herself, which is why he says it's hard to be "bon vivant" so far away from home. Her home is France, after all. But the bridge of the song seems to be Paul's own. He dreams he is dying. His soul rises and smiles back at him, and looking out to sea watches the Statue of Liberty sailing away. This death is not his own but his nation's. In the dream-vision, time is running backward as the emblem of the huddled, yearning masses returns to its origins abroad, while time runs back until it lands in 1620. There they are, immigrants, on a ship called the *Mayflower*, and then suddenly the whole *idea* of America is placed between two bookends, two ships: one to the New World and one to the Moon. Immigrants all. These people lived so well for so long, but now the hour is most uncertain, Paul writes. I guess everything dies.

The uncertain hour was Watergate, back then. And we had learned that "peace with honor" meant "we lost the war." I'm not sure the nation ever really recovered. Not my point. We have had any number of uncertain hours since and before. Sartwell points out that there is a profound beauty in things that are passing from existence. He quotes Leonard Koren: "the closer things get to non-existence, the more exquisite and evocative they become." It's like that chipped vase I was harping on about. What of *nations* that approach non-existence? That is the sad beauty of Paul Simon's song, not just the subject matter, but the melody and the quiet drama of the dream-vision. It transforms a hymn into something that both flies and floats gently away. This falls short of being a lament or an elegy. It isn't sad enough. There is acceptance of the uncertainty. It isn't pretty, and the majestic feel of the Bach chorale is undercut by the plain and weary feel. The song is *wabi-sabi*, that worn and used-up quality that marks the highest aesthetic value for Japanese art. I mentioned it above, but now a bit more detail.

Sartwell says that the "Japanese language possesses a vocabulary of aesthetic experience that is or ought to be the envy of the West." (*Six Names of Beauty*, p. 112). The idea of *wabi-sabi* has to do with the beauty we find in imperfection. Sartwell offers this list: "the withered, weathered, tarnished, scarred, intimate, coarse, earthy, evanescent, tentative, ephemeral" (p. 114). The first four are like the nation Paul Simon sings about. And the *Mayflower* is coarse, the narrator is an earthy working (wo)man, the musical feeling is tentative, the dream is ephemeral, and the song itself, intimate and evanescent.

We can go further. The Zen masters have simplified *wabi-sabi* in seven principles. First there is "fukinsei," asymmetry. Our original melody is beautifully asymmetrical, interval leaps and bending chord pattern that wanders away from home and never quite comes back. The song is made still more ungeometrical by the bridge, the dream, and the vision, a completely different rhythmic feel and melody. The dream interrupts the progress of the music and the story.

Second there is "kanso," or simplicity, and here it is the orchestration, just the singer and one guitar. Then there are "yugen," a subtle and profound grace, and "shizen," a natural unpretentiousness. It is "datsuzoku," free-flowing and not bound by convention, and also "seijaku" or tranquil. And although the song was new once, it was already weathered, as a melody, and as a poem, by centuries of use. And now even Simon's song is weathered or "koko" in its own right. As the song has taken on a patina, so has the singer. It sinks further into *wabi-sabi* as the singer himself nears nonexistence. It was hard not to think about that as I watched Paul Simon sing "The Sound of Silence," alone with his guitar, seventy-five years old, at the somber observance of the fifteenth anniversary of 9/11/2001. Somewhere, over his shoulder, the Lady still stood in the harbor. Or was she sailing away? Both, I think.

Weaving a World

I said I wasn't going to talk about this or make comparisons. This is a chapter about Paul Simon. There is no chapter in this book about Bob Dylan. So why does he keep coming up? Well, dammit, Bob Dylan won the Nobel Prize for literature. *Folk* music is hereby raised to fine art? Bosh. The division between fine art and "low" arts is artificial. Some of the best art I have ever seen (or heard or eaten) was made by people smugly labeled "artisans" by the mavens of *haute couture*. There should be a Nobel Prize for cooking, in my opinion. Anyone who doesn't see that "folk art" is among the highest expressions of meaning isn't paying attention. On the other hand, Nobel Prize? It's incongruous. Next thing you know they'll give a Peace Prize to a US President who is actively waging war in several countries . . .

The Navajo speak of the creation of the world itself as the weaving of Spider Grandmother and her mate. Is *that* low art? The "holy ones" created them the ancient pair as spirits and then later physical bodies were made to hold those spirits. Spider Woman discovered by accident that she had "string" within her, a spiritual power to make physical things, and she only gradually came to see that just by acting spontaneously, she creates patterns. Then Spider Man builds her a loom and she spins the human, cultural world too, which the Navajo call the "fourth World" or the "glittering world."

And that is what we do when we make things from within ourselves. Our bodies direct the spiritual energy within us, and then, a pattern begins to emerge. Sartwell says that for the Navajo "most people were artists as we would understand the term: designing and weaving blankets, composing and preserving and performing songs, making ritual sand paintings" (*Six Names of Beauty*, pp. 135–36). Then Sartwell says: "according to [Gary] Witherspoon, a person's wealth was measured by the songs she created, which are bound to her identity in the way some cultures use names. Songs can actually be exchanged and form a kind of currency." Cool!

So Bob Dylan is really named "Mr.-Tambourine-Man-Blowin'-in-the-Wind-Masters-of-War-Desolation-Row-Don't-Think-Twice . . . " He has a very long name, so he must be a very wealthy man. I assume this is what the Nobel committee recognized. Paul Simon's name is a good bit longer, if a bit less ostentatious. You may scoff at the idea of swapping songs for payment, but I know a place where that economy actually still exists, as an economy. The Kerrville Folk Festival is the yearly national convivium of poet-songwriters, eighteen days (twenty-three if you come for pre-Fest) camping on a ranch in Texas and exchanging songs like money. These folks are rolling in the wealth of soul-webs spun from the strings of five thousand guitars and fiddles, and of course, vocal cords. Entry to a campfire circle costs you a song. A plate of lunch costs you a song. Even *leaving* a camp costs you a song.

The Navajo have a word for the times and places when all this making begets beauty: "hozho." Sartwell says it is the most "comprehensive" word for beauty: all that is healthy and balanced and harmonious. The idea overcomes the binary oppositions we moderns tend to peddle. Light is very hozho, but so is darkness. Life is hozho, but so is death, in its season. Not everything is hozho, but anything *can* be, depending on its relations. There is no "outside" or wholly forbidden thing, since everything we make comes from *within* us, including what we make *of* that which we *did not* make. Time is hozho, especially the cycles of seasons into years, day into night, youth into maturity.

So, for us, the sunshine can be hozho, but also the storm. The Navajo are known for many things, but their weaving of rugs is especially admired. Perhaps the most popular pattern for such weaving is the "storm pattern," which has a trillion variations but is easy to recognize. There is a square in the center, which is the weaver's home, or her loom, and it is connected to the four directions, and the four worlds, by lightning. There is rain and flowing water and the four sacred mountains of the Navajo homeland. Storms are dynamic and scary and also welcome in the dry Nation. Hozho.

Such a rug, as with any the Navajo weave, is just *one* complex thought. To *think* the storm is to live through its gathering, its onset, its duration, its passage, and its aftermath. There is no way to think "the storm" without its place, its hereness and its thereness, its height and its depth, the way it runs and the way it stands. It's all in the thought, in the weave and in the weaving of it. The storm is the idea of the rug and thus, the rug *is* the storm, *for us*.

Writing songs is like that. There must be *an* idea, but there are limitless ways to frame it. Sometimes it's hard to see what the idea is because of the way it is woven. Paul Simon's song "Under African Skies" is *hozho*. You can feel it in the balance, the harmony, whether he is singing it with Linda Ronstadt (as on the studio recording), or, better, with Miriam Makeba at the Concert in Zimbabwe, when Paul changed some words for the context. I like those words better: music rang "round my grandmother's door," and the prayer is to take this baby girl from "the Township of Mofolo," which is a part of Soweto. The song is about "place," in the strongest sense, but a storm is brewing there.

It is a Navajo rug of a song. One thought, many parts. The song sort of grows into existing. A single guitar arrives from a distance and is joined by the rhythmic steps of one walking. It breaks into language describing Joseph, who walks his days under the skies of Africa. Then there is a koan about memory and how it lives in the roots of rhythm, about falling into this life and pulsing with the power of love. Then comes the center, the eye of the storm, a lament about a displaced child, not home, and a prayer for "wings to fly through harmony." This prayer granted, the one who prays vows to ask for nothing further. This child will *never* be home (Tucson, Mofolo, it doesn't matter), but still may be *hozho* by singing, living, acting from and with and through harmony. Harmony in our world is woven from within and adorns the glittering world *wherever we are*.

After this thought, Paul repeats the koan about memory and rhythm, followed by (what I take to be) the granting of the prayer, a flying harmonic dance of sky and earth. Spider Man builds, ummmbada ummmbada, Spider Woman weaves, woooo. A musical swell and then quietly we see Joseph, walking into the distance. The last two verses are exact repetitions of the beginning, but now the storm has spent its fury and the words take on a different meaning. The song drifts away into silence like a storm passing, like a painful memory that stirs an anguished emotion and then fades.

I think Paul originally saw in his mind's eye an image of a Native infant, a girl, displaced from her home, by Missionaries; yes, Tucson is Linda Ronstadt's home town, but that's only the proximate reason, that and the name is poetic. But the little girl child in the image isn't a famous singer, she is an un-famous one, vulnerable and almost powerless. Almost. How will she weave here, in this place she doesn't belong, and with no thread? Ah, but she *has* thread. She will sing and the melodies and the time that carries them will weave in the air, and through harmony she will fly. The South African situation is only marginally different. All these cities, teeming with dis-placed people, Tucson, Johannesburg; they most certainly don't belong under these crowded, clouded skies. They were put here by strangers and it has made strangers of everyone. We see the faces and are reminded of where we long to be. Those strangers are not beautiful or healthy. But the music almost redeems us.

I don't think Paul Simon will ever win a Nobel Prize. There are too many questions about credit for those who helped him weave the songs. These questions pertain to a time and a civilization that isn't hozho when it comes to owning things. I think I'd like it better where songs are the currency and making them is the way of life, but I know it can't always be that way.

Of Teaspoons and Waves

Paul Simon wrote (over a happy chord and floating rhythm) "she makes the sign of a teaspoon, he makes the sign of a wave." That's cryptic. But we *see* it in the official video for "Diamonds on the Soles of Her Shoes." What does that sign mean? These two people Paul is depicting seem to understand the sign language, after he puts on aftershave and they spend a night sleeping in a doorway on Upper Broadway. At first *she* has diamonds on the soles of her shoes and he's "empty as a pocket." By the end, he has traded his sanity for diamonds on the soles of his own shoes. Holy cod. I haven't ever *been* in that particular romance, but I think I know some who have.

This is another story about how we begin to remember. There was this girl, and people called her crazy. But there's something different about her. Creativity is like that, like those diamonds. And poor boys *know* their ordinary shoes, put on aftershave to compensate. They want some of that action, some of that freakish light that only glints and glimmers and glitters in that crazy girl's transient steps. You *gotta* take that gal dancing. Watch the shoes. There is an idea here.

This will now seem like a jarring change, but trust me. I hate to do this, but somebody has to do it.

The line goes: "Life's like this: You fall and you crawl and you break and you take what you get and you turn it into honesty." Avril Levigne's friends smash up a mall because it *isn't* reality, and they are surprisingly realistic about what a working class kid can expect. They demand that whatever comes at you, your challenge is to be authentic. And have some fun, by the way. I am not saying Avril is the epitome of authenticity.

There's a good point here. Which will it be? Will you go crazy, even after all those years, for your aesthetic vision, like

Paul Simon? Or will you relax because it's all been done before, as the Canadian kid counsels? Will you try to be somebody else, get some of those diamonds, or will you let it be? So many questions, so little time to watch YouTube.

Sartwell (yes, him again) suggests that our love of beauty, when we turn *ideas* into *ideals*, gets locked into an unhealthy dance with perfection. It's our inner Platonist becoming tyrant over the *to kalon*, Ancient Greek for "beauty." That's not a good translation. It's more like what is "nobly fine." No sooner do we *imagine* what *is* than we set about *perfecting* it to match our sweet imaginations. And having perfected it we can't measure up to it and want nothing better than to be free of whatever we have created. The perfect is the enemy of the good enough. But after you've been around the block on this paradox a few times, well, wherever you are, you want to be elsewhere . . .

It reminds me of that "blonde joke" (told me by my blonde wife who finds these jokes very funny): a man comes to a river bank, looks left and right and sees no bridge. But there is a blonde across the river, so he yells "how do you get to the other side?" There is a pause. Then the blonde yells back "you *are* on the other side . . . " Then she makes the sign of a teaspoon and he makes the sign of a wave. (I added that myself, but hey, *maybe* she does and maybe he does, you know?) I wish I knew what I'm talking about, but sometimes you gotta let go. And any day now . . .

I think we do have a clue about how to be released from our ideals, when they ensnare us. There are two possibilities. First, learn to be where and when you are, like when you're drivin' in your car, with her, one on one, and don't become somebody else, unless you want to frustrate your unimaginative skatepunk girlfriend. (To be fair, Avril never liked that song . . . at least so she said *after* it put diamonds on the soles of her shoes.)

The second option is the freakish decompensation. We take the Seventh Avenue Line to the doorways of Upper Broadway and swear off what the world may think. If we can't find the dance club, we just sleep with the freaks. We embrace our own special insanity, with those who can share it. People look at us and make the sign of a wave.

In 1932, Tod Browning, after he got his own sole-diamonds for his acclaimed film *Dracula*, had a moment of insanity that became an impossible aesthetic project, a film called *Freaks*.

His idea was to employ the actual freaks who were working in the sideshows of his times, the "midgets" and "human caterpillars" and "pinheads" and "conjoined twins" who had reminded the grandfathers of Kansas and the suicidal wolves of Wall Street that not *every* life *can* be idealized. Sometimes we fall and we crawl and we take what we get and turn it into . . . well . . . a closer and more honest look at the human condition.

So Browning put the freaks in a scripted film. It should have been called "Revenge of the Freaks," perhaps. It was widely banned as unfit to watch. They sort of smashed up the mall, those freaks. "If you offend one of them, you offend them all," the ominous voice says in the trailer. It's *not* sweet imagination, it's the back side of the ideal, in black and white. Paul Simon's video for "Diamonds" shifts constantly between scenes of making the video and the video they made. The first is "reality" in black and white, and the second is sweet imagination in Kodachrome color, the idea made artistically into an ideal. But Paul still can't dance. There is a freak hiding in there, and the freak's still got those the walking blues. Watch the video sometime.

These paradoxes are monsters of our own passion. Sartwell observes that we chain ourselves to anything that takes possession of our imaginations. Eventually we must decide whether we want a Kodachrome dream or a B&W life. In the second after it rains, well, there's a rainbow, but all of the colors are black; the colors aren't there, of course, "it's imagination they lack." The first world is nice bright colors, the greens of summers, making us think the world's a sunny day, how it looks from behind the Nikon camera of sweet imagination. It's understandable if we prefer it. I mean, everything looks worse in black and white, right?

In the Concert in Central Park, in front of half a million people, Paul Simon decided to reverse himself and sing "Everything looks *better* in black and white." He made Artie sing it too. I have heard Artie didn't like it. And I don't like it when people over-analyze song lyrics, but that change was a conscious decision.

The black and white world, devoid of Kodachrome and all it symbolizes, is like a mall Avril's friends want to smash. No illusions, dude. The world's in color. Don't heavy me out with your artful reductions, okay? Sometimes we want to be freaks and to see freaks, and that's exactly the world as it is. Life's like this, she said. We do substitute our imaginations, our personal Kodachrome, so maybe we put on colorful clothes, live like the rainbow isn't black. Because it isn't.

Beautiful word-images by any standard. Ironically, they are made real by being presented *as* unreal. I watched that Avril Levigne video more times than I should admit. It's awful. But it's a moment in time. I also watched that Paul Simon video a thousand times—the black and white is pretentious, but maybe he's being ironic? A quotation of Kodachrome? Look, that white boy has ordinary shoes and can't dance. It's good that he doesn't try very often. That would be freakish. Now, watch the white boy make a video. Worse in black and white. Or maybe better.

But maybe we could put the empty boy on a skateboard . . . I think I saw Avril make the sign of a teaspoon somewhere in that video. Can I make it any more obvious? As if anybody here would know exactly what I was talking about? Well, I guess every generation throws a hero up the pop charts. But maybe she's just trying to keep her balance. Maybe that isn't the teaspoon sign after all. Nice colors though.

Out of the Pure Blue

Every time I go to central Texas I'm amazed by how ugly and hateful the grackles are. But this bird shimmers and shines iridescently and is often the color of deep indigo, which many regard as the most beautiful blue there is. Something has gone awry with the Divine creation here (although evolution seems quite serviceable in this case). This thing has googly yellow eyes. It makes loud sounds, and unnatural, like a buzz saw or someone tuning an old radio. Seagulls are plenty annoying, but if Hitchcock *really* wanted to scare people, he should have set his movie in Texas, in the H-E-B parking lot.

But compare the one iridescent bird to another. The elusive indigo bunting sometimes negotiates with the cardinals to hold off the kestrels. Now a cardinal is a small bird, but it is twice the size of that little bunting. People say various colors are "happy" (yellow) or "cool" (blue and green) or "hot," (red), but there is so much more than that to say. It seems like a disservice to our experience to put a color in a pigeonhole (since we are speaking of iridescent birds). Sartwell writes: "Yesterday I saw my Indigo Bunting playing or battling with a cardinal across my yard, in an astounding and continuously transforming juxtaposition of color, and I wasn't thinking of hot and cold or happy and sad or Mahler: I was completely absorbed in the scene, working just to keep track, with no time for or inclination to interpretation. It was a call to the present moment" (*Six Names of Beauty*, p. 33).

That "call" to be in the moment is something we all know. It has to do with the fleeting moment and the impending sense of loss while every nerve in our bodies is absorbed in what cannot last. Sartwell says:

> I have no evidence . . . but it seems to me likely that the human aesthetic sense arose not, for example, from some awesome majesty of a forest, mountain, sunset, but by the sudden burst or blossom of energized color across a field of vision: the flower, the fruit, the butterfly, the bird . . . beauty arises first in what stands out from the environment because of its unusual shape, bright coloration: the arousal of the senses. Too, the sense of beauty must be associated with loss, and the temporal boundedness of the flower, butterfly, bird are proverbial. (p. 28)

The Hebrew word for this is "יָפַע" which is transliterated as "yapha." In Deuteronomy 33:2, in Moses's last words before his death, he says: "God came from Sinai, shone forth (yapha) to them from Seir, and made an appearance from Mount Paran. From the holy myriads, He brought the fire of a religion to them from His right hand." (*Living Torah* translation).

In its own way, this is Sartwell's shining burst of color. Surely the visible spectrum, and all of its glow, was in the command, "Let there be light," but our ability to notice such things is limited by both time and place, and by what we *are*. But when a color calls to you, it is the fire of a religion.

Every artist and every performer understands. A burst, a shine, and an energy, in their fleetingness, can be captured in many ways. I am reminded of Paul Simon's famous Graceland concert in Harare, Zimbabwe, in 1987. There were a million aesthetic decisions to be made. Simon was under tremendous pressure for violating a UN sanction held to be sacrosanct by the cultural forces of that time. We must isolate South Africa in every way, to end apartheid, they believed. Simon was taking upon himself a unilateral, unearned moral authority for the sake of having a collection of pop music that would revive his career. He was not being political, just looking for a new sound. Everyone knew it.

There were incidents and accidents and hints and allegations, but gradually the *Graceland* project took on a social importance no one foresaw. It was an opportunity. By the time the concert in Zimbabwe happened, Simon had a pretty clear idea of what he had done, largely unintentionally, if Peter Carlin's account is accurate in his biography of Simon. Paul decided that "something" was going to flit across our field of vision with a burst of sound and color, and *THAT SOME-THING WOULDN'T BE HIM*. If you watch the film, especially the opening of the concert, "Township Jive," you can't help noticing that all the *color* belongs to the other performers. Simon wore a pair of black jeans and a plain white t-shirt. He stood front and center, more in the role of a presenter than to be admired. The plain white shirt says, "*You* fill in what my role is here." If he had pranced out like Elton John, or even just put a slogan or image on that t-shirt, he would have missed the moment, the aesthetic demand that *something* **true** and **good** be done.

It is a dicey thing when the **beautiful**, especially what is *yapha*, bursting forth temporarily, leads the true and the good by the hand into the future. There is no way to ensure its guidance is sound. The fire in its right hand burns as well as illuminates. Many people now see Simon's bold decisions as the beginning of the end of apartheid. There was a call to the present moment in what he did *with* what he had done. The momentum of that struggle turned. Millions of people bought the record, millions all over the world watched the concert, and Miriam Makeba's role was especially important. Mother Africa. She had been in exile for over a quarter century on that day in Zimbabwe. The climactic moment of the concert came when she sang "Soweto Blues." That performance was deep indigo, if you know what I mean, but it was followed with this amazing statement of solidarity when she sang (and translated, I think) "Under African Skies," as a duet with Simon.

They sing, as I said above, the story about how we begin to remember, and about the remnant, the remainder of the roots of rhythm. It is a song about Joseph, every Joseph, whose face is as black as the night, and Africa is *his*. This is not a threat, it's a promise. The concert is in broad daylight so that everyone across the border can have no doubt that this diverse, celebrating crowd, bursting forth in fleeting color, is beautiful, and sooner or later, this *is* what South Africa *will look like*. The bonds *will* be broken. The world saw and finally understood. Pressure on the politicians from the dull, satisfied middle class of the Western world grew. The politicians could act. I wouldn't be surprised if the keepers of apartheid watched this concert and thought to themselves "We're done for." And they were, even though it took *much* more to make it happen.

The famous British promoter Tony Hollingsworth, and others, recognized before Simon did that staging huge concerts could bring the plight of black South Africans increasingly into the light. There wasn't sufficient support to do it until after Simon did his Zimbabwe show. In 1988 they did another big show, and then in 1990, Miriam Makeba sang at the second, broadcast to over sixty countries. The regime decided to visit Nelson Mandela on Robin Island immediately after that concert. He was the only person who could lead the transition without a horrendous war. And that war was coming if the South African government did nothing. They chose life for South Africa.

I believe that the tone of beauty, of bursting forth, of affirming life, was *set* by Paul Simon, by his decisions. In the midst of a sensory feast, as the humble presenter, he made a difference in *how* it all happened. He was saying: "Don't you see how beautiful this is? Don't destroy this beauty with violence. Work with it, follow the lead of your senses and your heart, and **truth** and **goodness** can also be yours." If he had shown up angry, accusatory, self-righteous, nothing would have changed. I believe Paul Simon *knew* that his was his message was life, color, beauty bursting forth. South Africa looks today as Zimbabwe looked that golden afternoon. A moment in time? Yes. But the roots of rhythm remain and help us begin to remember.

I never saw an indigo bunting until I was almost fifty. It was astonishing. Could that bird actually exist? Nothing in my history prepared me for this sudden renewal of "innocence" in my senses, as Sartwell describes such experiences. The older we get, the harder it is to recover the innocence we had as children, when the whole world was a colorful show. But then in moments like that, or like the Graceland concert, we begin to remember, we are absorbed, and we play and dance in our hearts like children, like the crowd in Zimbabwe that day. It is . . . and I want to shout it, to exclaim it . . . it is Yapha! from the pure blue. Thanks for that, Paul.

BONUS TRACKS

Growing Older but Not UP

15

Christ in a Sidecar: An Ontology of Suicide Machines

We now enter the domain of the rock lifestyle. Apart from sex and drugs, there is image—things that go fast, things that sail free, loud concerts, life on the road, and trying to make a living (at music). Rock isn't just music, it's life, for our rock heroes; it's about the way things look and feel, what's cool and what's not. There will be more autobiography here than earlier. I hope the stories make you remember things in your life. This is a day's ride on a good bike. But we aren't quite ready to depart. Right now our trusty steed is up on blocks in the living room, so be patient. We have work to do first, but you won't be disappointed.

Workin' on a Hog?

We need some tools, and tools are not very exciting. Here's something boring to consider: Philosophical discussions really need to begin with an explicit "ontology," that is, an explicit specification of what entities, processes, and modes of existence will be under discussion. Not only does good ontology inhibit needless verbal disputes later, but it also forces us into a reflective frame of mind, a frame of mind in which we ask ourselves what Martin Heidegger called "the Question."[1]

---

[1] Many trees have given their lives in service of discussing the Question of Being, but the first trees to offer themselves in sacrifice probably came from the Black Forest in about 1926, since Heidegger's book, *Sein und Zeit*, first

In the coffee houses they would say it in German—*die Frage*, or *die Seinsfrage*, if they are feeling especially full of themselves.[2] One rule of the coffee house is that one should never say anything in English that could be expressed with greater *gravitas* in a dead language; failing that, use German for the ominous ideas, French for the dismissive ideas, and while Italian is only for the posers too *gauche* to realize that Italian is not *chic*, at least it isn't English.

Returning to "the Question," it is a way of launching a sneak attack on things we already vaguely understand (and presume in our thinking), but which we have failed to make explicit. When we have slunk quietly behind our quarry (the quarry is our own vague awareness), we pop up, say "boo!" and then wait to see what comes running our way. But there are lots of ways to sneak and slink, lots of ways to say "boo!" and still more ways to list and count the things we catch sight of as we flush out the truthy little frightened quails.

In the case of the splendid Dr. Heidegger, he did something he called "fundamental ontology," which outlines the bare essentials one must assume in approaching the Question of Being, oh, wait, I mean *die Seinsfrage*. He transforms that venerable question from "why is there something rather than nothing?" into the slightly less obvious "what sort of being asks such an impossible question?" It turns out, after much hand wringing, that the answer is, "well, the sort of being who asks that question is one that has a problem with its own being—and that would be me, and maybe also you, but definitely me."

But according to Heidegger's zealous and numerous followers, none but the Master himself is deep enough or smart enough to carry out the weighty task of Fundamental Ontology (the capital letters are my own, but I think I can hear them in their tone of voice when I am in the presence of such self-

---

appeared in 1927. The two-part introduction to this work sets out Heidegger's phenomenological method and raises the Question of Being. For a recent translation, see Martin Heidegger, *Being and Time*, trans. Joan Stambaugh, Sections 1–8, 12–36.

   [2] Of course, one question leads to another, so if you are very adventurous and would like to investigate the Question surrounding the Question, see Jacques Derrida, *Of Spirit: Heidegger and the Question*.

importance, all of them driving BMW cages in blissful ignorance of the fact that Bayerische Motoren Werke ever even
made a motorcycle). I am inclined to let the snobs have their
Fundamental Ontologies (and if you are one of them, you are
not welcome to ride with me, let alone work on my bike) while
I go after something more suited to their estimation of my
depth, or lack thereof (estimation, I mean, not depth).

As William Blake noted, it is a better testament to your
character to count some kinds of people among your critics
than among your admirers.[3] I think Blake would have fared
poorly at a Harley rally, but that doesn't mean he was wrong.
His trouble was that he whined about his critics all the time
and made enemies needlessly. Perhaps the Blake scholars (and
there are many more of these than the world really needs)
would be offended, but sometimes I just want to shake some
sense into the odd little guy: "Just do the pictures, Bill, write
the words. Don't waste your energy on the idiots who don't get
it." But no, he couldn't let it go, and so he immortalized his own
enemies, none of whose names would even remain to us but for
his whining. So I won't bother calling the Heideggerians by
name; let history swallow them if it wants to, or me, or both.

Ontological Questions

Ontologics of the sort I want you to consider are motivated by
questions. Whenever you find a question that you know the
answer to, but you don't know why you are so sure of yourself,
you have the makings of an ontology. But there are so many

---

[3] Blake had lots of ways of saying this, but one of my favorite is: "Thy
friendship has oft made my heart to ake: / Do be my Enemy—for Friendship's
sake" (Rosetti MS, LXXXIV). Another nice one is "To H[ayley]: You think
Fuseli is not a Great Painter. I'm Glad./ This is one of the best compliments he
ever had." One may find tasty little epigrams like these scattered in Blake's
manuscripts that immortalize names such as Flaxman, Cromek, Stothard,
Macklin, Boydel, Bowyer, and Hayley that we surely would have lost but for
Blake's scribbling complaints. See John Sampson, *The Poetical Works of
William Blake*, pp. 204–210, 212–16 (Rosetti MS, L–LXX, LXXVI–LXXXV). In
Blake's defense, he never published these remarks, but he did set them to the
page. As for whining, I guess I should go easier on Bill—after all, I was never
tried for High Treason. I am confident that it is a drag, and I might whine a
little bit myself about that.

questions and so little time. We should choose our questions carefully. I have thought about various possibilities for a guiding question in this chapter. I must have settled on a question or you wouldn't be reading this. I think most people will quickly see that this question has a lot of torque; it is indirect, but it will take us far if we can free ourselves for the trip.

My guiding question is: "Would Bruce Springsteen ride a Honda?"

First off, I don't mean "Has Bruce ever ridden a Honda?" Maybe he has, but ours is not a factual question about Springsteen's biography, it is about two cultural icons, Springsteen and Honda, icons that press upon us an immediate contrast. Our imaginations try to place Bruce on the Honda, and we have a sense of what Walt Disney called the "plausible impossible."[4] We feel we are imagining a fiction when we try to place Bruce on the Honda. We all know Bruce would not "ride a Honda" in the intended iconic sense, even if curiosity or circumstance might have led him actually to try one out at some point. But how do we know the answer to this question with such confidence? It seems like a Hog of a question, and everyone knows that taking ownership of a Harley means a commitment to learning how to work on it, but even lesser bikes have maintenance issues. I mean, you don't want to be at the mercy of the guy who owns the repair shop, right? The quality of his mercy is pretty strained, nay, it fairly tears a ligament in giving you what you deserve.

In what follows we will first explore this answer to our principal question and collect our insights like needed parts (and I do not mean cheap after-market knock-offs; let the shade-tree mechanics use those—we work only with parts that would make Milwaukee raise a glass—or at least Tokyo), and one by one install them. Eventually we will have a question that purrs, and

---

[4] Walt Disney explained the principle of "the plausible impossible" in Episode 55 of *The Wonderful World of Disney*, originally aired on ABC (31st October, 1956); it is part two of a trilogy called "The Art of Animation," and is currently available to download in several places, including
<http://tv-episodes.prettyfamous.com/l/7123428/The-Plausible-Impossible>.
Unfortunately it doesn't appear to be on YouTube or any other free site I can find, but I'm no expert at finding such things.. For the phenomenological basis of Disney's principle, see Edmund Husserl, *Ideas: General Introduction to Pure Phenomenolgy*, §23, pp. 90–92.

later we may take it out for a ride, but what more did you really expect? You want the meaning of life? Go see the Dalai Lama.

The Passion of the Boss

Would Bruce ride a Honda? No. But before we can get to the stuff that is so boss about the answer, we need to spend some time tinkering with the question while we're still in the onto-logical living room (yes, we work on this bike in the living room, not in the garage; if you are worried about the mess, go read a different chapter). Put on some old clothes in case you get sub-stances on yourself.

We learn much about the value of the question when we imagine variations. Ontologists always imagine variations.[5] I think the question needs to be formulated just as it is, and not, for example, "would Bruce ride a Harley?" to which the answer is "duh." That question leads us nowhere we have not already been, many times, although maybe we could have an interesting chat about what model Harley Bruce should ride, if you only knew more about it. The question also cannot be "would Woody Guthrie ride a Honda?" which is a jarring enough question, but I fear it is too great a project for any but Heidegger and his most profound followers. Indeed, that Woody Guthrie question is just one short step away from the *Seinsfrage*.

A much more predictable conversation could be had if we asked "would Jesus ride a Honda or a Harley?" To this one, we can all agree he wouldn't ride a Honda (see below), but I fear we would be split over the Harley question, with a small minor-ity insisting not only that Jesus would ride a Harley, but that he actually did enter Jerusalem on a Hog (which may explain why things soon started looking like Glen Hanson's demise in *Easy Rider*—am I the only one who has noticed the similarity between that scene and Mel Gibson's *Passion of the Christ*?). This is my own view, in fact; not that Jesus would ride a Harley, but that he actually did. But let's keep it light. I think we can

---

[5] For an explanation of the method of imaginative variation, see Husserl, ibid., §§68–70, pp. 195–201. For an explanation of the explanation (trust me, you'll need it), see Erazim Kohák, *Idea and Experience: Edmund Husserl's Project of Phenomenology in Ideas I*, pp. 143–47.

easily agree on the Bruce part of the question. Maybe Jesus on a Harley, definitely Bruce, no Honda for either one.

The "Honda" part of the question is equally crucial. It's an uncomfortable truth that there are two manufacturers of real motorcycles in the world today. One is Harley-Davidson, the other is Honda. The rest are wanna-be's. I am not saying Suzuki and Yamaha have made no real bikes. They made and make inferior Hondas.[6] I am not saying BSA, Triumph, Norton, and Indian never made real bikes. They made and make inferior Harleys.[7] Here is another uncomfortable truth: Honda knows how to make a motorcycle.[8] Hondas are fast, they are efficient, they last forever, they require very little maintenance, and yes, they even look good (to the middle-class, suburban eye). After some initial experiments, Harley-Davidson made the decision soon after Hondas appeared in

---

[6] I use the word "inferior" advisedly, being well aware of the excellence of some other bikes, especially Yamahas. Honda and Yamaha fought it out for world pre-eminence among the Japanese manufacturers in a war that nearly buried Harley-Davidson in the early 1980s, but I speak here not of the specific history but of the battle for supremacy in the public mind, for the status of "cultural icon." If this were a matter of history rather than philosophy we might pursue these issues, but my claim has to do with things everyone knows, which is that history has proclaimed Honda the victor, regardless of whether there may be some Yamahas that were in some sense superior. That's why "Yamaha" is a friggin' piano in the mind of John Q. Much has been written on this historic battle between Honda and Yamaha, but for something suitably compact, see Greg Field's short essay "H-D vs. Japan," in *The Harley-Davidson Century*, edited by Darwin Holstrom (St. Paul: MBI, 2004), pp. 206–07. I certainly confess that Suzuki, Kawasaki, and Yamaha have made some impressive crotch-rockets, but the later agreements with Erik Buell have lifted Harley into a position of great respect even among the sport-bike enthusiasts. Buell and Harley certainly are of a feather, even if H-D was slower to recognize Buell's genius as an engineer than they should have been.

[7] As above, this is a matter of the historical outcome in the battle for cultural supremacy, not a judgment about technical achievement or actual history, regarding which more subtlety of argument is needed.

[8] I do not deny that a wealth of literature and judgment exists from Harley partisans that trashes the quality of Hondas, but there is a more balanced and sober literature that recognizes in the words of Greg Field, "Soichiro Honda's genius," and while Field specifically had in mind the electric starter in saying this, he adds that Honda knew "motorcycles would never appeal to the masses until they were just . . . as reliable as a car" (*The Harley-Davidson Century*, p. 127).

the U.S. market not even to compete, and Honda reciprocated (initially at least).[9] It was a sign of mutual respect, and while Harley-Davidson learned some lessons from Japan, and taught Japan as many, H-D also showed a great awareness of what makes a Harley a Harley, that ineffable something (that *je ne sais quoi*, if you need a phrase to go with your *cappuccino*) that would be lost if certain paths were followed. Harley-Davidson was unwilling to make McMotorcycles. It is worth noting that Honda also makes the best cages in the world. Harley-Davidson will not be trying to compete there either. Our first needed parts in this rebuild project: most battles are won or lost in the choosing, and there is no dishonor in letting someone else make a buck you never needed anyway. How different corporate America would be if it grasped this lesson!

Thus, I claim, we ask "would Springsteen ride a Honda?" precisely because it's the most informative contrast available to us. Honda makes an outstanding bike and they always did. But do they rock? The question is about a profound relation between, on the one side, very defensible, conservative, thrifty middle-class values and on the other side, well, a somewhat impractical craving for freedom from those same values (not to reject them wholesale, but to take or leave them, as conscience and the sense of self may demand).

So what does Honda mean? Again, we seek contrast. By way of illustration, for instance, we intuitively recognize the ridiculousness of a Honda with extended forks. There are some things that just ought not be tricked out, like June Cleaver in a thong and pasties or a Honda 750 with extended forks (the 750 is still the "manliest" bike Honda ever made, but even it is something that could be respectably featured in an article for *Good Housekeeping*). The Honda as an icon helps us understand that this is a contrast not just of values, but of fundamental—even existential—relations. The truth is that Bruce could never love a Honda with all the madness in his soul, and the reason can be summed up in this phrase: Honda cannot make a suicide machine.

Honda cannot make a suicide machine because that would contradict every value they have poured into their bikes from

---

[9] The history is complicated, but again, please refer to Greg Field, "H-D vs. Japan" in *The Harley-Davidson Century*, pp. 206–07.

the first. In fact, this is part of the reason we all know Jesus wouldn't have ridden a Honda. He had no use for middle-class values of this sort. What we may disagree on is whether he went into Jerusalem in a final act of defiance and there committed suicide willingly by the hands of others. But if he did that, he did it on a Harley, because a Harley is not first and foremost a bike or even a machine. A Harley is a decision about life and what makes it rock, and how it needs to be lived. When that decision comes to be embodied and epitomized in a machine, we call it a Harley. Here we have another needful part: Harley-Davidson, as cultural icon, represents not a machine first or foremost, but an existential decision and the life that follows upon it. We will seek to understand that decision and the philosophies that accompany it with Bruce and JC, when we hit the road, but we are not quite finished tinkering with this question. We have seen "it's not just a bike, it's a choice," but have we understood it?

The Moment of Truth (or Falsehood)

A narrative may help to bring this point into greater relief. With your indulgence, I want to rehearse a scene from my own youth that has been replayed tens of millions of times in other lives in the last fifty years, with incidental variations. Many of you will recognize the story. My father, like so many men of his generation, rose to become a successful professional from a humble background. He capitulated in 1975 (year of "Born to Run," and no mere coincidence) to my adolescent pleas for a motorcycle. Like any father of that day and age, he would "make this a learning process" for me. I would learn about all the different motorcycles available, within a determined price and power range, and then we would make an informed purchase. After reading the available materials, a Wednesday was designated during which we would visit each dealership, but we would not be buying a motorcycle that day—this was made perfectly clear. We would narrow our choices and return to the dealers whose offerings impressed us, and we would pay a fair price, and we would know what a fair price was. Such were the preordained values. And while the best trade plans of micely men can sometimes turn askew, sometimes they don't.

Now, there are two types of fathers in such situations: there are those who take their sons to the Harley-Davidson dealership, and then there are fathers who are willing to be taken there. No father who consents to having an adolescent son of his on a bike at all is likely to rule out the Harley in advance. Those Harley-less fathers and the ones who simply say "no" to their sons' pleas for a bike are the same class of fathers. Their sons, on account of the fathers' restrictions, will eventually learn on their own (or spend the rest of life wishing they had), that it takes a minimum of two men to bring a boy to manhood, and that the boy chooses the second man, not the father. Saying "no" to a son who is serious about his request for a bike is a fast way to insure that the boy will choose a mentor whose values are quite unlike his father's; he will certainly choose a mentor whom his father would reject, perhaps for the very reason that his father would reject such a spirit guide. Fathers reading this, be advised: If the boy wants a bike, you will do well to make that possible for him. If your girl wants a bike, best of luck. I have no advice for you. Girls on bikes and girls on horses are all quite appealing—even unappealing women become strangely intriguing astride a great beast or a great machine, for reasons I would do better not to investigate too closely, but I have the sense that it is for the girl and her mother to work out the wherefores.

My own father was willing to be taken to the Harley dealership. The one quirk in my personal narrative is that the episode occurred during the one year that H-D offered a 90cc bike.[10] In some ways, 1975 was the pivotal year not only for me, but for Harley-Davidson and Honda, because the territory of the imaginations of American mass culture was being divvied up at just that moment, and my own decision about a bike illustrated the moment pretty nicely. A few years before, Honda had introduced its SL 70cc enduro bike (street legal, but suitable

---

[10] This bike, the Z90, was actually made by Aermacchi, an Italian manufacturer with which H-D collaborated for a number of years after 1960. It was quickly apparent that competing with the Japanese on smaller models was a losing proposition in many senses for H-D, and the 90cc bike was never offered again, nor was there anything else smaller than 54ci until after 1995. See *The Encyclopedia of the Harley-Davidson* by Peter Henshaw and Ian Kerr, p. 172.

for trail riding, which was then a growing craze), and Harley had entered the fray with the 90cc enduro bike made by Aermacchi. The latter bore the Harley name, however, and the name already meant what it still means today.

But I Digress

I will return to my narrative in a moment, but we have a bolt stuck here and we need an impact wrench. Peter Fonda's "Captain America" seems to have clinched the iconic standing of the Harley, which had long been associated with a certain conception of freedom and individualism, but in the wake of *Easy Rider*, the popular imagination had crystallized around this idea. Part of the genius of Captain America was its symbolic insistence upon the association of patriotism with this very notion of freedom and individualism—this bike gave us permission to think for ourselves about what devotion and loyalty to the ideals of America really means, and the irony that this bike conveyed its rider toward making a drug deal (outside of the current laws) is also a source of creative tension. Brilliant. It's worth pausing to consider how Dennis Hopper's film and its impact would have been different if Fonda had ridden any other bike (not just a non-Harley, but even any Harley other than Captain America). It is dangerous to make assertions about "might-have-beens," or what analytic philosophers like to call "counterfactuals," because no evidence can exist that fully demonstrates the falseness of such assertions. But with that disclaimer noted, I want to suggest that the film becomes close to meaningless without the rolling American flag. That bike is the iconic key to the kingdom, not only of that one film, but to the kingdom of America the Paradoxical. It is not an accident that our celluloid sacrificial lamb, Glen Hanson, is a rogue lawyer incognito, and that, symbolically, it is precisely the law that suffers a brutal death at the hands of those who believe themselves to be defending it and its ideals, because, after all, the letter kills the spirit, according to Jesus, just as surely as the rednecks kill Glen Hanson.

The Story of the Moral

Predictably, the Honda and the Harley were the finalists in my father's version of bowling-for-buddy-pegs. The Wednesday for purchasing arrived, about as slowly as Christmas (another notion we wouldn't have without Jesus, not so much Christmas, but the idea that it is slow—he sure took his sweet time showing up, what with Babylonians and Assyrians running amock, and all those depressing lamentations, I mean, incarnate already, would ya? Christ in a sidecar!).

We went to the Honda dealership first. Immediately the salesman (wrongly) guessed that the decision would actually rest with my father. He proceeded to explain the practicality of the (new) XL 70, its four-stroke engine, its low maintenance requirements, its reliability, its lower price, its superior resale value, its safety features (he even dared to offer my father the optional governor for the carburetor that would keep me below 35 mph). Upon learning that the Harley was his competitor in our case, he freely trashed it. "That Dago junker? . . ." he said, after checking my dad's card to make sure our name wasn't Delvecchio or Altabello. The Honda dealer had an impressive command of the factors bearing upon WASPish middle-class values, and an equally impressive set of prejudices to back them up. But he also had a pretty good little bike.

At the Harley dealership, the salesman was a biker. He correctly surmised within two or three minutes of observing me and my father that the decision was actually mine to make, although my father had never said as much to me—I guess dad was watching to see what I would do, and the biker recognized it. My Harley salesman was therefore speaking to a fourteen-year-old kid. He never had a bad word to say about the Honda XL 70. He was asking me what I wanted without making comparisons. I learned that the Harley was quite powerful, had a much higher top-end speed, and I already knew it was cooler by far. Without saying so, the Harley salesman helped me understand that this decision was about who I was and wanted to be. The Harley had a two-stroke engine, requiring me to mix the oil and gas. It sat higher off the ground. It was very cool. I still want a Z90.

I chose the Honda (without the governor, thank you very much, top speed of 50 m.p.h.). I apologize to the readers who would have wished for the opposite choice. If I had chosen the Harley, someone else would be writing this chapter, or maybe no one would write it. I would be doing something else, or be dead. To make matters worse, I subsequently chose five or six more Hondas over the next thirty years (there's one in the garage right now). My father would have allowed the Harley choice and supported it, but his personal values had been imparted to me without being forced on me, and he was pleased with my choice. I could tell.

And I was actually honest with myself—in the sense that I realized I could not self-honestly ride a Harley. At fourteen, I liked Peter, Paul and Mary and Don McLean at least as well as Led Zeppelin and the Stones, but Springsteen's ode to Highway 9 was changing me. Would I compensate for my own sentimentality with a big bike, or just confess it? I belong on a Honda. I am pleased that I look just as comfortable on a ratty Honda as on a sleek new one, but a Honda it must be. I always admired the guys who belonged on the Harleys and I wanted their friendship. And I detested the guys who chose Harleys and did not deserve to ride them.[11] It quickly became evident to me that there is room in the world of rockin' loyal bikers for a guy who belongs on a Honda, so long as he knows who he is and does not pose or make a fool of himself by lying to others or to himself about it. This is the part we need to get our bike running, that and our metric ontological tools, for, as you can see, we've been working on a Honda. I just put it in the living room to scare you. You can rock a Honda. Sort of.

But that Harley dealer could see that I did not care how the motorcycle really worked, I just wanted the ride. He did not say "buy the Honda," but he knew I would. I was headed for the coffee house already. I can easily recall that the reason I gave myself at the time was that the Harley sat a little too high off the ground (in retrospect, the symbolism of that seems right), and that the two-stroke engine would be a has-

---

[11] So I wrote this essay mainly while camping at the Kerrville Folk Festival (which should be pretty telling, I mean, it's not exactly as cool as Sturgis or even Bonnaroo), and parked down in the RV lots is this guy with the biggest RV I have ever seen, and I walk by one day and he's got this tricked out purple Harley parked by his home-away-from-home (I am well aware of this practice at the actual rallies, but hear me out). So I pause as he is lounging by his rolling Biltmore, drinking a pretty pricey pinot noir: "Nice RV," I say, with ascending intonation. A pause. "Thanks," said he. Another pause. "Nice Harley," descending intonation, just a hint of a sigh. I walk on. I'm thinking, "I wonder how he pulls that RV with 54ci. . . ." Enough said.

sle. What kind of kid is deterred from buying his first Harley by a two-stroke engine? The sort of kid who needs to be riding a Honda and buying Don McLean records. This is not merely about convenience or predilection, it is about sense of self, core values. Springsteen's work was cut out for him.

It's true that some choose to serve appearances in making such decisions, some chasing after what they believe others will see as "cool," others attempting to please the expectations of a parent. Such persons will have more complicated journeys to self-understanding than those who confront the decision for what it truly is. The ones who choose their rides based on appearances have been consumed in what Heidegger calls the "they self," or in German (since this is a very ominous idea) *das Man*, which is the self that conceals its own fundamental modes of existing in order to live inauthentically, caught up in the world of images and slogans and RVs. Bikers have more straightforward terms for such people, such as "assholes," but the nomenclature isn't crucial here. We will leave such persons to the things they believe are important. But in the domain of those who confront existential issues more directly, Robert Frost would have appreciated the depth of the choice between a Harley and a Honda and would have been able to summarize it better. For me, the road more traveled was the right call, but it still leaves one many delightful miles to go before one sleeps.

Yes, this seems to be the spare part we needed to get our question running. I might be too lazy to mix gas and oil, but there is more than one kind of laziness. We haven't been lazy about our question. Let's check it over, see if this beast will start before we take it on the open road. We asked: would Bruce ride a Honda? We knew he would not. We considered variations on the question. We discovered that Bruce and Jesus have something in common, which can be summarized as: "live free or die," as they say in New Hampshire. Both Jesus and Bruce have a passion, meaning they are open to the world, a certain intense ontological longing, they "want to know love is wild" and "want to know if love is real." That mode of existing, the "passion of the Boss," is compatible with mounting a suicide machine, whether it takes one to the "mansions of glory," or Highway 9, or Sturgis, or Golgotha. The cultural ontology of the suicide machine shows us something about identity and the moment of decision. It has shown us America the Paradoxical and the ambiguous relationship between freedom and self-knowledge. If *you* are ready for a ride with Bruce, now, read the Epilogue to his autobiography. It's a ride with the Boss. He likes to go over 100 mph, and says he's on a V-Twin ape-hanger with a spring seat, but he didn't mention whether it's a Harley. I'm guessing it is, but I have an old Honda and it won't go that fast.

16
Yesterday's Tom Sawyers

It was October of 1977, the Farewell to Kings Tour, and Rush was coming to Memphis. They went almost everywhere but Parsippany on that endless tour—I mean, they made it to Dothan, Alabama, and Upper Darby, Pennsylvania, where they split the bill with Tom Petty (now there's a case of musical cognitive dissonance). I hadn't really heard of Rush. Like an idiot, I was still listening to the last band my friend Brent got me into three years before, Led Zeppelin (and I'm still listening), and in the week of which I will speak, I also had out my old Lynyrd Skynyrd albums, mourning the sky plunge of Ronnie van Zant and friends. ("Old" is a highly relative thing; my favorite Skynyrd albums were simply ancient, you know—I got them when I was fourteen, two years before.)

Rush's *2112* had caught the ears of all the teen-aficionados-of-what's-next, and I certainly wasn't one such. But way across town, some thirty miles from my digs in a humble part of town, my friend from elementary school, "Brent C," was experiencing a serious meltdown. Brent C. is not his full name, which he said I can use, but, well, now he's a Republican, and they don't rock unless it makes them some money. I now understand why he made me play all these board games built around financial transactions, like *Monopoly*, and *Masterpiece*, and *Stocks and Bonds*—he taught me what leverage was and then amortized my ass, but good. Anyway, he was the guy, and every school had one, who really knew music, sort of what Chuck Klosterman must've been like in high school. This attention to the details and fringes of music actually makes you geeky at that age (or, in Klosterman's case, geeky, narcissistic, annoying and self-indulgent, even if your taste in music is unmatched).

The meltdown came to this: Brent had somehow scored second row, center section seats for the Rush concert, and his very strict (and sometimes arbitrary) parents had just denied him permission to go to said concert. They had their reasons, I'm sure. Those were the glorious days when the rule was: the lights go down then the people light up. Even Brent's parents had caught on to that little feature of the youth culture. And unlike parents today, they could truthfully report they never themselves inhaled.

It's embarrassing in any generation to still be asking your parents' permission to go somewhere at sixteen. I mean you're just getting to the point that they sort of couldn't stop you, except with the "I pay the bills argument," an idle threat which invites one's own flesh and blood to contemplate homelessness and is oh-so-easy to see through. But old habits die hard, and at sixteen you don't quite want to test those waters, at least if they've been fairly good to you. I wouldn't say Brent's parents had been exactly "good to him," yanking him as they did from the public school system when bussing started and sending him to a very expensive prep school for boys. I mean, no girls, and rich assholes establishing their pecking order with no girls to make them feel insecure about it, and did I mention no girls? Frankly, I'd rather go to military school to be made into a man, and I think no jury of sixteen-year-old boys would have convicted Brent of failing to honor his mother and father if he'd told them to piss off. But Brent wasn't quite to the point of openly defying the elders. Rather, unbeknownst to them, he had, of necessity, become Tom-Sawyer-devious.

Philosophical Moments

Among fans, the themes and lyrical motifs in Rush's important early songs, especially on *2112*, are widely recognized as being driven by philosophical concepts. Unhappily, the "philosophy" they are supposedly advancing is the ideological individualism and "objectivism" of the pseudo-philosopher Ayn Rand. Now, before you go either grinning in approval or snarling at me, I don't call Rand a pseudo-philosopher as an insult. Like absolutely everybody else in the world, Rand had some philosophical ideas, and, being an aspiring novelist, those ideas informed her narratives and characters in thematic ways. But even a Hardy Boys mystery has that much philosophy (and as I now consider it, I'm pretty sure the Hardy Boys probably grew up to be Republicans too). I doubt it initially dawned on Rand to try to be a philosopher—up until people began to respond favorably to the philosophical aspects of her writing.

It's sort of like what happens when several people tell you independently "I like that hat on you." You're likely not only to wear it more, but to start buying hats based on their proximity to the one people like. It's only human. But that doesn't make you so much as a hatter, let alone a maven of fashion. If you then present yourself as hatter or maven, and ignorant people believe you, don't be surprised when the hatters are pissed and the fashion mavens are laughing. (This, by the way is called an "argument from analogy," and one difference between a follower of Rand and a philosopher is that philosophers both know and admit that analogies settle nothing, and also know when they are relying on one. Rand's entire philosophy is built on questionable analogies, and her following consists of people who either don't know that or won't admit it.)

All people have philosophical moments, but most people don't credit their own philosophical thoughts. They forget them quickly and certainly don't do anything about them. What is there to do about having a philosophical thought? Well, plenty, but like anything else, you'll have to practice, and learn, and read, and work at it to do anything very good with such ideas. Now some people have lots of philosophical moments, but not all of them become philosophers. Rand had a handful of philosophical ideas that she visited over and over, none of them original (but that isn't important in philosophy), and she also learned in a superficial way to stitch them together into the rudimentary semblance of a "philosophy." In this respect, Rand was like Mark Twain, George Orwell, Émile Zola, and even Tolstoy and Dostoevsky (who were operating on a higher plane), in that she had a lot of such moments, credited them, and put them to work in a more or less co-ordinated way. She was by a long stretch, as a writer and thinker, the inferior of all of those mentioned above, but in terms of successfully combining philosophical ideas with fiction writing, she was better than the average bear.

No one likes Rand better than tweenage males who think themselves misunderstood geniuses. It's a shame that people have hung the Rand-albatross on Neil Peart, just because he read some Rand at an impressionable age. It's especially unfortunate since, unlike the hordes of other infantile, self-regarding tweenage males so affected, Neil actually was a misunderstood genius. The hordes don't usually have much to show for their supposed genius, except a few, like Alan Greenspan, who have more to apologize for than to prove their pretensions of genius. It is far better to have a modest self-estimation and exceed it than to have a grandiose one and make others pay for the deficit.

My point is that when you look at Neil's lyrics from that time period (part of the proof of his genius is that he rather quickly outgrew all of this), what are you looking at? How is it that the lyrics and the music from Rush's "literary era" combine to make something that has, well, philosophical value, even if it isn't quite "philosophy"? Rush's music is way, way better and more valuable as a cultural contribution than anything Rand ever managed, in my opinion. I do think that there's something in that literary era of Rush that opens minds and that elevates the fans to places, good and worthy places, they might not otherwise go.

Halloween Traditions, or, Are You Down with What You're Up For?

The concert was scheduled for an inconvenient Sunday night, October 30th, downtown at Dixon-Myers Hall, which was where the Memphis Symphony Orchestra performed at the time (hell, maybe they still do). This was a concert hall, not a coliseum or arena. It promised incredible sound and proximity. UFO and Max Webster both opened. That was going to make it a late night. I have no memory of Max Webster and only the vaguest memory of UFO, that the lead singer, in mascara and bright green pants, spit a lot as he vocalized and we were in the danger zone.

Maybe you've got a similar experience in your history, but Brent and I were finding less and less to talk about after he moved to the rich side of town. As usual, friendship had been built on dozens of common activities—sports, playing board games, collecting football cards, and especially music, as I struggled to keep up with his ever expanding taste for progressive rock. To this day my album collection (yes, I still have it—hope you kept yours too) bears Brent's stamp. I felt sort of like a musical contrail behind his Lear jet. But now I was more like Roger Waters, finding all the talk about cars and money and rich people stuff a little off-putting.

Yet, since he moved, Brent and I had sort of started spending Halloween together. Two years before Rush, he came to my house for a sleepover (and neighborhood marauding), one year before Rush, I went to his neighborhood for the same. I don't think we were actually planning to make it a tradition, and I had already become, I think, something of a wrong-side-of-the-tracks embarrassment for him in his new social circles, but then came those amazing tickets and his parents' unbearable denial of concert privileges.

Now yesterday's Tom Sawyer was a modern-day warrior, and his mind was not for rent. So it occurred to Brent that there might be a way, just maybe, to get to that concert after all. His folks would surely believe that he was at my house for the now annual Halloween exchange, and since Halloween was on an unworkable Monday, well, we'd just have to do our annual get-together on Sunday (concert day). It probably crossed Brent's mind to try the whole plan without calling me at all, since another friend, let's call him "Jim" (whose emerging worldly values were closer to Brent's), was already promised the second seat. But Brent believed in hedging his bets, and Jim would just have to understand.

So Brent called me with the offer of a seat in exchange for, well, a willingness to join a conspiracy (displacing Jim, who eventually ended up further back in the crowd, with a one-off ticket of some kind). Now I'm no one's Huckleberry friend, but I was up for this. Brent proposed to make a weekend of it: Friday, Saturday, and Sunday, and this was intended to throw his folks off the trail, I believe. And I was down with that. But there was a problem. My parents would be out of town Friday and Saturday, and while they would willingly leave me for a weekend, no way would they leave someone else's kid, for whom they'd be responsible, etc., and no way would Brent's folks let him come to my house with the folks out of town . . . blah, blah, blah.

But I'll bet you've already figured out what we told them. You've seen *Risky Business*. This would be like that, minus Rebecca De Mornay, plus Brent C, minus Chicago, plus Memphis, minus Bob Seger, plus Geddy Lee. It's funny how parents' perceptions run. My folks thought Brent was probably a good influence on me, and his folks suspected I was a bad influence on him, when the truth was exactly the opposite. Parents, if you are reading this, be chastened, be very chastened. You really don't know. Remember your own youth and tremble.

Lyrical Motifs

It has crossed your mind many times that song lyrics are not something you usually grasp the first time you hear them. There are exceptions to this, of course—especially funny songs and story songs, where the music is just there for effect and the whole point is the words. You can recognize such songs almost immediately and then you sort of quickly decide whether you want to follow along or just tune it out. That quick decision process is a relatively recent phenomenon in human history. Music is so ubiquitous in our culture (God, I love having an excuse to use words like "ubiquitous"—I once managed to get antidisestablishmentarianism into an article, and have now managed it again, except that the last time it was legit and here it's utterly gratuitous and annoying), where was I?

Oh yeah, the ubiquity of music in our culture makes it easy to forget that not very long ago, music was a pretty special thing, not heard everywhere and anytime, but rather planned for, hoped for, anticipated, relished. Real instruments were expensive and actual musicians relatively sparse. The presence of music a hundred years ago rendered people rapt or ecstatic, or both in turns. It still has that effect on traditional peoples whose ears aren't ruined by the noise of modernity. In the days of yore, you wouldn't have decided whether to follow a story song. Rather, your body would grow still, unbidden, and everything but the ear, and its peculiar power of focus, would simply fall into the background.

You know it's hard work to follow lyrics, and the music has to be arranged to create the right sonic space for lyrics to punch through to the surface in perfect clarity. One thing that has to be pulled way back, almost to silence, is the bass. The rumbling in those sonic ranges created by bass cancels all clarity, takes the fine point off of enunciation, and it doesn't take much bass to prevent people from understanding the words entirely. On the other hand, when the bass ranges are prominent, it has the effect of blending and melting all the other ranges together; bass can unify the music and weld the percussive to the melodic.

The bass in Rush's typical music is actually mixed loud, but along with the kick drum, it is equalized thin to minimize this "cancellation effect" on the clarity of vocals and other instruments, but still you aren't going to get all the words in a Rush song. In fact, even with special attention and cranking up the stereo at home, you'll never understand them all until you read them somewhere. Rather, what happens is that when the music pulls back for a dramatic moment, you'll pick up a few words, usually the repeated ones, and then the music will swell and take the rest away from you. Go ahead, sing with me: "The world is, the world is love and light hmmm, hmmm. . . . Today's Tom Sawyer he gets high on you, hmmm hmm, hmmm, he gets by on you." I know you're with me.

Resistance Is Futile

This thing I just described actually has a name. The philosopher Susanne Langer (1895–1985) calls it "the principle of assimilation." Her claim is that wherever two or more fundamental art forms are mixed (in this case music and poetry), one of them must assimilate the other to itself. For example, where painting or sculpture is used to decorate a building, they would be assimilated to the art of interior design, or, if the sculpture is outside, to architecture. Most painting and sculpture really is just decoration, after all. An extreme case of this tension between art forms and assimilation is Frank Lloyd Wright's Guggenheim Museum building in New York, which assimilates interior design to architecture, and then ingeniously assimilates even the greatest painting and sculpture into simple decoration for his architecture. This is what Wright intended. That pisses off the interior designers and painters and sculptors, of course, but to the architects it seems about right.

On the other hand, if you visit the Academia in Florence (where Michelangelo's David is on display), you will see an entire architectural edifice assimilated to the purpose of showcasing Michelangelo's sculptural works, especially his David, which was originally commissioned to stand outside at the entrance of a government building, assimilated to the art of architecture or urban design, but was later deemed by a later generation to be too good for that pedestrian function and made into its own *raison d'être*. Does this "assimilation principle" hold true in every case? That's a long argument we can have some other time, but there are certainly many examples of it. It is clear that differing art forms are constantly in tension when combined. Some art forms, like film, are ravenous in their appetite for assimilating other art forms to their own primary structures. Film gobbles up drama, acting, photography, painting, writing, music, interior design, urban design, architecture, and more, turning them all into filmatic effects.

In music where words are being employed, there is a tension between poetry and pure music. In the singer-songwriter genre, generally the music just supports the poetry. With the music of Rush the lyrics are assimilated to the music, most of the time. "The Trees" and "Closer to the Heart" are exceptions, and there are some others, but for the most part let's just say you are not being encouraged to sing along. Rather, Geddy's voice is being used as a somewhat shrill lead instrument and the lyrics simply cause the aesthetic qualities of his voice to vary in interesting and pleasing ways. It doesn't matter very much what he is singing about; the point is what it feels like and sounds like to hear him sing. You may know that Neil was writing the lyrics because neither Geddy nor Alex had any real interest in doing so. Whether they had any talent for it I don't know, but lyrical talent wasn't really needed, only lyrical competence. This band wasn't going to be about lyrics, it was about music. So Neil got the job by default.

Now Neil Peart is not exactly the possessor of a great literary pedigree, but one thing I have noticed about songwriters of all sorts: nearly all of them are avid readers. They love words. Earlier I mentioned the autobiography of Keith Richards, and one learns near the end that he owns a massive library and is addicted to (among so many other things) British and Roman history. Keith Richards. Next to him, Neil Peart looks like a

Harvard professor. So Neil was always a reader, and he read this and that, and found that he liked mythology, ancient history, and, unfortunately, in callow youth, before he had time to read widely, also Ayn Rand. No one who reads widely, and who gets the benefit of that reading, is likely to hold her in very high esteem for very long. Emotionally damaged people and those who simply cannot grow up are the exceptions, but then, they don't get the full benefit of their reading, do they? And in this they follow their heroine.

By the time of *Moving Pictures*, three years and some months after my night out with Brent, Neil was writing lyrics about what he really knew: his own experience. He still wasn't much of a poet and it still didn't matter. In 2011 Rush reprised *Moving Pictures* in a lengthy world tour, playing the original track list in order to appreciative packed houses. It was their best album and they know it. No Ayn Rand on that masterwork. Neil's lyrics are so much less contrived and closer to the heart even beginning with *A Farewell to Kings*, so the flirtation with objectivist ideas was pretty brief.

But even on *Moving Pictures*, if you try it, I think you'll see that the lyrics can't withstand the test of being pulled from the music and examined as poetry. Some lyricists do pass that test—Robert Plant writes in the same vein as Neil, for example, but is a much better poet; and Roger Waters is a bit like Neil in his minimalist mood, but far better poetically. Still, even the best lyricists have a hard time being taken seriously as poets because they often try to rhyme things, which just isn't hip in poetry these days. And thinking of Plant and Waters as other progressive rock lyricists, it is interesting that in Zeppelin, the lyrics are almost always assimilated to the music, while with Pink Floyd, most often the lyrics dominate the music whenever they are present. There isn't a single formula here, but a dynamic tension between two art forms.

It's natural for these musicians to put in the audible foreground whatever is artistically best at any given moment. When you've written lyrics as good as "Stairway to Heaven" or "Comfortably Numb," you don't drown that out with bass. When everything in a piece is outstanding—music, lyrics, melody, groove, tonal textures of the voice and guitars—well, in that situation, something is going to have to be sacrificed to the whole. One of the most difficult moments in the production of a recording is the moment when a musician has hit a riff that is so amazing on its own but it distracts the ear from some other musical element that is more necessary to the whole. Such a riff has to be left out (or, as we sometimes can do these days, moved to another place in the recording). It is tragic, but it happens constantly in the art of recording. Live performance presents similar dilemmas, and the visual presentation just complicates matters more.

Returning to the issue of assimilation of lyrics to music, as Rush favors, it creates a lower standard of poetry needed, and that's just fine. To provide another analogy: if you're part of the crew building the Notre Dame Cathedral and your boss says "sculpt me a Madonna for the roof," you don't need or want a Michelangelo for that spot. It would be a waste to put in that kind of time and detail for something no one ever sees up close. You want something that feels right from a couple hundred feet below, and while you can't afford to hire a sculptor who sucks, you do want one who understands that this is about the building, not his statue, and who sculpts accordingly. Rush's music is a veritable Notre Dame of both living and processed sound, and it just isn't about the lyrics, at least not very much.

J-Wags, or, Are You Down with What You're Up For?

The plan for Friday night (Rush, T-minus forty-eight hours and counting) was in Brent's hands. We were staying at my house, of course, while his folks believed my folks were home and my folks believed I was at Brent's house (and my sister was also gone somewhere that weekend, I don't remember where, but her absence becomes relevant at T-minus twenty-four hours). Brent actually knew of a bar where they wouldn't ask for our ID's (drinking age was eighteen back then). This is one reason to keep old friends even when you have little left in common; you might discover new uses for each other. A bar? That was way beyond my ken. I didn't think of myself as an innocent (I was, sort of, but I didn't like to think about it), but I had never been in a bar, and I certainly hadn't heard of this place called "J-Wags Lounge" in mid-town.

Anyone who knows Memphis is now saying "Oh my God." J-Wags, which closed in 2012, later became a famous bar—a famous gay bar, that is. And here we were sixteen, straight, and clueless. Now I want to be very clear that when it comes to gay bars, I am totally down with it, even if I'm not up for it. Still, the worry is irrelevant because in 1977 J-Wags was just a neighborhood bar, not yet having evolved into its future niche, and I now know how very ordinary it was.

I was instructed by Brent to wear a powder blue pinpoint Oxford shirt with a button-down collar and khaki pants, and docksiders. This was all very important, I was told, because if you aren't dressed right, they might ask for your ID and then everything is ruined, right? Well, I was down with doing as told to by those attempting to corrupt me, and I was pretty much up for some corruption. But I had none of these clothes, so Brent lent me a shirt and I made do with that and Converse All-stars and jeans. Thus shod and shirted, we set out.

Brent's very cool and discreet older brother (he played a blue Stratocaster and was the prime source of Brent's cutting edge intelligence on what would soon be hip rock music among our younger and more ignorant masses) took us to within a dozen blocks of J-Wags (we hadn't told him the destination, so he had deniability), and from there we hoofed it a pretty fair piece to J-Wags. Jim (of the displaced ticket) had a car and was supposed to meet us there. And so he did. The concept of a "designated driver" did not exist in 1977, but Jim was far more interested in getting stoned than getting drunk, and a stoned driver, aged sixteen, is probably safer on the roads than the average sober adult: our average speed home, probably thirty miles per hour.

The evening was passed, and you just won't believe this, drinking actual beer in an actual bar and playing pool with actual bar patrons. Doesn't take much to thrill you at that age, does it? But the anticipation of a whole weekend of such forbidden adventures, to be culminated in a Rush, well, it was quite enough. Did I get drunk? Well, I had, like, four draft beers in three hours, with no resistance to alcohol, at 5' 7" and 115 lbs. You do the math. Did Brent? I actually don't remember much. I woke up in my own bed (alone). Jim must have somehow made it back to the rich side of town because he wasn't at my house Saturday morning, and somehow we were, and Jim was still alive Sunday night when Rush came to town. He must have puttered back to the rich side. (I never saw Jim again after that

Sunday night, so I hope he turned out better than it looked like he would. But I'll bet if he's alive, he's a goddamn Republican.)

The Virtues of Virtual

Langer says that every basic art form accomplishes its "work" by taking some aspect of our actual experience and making a semblance of that experience in a virtual space and/or time. Now, I'm going to be honest with you, this is one honking big philosophical idea. It isn't quite as honking big as the idea of God, or freedom, or eternal life. (I'm not saying whether those ideas have any concrete reality corresponding to them, only that at the very least they are ideas, and you can think about them.) Those big boys would sort of be the Beethoven symphonies of philosophical ideas. This idea of Langer's is sort of more like a bitching Rush album of an idea. And hearing an idea like this just once is akin to trying to take in *2112* and "get it" the first time through. It isn't going to happen. But I've spent about twenty years thinking on this idea of Langer's, turning it over, trying to decide whether I agree with it, so maybe I can save you some trouble. You decide. I still haven't made up my mind, but I think it's a serious thought, sort of a way of cashing in on the claim that art imitates life, but richer. So I'm going with it.

What does that idea mean? Basically she's saying that the reason we recognize something as art when we encounter it is that it reminds us of something in life that it recreates in a virtual way, as an illusion. For example, painting, as an art form, makes a semblance in two dimensions of what it is like to actually see things in three-dimensional space. Its "primary illusion," then, is to reduce that experience of seeing to two dimensions and to use pigments and geometrical tricks of the eye to create the illusion. The "virtual space" is the space inside the painting. It sort of invites you to step out of your actual space and into the virtual space of the painting, at least if it's a good painting. This is true even with abstract paintings: they exist in a virtual space, enclosed by a frame of the edges, and if you stepped into the odd space occupied by an abstraction, I suppose you'd either become abstract yourself or be in a pretty strange mixed space.

Sculpture, as an art form, recreates in a semblance the experience of the bodily traversal of the lived space of action, the space of bodily movement. When you look at a sculpture, if it's a good one, it feels as if it has moved into the position it currently holds, and could very well move beyond it. To compensate for the fact that the sculpture really doesn't move, you move around it. The artwork exists in a virtual space-time of a history of movements it never actually made, leading to its current pose, and a virtual future of possible actions never to be enacted. The work invites you to furnish in your imagination the movements leading up to the pose, and to finish those actions proceeding from its frozen present. And you do that, in your imagination, whether you want to or not. The virtual space and time of physical movement is the sculpture's world, and it reminds you of your actual world of movement when you see it.

But music, and pay close attention here, music creates the illusion of what it feels like living in time's flow. Nothing in music actually moves or lives, biologically, or has real feeling. Yet, music feels to us as if it's alive. Yes, the musicians are alive and they do move in actual time as they play their instruments, but that is not "the music": it's just the physical activity in actual time that creates the illusion of virtual time in the virtual movement of the music. Just as the brush strokes are not the painting and the hammer strikes are not the sculpture; they create the illusion but are not themselves illusory. This is pretty hard to understand, especially with music, but an example may help.

Imagine that Geddy is working up to singing a sustained high note; his vocal chords are tightening, his throat is constricting, his breath is being forced through a smaller space, and sound issues forth. (I hope he's had a breath mint.) But nothing actually "goes up" when he hits a "high note." There is nothing in the physical activity of singing or playing an instrument that makes one note "higher" (closer to the sky) than another note. Nor does anything actually move from "lower" to "higher" notes in an "ascending" scale. Rather, one sequences individual tones in such a way as to produce the illusion of rising; it feels like something is ascending when you hear it, even though nothing actually rises. What's really altered, in effect, as Geddy sings the high note, is the peaks and troughs of the sound waves, propagating in actual space and time. The actual propagation is in actual time and space, with the illusion of "higher" and "lower" pitch, is a part of the virtual character of music.

In the same way, music employs the actual passage of time as its physical basis for the sequencing of varied sounds that provide us with an audible series of (oft repeating) virtual markers, called tones, that remind us of the actual passage of time. The tones have individual duration, but they don't move. Tones are made of sound waves vibrating within a regular frequency of peaks and troughs (with slight variation), but as tones, they offer only an illusion of stability for the duration during which they exist. The sounds are actual, but treating them as tones is a virtualization of sound, a step from what it actually is (sound) to its virtual temporal relations with other sounds that we will also treat as tones. You recognize the difference between music and noise when you hear it, but you may not realize how much of the difference between them lies in your willingness to treat the sounds as tones. My folks were disinclined to treat my Rush albums as "music" way back when—it was an awful noise they said. My mother, who was a voice teacher, was horrified by what Geddy Lee was doing with his voice. Shrieking, she called it. They weren't willing to virtualize what they were hearing.

Now, if you think about it, you'll agree that the tones do not make the actual time any more than the sound does, and neither sound nor tone is one with the actual time; rather, unlike mere sounds, which seem to be at the mercy of actual time, the tones use the actual time to create an illusion of movement and repeatability within the relentless flow of our experience. The truth is that the flow of our experience renders real actions unrepeatable. You cannot genuinely repeat any action, in the sense of making one action identical to another action, because the time when any action was first performed is now past, and unrecoverable. The best you can do in actual time is to perform an analogous act and then pretend the time passage between the first and second enactment doesn't matter. This is the basis of virtualizing time, and music does it amazingly well.

Run That by Me One More Time

So we know that tones arranged in various combinations and series use time to create an illusion that reminds us of our own flow of felt experiences: the music sounds like what it feels like to be alive, to have a rhythmic heartbeat and a breathing pattern, to move our bodies up, down and all around, to be obliged to anticipate the next moment and join it to the last moment by means of our present sensing and feeling. But there are rules about how music has to do this in order to maintain the illusion.

Like so many things, the illusion music creates exists only between two extremes. Too much automatic repetition in rhythms or tones kills the interest: the time is over-virtualized and does not remind us of what it feels like to be alive, but sounds like a machine instead. The musical illusion is broken and becomes mere sound. Too little repetition in the rhythmic or tonal scheme kills the experience of the illusion of living (which does incorporate much repetition), and starts to seem like actual, unrepeatable time. Music, the illusory semblance of our life of feeling, exists, then, between these extremes; it is virtualized time.

Now I have to report something weird and kind of shocking. If Langer is right, the way humans become conscious of actual time is by attending to the ways that music can use actual time to suspend certain moments and contract others; the tension and release of energies in music points us to the otherwise uninterrupted continuity of our flowing experience. Consciousness itself is a virtualization of experience, and we become aware that we are conscious by way of music—not so much its successful semblances, but at the points where semblance breaks down and actual time retakes us. She actually believes that music is the key to our kind of consciousness (a self-reflective kind). If we had nothing that was like time, but not time, how would we ever become aware of its passage? It's a fair question. So music is virtualized time, and the virtue of it is that it teaches us an awareness of real time precisely because music just is illusory time.

Now the music of Rush (like all progressive rock) diverges from other rock music in using repetition more sparsely. Most rock music is built on a virtual repetition of four beats, called 4/4 time, or "common time." Whatever syncopation (that is, the violation of the evenness of the pulse created by "early" attacks and the uneven sustaining of tones for rhythmic effect) regular rock music contains is simple variation on the repeating four beats. It is there to punctuate the driving, regular and repeating beat. There are thousands of regular grooves into which ordinary rock music can fall, but all built on the matrix of common time.

Rush in particular and progressive rock in general is partly defined by its habit of hopping from one time signature to another; the rhythms are driven and herded around in community by what seem like almost mystical forces. The gods and demons subtract a beat here, add one there, squeeze two into one, and take us just a bit beyond the predictable recurrent rhythms of ritual dance, or of our living bodies. It feels sort of like being on a rollercoaster. It isn't for everyone. In progressive rock, the regularity of rhythmic order is sacrificed for the sake of a different way of virtualizing time. Rhythmic patterns do exist and come back around, but they catch the listener unaware, and the standard AB/AB/CB song structure of verses, choruses, and bridges is totally out the window. Even the concept of a "song" isn't always the basic musical unit. See Yes, *Tales from Topographic Oceans* for some alternatives to the "song" concept. In this regard, progressive rock owes a lot to jazz and even to classical music.

Interlude

So I'm writing this in a bar in Carbondale, Illinois, on a cold December day, and as I just typed that last line, I look over, and the barkeep (a young blonde woman with a two-foot pony tail) is being accused by the owner of playing him "like Tom Sawyer" by convincing him to shine the brass fittings on the beer taps because she "isn't sure how to do it right." From this we learn two things. First, that I'm a lot more familiar with bars these days than I was at sixteen, and second, that there is a fair case for synchronicity.

The Sign of the Three

Something must be done to make sure the "center holds" when music is being played with little so respect for the repeating latticework of a 4/4 beat. The center of Rush's sound is and always has been a little trick they use. So long as the bass line and the kick drum match exactly, and so long as the actual tempo of the song (the number of beats per minute) does not vary too much, any amount of syncopation (that early and late emphasizing of beats) and violation of time signatures can be workable. So Neil and Geddy synch up the bass and kick drum and rehearse it as many times as necessary, until it seems like that pinpoint precision happens on its own (which is also an illusion), and then the more melodic elements can move whither they will without the whole thing feeling confusing to the ear and body of a listener. It still feels like the passage of time, but with fits and starts, just about where you want them. Classical and jazz composers also exploit our desire for more temporal variation in our virtual time, which reminds us of the variations in the succession of our actual feelings, but classical and jazz composers never, ever synch the rhythm of the bass and drum movements as Neil and Geddy do.

I say this is a "trick" because all rock and blues and country musicians draw on the strategy of using the kick drum to reinforce the movement of the bass, below the other instruments, but most of them do it while respecting the regularity of four beats per measure. Of course there's a lot more to the Rush sound than the two characteristics I've mentioned: mixing the bass and kick drum hot with a thin equalization, and synching them precisely. Rush is a three-piece band, and three-piece bands face certain challenges that don't emerge in larger bands. All three-piece bands have to find ways to keep the sound full and fresh with limited hands and voices. There are dozens of ways to accomplish the task.

It's good to remember that having a lot of "empty space" (this is a metaphor of course) in a piece of music is not always a problem. The early recordings of the Police show how three instruments can do the same things Rush does, but in the spacious (as opposed to full) mode. Van Halen (when they were three-piece) synched the bass and kick, kept the drums simple, fattened the bass sound and kept it sustaining, and then let Eddie do the rest. The Who and Led Zeppelin never adopted the strategy of precision synching of bass and kick drum except when it occasionally pleased them, while ZZ Top just made up for its sparse instrumentation with volume and energy.

On the other hand, Rush isn't exactly a three-piece band, since Geddy plays so many instruments and sings at the same time, and Alex and Neil kick in the processed sounds as needed. But the music has to be closely arranged so that the ear cannot detect when Geddy has moved off of the bass guitar and is playing the bass line with his left hand on a keyboard or with his feet on the Taurus pedals, which sometimes Alex also does. There are lots of pieces, but just three people, so the name is a bit misleading. And there are three piece bands with four people (like The Who), so the point is, that's a lot of music for just a few fellows to be making.

To do all that Geddy does while singing the lead vocal is pretty freaking impressive. Lead singer-bass players are rare enough—count 'em, go ahead. Sting, Geddy, Paul McCartney, Roger Waters, Richard Page, and who the hell else? There is a reason for this paucity. Unlike the guitar and the drums, the bass generally plays against the melody, even in ordinary rock music, let alone progressive rock. Singing while playing bass requires something quite beyond patting one's head while rubbing one's stomach. To add in keyboards and pedals, and an occasional guitar, is something more than human. It may look relaxed when you see Geddy do it, but that appearance is as illusory as music itself. The boys have rehearsed this stuff into an automatism. They play it exactly the same way every time, and they pretty well have to, to get it to work. They have been criticized for this. I'll take that up later.

Saturday Night's Alright, or, Are You Really Up for What You're Up For?

I don't remember the day after J-Wags. I'm pretty sure me and Brent slept in and then probably ate junk food and played board games, in which he probably whipped my ass, as always, and celebrated said ass-whoppin' insufferably. Unfortunately I can't reveal everything about Saturday night (Rush, T-minus twenty-four and counting), even at this late date. Too many of the principals are still alive and haven't given their permission (and they wouldn't give it if I asked them—not for this night). Brent probably wouldn't mind, since on the scale of things he did later in life, this night probably doesn't even register a 1 on a scale of 1 to 10, (10 being the most unimaginable bad behavior). But on my personal scale, this was about an 8.

Here's what I can say. A lot of young people were celebrating Halloween that night. We actually stayed home, at my folks' (otherwise vacant) place. Brent had somehow procured for our enjoyment a big bottle of Jack Daniels black label, maybe two, I don't rightly remember. It was more than enough in any case. By late afternoon the seals had been broken. We handed out candy to the kids as they came by, rather more cheerily than would be usual. As the night wore on and various other activities began to unfold, we were interrupted in our Bacchanal (which involved Rush albums at extreme volume) by a knock on the front door. This led to a staggered scurrying and stowing of contraband, forbidden literature, and other things that shan't be mentioned.

It was two of my sister's friends at the door—her friend "Carrie" and a fellow named "Bill," whom I barely knew from earlier days when he dated my sister instead of her (very attractive) friend. The friendship survived his transfer of affection, and indeed, the switch led to a marriage of over thirty years duration (and still going), with many kids. Must've been a decent trade. But in 1977 Carrie and Bill were all of seventeen. They were looking for my sister to go driving, or whatever. But she was gone (I still don't remember where). Yet, here we were, Brent and me, and as they peeked in, it was pretty clear to them that, well, we had the "stuff." And they had nothing in particular to do. Let the Bacchanal resume.

What followed I just can't quite describe, except that it probably isn't as bad as you're imagining—and I didn't lose my virginity until some time later, after I got my own car, so get your mind out of that particular gutter. Another word to parents: if you want to hasten the loss of your children's virginity, by all means get them cars. This provides a mobile version of precisely what they lack, which is a place to do what all of nature is encouraging them to do. Parents who won't leave their kids for Risky Business weekends, but who tell themselves it's okay to get the kid a car, well, there is no virtual space virtual enough to contain your self-deception. Do the right thing, I say. Get them pills and condoms and tell them to go at it. They're going to anyway. And of course, some won't. It's up to them. If you do the right thing, it doesn't matter about the car. None of this is philosophy. It's just a reminder of what you already know.

The only issue is whether you're going to screw up their young minds with guilt. Abstinence my ass. And what is with this puritanical culture? We declare wars on weaker peoples and massacre them without reservation or conscience, and then depict it in all its gore in movies and news stories for the public, and you (neo-Puritans) have the audacity to tell me that sex is obscene? I'm sorry, but fuck you. (This also is not a

philosophical argument, it's just a rant.) And while we're inter-
luding, I notice that the Tom Sawyer routine of the barkeep
worked for about five minutes before she ended up polishing the
brass by her lonesome. Tom Sawyer ain't what he used to be. It
seems that everyone is on to his scam. But he's become mean.

Aftermath: Not Down with What I Was Up For

No more about the proceedings that night, but when I woke up,
after daylight, I was in better condition than anyone else. Brent
was hanging over the toilet in one bathroom, either unconscious or asleep (who could tell?), and Bill was motionless in a
pool of his own upchuckings in the other bathroom, arms
crossed over his chest in the attitude of a corpse. Carrie was
passed out on the living room couch (I didn't look too close), and
I was the only one who made it, part-way at least, to an actual
bed. I remember praying that the room would stop spinning. I
woke up because, well, my urgent choices were either to move
Brent from his perch or to hazard stepping over Bill on my way
to transact a similar business in pink porcelain.

I swore to God in heaven (if there is one), as I gave up my
insides to the sewer lines of Tennessee, that never, never again
would I become that intoxicated. So sincere was I in my repen-
tance that I even swore off all hard liquor then and there. I
actually kept that pledge (it still tastes like cough medicine to
me). It was one of those deals where you're still drunk when
you wake up. I'm no goody good, but I also don't need to cut off
a second finger to be absolutely certain I didn't want to lose
the first one. If you've been sick-drunk and hung over like that
more than once, well, all I have to say is you're not a very
quick study.

My folks were to be home in the early afternoon, and one
can't take chances, so with much groaning, general bleariness,
and a bit of blaspheming, there was the gathering and dis-
patching of Bill and Carrie, and then there was some serious
cleaning, airing, and stowing to do. In our condition, it took
quite a while. My first hangover. Remember with me now,
brothers and sisters, your first hangover. Where were you?
And how old? Yes, that's it, let it all out. I'm here to heal your
memories. And Jesus protect us from the next hangover. And

the one after that too. I now understand the magical power of water and need Jesus less than before, but everybody needs a little Jesus now and then, so I'm not abandoning the faith.

Processed Processes

Rush has been criticized for the full duration of its long career for mixing processed sounds with sounds being played at that moment, on stage. It is actually pretty hard to tell sometimes what is being played and what is being triggered by one of the band members that has been sampled or recorded or sequenced in advance. But it is a fact of technology, up to the present (and this will change eventually), that the processed sounds do not respond to the band's musical activities; so the band has to play along with the processed sounds.

That, friends and neighbors, is not easy to do. Not only must the processed sounds be triggered at the precise moment needed, but the band has to be playing at the right tempo, or at least, they must adapt to what they know the processed sounds will do. If a chord change has been sequenced, for example, the band has to change chords with the sequence, and to know the precise moment. Only mathematical precision on the part of the live players makes possible the mixing of processed sound with live sound, at least if those sounds go beyond mere "sound effects."

Armed with Langer's ideas about virtual space and time, this endless debate takes on a new dimension, so to speak. Given that music is already an illusion that reminds us of the flowing life of our feelings, and given that this illusion is maintained within limits, we confront here the issue of whether the processed sounds, which are illusions of illusions, or second order virtualizations, do or don't belong in live performance, and if so, whether they belong in the genre of progressive rock, and in the music of Rush particularly. You are all aware of how Rush maintains its artistic integrity by recording only what it can reproduce in live concerts without depending on extra musicians (and that would include allowing sound engineers to trigger the processed sounds).

Clearly the band wants to maintain aesthetic and artistic integrity with regard to the limits of processed sounds. They clearly realize that once you begin messing around with processed sounds, there is always a danger that the first order virtualization will be swallowed by the second, and if that were to happen, well, they might as well lip-synch the whole thing, and we won't want to pay the price for the tickets to see that. On the other hand, Rush made it clear from the outset that they intended to use processed sounds to create their music. There is no chance that they can be accused of shifting their ground, but as the technology has progressed, so has the sound (at least until they decided to do just a bass, drums, and guitar thing with Vapor Trails in 2002).

If you think about this, from Langer's point of view, all music is in some sense "processed sound," because the jump from actual sounds to virtual tones is, itself, a kind of processing. Indeed, that is the crucial step because it is the move from actual to virtual time. Simply amplifying the music is another step away from mere sound, but not as radical a step as from sound to music. So the issue is not really whether the music is processed but how and how much. And this, like any other question in the criticism of art, actually comes down to whether the art is good. The use of new technologies in any art may or may not lead to better art. Usually the first attempts to accentuate an art form with a new technology are quickly surpassed by later efforts, when the possibilities have been better understood and mistakes have been made.

Once in a while some artist will really just know what to do with an innovation. For instance, the 1939 *Wizard of Oz* was the first feature-length film in "Technicolor," which required quite a lot of adaptation of sets and costumes so that the final film would look right—did you know that the ruby slippers actually had to be orange in order to appear red in Technicolor? And so with Rush. Those Moog Taurus pedals were only the beginning. Consistently Rush has been on the cutting edge of technology and has also occasionally reminded fans and critics that they don't really need all that technological support to do what they do.

So I take myself to have settled a long standing question. Asking whether Rush should use all those processors to make their music is closely akin to asking whether they should make any music. They have communicated their aesthetic standards and the principles that maintain the integrity of their art and their live performance. Everyone agrees that they can execute their music in concert, flawlessly. The only appropriate question, then, is whether the music is good. To this question I will offer a short answer. It is not all equally good, and there are times when the mathematical precision, from kick-drum/bass matching up through processed sound, does kill the life in it. (In Langer's terms, the music sometimes becomes "discursive.") But some of it is so very good that life bursts out of it, and here I would mention my two favorite Rush songs. I hate to be predictable, but I never tire of "Tom Sawyer" and "Limelight." Great music. Even if I never can remember all the words.

Houston, We Have a Problem, or, What Goes Up Must Come Down

It was concert time. Brent and I had finished our Rush "homework," and oh so much more. My parents had returned on schedule, and of course, as far as they were concerned, we had arrived only shortly before. I didn't lie. We went to the store and arrived back at the house shortly before the parents, which makes it technically true to say "we got here just a few minutes ago." Parents, it is good to be aware when your children have achieved "sophistication" with language. As with all human achievements, this cuts both ways. If they've come to have a fair command of "nice distinctions," and if you think that niceness won't be used in the service of narrow self-interest, then I suggest you buy your kids cars and trust them to remain chaste and sober in the operation of those machines. You'll get what you deserve down the line.

I had never had such tickets, but sort of suffered through the first two bands, knowing nothing of their music and being quite ready for the main event. And then, there they were, within a few feet, doing, well, God knows what, in order to create all that sound. What did they play? Well, I wouldn't have been able to tell you exactly, except for the invention of the Internet and millions of people with too much spare time. The list was:

- "Bastille Day"

- "Lakeside Park"

- "By-Tor and the Snow Dog" (abbreviated)

- "Xanadu"

- "A Farewell to Kings"

- "Something for Nothing"

- "Cygnus X-1"

- "Anthem" (Arrggh—but I had never heard of Ayn Rand back then and couldn't understand the words anyway)

- "Closer to the Heart"

- "2112" (minus "Oracle")

- "Working Man"

- "Fly by Night"

- "In the Mood"

- Drum Solo

- Encore: "Cinderella Man"

That's how it went, I'm pretty sure. It's a pretty awesome list. I'd pay a lot to see that show again, and in fact, to have back the night (if not the morning that followed). Me and Brent and Jim and about half a million other people saw that show in the course of that year. Maybe you're one of them. I was certainly hooked. Glorious show, definitely in the top ten I've ever seen.

But there was a problem. We arrived at my house euphoric from music (and the contact high we'd managed), only to hear "Brent, call your parents." I could tell by the tone that we were screwed. There was something we hadn't figured on. His mother called during the concert. My mother said, "Oh, they're at the concert." I hadn't lied to my parents about that part. I mean, they never would have denied me permission to go to a concert, so why lie? Shit. Double shit. You can see how it unraveled from there . . . "Oh, we thought Randy was over there" . . . "no, he wasn't here, we thought they were there" . . . "No, we went to Nashville" . . . Screwed. Totally.

But there was a difference. When you start listing and assessing the (known) crimes, you'll see why I wasn't in nearly as much trouble as Brent. He disobeyed a direct order and created an elaborate ruse to do it. I just did a Tom Sawyer meets

Tom Cruise kind of thing. I was grounded for a week or two, and still got my first car a month later as a Christmas present. And you know what cars lead to. But in order to prevent themselves from killing him, Brent's folks blamed the awfulness of it all on my bad influence, and that was it for me and Brent. Never allowed to visit or communicate again. The next time I saw him we were juniors in college, and well, we really had nothing in common by that time. Except we still loved Zeppelin and Yes, and Rush, and our memories.

17

Dead Reckoning and Tacking in the Winds of Fortune and Fate

Fortune favors the bold.

—Latin Proverb

When it comes to the basic questions of life and death, I have never considered myself a really deep thinker.

—James William Buffett, *A Pirate Looks at Fifty*

Others disagree with Jimmy's assessment of Jimmy. Our basic argument follows Jimmy's own logic. We can question whether all those allegedly "deep thinkers" are paying "way too much attention . . . to something that just can't be changed" (*A Pirate Looks at Fifty*, p. 35). To the list of things that just can't be changed, we can add taxes and bullshit, but whereas taxes and bullshit crop up all the time, it does seem like we're all going to get just one true shot at the bucket-kick, regardless of what may or may not come after it.

But speaking of life, rather than death, I guess this is where we find the questions that trouble us so. Here is where Jimmy has some thoughts for us, and I, for one, find them deep enough to ponder with appreciation. We can't take on every question, so I'm settling for one that I think every Parrothead has considered, and certainly Jimmy has. It's really one question, but philosophers use a number of different terms to describe the dilemma.

On one side we find the ideas of chance, luck, contingency, and freedom; on the other side we find destiny, fate, necessity and determinism. Our little brains get caught betwixt and between, which is one good reason to saturate those neurons with a good red wine from time to time. Administered in the right proportions, certain libations become catalysts for a cerebral emulsion. We find an elevated, or at least altered, form of consciousness, and the conflict between fortune and fate becomes pretty funny. So if you don't mind, or even if you do, I'm opening a bottle of my favorite stuff; I recommend that you do the same. If I start making sense to you along the way, you'll know you're gills are the right color of red (or at least the same color as mine).

A Dead White Dude and an Incarnation

Just about every philosopher who ever lived took the trouble to register an opinion about necessity and contingency—when something cannot be otherwise (which is necessity), and when something can be other than it is (which is contingency). The same is true of the issue of free will and determinism. Pretty much all the dead dudes talk about it. The discussions get tedious pretty fast, and nothing gets settled.

Jimmy has also weighed in on these subjects. On necessity and contingency, he chooses the hokey-pokey, on the suspicion that we are complicating the questions beyond what is advisable. Just put your head in, pull it out, shake it all about, and turn yourself around. On freedom and determinism Jimmy expresses his agreement with Forrest Gump: "he didn't know whether life was some kind of predestined plan or whether we were just floating around like a feather on the wind, but he thought it was probably both" (*A Pirate Looks at Fifty*, pp. 35–36). These may seem like contradictory answers, but as Jimmy confesses, "I can't help but be / Ruled by inconsistency" ("Distantly in Love"). This crap doesn't have to be worked out. We live the same way regardless of the answer.

On the other hand, relatively few philosophers, past or present, speak seriously about fortune and fate, but the list of those who do have something to say is intriguing: Aristotle (382–324 B.C.E.), Niccolò Machiavelli (1469–1527), and Giambattista Vico (1668–1744). The discussion of fortune and fate is not nearly so boring as those other topics. I think philosophers avoid these subjects because they have a vague feeling of superstition about them. Philosophers don't like to be seen as superstitious; they want to be Reason Incarnate, no matter how boring that makes them. And indeed, there is an important difference, however slight, between the ideas of "fortune" and "fate" and the other more "rational" ideas of necessity and contingency, freedom and determinism. Fortune and fate poke their conceptual fingers into the ribs of our primal ignorance. Sometimes that tickles, but Reason Incarnate isn't ticklish, and it isn't easily amused. Those other more "rational" ideas try to build our knowledge up from what we really can learn about ourselves, and our universe, by observation, experimentation, measurement, reasoning and the like. We may not come to any conclusions, but at least we feel like we know something when we're finished studying. But there aren't any "experiments" with fate and fortune, and even first hand experience with them isn't a reliable teacher.

There but for Fortune . . .

Aristotle had nothing to say about fate, but he spent some time wondering whether good and bad luck could actually determine a person's happiness in life. After a long discourse about it, he came to the conclusion that virtuous habits in both public and private life are the best defense against bad luck. Actually, he doesn't use the word "virtue," because he was Greek, and that isn't a Greek word. I'm saving the word "virtue" for something else in this heap of verbiage. Aristotle said that what you want to ward off bad luck is *arete*, which sort of means "excellence," and in this case, not just an excellent fishing hole, but moral excellence. He pointed out that an "excellent" person could weather bad luck better than a person with all sorts of bad habits, vices, and moral failings. Even with tons of bad luck, a good person could still find ways to feel blessed and happy in life. On the other hand, a person of uneven character couldn't be contented with life even when all his luck was good, let alone when it was bad.

This sounds right to me, but I don't really want to do all the hard work required to be a genuinely excellent person, so Aristotle does me no good. And I'll bet I'm probably just like you (correct me if I'm wrong). I want to be selectively moral, and I also want the favor of good fortune to make up the difference between my vices and their natural consequences. In short, I don't want either justice or mercy—I don't deserve the latter and can't bear the former; I want to escape the natural order by just enough to enjoy my favorite toys, keep my vices, and die in my sleep. As Jimmy says, "a little escapism never hurt anybody. I should know, I've been selling it for years" (*A Pirate Looks at Fifty*, p. 58). Aristotle is right, but he's too austere for us. We want an easier way.

Machiavelli, on the other hand, might be just the ticket. He also has little to say about fate, but he says a lot about fortune. I know you've all heard of Machiavelli, since his name has become synonymous with ruthless politics and strategizing to take advantage of people. But there's a lot more to Machiavelli than that, and he deserved a better fate than to have his name become the ready-made epithet for all conniving assholes with limitless ambition and no scruples. I'm going to take a few tips from Machiavelli in what follows, because he may have the advice most needed by people like us—me, you, and Buffett (that is, people who don't want to sacrifice all of our vices just so that we can be serene in the face of all the bullshit that might or might not come down A1A).

An Over Forty Victim of Fate

Giambattista Vico also has a fair amount to say about fortune, cutting sort of a middle course between the ample wakes of Aristotle and Machiavelli, but what's more interesting and useful is what he has to say about fate. Vico carefully avoids saying there is "no such thing" as fate. I mean, how could we know? What he does say is that, "to be useful to the human race, philosophy must raise and direct weak and fallen man, not rend his nature or abandon him in his corruption." I don't wish to be rended or abandoned in my corruption, so Vico says I will have no use for those nasty old Stoics who are "chaining themselves to fate" or for Epicureans who are "abandoning themselves to chance" (*The New Science*, Cornell University Press, 1968, pp. 129–130).

The reason we need to look at this is because of what Jimmy has to say about fate. It doesn't show up too often in his songs, but it shows up famously: he was born two hundred years too late, and that was the work of fate. And Jimmy can't quite decide which way the wind blows on this—he has described the winds that fill life's sails as both fate (*A Pirate Looks at Fifty*, p. 15), and fortune (see "Mental Floss," his ode to the jellyfish). We need to find our way among the winds of life, to tack the craft toward one particular harbor.

Methinks There Is Madness in His Method

How to get at this? We need to get our bearings. Jimmy has always prided himself on having learned the art of dead reckoning, but even so, we have to have a fix on a position, a speed, and a distance. We can reckon our way through Buffett's philosophical moments if we can get a fix on them. I have noticed that Buffett songs follow sort of a pattern—it's not quite a "formula," but it's more than chance. Most of his songs contain the following: (1) a place, (2) a time, (3) a meeting, (4) a sentiment, and (5) a thought. Five things (I can still count the fingers on one hand, so no emulsion yet). Now there's plenty of variation in these five, so they aren't the fixed stars of the Buffett firmament, and I want to say something about the first four before we get to the last one, the thought, which is the part I'm really pondering. But first a story—or at least the beginning of one.

Meet Me in Memphis

A Place: Memphis. A Time: May 7–10, 1981. A Meeting: I was roped into working alongside that Parrothead. I won't name him, but the situation is worth recalling. If you're in the flower business, like this one particular Parrothead, Mother's Day is about the worst weekend of the year (Valentine's Day is the other main competitor). Every florist recruits friends, relations, acquaintances, and a few people off the streets to deliver flowers. I wasn't so much a friend of the Parrothead; I was more like a friend of an acquaintance of a cousin of a guy they pulled off the street. But every town has its own coconut telegraph, so I got a call to deliver flowers and pick up a little extra coin, which every thirsty student can use, for good ends or ill, or both. Final exams were, well, almost over. What followed was four straight days, Thursday through Sunday, in a ragged cargo van with a rabid Jimmy Buffett partisan, the first of that clan I'd encountered in all my twenty years. So while I knocked on doors with flowers for the resident matriarch, my new compadre charted a course for the next destination.

Like just about everyone, I had heard Buffett's hit songs. I liked them, even knew the words. But I didn't own a record and I'd never been to a concert, and I guess I would describe myself as "neutral" on matters pertaining to Buffett. That was about to change. The Parrothead had all and only Buffett recordings in the van, and it was his van. Our first conversation went something like this:

> PARROTHEAD: You like Jimmy Buffett?
> ME: Sure.
> PARROTHEAD: He's the greatest songwriter who ever lived.
> ME: Better than Bob Dylan?
> PARROTHEAD: Way better.
> ME: That's absurd.
> PARROTHEAD: Listen to this . . .

He cued up "Why Don't We Get Drunk (And Screw)?" I had to admit that I'd never heard a Dylan song quite like that one, unless it was "Lay Lady Lay," where the message was a little more between the lines, the bed was brass, and Dylan was interested in a "lady." Jimmy wasn't talking to a "lady" in any but the loosest sense. Then my new friend played "God's Own Drunk." That was different. Then "Fins." I began to feel like remora. Then "Livingston Saturday Night." I was forming a notion that Jimmy Buffett was fond of a party, and who isn't? I found little in the next four days to disconfirm the hypothesis. But here was something weird, and I'll bet you've had the same experience. I actually didn't like this Parrothead guy very much, and I'm pretty sure he didn't care for me either. He would have to educate me, which was a bother, but I would do in a pinch, and this was something like a four-day pinch.

All of the Places

Back to the method. The places in Buffett's songs are just places that have been special to Jimmy—Paris, the Islands, Alabama, Florida, you know them. Once in a while he sings about places he doesn't like, such as the list of places he doesn't want to land when the volcano blows, but mainly he sings about places that have meant something good to him. It's a long list. Somehow though, there are places that are Buffettish and places that just aren't, and it's not easy to explain how we know which is which. It isn't just the weather. For example, Montana is cold, but it's Buffettish, while Vermont is cold too, but it isn't. It's the same with cities. New Orleans is extremely Buffettish. Houston isn't. And with countries, France is, Spain is, Germany isn't. It's not easy to say what makes a place suitable, but here is a litmus test: try to imagine whether Frank and Lola could get together again there, and if so, it's probably a Buffett place. This test explains why, for instance, San Diego won't work, but Paris will. But it isn't failsafe. You also have to study up to find out where Jimmy crossed paths with some assholes, since assholes are nearly everywhere, even Key West. When you know his stories, you'll see why some places make the grade and others don't. But any place that people are in too much of a hurry for Frank and Lola to rekindle their marriage, or too caught up in the future or the past, that place isn't worth your time.

Makes Me Want to Go Back Again

The times in Buffett songs are everything from times of day, to days of the week, to seasons, to whole swaths of years. These might be in the present or the past, but Jimmy will tell you when it is or was, just like he'll tell you where he is, was, or would rather be. He has a pretty consistent set of attitudes about these things. He likes the night time, but not the morning after; he likes summer, but not winter; and he likes the past, but not as much as the present. And most importantly, Jimmy is deeply ambivalent about the future. He tries to avoid hoping, wishing, predicting, or trying to control the way things turn out. This will be good to remember when we get around to discussing the "thoughts" about fortune and fate, if we can still remember our own names by then. But the "past" for Buffett isn't really history (in spite of his degree in it); it's not songs about the French Revolution or even the Civil War, it's the past as remembered, in personal experiences or in the way others have told him their own stories. Past times in his songs and books are times ripe for a moment of reflection, a memory, a realization. But we can't look backward too long. You may miss what's in front of you in the present.

The good "present" times are of three kinds: solitude (that's mainly fishing, flying, or sailing alone), a conversation, or a party. That's about it for the present, and so if you're wondering whether a given time, day, or season belongs to Buffett temporality, just ask whether it would be good for a conversation or a party, since time disappears in solitude—which can be a very good thing. That's your acid test, conversation or party. So "morning" is fine for a conversation, even very, very early, when the fish aren't biting, but not the morning after. Summer is always good for a party, but fall, after the tourists are gone, is better for a conversation. Winter isn't good for very much. Spring just doesn't seem to show up at all in Buffett's songs or books, maybe because spring is all about the future. The only time always to be avoided is the future. If you start worrying about the future, bullshit is sure to overtake you. I admit that there are a couple of songs about the future—near future in "Come Monday," and distant future in "Little Miss Magic," but these are the exceptions that prove the rule. The point is not to fret about the future when it comes up, and it's wiser to avoid the subject as much as possible.

All of the Faces

The "meeting" is a constant in the Buffett song catalogue. It's in just about every song. Often the meeting is remembered, like his African friend, or the bear in "God's Own Drunk," or Jimmy's partner in crime in the peanut butter conspiracy (do you think they ever paid the Mini-mart back? I'm thinking not.). Sometimes it's a present meeting, and occasionally the meeting is missed, like when the phone doesn't ring. But whether it's a gathering of friends or a romantic encounter, what we get from these meetings is a cast of characters filling Jimmy's life with the weird, the wonderful, and even the worrisome meeting that may cost him two good years.

Before we get to sentiments and thoughts, let's take a drink and do a little experiment. Think of your favorite Jimmy Buffett character. I have to admit, mine is the bear . . . buddy bear in "God's Own Drunk." Now choose another one. I also have a soft spot for the old man in "He Went to Paris." You choose your own favorite characters. Now let's have a little fun. Choose a Buffett-place and a Buffett-time, and have them meet. What, maybe a bar in Bimini, long after dark. The bear bellies up, orders a plate of raw fish, the old man says "I can't recall your face, but you smell like a Scotsman I used to know . . ." You take the story from there. I think it ends with the bear selling the old man a homemade still. This much—the place, time, and meeting—might get you a story, and maybe you could make it rhyme with the heroic couplets Buffett is so fond of. But I think you'll see that it won't quite make for a song. There are two things missing, and those two things are the beating heart and the thinking brain of any Buffett song—the sentiment and the thought. And when we've taken a look at those, and how they fit together, we're getting pretty close to tacking the winds of fortune and fate.

"It's Five o'Clock Somewhere"

Suburban streets of Memphis. May 7, 1981, 11:00 A.M., or thereabouts. You might not be surprised to learn that, among the many uses of Buffett music, it makes a good accompaniment to delivering flowers for fourteen hours a day, four days in a row. By now I've heard the whole of A1A, and White Sports Coat, and I'm wanting to go to Key West. "Nautical Wheelers" has imprinted itself as my new favorite song. I still don't like this Parrothead, but I'm beginning to feel something like gratitude (and that's my sentiment for this story). There was something carefree, something ineffably fun about the feel of the music; just turns drudgery and repetition into a party. I mean, why shouldn't there be a party? But I wasn't altogether comfortable when *mon ami du jour* began to drink beer (while driving) before lunch, which is part of the reason I am not naming him. I am not certain it was even illegal to do that back then, but it wasn't wise in any case, and I certainly shouldn't have joined him. My main memories of the weekend are all from before noon. I think it went by pretty fast, but I can't say for sure.

Even four albums in, I wasn't prepared to allow that Jimmy Buffett was either the greatest songwriter ever, or better than Bob Dylan, and I'm still not, but I no longer think the idea is absurd. It sort of depends on what you're looking for in your music, and here is what I think I can say: nobody does what Buffett does better than Buffett, and that is partly because Buffett invented what Buffett does to suit what Buffett can do better than anybody else. It's actually kind of pathetic when anyone else even tries to do a Buffett-kinda-thing. I mean, for example, I'm sure Alan Jackson is a great guy, but the only, and I mean the only thing that makes "It's Five o'Clock Somewhere" an interesting song is when Jackson wisely defers to the much more interesting perspective of Jimmy Buffett. Jackson may have been to Margaritaville a time or two, but he didn't build it from his own imagination.

Alan Jackson, for all his ample integrity, and his admirable defense of traditional country music, is still one of a thousand Nashville frozen concoctions playing the part of the redneck with an attitude, or I should really say "the good ol' boy with a chip." The only difference between a "redneck with an attitude" and a "good ol' boy with a chip" is a two-year string of bad luck. I don't think Alan Jackson ever had such a string, but I'm willing to be corrected. And I think Alan is probably the real thing too—he actually is a good ol' boy from Georgia, writing and singing about what he knows, and doing it very well, and there's nothing in the world wrong with that. But that is what Nashville thrives on, new incarnations of the same persona. It's a tired persona if you ask me (and I realize you didn't).

Now, by comparison, how many Jimmy Buffetts are there? Nothing could be more obvious when Jackson steps on the stage with Buffett in that video—Jackson is the real thing, by Nashville standards, but any of a hundred Nashville stars could have filled his place in that song—Eric Church, George Strait, Toby Keith, Dierks Bentley, even Steve Earle. You choose and rewrite the video. You'll see that it works. But whoever you choose to play Alan Jackson, there is only one Buffett, and only he can finish the video. One of them created the whole genre of music he plays, and the other one simply stepped into a pre-fabricated role, adding his slight variations. That's my "thought" for this story, even if the story isn't over, and even if that silly song was twenty-two years away from making sense back in 1981, when that Parrothead changed my point of view. So, long before Jackson had emerged from the woods of north Georgia, the Parrothead was trying to help me "get it." He wasn't an articulate fellow—plenty smart, but not a word guy—and in the end mostly what he had to say was "listen to this" . . . and he'd fast forward to another tune.

Permanent Reminder of a Temporary Feeling

What sorts of sentiments does Buffett convey? Of course, it's almost the whole human complement, but we get no hate, wrath, anger, or rage. Rather than those, we get a bit of disdain, annoyance, and their close kin, but from Jimmy we get no blaming of other people, and precious little blaming of himself. We get considerable lust and nostalgia, but no remorse and only a bit of regret. He wouldn't do anything differently (except the great filling station hold-up), but he also doesn't want to do it over. There's only an occasional hint of light-hearted envy or revenge (I'm thinking of "Gypsies in the Palace" here). But what overall quality can we name that helps us recognize which sentiments do and don't belong in Margaritaville? I think I've figured it out, but let me get at it indirectly. Maybe the key to this treasure chest is hidden in Jimmy's way with words.

Shared sentiment is probably more important than like-mindedness in binding Buffett to his fans. Poets thrive on shared sentiment, but I don't think Jimmy Buffett is first and foremost a poet. He has a fine turn of phrase, and rumor has it that he's a pretty smooth talker, but when I consider the William Blakes and Dylan Thomases of our mother tongue, I think Jimmy is up to something else. Even among singer-songwriters, there are the "pure poets," Dylan, Springsteen, and the like, who seem to think of words in the way Van Gogh must have thought of hues and tints. For Jimmy, words are nice, but they are a means not an end.

The poet type wants artistic intensity in his relation to his audience, he wants to share his art more than his feelings, so his feelings get all arted up. It's hard to know whether to trust the genuineness of those feelings. I don't think Dylan has any feelings of his own, but if he does, he wouldn't share them with us. We aren't worthy. Poets are too much trouble to mess with. Jimmy wants a party. There's an art to that too, but it's not exactly art for art's sake. A really big difference between a Parrothead and, say, a Springsteen fan is that when we hear Jimmy talking about how he feels or felt, we say "yeah, I been there too," whereas Springsteen fans are more likely to hear the words and believe that Bruce somehow, magically, just knows how they feel. That's fine, but it isn't exactly the truth about life. Springsteen is an honest guy. He would never really claim to know how someone else feels, but he makes them feel like he does know, and that is the magic of poetry. Of course, a concert, whether Springsteen or Buffett, can be a party either way, but the two have a different overall atmosphere, I think you'll agree. If his songs and books are any guide, Jimmy isn't always even sure how he feels, let alone how we feel. So Parrotheads see Jimmy as an ideal drinking buddy and a potential partner in crime, not as a prophet or a pure artist. If Jimmy became too intense, too dramatic, too Springsteen-esque, it would spoil his mystique and the persona he has worked so hard to create. The key to his feelings does not lie in the poetry.

What about the stories? Some would say, and Jimmy has said this himself, that he's really a storyteller (*A Pirate Looks at Fifty*, pp. 12, 444). If that's true, then his words are toggles for telling stories—and you have to choose the right words if you want to tell a good story. There's surely some truth to saying Jimmy is a storyteller, but what kind? He isn't like Pete Seeger, old school, morality tales filled with mythic images and symbols. And he doesn't even tell very many tall tales, those fantastical yarns like his hero Mark Twain used to invent. There are only a few of those, and while Jimmy is not one to let the truth spoil a good story, he stays closer to fact than Mark Twain. Jimmy is really more of a journalist than a traditional storyteller—he has more in common with Hunter S. Thompson than with Seeger or Twain. He tells his own story, and does so in ways that entertain us, and that we can relate to.

So the feelings are, I think, of the sort you get when you read or hear a good story, first person, like a travel journal—and maybe that's why Jimmy liked Mark Twain's travel books, like *Following the Equator*, better than the more celebrated "tall tales" about jumping frogs and prince-paupers and Connecticut Yankees. So, thinking of Jimmy as a sort of travel journalist, what kind? He's not ebullient like Rick Steves or irritable like Bill Bryson. But he is a little like Tom Bodett or Garrison Keillor, if not quite so folksy. Yet, there's something common about the sentiments here. I have a name for it: "wistful." And that is like Bodett and Keillor, without the Yankee pathos. Any feeling that can be felt wistfully fits in a Jimmy

Buffett song, and things that can't be felt with wist don't belong. That's not to say that Jimmy's always wistful, only that the sentiments and feelings that show up in the stuff he writes would be ones that could be tacked to a wistful wind. So, go down the list of feelings that show up, add a little wist and you'll see what I mean. It may be that wistful habits of feeling give a person just enough detachment to laugh at the cruelties of fate—folly chasing death, as Jimmy described it (*A Pirate Looks at Fifty*, pp. 39, 449). If we couldn't laugh, we'd all go insane. The key to the treasure chest is cut wistfully, and damned if it doesn't fit the lock. It's better to be lucky than good, sometimes.

A Prince of a Guy

Adding up what we've got so far: places where Frank and Lola can get together again, times that are good for a conversation or a party, memorable meetings that make for good stories, and sentiments in a wistful key. We're ready for a lesson from Machiavelli, because these are the very tools of fortune. He has an interesting take on fortune. We usually think of 'fortune' as something good, but we also use phrases like 'a trick of fortune' and other sorts of verbal tics that show we don't always see fortune as favorable. The Latin goddess of chance is Fortuna. This is the same as "Lady Luck," upon whom Jimmy occasionally calls (*A Pirate Looks at Fifty*, p, 8). Following the sense of his times, Machiavelli sees Fortuna more as a playful trickster who throws up obstacles before any and all of us, and our success or failure in any endeavor depends upon how we meet those obstacles. Sooner or later, Fortuna defeats most people, but Machiavelli says that there are some things you can do to evade her wiles. But first, well, you have to marry her, he says, and then you'll need a big stick.

I don't like violence, and neither does Jimmy, but if anybody ever decided to marry Fortuna, Jimmy did. So let's hear Machiavelli out because, after all, fortune isn't actually a woman, and the stick you need to hit her with doesn't grow on a tree. It's just a metaphor. So what stick is this? It's "virtue," says Machiavelli. This was in Chapter 11, but just in case you forgot, it's the Latin "virtutem," which means moral strength, but also manliness, potency. The word "virile" comes from the same root, "vir," which means both a man and a hero. The sort of person who can marry Fortuna and then make her a co-operative partner is a kind of hero, a man's man—and by his own accounting, Jimmy has read dozens of books about heroes and crooks, and learned much from both of their styles. I wouldn't be surprised if Machiavelli is on Jimmy's book list, since the man wrote the ultimate travel guide for heroes and crooks. The point is that, since no one can avoid the tricks and wiles of Fortuna, it's wise to keep her close at hand, cultivate your strength and your boldness, and above all learn to read the winds—choose the right places, times, friends, and feelings, and when you think you have them, move decisively. Look before you leap, but he who hesitates is lost.

For example, you might decide to tell everyone in Nashville to just kiss your ass and go to the beach with Jerry Jeff. That seems pretty decisive to me. If you made the right move, you might even live to see Nashville come to your doorstep with a song praising your choice. You win Jimmy, you're a prince of a guy.[1] I wondered about the song "It's Five o'Clock Somewhere," and since one of its co-writers, Don Rollins, is a friend of a friend, I asked how much these guys plotted what they were doing, since it looked like the work of Parrotheads. It turns out that Rollins was not the plotter, but Jim "Moose" Brown was. As Rollins explained, he really didn't know how extensive Jimmy's fan base was, but since Moose Brown is friends with Michael Utley and Mac McAnally, he thinks that maybe Moose was more aware of how the scenario would play out. My suspicion is that Moose Brown knew exactly what would happen.

---

[1] But everyone knows that Nashville plays the game by Machiavelli's book, which is why we don't want to land there when the volcano blows. Fortune favors the bold, the Latin proverb says, but Machiavelli adds that Fortune also favors the young. Jimmy was young when he made his big move, and I'm not recommending this sort of huge step for most of you, and certainly not for myself. I'm only pointing out how it describes a certain brash and successful songwriter we all know. But here's a kind of virtue that can make full use of your own vices (and those of others). That's good work if you can get it. We could all do with some of this kind of virtue (indeed, I could do with more than I have).

I Really Do Appreciate the Fact You're Sittin' Here

Later in May, 1981; Memphis Comics and Used Records, toward the end of the "B" bin. You never know what effects a weekend may have. I know that you and I aren't intimate enough for 'my story' to be of much interest to you, and I promise this is not a prelude to a suggestion about a waterbed. But I'm almost finished with what I have now decided will be just my first bottle of Pinot Noir today, and if you took my advice earlier, we are drinking buddies by now. In any case, you're not looking so clear to me at this point, so if you'll hold me steady, I'm pulling in the anchor. We have a lot in common, you and me. We like most of the same times, places, meetings, and sentiments. We like Buffett. Maybe you'll put up with the rest of the story, even if I'm not quite your favorite drinking buddy, and this isn't really a pinch you're in.

The final exams went rather poorly—five F's that semester and I was on my way to dropping out of college. The flower deliveries went somewhat better, as far as I can recall, and I got hired part-time into the business with that Parrothead. That would put food on the table for the next couple of years while I foolishly tried to become a rock star. Fortune may favor the young, but it generally shits upon the talent-less. It's hard to say whether it's fortune or fate, but either way, I exercised my Machiavellian virtues, such as they were, and went semi-heroically to the best used record store in town. I bought every Jimmy Buffett album then available. Jimmy didn't get any royalties from me then, since I bought them used, but I was poor, and he has been spending my money foolishly ever since. I'm proud that I probably spent enough in later years to finance the port-a-potties for the workers building the first Margaritaville Café (or at least this was my thought, when I ate there). Anyway, I bought the records and, like many of you reading this, I started learning Buffett songs on the guitar—songs I still know by heart. It amazes me how many people learned to play the guitar for the sake of singing those songs, and fortunately, most are easy. But I meet other Parrotheads on a regular basis who did that. I've run across a couple of these who never even learned anything else.

The Fickle Finger

To make it in the brutal music business you need some luck, but you also have to be good (better than I was). There's no sense at all in saying that it was fate that sent Jimmy to the beach, although fortune may have had a good bit to do with it, as he readily admits. When Jimmy contemplates fate, he reserves it for matters that seem beyond control—like when his wonderful little hotel on St. Barts burned to the ground. He suspected malice at first, but "as fate would have it, the fire started in the deejay booth of the disco" (*A Pirate Looks at Fifty*, p. 450). I'll leave the interesting symbolism of that for you to ponder. Like Vico, Jimmy is careful not to say there's no such thing as fate, but if it really exists, maybe the thing to do is to twist fate by tricking fortune.

That's sort of the way Vico tells the story. He says that if you want to know why things happen as they do, you have to consider three main things: the "natural causes," the "moral causes" and "the occasions of fortune." Natural causes are things like, if you don't see the wake in time, your flying boat will go out of control—because that's how the wake affects flying boats, and no amount of Machiavellian virtue can help that. Moral causes are things like being prepared for the plane crash by some U.S. Navy water survival training. The "occasions of fortune" are like this (and look closely here at what Jimmy says): the crash "would have killed me if it hadn't been for the intervention of God, Buddha, St. Christopher, my guardian angel, my fishing buddies, luck, and the United States Navy water-survival training" (p. 42). You can see that Fortune is called by her other name here, Mrs. Luck (remembering that Jimmy married her), and that the moral cause is named too (Be Prepared), but the rest—God, Buddha, St. Christopher, and the guardian angel, all rolled together—has a different name. Vico calls it "Providence."

I'm not going to go religious on you here, I promise. "Providence," apart from being an un-Buffetish place in Rhode Island, is more like a way of seeing the cosmic balance between fortune and fate. It comes from the same word as "provide," and it has to do with the resources in life that are provided for us—including the order of nature (natural causes), the order of virtue (the opportunities we have for developing our own character), and the ways in which fortune can be seen as a series of obstacles that we can meet. And here's Vico's point: you're not utterly at the mercy of either fortune or fate, if you make use of what is provided, but you also can't foresee all the consequences of your actions. And here's the chorus to that song: no matter what happens, it can be turned to good ends, to the end of providing for others, even if not for ourselves.

So let's discuss a nightmare. What if Jimmy had died in the plane crash? (After all, John Denver did.) What would we have said? That isn't a hard question. We would have said: "He died the way he lived, doing something he loved, and by the way, thank you Jimmy for the music and the books and for your life. We love you, and your music and life provide us with the means for confronting our own lives, with wist and wisdom." That is what we would say. And if Jimmy could answer us from beyond, I know he would say this: "Some of it's magic and some of it's tragic, but I had a good life all the way." That is "providence." We provide for each other, at the very least, the means with which to confront the obstacles that Fortune sends on the wind. You could think of Machiavelli's "big stick" as a main mast and Vico's providence as the mainsail. Vico says that whatever courses of action we set out upon, no matter how wicked or wise, these actions can serve the greater purposes of providence. Tack it right, and any wind can get you to harbor.

We are weak beings, "fallen man," as Vico says, but we don't want to be chained to fate or abandoned to the winds of chance. We want something to hope for and to be grateful about, and when you focus on that, with enough detachment to laugh about it, you'll see that the wistful sentiments are the right ones. That's the gift, the "intervention" of God, Buddha, St. Christopher or your guardian angel. They don't bring you safety, they bring you a sense of perspective about things, at least if you'll think about providence as being greater than fortune and fate. That seems like good advice to me, especially since it lets me hold on to my selected vices, with a clear understanding that they may do more to deter others from taking the same course than they do for me. I may have to be contented as a good bad example for others not to follow, but I might also get off scot-free. And that word "contented" is the emotional complement that rounds out the feeling of gratitude. Think about it. I'll bring that up again at the end, which is very near.

Providence

July 12th, 1986, Clinton, Kentucky. A meeting of the dearly beloved. Indulge me one last time, so that I can finish the story. Luckily, within a few years, I was actually able to marry a Parrothead, which is the next best thing to marrying Fortuna. (I'm no hero.) I'm not saying I married her because she was a Parrothead, but that may have been the only reason she married me. Providence. I didn't have much else to offer at the time, so I gave her flowers that I got for free (from among the stock too old to sell at the Parrothead's shop), and I serenaded her with Jimmy Buffett songs on my dad's old Gibson. She already knew the harmonies. Between the two of us, she was the one who had a real job, so she bought me a Martin guitar (this is God's own truth). We are all looking for the right sort of stick to tame fortune. In this case, the stick had six strings and was fashioned with care in Pennsylvania. These days I don't believe in mixed marriages (one Parrothead, and one who doesn't get it). That union is doomed. No stick is big enough. This may be more important than religion or politics, because it bears on the following five things: (1) the right places; (2) the right times; (3) the right meetings; (4) the right sentiments; and (5) the right thoughts. The five-fold path to providence. Now you're beginning to understand the full wistful weight of my gratitude to that Parrothead, wherever he is.

I think most of you have a story like mine, because we Parrotheads don't become the way we are by the ordinary channels. You don't come to this passion by watching VH1 or listening to hit songs on the radio. There is some dumb luck involved, but it isn't just fate. This kind of providential understanding of life spreads by subtler means, first-hand experiences, and by recognizing a providential moment when it shines. Maybe somebody who "gets it" comes to suspect that you might have the makings of a good Parrothead and takes the trouble to educate you until you can squawk on your own. I don't know if it's more like Amway or Catholicism, but whatever it is that spreads the good news, you can't bottle it. Alan Jackson likes us, I think, but he is not one of us. Don Rollins and Moose Brown, who wrote that song, mischievously plotted Jimmy's final revenge on Nashville, but if the best revenge is living well, then the perfect revenge is to live better than the people you told to kiss your ass when you finally learned that life is too short to put up with their bullshit. Thanks to Rollins and Brown for making us all smile, and to Alan Jackson for playing along. He got in his own kind of jab with the song, no doubt. I certainly am grateful to those guys for holding Nashville down while Jimmy got to tickle it into submission. And being grateful, I find myself contented.

"Livin' and Dyin' in Three-Quarter Time"

Maybe the secret to it all is as simple as being contented to live and die in three-quarter time. This is not defeat or fatalism by any stretch. The two key ideas are "contentment" and "three quarter time," and the second idea is the basis of the first one. If you want contentment, then it's a good idea to take the gift of time and make it into a tempo, organize it into a rhythm that works for you. If you're a Nautical Wheeler (that was a square dance group in Key West, apparently), then three-quarter time may be the way you want to go about that. But we all need rhythms, and I think people who can't find contentment are of two sorts: there are the ones who can't decide on the right rhythm, and there are those who don't notice and appreciate the rhythm they've found.

That weekend in 1981, I think I heard the call of Providence, because the line I could not leave alone, in my thinking, was "everyone here is just more than contented to be livin' and dyin' in three-quarter time." It went round and round my brain. It still does, and that is still my favorite Jimmy Buffett song, and on the weight of that one line: words to live and die by, if contentment with your Fortune is what you seek, and gratitude is what you offer in exchange, to appease Fate. As Jimmy says, "You know I can't help but be / Part of my own philosophy."

18
Running on Empty

Stage Left

Musicians are politically liberal. I suspect it has been ever thus, in all ages and places. Some of you may wonder why. Yes, there are exceptions like Charlie Daniels and Ted Nugent, but they are despised by most of their musical brethren and sistren. In contemporary country music, there is often a *show* of patriotism, sentimentality, and right-leaning ideas, but the musicians and writers are almost all privately leftists. Some, such as Garth Brooks and the Dixie Chicks have damaged their careers by being open about it. It's not like Johnny Cash was a conservative.

Even the notorious Toby Keith is quite moderate; he says he has "never been a Republican" and had always been a Democrat, until the Dixie Chicks dust-up, at which point he registered Independent. He played the Republican National Convention because it was an excellent paying gig, not an endorsement. That's what he said.

There is a fair representation of socially liberal but economically libertarian musicians (i.e., capitalist individualists), from Neil Young to Jimmy Buffett to Gene Simmons. They tend to be merely unpopular and suspect among their peers rather than despised, and encouraged publicly to STFU if they talk too much (like Gene Simmons). If they are a little slicker, like Willie Nelson, they can become outlaw heroes.

For musicians, nothing I say here will be new at all. But music *lovers* come in all sorts of political stripes, because nearly everyone likes music and something like three-quarters of us *love* it. Music is part of what makes us human. Even *in*human humans like it. It's not as if Hitler didn't like music. He wouldn't have liked rock music, but then, I doubt Chairman Mao would have liked it either, and his politics differ from Hitler's by about 180 degrees, even if his policies looked similar in practice. Extremists of that sort tend to follow Plato's famous limitations on music: no blues, no rock, nothing feminine or emotionally watery, no torch songs, no murder ballads, no dissonance, no bent notes. Plato used different language, but this is what he meant. Musicians see it otherwise. They want to play what is interesting to them, and marches and hymns are *not*.

Lawyers in Love

I also want to talk about the economics of making music, especially rock music during its rise and heyday, in a capitalist, and increasingly corporate era. It's hard to talk about the politics without the economics. But economics is pretty boring –they call it the dismal science. I doubt it's a science, but it's plenty dismal. Musicians almost always hate the economic side of what they do. They tend toward socialism in sentiment, but the successful ones find ways to justify the demand for a living wage and the claim of ownership over their creations. Most professional musicians live either below the poverty line or have day jobs to keep them afloat. For the sake of being able to make music, they accept living simply.

The general poverty of musicians probably contributes to their liberal leanings, in complex ways, such as are best described by Dickens in every book he ever wrote (a bleeding heart if ever there was one). Musicians have to be generous with each other, to get by, as the poor usually are and do. When nobody has anything, there isn't much property to squabble over. Individually, you try to keep your instruments and gear functioning –the tools of the trade—and everything else is a luxury. Together you share what you have because you need people to play with in ensembles.

On the other hand, musicians usually have to travel light, in life as in work. Owning things means burdening yourself with stuff you can't transport and must return to, and that has to be maintained. So professional musicians don't accumulate anything except gear and instruments, and a means of transporting them. For people with little invested in "ownership," the concept is kind of vague and not very important. Musicians don't think about it very much, historically speaking, but . . . good ole capitalism has changed that in huge ways in the rock era.

Musicians "own" their songs and their music, sort of. Ownership, as an idea, is both political and economic, and owning something as fleeting and ephemeral as musical performances, and owning "property" as easily stolen as songs and recordings, is philosophically tricky. So I will talk about Karl Marx versus the British tradition of the idea of "property" and "ownership," mainly Adam Smith. The whole world pretty much falls between those two poles of thinking about ownership. Americans, excepting professing Libertarians, are far more socialist than you've been led to believe, unless you really study this topic closely. Yes, even Republicans are far closer to being socialists, on the whole, than hard advocates of individualized private property.

In spite of their Leftishness, musicians are a pretty good test group for the socialism of Americans as a whole. Many British musicians choose to reside in the US (or outside of Britain) for economic reasons—these include Keith Richards and Elton John, among many others. They like American socialism better than its British counterpart. The taxes are lighter and the trade-off in services is no biggie for the wealthy.

The main people who win when musicians do really argue about property are the lawyers. They *love* this collection of paradoxes. But even they have difficulty commodifying something that, by its very nature, is given away in the course of being created, such as a musical performance. Do you "own" the performance of the song you're singing *as* you sing it? How the hell is that supposed to work?

The Pretender?

Jackson Browne. Not really a pretender, in my opinion. I don't know him, of course, but I don't believe he was ever careful about crafting his "persona," especially regarding politics, to avoid offending his fans. He has been an outspoken defender of Leftist causes for his entire career, and if his lyrics are any measure, he's what Europeans would call a social democrat, with a few tendencies toward full socialism. These categories are respectable middle-of-the-road positions in much of the world, but feared and maligned in the US, largely from a generalized misunderstanding of what they mean. The word "liberal" is used by Republicans for this maligning, and they usually have to spit and grind their teeth while saying it. This is ignorance. Both major political parties in the US, are "liberal" in the proper sense of the word. More of that in a minute.

Jackson Browne is a "liberal," in the true sense of the word. He's very clear about his belief that corporations are not persons and ought not have the same rights that individuals have. That is liberalism—the individual rights part. He (and you and me and anyone) is also enmeshed in a system of ownership that treats individual human beings as the primary units of economic reality, and as the basis of "ownership." Combinations of human beings (such as municipalities, governments, or corporations) are capable of owning things only under legal restrictions. You, on the other hand, own things as a natural right prior to law and serving as one basis for law.

Take It Easy

Jackson is okay with this kind of individual ownership—he copyrights his songs and enforces the copyright. He sued John McCain and the Republican Party for using his song "Running on Empty" in a political ad in 2008 without permission (it was settled out of court, for money, but it also sent a message to the Right, and that was part of Jackson's motive). When Jackson parted with David Geffen, who had been his manager as well as his record company CEO (of Asylum, in those days), Geffen gave Jackson the publisher's rights to his songs (Geffen screwed everybody else, for instance The Eagles). Jackson accepted those rights, formed his own publishing company, which "owns" his songs, under law.

That "gift" from Geffen was worth a *lot* of money. "Take It Easy" was listed in 2014 as the sixteenth most played or performed song among the millions licensed by ASCAP (American Society of Composers, Authors, and Publishers).[1] Number 1 is "Happy Birthday to You," and number 3 is "White Christmas," to give you a sense of this rarified standing. It leads me to hear the title of Jackson's song anew, in this short conversation:

---

[1] <www.ascap.com/press/2014/0213-ascap-turns-100>.

DAVID GEFFEN: "Take it."

JACKSON BROWNE: "Easy."

Technically, anyone who owns an establishment where the song is played (as a recording or live) by anyone, owes Jackson Browne money. I have personally performed that song surely a thousand times myself, all over the country. When you add in the ten other Jackson Browne songs on my own performance list that I have been doing since the 1970s, I think I've probably bought him a car. Personally. I wonder if Geffen wants those songs back. He isn't known for his generosity. I'm guessing that Jackson does cash his checks from ASCAP. Yes, he gives tons of money to charities and plays benefit concerts all the time, and he is known for his generosity, but he hasn't assigned the rights to "Take It Easy" to a charity. Nor is it reasonable to expect that of anyone. But the song was *given* to him. I'm just sayin'. On the other hand, Jackson generously credited Glenn Frey (of The Eagles) as a co-writer. Frey said many times that at most he contributed a phrase and he can't even remember it. (It's sort of like Paul Simon and Los Lobos in reverse.)

I wonder if David Geffen would give me, say, "Hotel California." It's way down the list, number fifty-two all time. He can afford it. But if he gives it to anyone, it should be Don Felder, who wrote the damn thing. I've probably bought David Geffen a fleet of cars, and even though Don Felder is notoriously difficult to get along with, I'd rather see the clubs and venues pay him the money.

It's amazing how much these Leftist musicians care about the institution of private property when it comes to their songs. Indeed, the use of lyrics is so restricted by copyright laws that you will find very few of them in this book. If you pay close attention, you will note that throughout the book I have paraphrased and alluded, rather than quoted, to keep from running afoul of the law. If the musicians themselves could be approached for permission, that would be one thing, but all of the watch-dogging and subsequent other dogging of venue owners, and restaurant (and even elevator) owners, is done by vultures who don't give a shit about music and have little or no connection to the writers who published it.

Call It a Loan

My point is that the economic realities of the present day tend to make "liberals" of us all. That isn't necessarily a good thing. A liberal is someone who holds that the *human individual* is the most basic unit of social reality, and is the *only* legitimate basis upon which governments can be formed. Liberals believe in consent of the governed, and that human individuals trade their natural rights, including the right to own property, for civil rights, so long as the government (which may take life, liberty, or property under law) is legitimate (derives from the consent of the governed). That describes almost every government in the world, nowadays. Even welfare states, such as the UK and Norway and Sweden, insist on consent of the governed. The countries with dictators and military regimes are still filled with people who regard their own governments as lacking legitimacy due to the absence of their consent. Jackson's statements on his website imply this view.

It's pretty difficult to get anything done in the US without buying in (pun intended) to the economic presuppositions of the system, and these are supposed to be *political* ideals with economic implications. For instance, "liberty," or "the pursuit of happiness." In reality, as we have evolved, the roles have tended to reverse, which is to say that we are an economic system with a political structure designed to maintain that system. Some would say we always have been reversed. Those who say so were once mainly socialists or Marxists of some stripe, but these days the claim is harder to dispute and is made even by people who don't mean it as a criticism of the US. Yes, we get nervous when people "buy" private armies, but the difference between selling oneself into the US armed forces or taking a job with Blackwater is not that huge. A "volunteer" army must be paid, and if poorly paid compared to mercenaries, then expect a good deal of discontentment and poor morale and losses in efficiency and *esprit de corps*. But we don't seem to mind it when people buy our politicians, and that is what Jackson Browne has fought, vocally. He wants a clearer separation of business and the state, which ironically, is the position strongly advocated by Adam Smith, the great apologist of free trade.

Even though Smith is often quoted in snippets and cited as the father of capitalism, it isn't at all accurate to say his philosophy would support the system we now have. He advocates that government be energetic in regulating business, and that it should never be in the grips of either the landed interest or the financial sector. For the last 140 years, the US has been increasingly controlled by the alliance of business and government, and always at the expense of the land-interest. Donald Trump's election may reorient that trend, since Trump is not a finance or business guy, he is a land guy. That is part of the reason his political views are so hard to classify in the current milieu. But he speaks like a populist-individualist, and that is pretty much the rhetoric of the land-interest since the beginning of this nation. Jefferson would have no trouble understanding him. Hamilton would hate him. For those who think big business is happy to see that guy become President, think again. Let's just say the Koch Brothers can't buy him. That doesn't make him any less crazy, only differently crazy. And all of this is nothing but the very system Adam Smith described, as it seeks to rebalance itself after 140 years of struggle in which the land-interest lost every fight.

Some with Leftist leanings will say, disappointedly, that we all sell ourselves to something and we always have. It isn't so simple. Socialists think differently. They don't believe that the individual is the most basic unit of economic reality, and *for this reason*, also not the most basic unit of political reality. Socialists reject individualism as a political idea because interdependence (both physical and economic), for survival, health, and flourishing is basic to our natural way of existing and therefore any just political organization needs to acknowledge what they call our "species being."

Where historically, liberals subjugated economics to politics (in word if not deed), socialists never did. Socialism is a set of economic ideals that implies certain things for political legitimacy, but is consistent with almost any form of state or government, including the form of the US government, now and in the past. The economic ideals of socialism can be and have been enacted in laws and enforced by the government of the US increasingly throughout its history. *True* liberals do not like it and have fought it at every step—and have lost every single battle.

The liberal can counter that just because we have been interdependent in the distant past for survival does not mean we should be now. They like to refer to the attitude of socialists as "collectivism" and associate it with ominous words and doom-saying. You would think they'd call it "regressive," or "outdated," or "obsolete," but they don't. They could say that overcoming our interdependence is the key to our very freedom, and that interdependence is as limiting politically as it is economically. Only Libertarians ever talk that way, and precious few of them seem to see the matter this way. A missed opportunity for important critique, I'd say.

Lives in the Balance

Musicians are more accustomed to interdependence than most people, because making music is, in almost every facet of the business, a group undertaking. It is similar with filmmaking. Speaking as a bass player, I, for one don't think I'd have any fun, or that you would listen for very long, if it was just me playing. You might listen to Esperanza Spalding for a few hours, but let's agree she's a welcome exception to almost every rule. *I* need a band. Solo musicians still must have an audience. This is a social activity through and through.

Philosophers may function best as "lone beasts in their burrows," to use the phrase of William James, but musicians can't do that, and people who must create in solitude might become composers, but they will not become performing musicians. Thus, the idea of "property" for musicians develops in their minds as something shared, even commonly held, and they don't tend to get hot and bothered when the government treats such property as something that is subject to the due process of law.

The basis for such governing in the US Constitution comes in several places, primarily the Interstate Commerce Clause and the "Takings" Clause of the Fifth Amendment. Many people misunderstand that clause. It says the federal government (and adding the Fourteenth Amendment, also state governments) *shall not* take your shit *without* due process of law. It means they *can* take your shit *with* due process. We Americans have been arguing about it since long before the Constitution, especially regarding the power to tax. We hate taxes. That's why it took a Constitutional amendment to create the income tax. Nothing less than that level of agreement would do, and many people regard it to this day as a terrible idea. Many more try to avoid paying them, for as many reasons as you can imagine, from Thoreau's protest over slavery to Willie Nelson to Montana Freemen who claim the government isn't even legitimate on account of taxes. The latter come closer to the attitude of our Patriots during the Revolutionary era.

I'm a Patriot

Nothing brings the American Left and Right together faster than the government taking things from the People, and when it comes to taking land, strange bedfellows find one another in the political darkness. Let the feds take some land for a highway or pipeline or drilling in the wildlife refuge, and watch the Left erupt. Let them take land for preservation and restrict grazing or hunting rights and watch the Right erupt. Nobody seems to like the government when it comes to land, and nobody seems to trust big business, and nobody knows what to do to get these two powers out of bed with each other.

So we mainly bitch about things. I bitch, you bitch, Jackson Browne bitches. But he writes songs about it that sell lots of copies and are heard far and wide on the radio. He said these things when it was hip to be Left, and he got even louder when it wasn't. I have a bandmate who loves Jackson's music, but regularly remarks that the man ought to shut up about politics. A lot of people feel that way, but mainly I find respect among people who believe that the consistency of Jackson's viewpoint over so many years produces grudging respect among such critics and, in my case (since I agree with most of what Jackson says) immense appreciation that he didn't get Reaganized, or Bushified, or Clintonized.

But the man is no philosopher. Nor would he want to be thought of in that way, I would guess. I think Jackson Browne is a songwriter of the first order, the best of his generation, along with Dylan and Paul Simon. He never got the press they got, but I think of them as the American songwriting trifecta: one from the east, one from the middle, one from the west. All on the Left, but while Simon has a flip-flopping problem, and a very dicey history of screwing people out of ownership of things, Dylan is actually just as explicitly ambivalent about politics and economics. He always knew his bread was buttered on the Left-hand side, but he also never professed any deep-seated solidarity with those people. Dylan is comfortable with the institution of private property, but not known to worry overly about enforcing his copyright. He is generous to other musicians in the use of his name and, in contrast to Paul Simon, well-liked among them.

Was I Unwise?

Jackson Browne, on the other hand, is a hippie. He has always and without compromise been a creature of the political Left, and noisily so, and he's as serious about it as a hippie can get. He takes on cause after cause, using his celebrity and resources to promote humane and humanitarian ends, and to oppose overreach of ruthless business and mindless government. And he typifies the musicians' dilemma regarding economics, especially property. I'm almost certain he hates the economics of the music business, but he has succeeded in corralling those unruly doggies into *his* chutes and pens and sending *that* meat to the market. It's a fact. And it's a paradox. And it's actually very common among musicians who succeed, at all levels, to navigate the contradictions.

The music business has many facets, but the two principal pieces that have supplemented performing are writing and recording. They are very different in economic terms. Being good at any one of the three doesn't imply ability with the other two. Each aspect has its own infrastructure. They overlap at crucial points, but the people who dwell in the world of performing see recording as an artistic endeavor that helps to finance the musical life, while those who dwell on the recording side see performing as a promotional venture that sells products. These two sets of dwellers often clash but are generally symbiotic.

Between these two (one ancient, the other very recent), exists the middle child called songwriting or composing. As a business, it's fairly young (five hundred years or so). As an art, it's very, very old. The idea that a musical work could be "owned" is peculiar and arrived with capitalism. It grew up slowly. I have prepared you to think about it, if you have stayed with me this long. Writing music isn't quite performance and it isn't quite recording, as a business, but both performing and recording *depend* on it to a very great extent. In fact, under-standing that side of things is the key to getting the gist of the other two, these days. Since recording is a relatively new econ-omy, one that was added to musical performance in the age of Edison, I want to describe the economics of performing, and, if I can, show how the writing business and the recording busi-ness give us a refined view of performing, which, I insist, is the essence of music.

The Road

I think the reason Jackson Browne's *Running on Empty* struck such a chord with audiences, and especially with musi-cians, comes down to this: He tried (and succeeded) to show the whole spectrum of "the show." It was actually a concept album, like *Magical Mystery Tour*, except it *worked*. The deci-sion to present only new material on a live album was creative and risky. Untested stuff. But that's what performers face when they float their newest material. New songs settle in to what they *will be* gradually, as the performers find the right details and rests and attacks and crescendos. When the mate-rial is new, it's never quite the same twice, until it settles in to what it *will be*. Bands find those nuances together. Some nights are magic. Some suck. Jackson and his band had a really good night in Maryland that supplied almost half the tracks on that album.

Jackson also recorded loose-sounding stuff from the bus and a couple of hotel rooms. One can hear the roar of the engine and feel the late night haze in these famous cuts. Musicians have all been there. It connects. I don't know how non-musicians experience this part, but I'm guessing it's funky, cool, and it works. We all put ourselves there, with the band, and we feel like we're welcome, are a part. This was a brilliant idea. And in no way does it romanticize or glorify. It's gritty and feels real. Let's get to some of those realities. I will do something risky and speak from experience in what fol-lows. I don't harbor any illusions that my personal experience is inherently interesting to anyone else, but most people don't really know how the the performing thing works, and I think it has much to do with the Lefty tendencies of musicians, and their ambivalences.

You've Been Promoted

They say the music business is ugly. I know the truth about this "ugliness" when it comes to live music, although it's more sad than ugly. I did try to make a living as a musician. I have hundreds of friends (many very close) who have succeeded, for various stretches of time, in making ends meet. I have served (and that's the right word for it, not "worked"—it's service, trust me) as a small-time promoter, producer (in the sense they use this term for producing live shows), booking agent, impresario (as a writer, disc-jockey, presenter, and such), accountant, and entrepreneurial risk-taker. I have run a music venue, both for profit and not. I experienced all of these arcane functions from the side of a performer as well, both as a solo act and as part of many ensembles.

It takes a lot of people to bring you that show you saw. The economics of putting on live shows can be summed up in a joke (told to me by another concert promoter):

Did you hear about the concert promoter who won the lottery?

Uh, no.

They interviewed him, asked him what he'd do with the money.

Yeah? What'd he say?

"I guess I'll keep doing the shows until it runs out."

It's a sorry truth. Most people involved with live music just *love* music and believe it improves people's lives. Very few go into it for the money. The Bill Grahams of the world, who put on shows to make money, are few and not much respected. The promoter is the guy or gal who assumes all the risk for doing the show—renting the venue, or negotiating an arrangement with the owner, hiring the band, seeing to lights, sound, seating, insurance, and advertising. He or she works out how everybody gets paid and pays them. If your lazy ass doesn't show up to take in the show, we get stuck with the loss.

In my experience, promoters are about equally male and female, and come in all races and religions. They learn what they do by making mistakes. A young promoter is by definition an idiot and often uptight and unpleasant. People who are able to keep doing it into middle age become either bitter and awful, or wonderful and wise. There's no in-between. Non-musicians who promote shows are likely to continue making the same mistakes into old age and will not improve.

In the small time, the promoter is often a venue owner or someone hired by the venue to oversee entertainment. A bad night for such people is absorbed as part of the business of selling food and alcohol. It's quite common for the band to accept less money than was promised when business is slow, sometimes (albeit rarely) even at their own suggestion. It's not in *their* interest for the bar to go under or to be remembered as the band that took the money and ran. They want work. All concerned must make money for work to exist. They know that.

It's also common for the owner-promoter to increase the band's pay above what was promised when the venue or series has a good night. It isn't just generosity. We want *that* band back and we incentivize their return and try to motivate buzz from the band itself to bring a crowd. If the bar or other venue *doesn't* increase the pay after a big night, the band may grumble and refuse to return, or at least demand a significant increase before agreeing to come back. If the owner increases the pay once for a good night, it must be done the next time, if the crowd is the same. Both the band and the venue want to build a momentum, a feeling among people that this is the place to be. That's the symbiosis. When it works, everybody is happy, including the crowd.

So between promoter and musicians, it's friendly but it's business. If the band is too loud or is chasing away customers, there will be negotiation. In rare cases, the band doesn't fit the crowd and is paid and sent home early. That sucks for everybody concerned. But simply quitting early due to a lack of butts in seats happens *a lot*, more these days than in more glorious times for live music. It's no secret that live music venues are suffering these days.

Why? You're at home on your computer or playing video games. The musicians are playing to rooms that don't contain *your* body. And among those who are present, half are buried in their iPhones. They don't know how to *be* where they *are*. But sometimes they are summoning all their friends to the venue, so it's a mixed curse. Sometimes they are being summoned away. Times are tough either way.

My Personal Revenge

As the song title above indicates, there is depth in the best revenge—living well. Jackson's translation of that has to do with what is now called "transformative justice." First, you whip the evil-doers, with truth and without violence, and then you freely include them in the better world *they* couldn't imagine, back when they were torturing and killing your people. Presumably you do this by singing songs (and recording them), and that means writing them, since songs are nonviolent truth purveyors. Yes, that's a hopeless dream, but that is, according to all the evidence, how Jackson Browne sees the world.

The catch is that you have to *whip them*. That's the business end of this particular weapon. We don't reconcile with the bad people until we've transformed the situation. Reconciling with the bad ones never brings about a better world. So: Every band has to have at least one member with a fair head for business. This is a good person who understands evil people. If you're a solo act, that'll have to be you, or you'd best go find Colonel Tom Parker. For the Stones, that would be Mick Jagger, since about 1967. He actually went to school for it. For Bruce Springsteen, it is Bruce Springsteen. For The Eagles, it was Glenn Frey, although he got his ass kicked by David Geffen. For the Grateful Dead, it was *no one in particular*, which usually doesn't work, but hey, there's an exception to every rule. For Jimmy Buffett, Inc., it is most definitely Jimmy Buffett, and he is something of a shark. And for The Band, unhappily, it was Robbie Robertson, who took everything from his friends for himself.

Most musicians are sheep. They just want to play and get paid. They want no part of the business. In most bands, the person who handles the business side hates doing it, but is looking out for everybody. Sometimes that person gets a bigger cut, but it's tricky. People don't like being paid differentially in a band—that's the socialist moment in the artistic temperament, which goes way deeper than the capitalist moment. Musicians depend on each other to do what they do, and measuring the relative importance of any part is fraught with problems. The Eagles eventually had to kick out Don Felder because he couldn't be reconciled to making less than Frey and Henley. On the other hand, Felder did write "Hotel California" ... so maybe they should have showed a little more appreciation. Joe Walsh accepted the reduced pay, as did Tim Schmidt, without complaint. But they decidedly *didn't* write "Hotel California." It's art, but it's business, and when the people on stage begin to be mere mercenaries rather than artists invested in the art of the show, the atmosphere changes and the energy is drained from the performance. People play their best when they feel equal, even if they aren't. The E Street Band is an example of successful balance.

Having two band members with a head for business creates challenges and conflicts. It definitely works best when one person makes the decisions, with consultation and approval from the others. It's a pain in the ass, but it has always been done by someone, as soon as music was commodified. That happened in ancient times. Aristotle mentions it. So, to win the struggle for truth, justice, and the musical way, you have to survive economically, and that requires *trusting* someone who understands evil and is thus capable of choosing it (unless you're The Grateful Dead, and you aren't).

Looking Out at the Road

For most acts during the rock era, the touring and performing part is a break-even proposition at best. Yes, there are exceptions. Bruce Springsteen, the Stones . . . and that's about it. You're thinking to yourself: "I pay big bucks for that concert seat. And there's like thousands of people there, and *they* all paid big bucks. No way this isn't making money." Way.

The point of touring has always been about building a fan base, city-by-city, and promoting album sales. The imminent arrival of the band provides an occasion (or excuse) for an intense marketing campaign, leading to buzz, word of mouth, increased spins and requests on local radio, increased presence on jukeboxes in that area, and so on. The cost of all that promotion is immense, as is the cost of moving the crew and equipment and band from city to city, and paying all the people (from security to insurance to renting the facility to concession contracts) who make these events happen. Very few performers negotiate these costs from a position of strength. Then there's the cost of pre-production—an act might spend more on lighting *design* than it makes in two or three nights, if the lights are important to the show.

The band wants to be paid, too, but they don't get what you'd think unless they own themselves, like the Stones and Springsteen. Most bands don't. They have to convince people to finance the tour. Sometimes that's the record company or a company hired by the record company, but the musicians usually just get a per-night guarantee, a per diem, expenses (within limits), and the profits don't go to them. It's a paycheck for the musicians. And you might think this is fun work, but touring sucks. You're away from home, cooped up with people you don't necessarily like, keeping a beastly schedule, exhausted from too many shows too close together, unable to enjoy it or even remember where you are. You sleep on a bus or in an impersonal motel or hotel.

The Load Out

All of this information is on Jackson Browne's *Running on Empty* recording. Apart from being one of the two or three best live albums of the rock era (just my opinion, of course; the other two would be *Cheap Trick at Budokan* and Springsteen's five-volume set), it has an intensity, a communicative power, a feel of authenticity that no other live album in rock has (one must set aside the live recording of Miles Davis in order to speak of intensity, authenticity ,and communicative power in a recording, since his are in a league of their own). With *Running on Empty*, listen especially to "The Load Out." The depiction of restlessness among the musicians, wandering around backstage, bored with rural scenes and magazines, day after day— well, the musicians might be better off if they helped with setting up and breaking down. They've all done it a million times. It's second nature to help. It'd be hard not to.

The crowd that comes to the local bar to see a band also doesn't see them arrive two or three hours before the show for load-in and set up. Most listeners don't see the load-out either. A few folks do often hang around to help, usually people who also played at one time or another. By the time your favorite local band has played four sets over four or five hours, they've put in an eight-hour workday. Or more. They do everything themselves—the sound system, the mix, the lights (usually minimal), keeping up the instruments and equipment, not to mention the driving. They are often friendly but not friends.

The camaraderie is real, as are the smiles on stage, but the communication is a sharing of music, not of life. They won't be hanging out until there is another show. Then they'll catch up with each other's news, talk equipment ("gear"), sounds, schedules, rehearsal plans (this isn't always necessary, once you get to a certain level of proficiency), and all pitch in on what has to be done.

And it doesn't pay. Really. It's done for the love of music. When I began playing in local bands in the mid-1970s, we (four or five of us) would split $300 for a night at the Moose Lodges and the like. As you climb the ladder, up to being a "regional act," your band would make, at best, about 2K per night (frat parties at big universities), and be happy to get $800 for a showcase-type club (all the seats face the stage), and $600 for a popular rock bar. As of 2017, that rate of pay is about *the same*, for the bands operating at the level of "regional." For local bar bands now, the rate for four sets is $250 to $400 (in the South and Midwest, a hundred bucks more on the coasts). A hundred bucks in 1980 dollars is $290 in today's money. In thirty-five years, local and regional musicians have thus had their earning capacity cut by two-thirds.

So, today, if you have four guys in your bar band, you're working for minimum wage—like the roadies in Jackson's song. Tips make a *huge* difference. But it was possible to piece together a living in the past. Every city in the 1970s and 1980s had a passel of musicians who worked regular gigs, drew regular crowds, and had middle-class lives. The bigger the city (and more musical), the bigger the passel. Musicians always supplemented their performing incomes working at music stores, giving lessons, waiting tables if absolutely necessary. But it could be done. These experiences are shared by pretty much every musician you have ever seen in concert. The process of succeeding in rock music, as a performer, does not skip steps. It happens faster for some, but the overnight success mythology *is* mythology. You have to *do* all this to *learn* how to perform. You are paying your dues. It's an emotional rollercoaster at best.

These Towns All Look the Same

I saw Jackson Browne play in November of 2015, full band. He was touring in support of his (then) new recording *Standing in the Breach*. The album is great, he looks great, sounds great, and was able to fill (almost) a 2,500-seat venue. We had second-row seats. Not a soul there was under forty, and not very many between forty and fifty. Jackson hasn't managed to connect with a younger generation as Springsteen has done (sort of). But he seems okay with it.

After the initial round of songs, it came time to say something to the audience. Jackson was never talkative on stage at any point in his career, which is fine. Some performers aren't. But this night he decided to explain why he stayed in his room even though he had a day off on the tour. It seems that the last time he was in town he went to this great guitar store and spent too much on guitars. Everyone laughed. Surely he had been to Killer Vintage Guitars, on Ivanhoe. But as he unfolded the tale a little bit more it became clear that he believed he was in Kansas City. Catching confused faces in the front rows, he said something like, "I'm in Missouri, right?" Whole audience: "Yes, other side of the state." Even then it took him a second or two to come up with "St. Louis." He blushed, didn't handle it well, and . . . was immediately forgiven.

We all knew the line "These towns all look the same," and we know why he wrote it. He did sing "The Load Out" that night, saying he just can't do it every night, but tonight he would. (Raucous cheers, as the opening piano notes sounded.) I wondered if he wanted to sing that line to us. They *do* all look the same. They sell a sign in New Orleans with a quote from Tennessee Williams: "America has only three cities: New York, San Francisco, and New Orleans. Everywhere else is Cleveland." He only missed it by one. Miami isn't Cleveland, but yeah, St. Louis is Cleveland and Kansas City is Cleveland and Milwaukee is Cleveland, and I'll shut up about it. To natural-born coastals like Jackson, I'm sure the whole flyover looks like one big wasteland. It isn't, but you have to get specific about what is and isn't waste. Too specific for coastals.

If I Only Had a Dollar for Every Song I've Sung

The musicians love to play, but you might consult the final verse of John Fogerty's song "Lodi" for the downside of playing. The money makes it *possible*, but for most of us, it won't pay for a ticket home. So the money doesn't make it *practical*. The loved ones at home either have to adjust to this fact of musical life or separate themselves from the musicians they claim to love. The musician *will* play and would also like to have a life. If the life isn't provided by a supportive family, either the music will continue at the expense of the family, or the musician will wither under the prohibition of making music, which will also destroy the family, sooner or later. People who *can* adjust to *not* making music *aren't* musicians. The music is fundamental and ineradicable in musicians. It isn't a choice, its chord.

And here is the secret truth that has led musicians to poverty since the first Cro-Magnon drum circles: *We* would do it for free, but we feel *you* ought to pay us for it. Because *you* love it. It makes you feel good. It makes you sad when you want to be sad. It adds meaning and poignancy to your life and your memories, and you can't observe any important moment without us. We are needed anywhere anything is supposed to "count," in *any* sense. We play the national anthem, and the fight song, and we play the hymns, and we play reveille and charge and beat retreat, and the wedding song, and we made that woman fall in love with you and we made that man remember you with tenderness, and you should fucking *appreciate* that. Is that worth five bucks, asshole, with your one dollar tip? Can I possibly play "Free Bird" for you *again*? I'd *love* that . . . Sorry. I got carried away.

Just one problem. I probably *will* play that godforsaken song (it's a damn good song actually), and for free. Well, buy me a beer, okay? Or two. Two for "Free Bird." And I'll do it later, at the end of the night, if you stay and spend money to help out the bar. Just meet me half way here, okay? You want the song and you want it to be good, right? Okay, we'll see what we can do. And then we rock you. So pony up, okay?

Why Don't You Say What You Really Think?

We want you to listen, we want you to dance, we want you to remember the bar and the band and the night, and we want to be booked again. We may look like we're having fun, and hey, maybe we are, but it's business and you need to do your part. But we can't afford to piss you off, so we don't often say what we really think, unless we're, like, Bob Dylan, or Jackson Browne. And we aren't.

Last night I saw a regionally known and very popular musician play at a big brewery. It was a Friday night, the place was packed, and the musician involved can actually say what he thinks—has arrived at the level of acceptance and has so many devoted followers that they'll just accept "well, that's just him." I was in Alabama. This musician is from Alabama. During the (excellent, rocking) show, he went on an impromptu rant, while the band vamped, as he often does. But on this night, the rant would have been entitled "Fuck Football (and Be Nice to Each Other)." He attacked the game of football without mercy for seven or eight minutes, at high volume and with the oratorical timing of Jesse Jackson meets young Billy Graham. (Football was on every TV in the place.) Did I mention this was in Alabama? The Tide would play for the national championship the next evening. I know the politics of this performer. It's the same as Jackson Browne's, which is to say the same as almost every musician. Socialists singing for a living.

I'm guessing few hearts were changed or souls saved. The fellow next to me remarked "He's left politics and gone into attacking our religion." Most of us can't be outspoken like this—there's no reason to think our bandmates even share our political views, and if they do, they still want us to shut up. I noticed that the room was only half full for the next set. If I'd been the promoter, I believe I would have had a talk with that wonderful performer.

Later, I asked my brother-in-law, who is also a musician and was there: "Do you think the people left because of the rant against football?" He considered. "Nah, a lot of people leave at break. They probably just moved on to the next place." Man, I hope he's right. It didn't seem like it to me. Either way, now the seats are all empty and there aren't any roadies, even at this regional level. I wish people had stayed a little bit longer. That last set was fantastic.

Even though I've been outspoken my whole life, as a sort of socialist reluctant entrepreneur musician, I've never been brave enough to attack football . . .

Afterword: Long Live Rock

A Dialogue between Chuck Klosterman (As I Imagine Him) and Vance Druid (Who Doesn't Exist)

I suppose I could have had an actual dialogue with Chuck Klosterman. He is generous with his time, I hear. But then I wouldn't have control over what he says. This would become an interview. It is not an interview. It is a minor work of imaginative literature. Very minor. Chuck says a lot of what I say he says, if not quite these precise words. Vance Druid is a character Chuck created for his first novel, Downtown Owl. *I like that book. I wrote an essay about it for* Chuck Klosterman and Philosophy. *Vance Druid, with the unfortunate initials VD, will introduce himself, in an awkward bit of exposition.*

VD: So, Chuck, I am the aloof, good looking, twenty-something-and-very-cool youngest son of a North Dakota buffalo farmer, who lives outside the not-very-imaginary town of Owl.

CK: Yeah, I guess Owl looks a lot like Wyndmere where I grew up, population 418 and falling. So Owl is twice the size.

VD: I drive an old truck and I only listen to the Rolling Stones.

CK: Yeah.

VD: I'm headed for alcoholism.

CK: Like everyone else you know.

VD: And I don't say much.

CK: That's because you're cool.

VD: But you talk a lot.

CK: That's because I'm not cool.

VD: And that's really my point. Wanna know the *real* reason?

CK: I'll listen.

VD: Two things. (A) You gratuitously killed my love interest in the novel.

CK: She didn't crack the car window when she got stranded by a sudden blizzard.

VD: Yes, very sudden and all. Where was she from, Chuck?

CK: Milwaukee, by way of Chicago.

VD: And she didn't know to crack the window?

CK: I see your point. Okay, what if I revise? She was from, hell, Memphis or something.

VD: You'll need to hire a different reader for the audiobook, for her parts. The current reader sounds like Milwaukee by way of California.

CK: I'll get right on that. What's (B)?

VD: Not so fast. You stick me in 1984, at twenty-something years old, you parade a romantic prospect across my (fictional) vision, and then you take her away, leaving *me*, the coolest guy in Owl, to be the inferior little brother of the least imaginative people in North Dakota? And no girl?

CK: Owl doesn't have any girls. There are advantages you don't appreciate here. (A.) You don't have to suffer the insults of age. (You don't want to know what you'd look like *now*, so I won't tell you.) (B.) Julia was a silly person. You're better off without her. I killed her because she was silly. I don't regret it and you should thank me. (C.) Being the sibling of the least imaginative people in North Dakota is far better than being the sibling of the most imaginative people in many other places. (D.) The actual 1984 is looking better to me every day and you should be content to stay there. And the 1984 I reconstructed from memory in 2008 for you to live in is fucking paradise compared to now. Except for the blizzard, which I admit sucked for everybody. What is (B.)?

VD: (B) is Julia was silly.

CK: No, in the reasons I'm not cool?

VD: Oh, that's easy. (B.) You said rock is dead.

CK: Well, it is. It died in 2000, give or take a month.

VD: People have been saying that since, oh, about 1966. That was before *Exile on Main Street, Sticky Fingers, It's Only Rock and Roll, Some Girls, Tattoo You* . . . . I could go on.

CK: Yeah, but this time it's true. I have over sixteen years of shitty music to prove it's gone and it isn't coming back. By the way, the Stones have a new album, late 2016. It's all mid-century blues covers. Very good.

VD: Wow, I'm doing the math, wait. So, Bill Wyman is 80?

CK: Yeah, but he left the band in '93. The rest are still going.

VD: Keith Richards is alive?

CK: It is much discussed whether he really is, or whether he has been replaced by a vampire or pod person, but ostensibly, yes.

VD: Then rock music is alive.

CK: Are you listening to yourself? That isn't rock. It's Rest Home.

VD: I bet they rock.

CK: It's a good album. They're touring. People pay. Old people. I hate to break this to you, Druid, but the kids aren't learning to play guitar and bass and drums any more.

VD: I should have learned guitar. What do they do?

CK: Mostly the play video games.

VD: Pac-man? Donkey Kong?

CK: Those are still around, but everything evolves. You get to control cartoons now. Lots of killing and sex.

VD: What about music?

CK: They mix sounds. It's actually pretty amazing. It takes talent. Discipline. They make their own records from previous records and other sounds. It's called electronic dance music.

VD: Like disco?

CK: A bit. But now everyone's his own record producer.

VD: I bet it sucks.

CK: Look, VD . . .

VD: Druid to you

CK: Whatever. Look, the rock era was fueled by two things: (1) the invention of some new instruments that made a new range of sounds, due to the harnessing of electricity; and (2) a demographic bulge, a gigantic bunch of bored kids with disposable income to throw at the slightly older kids who were screwing around with the new instruments and learning to make those sounds publicly. When all the good sounds had been found and combined, and all the teen eros and angst gave way to virtuoso mastery of these sounds, and when all those possibilities had grown stale, and after two more decades of repetition (to be sure it was really all done and re-done), some new sounds were needed. They arrived. You Baby Boomers didn't get the memo. Your grandkids don't want to make derivative music. They want their own. They love your music, they listen, they respect, but they don't want to learn the guitar. It's over.

VD: I don't have grandkids. You killed my love life.

CK: She wasn't going to have your children anyway. She had her tubes tied after a teenage pregnancy. She thanked *Roe v Wade* and said "never again."

VD: You're making that up.

CK: Pinky swear, it's in my notes for the character. But yeah, I made it up. Sue me. Rock is still dead.

VD: You said it's not dead for listening.

CK: Oh, it's everywhere right now, being played for the people who remember what it was like. We'll listen to less of it as they die off. The kids listen. It's like the way you heard Big Band and Swing everywhere growing up, and they kept playing it.

But the swing era has now been reduced to one band and one song. Glenn Miller, "In the Mood." That's all anyone knows now. It's a pattern. Everything gets condensed to what history will hold in the popular mind, it isn't much, one musician, one song.

That's how the rock will survive in history. It will be played later about the way Sousa marches are played now. One musician, one march "Stars and Stripes Forever," and only the aficionados know more.

VD: Five old guys, on the town park gazebo playing "Brown Sugar"?

CK: Actually, "Satisfaction." Have you been to a small town Fourth of July lately?

VD: I haven't done *anything* lately. You need to write a sequel. Maybe I learned guitar in '85 and had a string of rocking hits beginning in '89.

CK: It never worked like that. You're still raising buffalo. Never married.

VD: Fuck that. And rock will never die.

CK: I have worse news. It may not be the Stones and "Satisfaction" that become the one song. It may be Journey and "Don't Stop Believin'."

VD: Bullshit. That's a shitty, stupid song.

CK: The reasons are complicated. It has to do with a scene from a TV series that will live forever.

VD: If you would just write me into a sequel I could stop that.

CK: I could change your future, but I can't bring rock back. No one can.

VD: How do you know there's no Mick Jagger and Keith Richards practicing in a garage right now who'll revive the whole thing? I mean, rock came back after disco, right?

CK: No one knows anything for certain. There will be revivals. But the confluence of circumstances is unlikely for anything so vital as rock was.

VD: But you said yourself we're probably wrong about tons of stuff we can't even imagine.

CK: This isn't like that. We are probably wrong about gravity, yes, but history doesn't repeat. The equivalent of rock music in fifty years will be unrecognizable to rock purists like you, like us.

VD: Makes me want a beer. Or twenty.

CK: And that, VD, is why you're still in Owl in 1984. Not the beer. But the things that make you turn to it. It's hard to keep moving. Eventually we all give up on that project.

VD: What about you?

CK: I like to remember rock. I like to think about it. I like to listen. But newspapers died, so I wrote for magazines. Magazines died and I wrote books. Books are dying, so I'll have to adapt. There will never be another Eddie Van Halen or Van Morrison. The best talent among the kids isn't applying its free hours to becoming like them. It takes a certain combination of cultural values to produce creativity in that extreme form.

VD: Well, what's important now, in music?

CK: We have a lot of hybrids. What was once called "country music" fills a lot of the sonic and cultural space reserved for rock in the past. That's where people who like guitars have to go now. No choice. Listen to Eric Church, the "Mr. Misunderstood" album. Listen to Miranda Lambert's "The Weight of these Wings." Hybrids –rock, country, rap, mix art. The same for EDM and hip-hop. Everything is trying on everything else for size.

VD: That's not an answer. What you're really saying is music *isn't* important. Not like in the rock era.

CK: There, you *said* it: The rock "era." *Nothing* becomes an "era" until it's over. Everyone in 2017 knows what "the rock era" means.

VD: Pretty sad. I'm not giving in, but I see your day sucks. How will people in the future know what it was like to rock?

CK: They won't. They'll imagine it in their own way, and get it wrong. But some stuff will be right.

VD: So, not fully dead?

CK: No, but no longer what we all ate and slept and breathed either. It's like rock music reduced by Alzheimer's. But it still has good days, now and then.

VD: Well, then. Long live rock.

References

Anderson, Christopher. 1993. *Jagger Unauthorized*. Delacorte.

Aristotle. 1999. *Nicomachean Ethics*. Hackett.

Augustine. 2006. *Confessions*. Hackett.

Auxier, Randall E., and Gary L. Herstein. 2017. *The Quantum of Explanation: Whitehead's Radical Empiricism*. Routledge.

Bachofen, Johann Jakob. 1992. *Myth, Religion, and Mother Right: Selected Writings of J.J. Bachofen*. Princeton University Press.

Barrie, James M. *Peter Pan*. <www.gutenberg.org/files/16/16-h/16-h.htm>.

Beauvoir, Simone de. 1986. *The Ethics of Ambiguity*. Citadel.

Buffett, Jimmy. *A Pirate Looks at Fifty*. Random House.

Camus, Albert. 1991. *The Myth of Sisyphus and Other Essays*. Vintage.

Cassirer, Ernst. 1944. *An Essay on Man*. Yale University Press.

———. 1955–1996. *The Philosophy of Symbolic Forms*. Four volumes. Yale University Press.

Danto Arthur C. 2003. *The Abuse of Beauty: Aesthetics and the Concept of Art*. Open Court.

Darwin, Charles. 2003. *The Origin of Species and The Voyage of the Beagle*. Everyman.

Derrida, Jacques. 1989. *Of Spirit: Heidegger and the Question*. University of Chicago Press.

Descartes, René. 1993. *Meditations on First Philosophy*. Hackett.

Dutton, Denis. 1999. Language Crimes: A Lesson in How Not to Write, Courtesy of the Professoriate. *Wall Street Journal* (February 5th) <www.dennisdutton.com/language_crimes.htm>.

Eisler, Riane. 1988. *The Chalice and the Blade: Our History, Our Future*. Harper.

Field, Greg, 2004. H-D vs. Japan. In Holstrom 2004.

Friedman, Stan. 2007. Magic. *Christianity Today* (January 1st).

Gimbutas, Marija. 1989. *The Language of the Goddess: Unearthing the Hidden Symbols of Western Civilization*. Harper and Row.

Goethe, Johann Wolfgang von. 2013. *The Sorrows of Young Werther and Selected Writings*. Signet.

Gracia, Jorge J.E., ed. 2004. *Mel Gibson's Passion and Philosophy: The Cross, the Questions, the Controversy*. Open Court.

Hanley, Richard, ed. 2007. *South Park and Philosophy: Bigger, Longer, and More Penetrating*. Open Court.

Harrison, Jane Ellen. 2010 [1912]. *Themis: A Study of the Social Origins of Greek Religion*. Cambridge University Press.

Heidegger, Martin. 1996. *Being and Time*. State University of New York Press.

Henshaw, Peter, and Ian Kerr. 2004. *The Encyclopedia of the Harley-Davidson*. Chartwell.

Heschel, Abraham Joshua. 1962. *The Prophets*. Harper and Row.

Holstrom, Darwin, ed. 2004. *The Harley-Davidson Century*. MBI.

Hume, David. 1948 [1779]. *Dialogues Concerning Natural Religion*. Hafner.

Husserl, Edmund. 1931. *Ideas: General Introduction to Pure Phenomenology*. Humanities Press.

Kant, Immanuel. 1987. *Critique of Judgment*. Hackett.

———. 2002. *Critique of Practical Reason*. Hackett.

———. 2009. *Groundwork of the Metaphysics of Morals*. Harper.

Kaplan, Aryeh. 1981. *The Living Torah: The Five Books of Moses and the Haftarot*. Moznaim.

Kierkegaard, Søren. 1992. *Either/Or: A Fragment of Life*. Penguin.

Kohák, Erazim. 1978. *Idea and Experience: Edmund Husserl's Project of Phenomenology in Ideas I*. University of Chicago Press.

Lampert, Nicole. 2011. Why My Wife Let Me Cheat on Her: Roger Daltrey on Why His Attitudes to Marriage Vows Are Far from Straightforward. *Daily Mail* (15th July).

Langer, Susanne. 1953. *Feeling and Form: A Theory of Art Developed from Philosophy in a New Key*. Scribner's.

Leigh, Wendy. 2014. *Bowie: The Biography*. Simon and Schuster.

Lesh, Phil. 2006. *Searching for the Sound: My Life with the Grateful Dead*. Back Bay.

Machiavelli, Niccolò. 1995. *The Prince*. Hackett.

Nietzsche, Friedrich. 1994. *The Birth of Tragedy: Out of the Spirit of Music*. Penguin.

Pirsig, Robert M. 2006 [1974]. *Zen and the Art of Motorcycle Maintenance: An Inquiry into Values*. Harper.

Plato. 2004. *Republic*. Hackett.

Richards, Keith. 2010. *Life*. Little, Brown.

Rolling Stone. 2011. *Rolling Stone* Celebrates Bob Dylan's 70th Birthday. *Rolling Stone* (May 26th).

Rosen, Stanley. 2014. *The Quarrel Between Philosophy and Poetry: Studies in Ancient Thought*. Routledge.

Rousseau, Jean-Jacques. 1995. *The Confessions and Correspondence, Including the Letters to Malesherbes*. The University Press of New England.

Sampson, John. 1978 [1905]. *The Poetical Works of William Blake*. Corner House.

Sartre, Jean-Paul. 1962. *Imagination: A Psychological Critique*. University of Michigan Press.

———. 1964. Sartre on the Nobel Prize. *New York Times* (December 17th) <www.nybooks.com/articles/1964/12/17/sartre-on-the-nobel-prize>.

———. 1991 [1940]. *The Psychology of Imagination*. Citadel.

———. 2013 [1938]. *Nausea*. New Directions.

Sartwell, Crispin. 1995. *The Art of Living: Aesthetics of the Ordinary in World Spiritual Traditions*. State University of New York Press.

———. 2006. *Six Names of Beauty*. Routledge.

Sawyers, June Skinner, ed. 2004. *Racing in the Street: The Bruce Springsteen Reader*. Penguin.

Snow, Mat. 2015. *The Who: Fifty Years of My Generation*. Race Point.

Townshend, Pete. 2012. *Who I Am: A Memoir*. Harper.

Twain, Mark. 2011. *Following the Equator: A Journey Around the World*. Twain Press.

Vannatta, Seth, ed. 2012. *Chuck Klosterman and Philosophy: The Real and the Cereal*. Open Court.

Verene, Donald Phillip. 1981. *Vico's Science of Imagination*. Cornell University Press.

Vico, Giambattista. 1968. *The New Science of Giambattista Vico*. Cornell University Press.

Warhol, Andy. 1975. *The Philosophy of Andy Warhol (From A to B and Back Again)*. Houghton Mifflin Harcourt.

West, Cornel. 1993. *Beyond Eurocentrism and Multiculturalism, Volume 1: Prophetic Thought in Postmodern Times*. Common Courage Press.

Whitehead, Alfred North. 1929. *Process and Reality*. Macmillan.

———. 1978. *Process and Reality: Corrected Edition*. The Free Press.

Wilde, Oscar. 1993. *The Picture of Dorian Gray*. Dover.

———. 2013. *De Profundis and Other Prison Writings*. Penguin.

Williamson, Nigel. 2007. *The Rough Guide to Led Zeppelin*. Rough Guide Reference.

Wyman, Bill, with Ray Coleman. 1990. *Stone Alone: The Story of a Rock'n'Roll Band*. Viking.

Young, Neil. 2012. *Waging Heavy Peace: A Hippie Dream*. Penguin.

———. 2014. *Special De Luxe: A Memoir of Life and Cars*. Penguin.

Bios

Auxier's Brief Bio: Not Brief Enough

Randy Auxier was raised on the banks of the Mississippi in Memphis, Tennessee, except for when the river was in flood stage. Then he would move up from the banks to the bluffs alongside the river. But then one evening while Randy was sorting through his collection of indigenous butterfly droppings, Elvis took pity on him and invited him to live in Graceland. During the years that Randy stayed there, Elvis taught him how to play the guitar and hold his liquor. It was during this time that Randy discovered his love for music, especially the soothing sounds of Zanphyr.

All was well until an incident involving Lisa Marie, a jelly doughnut, and a spatula caused Randy's ousting from Graceland. Asked later, Randy said, "I can now see that the spatula was a bad idea, but hindsight is 20/20." He considered moving back to the banks of the river, but Mud Island had been inconveniently developed right on his favorite spot, so instead he enrolled at Memphis State University.

While at MSU Randy formed The Shakes with some buddies. The Shakes were unique in that their drummer often performed naked and completely covered in Crisco. During one particular gig, the drummer's drum stick slipped from his Crisco-covered hand, went sailing across the stage, and struck Randy on the back of the head, causing a gash that required twenty-seven stitches. This ended Randy's stint with the Shakes and also caused him to question his life purpose. He thought to himself: "I want to make a real difference in this world—change people's lives—solve the world's problems—own a pair of sensible shoes. I shall become a Folk Singer, or maybe a Cosmetologist. No, definitely a Folk Singer. And while I'm at it, I'll become a Doctor of Philosophy. That should be handy for something."

And so off Randy (and his wife Gaye, whom he met while a counselor at a summer camp where they spent their days separating young loves and confiscating pot) went to Atlanta to attend Emory University. While searching for a place to live, they saw a quaint home they thought they would enjoy, so they moved in. You see, the current owner, Robert Hoyt, was away on vacation but had left the back door unlocked. Well, to make a short story longer, because of some turn-of-the-century "squatter's rights" law never removed from the books, Randy and Gaye became the new owners of the house. But Robert was a good sport about it and to show there were no hard feelings, agreed to form the Quixotics with Randy. Their claim to fame was their ability to play "Tambourine Man" non-stop for an entire forty-five minute set at each show, if they so chose. Needless to say, their popularity dwindled, most likely because they had no tambourine player and who can be expected to listen to "Tambourine Man" for forty-five minutes without ever hearing the tambourine? There was also a rumor they knew all the verses, but could not sing them in the allotted time. So Randy finished up his Doctorate at Emory and off to Oklahoma City they went.

As luck would have it, his Doctorate in Philosophy *did* come in handy, as Oklahoma City University needed a math professor. During the interview, Randy was able to convince them that teaching students math was far too "ivory-tower" and abstract and wouldn't Philosophy be a much more practical subject for the young minds? They agreed and so Randy began teaching about Tu Quoques and the Dewey Decimal system and other tenets of Philosophy.

One Saturday evening, while enjoying a half-caf-double-twist-full-nelson-latte and taking in the music at Galileo, a long-haired-hippie-communist-looking young man asked Randy if the extra seat at the table was taken. Randy said it wasn't, so as not to appear rude, but secretly hoping the guy would just move on. But he didn't and so since he was there, and the guy (Jim Preble) played guitar and sang pretty good, they formed Enough Rope. They had the longest running gig in town until the owner of Galileo finally figured out the same twelve guys were showing up at the Open Mic Night every week. That, and a job offer from Southern Illinois University ended the Enough Rope run.

Since moving to the Carbondale area in the Year of Our Lord 2000, Randy has become something of a musical jack of one trade, prostituting his meager talents for whichever musical john would pay the most, teaching philosophy for his daily fare. In the course of this effort to survive he was required by law to record and release his CD *Southwind* as part of a community service sentence laid upon him by a very twisted judge using something he called "the discretion of the bench." Go figure.

This bio is mostly lies, and even the lies are getting dated.

Corrected Bio of Randy Auxier

The truth about Randy is this: he doesn't have a collection of butterfly droppings at all; it was cicada exoskeletons, but he was afraid that wouldn't be interesting enough, but now even the cicadas are gone. The whole collection was in a bag next to the couch and his brother-in-law Bruce was watching *Star Wars: Phantom Menace* for the seventieth time, in the dark, and mistook them for his bag of pork rinds, and this is too painful to write about.

It wasn't Lisa Marie, it was actually Priscilla, and Elvis *gave* Randy the doughnut and asked him to . . . well, never mind the details, but the spatula was strictly damage control by the time it came to that. If you ever wondered why Priscilla went to Paris, well, there's a special doctor there. We all felt bad about this, but it gave her an appreciation for animals that really developed later on and led to the idea for that TV series.

It is true that the drummers for The Shakes performed covered in Crisco, but it was two different drummers, and they were scuffling over whether Paiste is better than Zildjian at the time the stick slipped. Randy was just in the wrong place at the wrong time. The performance was at a Rest Home, so there were supposed to be medical people on duty, but no one could find them, so the stitches were done by the quilting ladies. Randy still shows off his rocking-stitch scar if asked.

The truth is that Robert and Randy *did* have a tambourine that they used when doing the marathon sessions, but they were contacted by some lawyers claiming to represent Dylan who demanded that the tambourine be left out. Randy and Robert decided to fight the suit and won on a technicality when a post-modernist literary critic was called as an expert witness. He was trying to convince the jury that the song had *no* author when they all got up and left, except for two who had actually died of boredom. The aftermath was complex, but by the time anyone knew what had happened, it came to light that the lawyers did not represent Dylan but were actually the last living practitioners of New Criticism. At that point, Robert realized that Dylan left the tambourine *on purpose*, saw he could do stuff at least *that* profound, and began his solo career. He said, "sometimes a tambourine is *just* a tambourine, but don't bet the farm on it."

The stuff about Oklahoma City is true, except for the part about the latte. It was a full-caf-half-nelson.

Since the lying biography appeared on the web in 2003, some more untrue things have happened. Elevated (against his will and over his own confessions of incompetence) to full professor of philosophy with tenure, Randy responded by writing and recording a new CD, his third collaboration with engineering whiz-kid Bruce Chandler, entitled *Sp_r_t Gu_de*. During the project, Bruce received an electronic message from the Buddha that said "there is no self, leave out the I's." Bruce soon dedicated his life to the service of the self that *is not*, in hopes that it never will be, since evidently the self is still a possibility. Hence, Bruce's new production company handle: Buddha Joint (referring to the one remnant of the Buddha-self that yet remains, not a finger or finger bone, but the emptiness where the Enlightened One bent a finger when he tried to clap—it was shortly before he thought of a now famous koan).

So don't believe anything you read.

Brief Bio of Bruce Chandler
by Randall Auxier

Most people are not conceived in a test tube. Bruce Chandler is no exception, so the rumors are untrue—the ones about how he put a crack in the glass tube with his first effort at mitosis. The mitosis itself was successful, and Bruce now has many cells, so he did become good at dividing, but the idea that he was a prodigy is difficult to prove. It's also hard to disprove, given the thriving multi-cellular organism he has become. But my point is that there was no test tube. Bruce is from Kentucky. They didn't have test-tubes there in the late Sixties. Bruce was born without any shoes, calling into question the old spiritual that claims "All God's children got shoes," but that could still be true, assuming Bruce isn't one of God's children. But his mother was grateful in any case (about the bare feet).

Bruce had too much energy as a child. He would release it by beating with hands and feet on horizontal and vertical surfaces, and even some with obtuse angles. This tested the patience of his long-suffering family, at least until the invention of electronic drum pads and headphones (which came too late, but better late than never). In 1974, he wrote "Born to Drum," which Springsteen shamelessly adapted without crediting his fellow Bruce for the idea. And Chandler still has more cells than Springsteen, by about 17 percent (give or take, depending on what was for lunch). Bruce also took to electronic things—he had a knack for disassembling anything that was within reach (TI calculators, TRS 80's, other things beginning with T). Reassembling them took time and trouble (and other things beginning with T, like "telophase," the final stage of mitosis, without which, really, Bruce wouldn't have learned very much).

Speaking of learning, eventually there was college for Bruce at Murray State University, which is "Kentucky's Public Ivy," according to their website, and the obtrusive signs hanging all over campus. This is not Bruce's fault. Murray State was content to be a po-dunk school when he went there. There aren't enough po-dunk schools anymore. Everything is now Ivy League, by some sort of analogy or qualification. For example, Austin Community College is "The Yale of Community Colleges between I-35 and Red River Blvd," according to their website. Bruce never went there. But he did set up a four-track recording studio in his dorm room, where he was able to make an audio documentary of the very best thoughts and creative achievements of his Ivy League peers. Bruce has been contacted by the Smithsonian regarding the de-preservation of those tapes. This is part of a new initiative by federal institutions called "pre-emptive history."

Throughout high school and college, there were bands—bands of musicians I mean, not like "bands of hunter-gatherers" or "bands of thieves," but it does give me pause to consider that I can't think of many non-derogatory uses of the word "band." In compliance with the Smithsonian mandate, these bands have requested that they not be named in this book, but there were quite a few, take my word, and their desire to remain anonymous is commendable.

Have I mentioned that Bruce is a recording engineer and erstwhile producer? Well he is. There have been projects, oh yes, there have been projects. The trick has been keeping these projects from being de-preserved by the despisers of culture and art for art's sake. The strategy has been diffusion—not the wide dispersion of products, but rather, taking on so many projects that one is not sure exactly *what* one is doing. Interrogation of people like Bruce produces an honest "I don't know," and the polygraph machine is fooled. Or at least, that's the theory of "project diffusion." It's sort of like diversifying one's own psychological portfolio. Bruce can survive the liquidation of quite a few of his own mental assets with no noticeable loss of creative solvency. I'm not saying this *has* happened (I mean, who could tell?), I'm just saying it *could* happen safely.

Bruce plays keyboards when he's in the mood (for playing keyboards). And he designs websites, takes pictures, and of course, there is mitosis. A horse would have to eat Bruce's resumé very carefully to keep from choking on it. He moved to Texas in 2005, taking the resumé, but not the horse (which belonged to a neighbor). This made his family very proud. He took up with a lot of people his family doesn't know, mainly musicians, including many at the Kerrville Folk Festival where for a decade or so, Bruce headed the scattered efforts of a large Recording Krew, now relaxing in the service of a different chief. He (Bruce, not the chief) was hanging with some refugees from Pennsylvania for a while, but they eventually moved home to vote for Obama. That was 2008. They wrote him in for 2016, but without result, since they used the Russian alphabet. These days Bruce shaves more or less regularly.

Luke Dick Bio
by Someone

Luke is an imposing figure. Not as imposing as, say, a million, or even a couple hundred thousand, but it's more than you make, trust me. Luke stands well over four cubits in height, without the cowboy boots, and weighs in at over seventeen stone, but he had the boots on when I checked that. They are custom-made, lead-lined due to the radioactive dust around Luke's homestead, in a uranium mine in rural Oklahoma. Everyone wears the same boots there, so they have to take turns leaving home. Luke is proud of his origins, sharing them as he does with a whole species, and the only surviving branch of that species at that. Like everyone else from home, he played a little football, served a little time, got the boots.

Not many people picked Luke for a scholar and boy were they right. He studied philosophy instead, which is recommended by Dave Barry in one book, along with sociology, as ideal majors, since there are no facts to worry about. Luke started futzing around with guitars pretty early. That didn't take him anywhere, so he tried puttering around instead. Same story. But one day he was watching a Dire Straits video and noticed, in Luke's words, "that dude's not futzing around, he's *gettin' on* it." So Luke got on his guitar and that was the moment his life changed. No more philosophy for Luke, no sir-ee. So he moved to Nashville and when some music publishers were out for a wild night, they saw him and said "Man, you're really *on* that guitar." Luke answered, "yeah, it's my second one; lead boots kind of ruined the first one."

They were impressed and signed him to a publishing deal, which is all they could do, because they were publishers and they weren't really anything else. Except one was a lawyer, but had forgotten about it. That went pretty well. Luke stayed on the guitar, learned to surf the Cumberland, which at his stature attracted attention, much to the delight of his publishers. But in 2010 the river rose and people mistook Luke for a Red Cross pontoon and swamped his ES-335 (Telecasters and SGs will float, but not with someone seventeen stone on board—the displacement just isn't there.) Anyway, Luke said "I'm shed of this scene," and shook the mud off his heels.

There was nowhere to go but New York, and this is where things get dicey. Luke kept writing songs, but he was caught in a raid for making non-pornographic videos that were perfectly acceptable for network television. One was a freakin' McDonald's commercial for crissake. He was also seen teaching philosophy in the Bronx. The lengths some people will go to, sheesh. It cries out for a better correctional system, for sure. With his reputation in tatters, he put his tales between his legs and went shopping for boots that would take him home to Nashville.

He's been in Nashville a few years, and hence happy. "Hence" is actually one of his dogs, the others being Whence and Whither. He has a family too. Luke, not the dogs. They're fixed. The dogs, not Luke's family. He's finally off the guitar, but it served him well for that stretch of his life. Now he gets on a piano. Way sturdier. These days he writes songs and records songs and sings songs and feeds dogs. He seems to have recovered from the New York ordeal. He visits home often and is doing well enough to pay for an on-site oncologist. Everybody has boots. He owed Randy a favor. Randy was the one who played the Dire Straits video for him back in Oklahoma. Luke doesn't owe Randy anything now. They're even-steven, got it?

Index